Food Tourism Around the World

Food Tourism Around the World

Development, management and markets

Edited by
C. Michael Hall, Liz Sharples, Richard Mitchell,
Niki Macionis and Brock Cambourne

AMSTERDAM BOSTON HEIDELBERG LONDON NEW YORK OXFORD
PARIS SAN DIEGO SAN FRANCISCO SINGAPORE SYDNEY TOKYO

Butterworth-Heinemann
An imprint of Elsevier
Linacre House, Jordan Hill, Oxford OX2 8DP
200 Wheeler Road, Burlington MA 01803

First published 2003

British Library Cataloguing in Publication Data
Food tourism around the world: development, management and markets
 1. Tourism   2. Food   3. Gastronomy
 I. Hall, Colin Michael, 1961–
 338.4'791

Library of Congress Cataloguing in Publication Data
Food tourism around the world: development, management, and markets/edited by
C. Michael Hall . . . [et al.]
    p. cm.
Includes bibliographical references and index.
ISBN 0 7506 5503 8 (alk. paper)
1. Food.   2. Tourism.
I. Hall, Colin Michael, 1961–
TX357.F675 2003
338.4'791–dc21   2003041453

ISBN 0 7506 5503 8

For information on all Butterworth-Heinemann publications visit our website at
www.bh.com

Composition by Genesis Typesetting Limited, Rochester, Kent
Printed and bound in Great Britain

Contents

List of exhibits   vii
List of figures   ix
List of tables   xi
Acknowledgements   xiii
Contributors   xv

1   The consumption of experiences or the experience of
consumption? An introduction to the tourism of taste   1
C. Michael Hall and Liz Sharples

2   Consuming places: the role of food, wine and tourism in
regional development   25
C. Michael Hall, Richard Mitchell and Liz Sharples

3   Consuming tourists: food tourism consumer behaviour   60
Richard Mitchell and C. Michael Hall

4   The demand for halal food among Muslim travellers in
New Zealand   81
Melissa Wan Hassan and C. Michael Hall

5   The world of cookery-school holidays   102
Liz Sharples

6   The lure of tea: history, traditions and attractions   121
Lee Joliffe

7   Food and tourism in Papua New Guinea   137
Geoffrey Le Grys and Peter Van Fleet

8   Food trails in Austria   149
    Kim Meyer-Czech

9   Food tourism in the Niagara Region: the development of a
    nouvelle cuisine   158
    David J. Telfer and Atsuko Hashimoto

10 The lure of food: food as an attraction in destination marketing
    in Manitoba, Canada   178
    John Selwood

11 The Bluff Oyster Festival and regional economic development:
    festivals as culture commodified   192
    Kristy Rusher

12 Food tourism in the Peak District National Park, England   206
    Liz Sharples

13 Valorizing through tourism in rural areas: moving towards
    regional partnerships   228
    Jane F. Eastham

14 Restaurants and local food in New Zealand   249
    Angela Smith and C. Michael Hall

15 Linking food, wine and tourism: the case of the Australian
    capital region   268
    Brock Cambourne and Niki Macionis

16 Managing food and tourism developments: issues for planning
    and opportunities to add value   285
    Steven Boyne and Derek Hall

17 New global cuisine: tourism, authenticity and sense of place in
    postmodern gastronomy   296
    Rosario Scarpato and Roberto Daniele

18 The experience of consumption or the consumption of
    experiences? Challenges and issues in food tourism   314
    C. Michael Hall, Liz Sharples and Angela Smith

References   336

Index   371

Exhibits

1.1   The ancient festival of cheese rolling *Liz Sharples*   6
1.2   Revolving restaurants *Tony Stevens*   8
1.3   Portuguese food image among UK residents *Kevin Fields*   14
1.4   Restaurants in the sky *John Clark and Liz Sharples*   20
2.1   The Talbot *Liz Sharples*   26
2.2   Eat the View project *Liz Sharples*   29
2.3   Ludlow Marches food festival *Liz Sharples*   49
3.1   High interest in wine and cuisine tourism among the US
      and Canadian populations   65
5.1   Ballymaloe Cookery School *Liz Sharples*   104
5.2   The Padstow Seafood School, Cornwall *Liz Sharples*   106
5.3   Le Manoir Ecole de Cuisine *Liz Sharples*   111
11.1 Risk management planning: insurance, regulations, licences
      and permits *Kristy Rusher*   201
12.1 The Chatsworth Farm Shop *Liz Sharples*   209
12.2 The Hartington Cheese Shop *Liz Sharples*   213
12.3 Caudwell's Mill *Liz Sharples*   216
12.4 The Old Original Bakewell Pudding Shop *Liz Sharples*   219
13.1 Shepherd's Purse *Jane Eastham*   242
13.2 Peak Eats Ready Meals *Jane Eastham*   244
18.1 Tourist attitudes towards regional and local food in the UK
      Liz Sharples and C. Michael Hall   315
18.2 Farmers' markets in the UK *Liz Sharples and C. Michael Hall*   319
18.3 Oktoberfest in America *Robert Janiskee*   331

Figures

1.1	Food tourism as special interest tourism	11
2.1	Different supply chains and local food systems	41
2.2	Relationship between national, regional and local food, tourism and regional development strategies	58
5.1	Cookery holiday spectrum	116
7.1	Outline map of Papua New Guinea identifying major centres, provincial capitals and major roads	139
15.1	Reasons reported by Canberra restaurants for not using local wines in their establishments	275
15.2	Factors influencing choice of wines on restaurant wine lists	277
15.3	Factors that would encourage Canberra restaurateurs to use regional wines	278
18.1	Strengths	322
18.2	Weaknesses	324
18.3	Opportunities	326
18.4	Threats	328
18.5	International commonalities	330

Tables

1.1 Leisure/recreational activities of all US resident travellers to overseas destinations 5

1.2 Respondents' visits to European countries 15

1.3 European destinations for UK residents in 2000 15

2.1 Farm value as a percentage of retail price for domestically produced foods in the USA, 1987 and 1997 42

2.2 Benefits of farmers' markets according to the UK National Association of Farmers' Markets 44

2.3 Most important reasons for shopping at the Orono farmers' market by non-first time consumers 45

2.4 Factors favouring patronage of farmers' markets in San Diego County 46

2.5 Reasons why region of origin encourages purchase 56

3.1 Eating out/restaurants as an activity while on holiday in New Zealand (year ending June 2001) 63

3.2 Demographic characteristics of US direct farm outlet customers 64

3.3 *Australian Gourmet Traveller* readership profile 68

3.4 A typology of food tourist behaviour 78

4.1 Participants by age group 92

4.2 Participants by ethnic groups 93

4.3 Languages spoken by participants 94

4.4 Type of traveller: domestic vs international inbound 95

4.5 Number of participants by current position 95

4.6 How easy or difficult is it to find halal food while travelling in New Zealand? 96

4.7 In terms of your ability to find halal food, how would you rate New Zealand in comparison to Muslim and other non-Muslim countries? 96

4.8	How do you manage your meals while travelling in New Zealand?	97
4.9	While travelling in New Zealand, I always look for halal food	99
5.1	Analysis of selected European cookery schools	117
6.1	Tearooms on farms – Leicestershire, England	128
6.2	Typology of tea attractions	131
6.3	Tea museums	132
6.4	Tea tourism festivals	134
6.5	Examples of tea destinations	135
7.1	Major foods in Papua New Guinea	146
9.1	Selected success stories in culinary tourism in Canada	163
9.2	Recommended wine and culinary strategy for the Niagara Region	169
9.3	Dishes, restaurants and producers for the 2002 Tastes of Niagara Showcase	172
9.4	Tastes of Niagara membership	173
13.1	Local sourcing survey results	234
14.1	Restaurant type	253
14.2	Restaurant type by region	254
14.3	Cuisine style of restaurants	255
14.4	Region of origin and description of cuisine characteristics in menu items	257
14.5	Cuisine style by percentage of local products used in dishes	260
14.6	Difficulty/ease of sourcing local products	262
14.7	Importance of regional cuisine brand	262
14.8	Importance of supporting farmers'/growers' markets and buying local	263
14.9	Relevance of food and wine tourism to respondents' business	264
14.10	Interest in working with others in region to promote food and wine tourism	265
14.11	Information provided at restaurant	266
15.1	Trends in the development of food and wine tourism	272
15.2	Consumer demand for Canberra wines in Canberra restaurants	273
15.3	Responsibility for wine list construction	276
15.4	Reasons nominated for changing wine lists in Canberra restaurants	279
15.5	Supplementary wine marketing techniques used by Canberra restaurateurs	280
15.6	Nature and focus of restaurant wine training provided by Canberra restaurants	281

Acknowledgements

This book is written as a companion to our book on *Wine and Tourism Around the World* (2000). As with the 'wine book' this is also a book written by people who are interested and involved in food, from both an academic and a business perspective, and the editors and authors clearly hope that this book will be of interest as much to people in the food and tourism industries, as it is to those with a general interest in food. We would like also to note that research on food tourism is not always as glamorous and attractive as it seems. This stated, the editors would like to thank all the individuals and businesses who gave so freely of their time and expertise throughout the evolution of this book. We would also like to thank and acknowledge the input of all our contributors, whose knowledge and passion have made this book truly international in scope and focus, as well as the tremendous support provided by our publishers in Oxford.

In finishing the book, Michael would like to thank not only those who have sampled ideas regarding food, wine and tourism, but also those who have sampled his cooking over the years or who have fed him on culinary travels. In particular he would like to thank Dick and Margaret Butler, Dave Crag, Cam and Mel Elliott, Thor Flognfeldt, Derek Hall, Atsuko Hashimoto, Sandra James, Alan Lew, Carleen and Richard Mitchell, Dieter Müller, Stephen Page, John Selwood, Dave Telfer, Dallen Timothy and Allan Williams as well as Campbell's Butchers, Fortnum and Masons, Fresh Freddy's, Mr Johnsons, South Island Gourmet, the tomato and vegetable growers of Kakanui and 'the Girls'. He also very gratefully thanks Jody for coping with a book on food and tourism and looks forward to cooking dinner at more sensible times.

Contributors

Steven Boyne, Leisure and Tourism Management Department, Scottish Agricultural College, Auchincruive, Ayr, Scotland.

Brock Cambourne, Centre for Tourism Research, University of Canberra, Canberra, ACT, Australia.

John Clark, School of Sport and Leisure Management, Sheffield Hallam University, Sheffield, UK.

Roberto Daniele, Department of Hospitality and Tourism, Queen Margaret University College, Edinburgh, Scotland.

Jane F. Eastham, School of Sport and Leisure Management, Sheffield Hallam University, Sheffield, UK.

Kevin Fields, Birmingham College of Food, Tourism and Creative Studies, Birmingham, UK.

C. Michael Hall, Department of Tourism, School of Business, University of Otago, Dunedin, New Zealand.

Derek Hall, Leisure and Tourism Management Department, Scottish Agricultural College, Auchincruive, Ayr, Scotland.

Atsuko Hashimoto, Department of Recreation and Leisure Studies, Brock University, St Catharines, Ontario, Canada.

Robert Janiskee, Department of Geography, University of North Carolina, Charlotte, North Carolina, USA.

Lee Joliffe, University of New Brunswick, St John's, New Brunswick, Canada.

Geoffrey Le Grys, Centre for Food, School of Sport and Leisure Management, Sheffield Hallam University, Sheffield, UK.

Niki Macionis, Tourism Program, University of Canberra, ACT, Australia.

Kim Meyer-Czech, Institute of Spatial Planning and Rural Development, University of Agricultural Sciences, Vienna, Austria.

Richard Mitchell, School of Tourism and Hospitality, La Trobe University, Melbourne, Victoria, Australia.

Kristy Rusher, Department of Tourism, School of Business, University of Otago, Dunedin, New Zealand.

Rosario Scarpato, School of Tourism and Hospitality, La Trobe University, Melbourne, Victoria, Australia.

John Selwood, Department of Geography, University of Winnipeg, Manitoba, Canada.

Liz Sharples, School of Sport and Leisure Management, Sheffield Hallam University, Sheffield, UK.

Angela Smith, Department of Tourism, School of Business, University of Otago, Dunedin, New Zealand.

Tony Stevens, Academic Palliative Medicine Unit, The Royal Hallamshire Hospital, Sheffield, UK.

David J. Telfer, Department of Recreation and Leisure Studies, Brock University, St Catharines, Ontario, Canada.

Peter Van Fleet, Tribal Tops Inn, PO Box 86, Minj, WHP, Papua New Guinea.

Melissa Wan Hassan, Department of Tourism, School of Business, University of Otago, Dunedin, New Zealand.

1

The consumption of experiences or the experience of consumption? An introduction to the tourism of taste

C. Michael Hall and Liz Sharples

Food is one of the essential elements of the tourist experience. Yet it is such an integral part of the experience that it is only in recent years that it has become a subject of study in its own right. At first glance this may seem somewhat surprising. However, arguably it is the very fact that it is such an integral component of everyday life that food has for so long been missed as an area of serious research and analysis. Food, just like tourism, was for many years a fringe academic discipline, and was frowned upon as an area of research by students of more 'serious' disciplines, unless of course, you could splice genes into it, apply more fertilizer to it or get a greater economic return on it per unit of production. Nevertheless, this situation is changing. The social and cultural significance of food is finally gaining the recognition it deserves (e.g. Arce and Marsden, 1993; Bonanno et al., 1994; Cook and Crang, 1996; Fishwick, 1995; Goody, 1982; Pilcher, 1996; Probyn, 1998; Ritzer, 1993; Seligman, 1994; Sokolov, 1991), as is the role of food in tourism (e.g. Bessière, 1998; Cutforth, 2000; Hall, 2002; Hall and Macionis, 1998; Hall and Mitchell, 2000, 2001; Hjalager and Corigliano, 2000; Hjalager and Richards, 2002; Reynolds, 1993; Seydoux, 1986; Wolf, 2002). Moreover, the media is now full of magazines, e.g. *Cuisine, Gourmet Traveller, Australian Gourmet Traveller, Food & Travel*; radio shows, television shows and even entire 'lifestyle channels', such as the North American *Food Channel*, dedicated to food and the places that food comes from, that explicitly connect food and tourism. To an extent this is a reflection of changing lifestyles and the role of some goods and services as status symbols and as signifiers of identity, as well as recognition of the business opportunities to support such lifestyles. Issues of taste, image, freshness, experience and quality are now recognized as important, not only because of the role of food in the local economy, but also because what, why and how we eat says something about ourselves, why we travel and the society we live in.

Why study food and tourism?

Several reasons can be put forward for the growth in attention to food as an area of interest for tourism studies (Hall, 2002; Hall and Mitchell, 2001; Hjalager and Richards, 2002). Since the early 1970s rural regions in industrialized societies have been very substantially affected by successive rounds of economic restructuring. In response to loss of services and traditional markets, and removal of tariffs and regional support mechanisms, rural areas have sought to diversify their economic base, with new agricultural products and tourism being two such responses. Food tourism strategies are therefore a significant instrument of regional development particularly because of the potential leverage between products from the two sectors (Hall, 2002; Taylor and Little 1999; Telfer 2001a; 2001b). For example, in New South Wales (NSW), Australia, former NSW Tourism Minister, Mr Brian Langton, stated that 'NSW will embrace food and wine as an integral part of the visitor experience, and the focus of food and wine will broaden the destination appeal of NSW, and encourage more first time visitors to come back for seconds' (Langton, 1996). As part of the food initiatives the state government developed a *Food and Wine in Tourism Plan* and established a culinary tourism advisory committee (Hall and Macionis, 1998).

Undoubtedly, the extent of expenditure on food as a component of travel and tourism is significant and helps explain the interests of both government and business. For example, tourism spending on food and dining out in South Africa by international tourists averages 8 per cent of total spending, while the domestic tourist spends on average 24 per cent (du Rand, Heath and Alberts, 2002). In Australia, international visitors spent an average of A$4066 on each trip in 1999–2000. Visitors from China spent the most, averaging A$6070, followed by the USA ($5899), 'Other Europe' (A$5411) and Indonesia (A$5279). The lowest average expenditure, A$1808 per visitor, was by visitors from New Zealand. The largest expenditure items for visitors from Canada, the UK, Europe and New Zealand were prepaid international airfares and food, drink and accommodation. The only exception was visitors from Germany, who spent a quarter of their total expenditure on package tours. Visitors from the USA spent about one-fifth (18 per cent) of their total expenditure on food, drink and accommodation, around one-quarter (26 per cent) on package tours and just over a third (35 per cent) on prepaid international airfares. People visiting for 'other' reasons (e.g. education, employment and health) spent 26 per cent of their total expenditure on food, drink and accommodation. The largest expenditure items of business visitors were prepaid international airfares and food, drink and accommodation (42 per cent and 27 per cent of total expenditure respectively) (Australian Bureau of Statistics, 2000).

The Australian figures on tourist expenditure are broadly comparable to those derived from a study of per capita daily visitor spending in San Francisco undertaken in 1995 (Economics Research Associates, 1996). The survey was conducted over a twelve-month period using almost 3000 personal interviews with 'traditional visitors' who travelled from beyond the Bay Area (more than 100 miles). The interviews were conducted in twenty-five different locations at varying times of the month and day. Total estimated average per capita daily spending of all visitors to San Francisco was $130.40 with expenditure broken down as follows:

- 36 per cent lodging
- 28 per cent food and beverages
- 16 per cent retail stores
- 11 per cent local transportation
- 9 per cent entertainment and sightseeing.

Interestingly, food and restaurants were also highly ranked in terms of what was most enjoyable about San Francisco (Economics Research Associates,

1996). A visitor expenditure study used for the master plan for Las Cruces International Airport in New Mexico (Center for Economic Development Research and Assistance, 1997) arrived at a similar figure for expenditure on food and beverages. The following percentage breakdown of expenditure per visitor was identified: hotels and motels (46.3 per cent), eating and drinking establishments (25.5 per cent), entertainment (8.1 per cent) and retail, transportation and recreation (20.4 per cent). Although the expenditure study was conducted across all tourists visiting the area regardless of the method of transportation that was used to arrive in Las Cruces, the master plan noted that the percentages are very close to those recommended by the Federal Aviation Administration in assessing airport economic impact as well as percentages used in other airport studies (Center for Economic Development Research and Assistance, 1997).

Related to the issue of regional development identified above, policymakers have become especially concerned with maximizing the returns available from tourism development. This is especially the case in the less developed countries and island microstates where there is often significant loss of revenue overseas because of food imports. Therefore, growing food for the hotel and restaurant sector can be a significant income earner and employment opportunity (Reynolds, 1993; Telfer and Wall, 1996), given the extent to which international tourists may eat out at restaurants (Table 1.1). For example, the Government of South Africa (1996) in their White Paper on *The Development and Promotion of Tourism in South Africa* noted that tourism had the potential to influence visitor tastes and create export markets:

> Through tourism, South Africa becomes the supermarket or boutique to which visitors are drawn. Apart from the normal consumption of sun, sand and sea, wildlife, wine and water sports, tourism allows its clients to inspect other goods and services for sale in South Africa. Tourists to South Africa have the opportunity to sample the local fare (e.g. wine, beer, food, craft, entertainment, etc.). Moreover, they have the leisure, time, usually the money as well as the convenience (plastic cards) to pay for local goods and services. The potential for South Africa to influence visitor tastes and create permanent export markets is very real. (Government of South Africa, 1996: s.3.2xiii)

The tourism industry was therefore seen by the South African government to have enormous potential to create linkages and to:

> dynamise other sectors of the economy – agriculture, manufacturing and services. South Africa, more than any other country in the rest of Africa

Table 1.1   Leisure/recreational activities of all US resident travellers to overseas destinations

Leisure/recreational activities	All US travellers (%) (26 853 000)	For leisure and VFR (%) (21 080 000)	For business and convention (%) (9 425 000)
Dining in restaurants	87	86	91
Shopping	76	80	69
Visit historical places	55	61	43
Visit small towns/villages	45	51	28
Sightseeing in cities	44	49	34
Touring the countryside	37	42	25
Cultural heritage sights	32	36	21
Art gallery, museum	29	32	21
Nightclub/dancing	23	25	17
Water sports/sunbathing	22	26	12
Guided tours	17	19	10
Concert, play, musical	15	17	10
Ethnic heritage sites	12	14	7
Amusement/theme parks	10	11	4
Visit national parks	9	10	5
Casinos/gambling	8	9	4
Golf/tennis	6	6	6
Cruises, 1 or more nights	5	6	2
Camping, hiking	5	6	3
Attend sporting events	5	5	4
Environmental/ecological sights	5	5	3

Source: derived from Office of Travel & Tourism Industries (2000)

or in the developing world, has the potential to supply almost every need of the tourism industry – from meat and poultry, beverages and wines, to vehicles, machinery, furniture, cut flowers, jewellery, diamonds and more. Tourism will generate demand and production in other sectors of the South African economy. (Government of South Africa, 1996: s. 3.2xvi)

Food has also become recognized as being expressive of identity and culture and is therefore an important component of cultural and heritage tourism (Bessière, 1998; Cusack, 2000; Ritchie and Zins 1978) (see Exhibit 1.1). For example, Hall and Macionis (1998: 199) suggest that: 'Wine and food can . . .

be expressive of a regional culture as well as a regional environment. Such a relationship is extremely significant for tourism because of the possibilities of utilizing wine and the associated vineyard landscape as a means of establishing strong regional identity in the tourism marketplace.'

In addition, substantial concerns exist over tourism's role in globalization and the potential for cultural homogenization, including food, has led to debates about tourism's role in the 'McDonaldization' of culture (Page and Hall, 2003; Ritzer, 1996). Indeed, the very fact that food is expressive of a region and its culture has meant that it can be used as a means of differentiation for a destination in an increasingly competitive global marketplace. Therefore, there is significant interest in the role of food in place marketing and the imaging of destinations as well as of particular tourism products (du Rand, Heath and Alberts, 2002; Elmont, 1995; Williams, 2001) (see Exhibit 1.3). Perhaps, surprisingly, Frochot's (2002) study of the use of food in regional tourism brochures within France did not show strong differences between the various regions even though different provincial food ingredients, dishes and styles remains one of the central tenets of French cuisine. Indeed, most regions appear to be using similar food images, which concern mostly raw products, products in their environment, countryside dishes and countryside products. The notable exceptions are wine and cheeses, which are heavily used but only by regions that are their main producers. In other words, the main message that French destinations want to portray is mostly that of their authenticity through images of 'real' foods, country traditions and of natural products. As Frochot (2002) noted, the types of images used in those brochures can certainly be used by other destinations if they wish to achieve a similar positioning; or they might wish to adapt it to their own national or regional positioning.

Exhibit 1.1 The ancient festival of cheese rolling

Each year thousands of spectators gather to watch the ancient sport of cheese rolling at Cooper's Hill in Brockworth near Cheltenham in the UK. No one knows the exact origins of the ritual but this spectacle reputedly dates back at least 200 years and possibly has its roots in Roman times.

A whole Double Gloucester cheese is hurled down the one-in-two gradient hill and competitors take part by chasing down after it, in an attempt to catch it. The first person down the hill wins the cheese! There are usually four men's races and also a women's and young competitors' race ably stage-managed by the master of ceremonies. Competition is fierce, but friendly, and some entrants are veterans having been involved with the race for many years. Injuries such as twisted ankles are commonplace but fortunately serious injuries are rare.

Spectators, entrants and the media travel from around the globe to marvel at this strange custom. One German television spokesman reported: 'We have nothing similar in Germany. We are here because it is such an eccentric thing to do' (http://www.ananova.com/).

However, cheese rolling is not limited to the Double Gloucester. For example, in the English village of Stilton, cheese rolling is an important part of their May Day celebrations (http://www.festivals.com).

Liz Sharples

Another reason for interest by students of tourism in food is that it is an attraction in its own right for travel. This can be both for the purposes of visiting a specific event (e.g. Exhibit 1.1) or a built attraction, such as a brewery, cheese makers or restaurant (see Exhibit 1.2). Tourists may also travel to a particular destination which has established a reputation as a location to experience quality food products, e.g. the Napa Valley in California, Provence in France, Tuscany in Italy, Niagara in Ontario (see Telfer and Hashimoto, Chapter 9 in this volume), or the Yarra Valley in Victoria, Australia. Significantly, in her study of the interdependence of farming and tourism in Vermont, USA, which had a very significant food tourism component, Wood (2001) found that that 84 per cent of respondents value the farm landscape of Vermont and 59.4 per cent say they would be less likely to visit Vermont if there were very few farms. From this perspective food tourism may therefore be regarded as a form of speciality travel or special interest tourism (Hall and Mitchell, 2001).

Finally, because it is integral to the tourist experience, food has become an important element in the marketing of tourism (Hashimoto and Telfer, 1999) and in determining visitor satisfaction (Nield, Kozak and Le Grys, 2000; Rimmington and Yüksel, 1998), as well as an important component of hospitality studies (Wood, 2000). However, as pointed out by Mitchell, Hall and McIntosh (2000: 123) in relation to wine tourism, 'profiles of wine tourists in one region should not automatically be assumed to be the same as in another, or even from one winery to another'. Understanding the differences between visitors becomes very important for marketers and operators in targeting potential food tourists (see Chapter 3).

Exhibit 1.2 Revolving restaurants

Scarcity has value. Some people collect train numbers or beer mats. Some plan their vacations visiting particular vineyards. And with only about 200 revolving restaurants in the world it is perhaps not surprising that they have become a significant tourist attraction in their own right. Even package deals have got in on the act. Brochures espouse the attractions of revolving restaurants: 'enjoy dinner from the best view in Toronto', 'the soaring CN Tower with its revolving restaurant stands as a futuristic testament to the forward thinking optimism of this great city' and 'enjoy the neon of Las Vegas with a meal at the revolving restaurant in the Stratosphere Tower'.

But is there any other added value in a trip to a revolving restaurant besides ticking another one off the list? On the face of it the whole concept seems a poor thought-out idea. Who wants to eat in a spinning restaurant? Why would you even think that would be popular, given the fact that moving while eating will at best give you indigestion and at worst probably make you very ill. Is it a gimmick to overcharge customers to consume some fairly average food? Or is it possible to justify the environmental impact of some of these restaurants – for example, the one which sits right beside Niagara Falls?

But many people do find them attractive and plan specific visits to cities that have revolving restaurants. Despite that unnerving feeling of being unable to find your table when you've visited the toilet (the restaurant floor rotates round a fixed central service section) and the faint nausea when you leave, there are many revolving restaurants in some stunning locations serving gourmet dishes of the highest quality.

The idea of dinner accompanied by a high-altitude view dates back to the Eiffel Tower, which has had a restaurant at its second 'platform' since it opened in 1889. The notion of sedentary consumers taking in a mechanized 360-degree view of their environment is also a nineteenth-century creation: at panoramas, people sat in circular theatres and watched as painted scenery of London or Paris passed before their eyes.

However, the revolving restaurant itself is an American idea. In 1961 John Graham, a Seattle architect, an acolyte of Buckminster Fuller and an early shopping mall pioneer, built the very first revolving restaurant, La Ronde, atop an office building at the Ala Moana Shopping Centre in Honolulu. These spinning dining rooms became symbols of optimism and success, and they have since spread to almost every corner of the globe, atop broadcast towers like the Space Needle and crowning modern glass-and-steel hotels. Rotation, not location, is central to many examples of revolving restaurant real estate.

To understand their appeal, one must now look to Asia, Africa and the Middle East, where the revolving restaurant is still seen as a sign of progress – an emblem of prosperity, not kitsch. Indeed, they have become more indicators of economic development than adornments to the skyline. During the 1990s, a new wave of revolving restaurants swept around the world, from Lebanon to Jakarta to Cairo, their openings often occasioned visits by heads of state and much adulatory press. Yet Americans have cooled to the dynamic dining they helped popularize. Some revolving restaurants have simply stopped rotating, others have been refurbished into conference centres, their novelty surpassed by Rainforest Cafés, IMAX theatres and corporate sky-boxes. But revolving restaurants offer something beyond kitsch appeal or the pretensions of fine dining. They offer the city itself, arrayed as a subtly drifting panorama, viewed from a circular dining car where distance is transformed into time, with departure and arrival points fixed like points on a clock. In the world's fresher skylines revolving restaurants are still symbols of arrival.

Tony Stevens

Defining food tourism

In defining food tourism there is a need to differentiate between tourists who consume food as a part of the travel experience and those tourists whose activities, behaviours and, even, destination selection is influenced by an interest in food. The definition of food tourism can be closely related to the established literature on wine tourism (see Hall, Johnson et al., 2000a). Wine tourism has been defined as visitation to vineyards, wineries, wine festivals and wine shows for which grape wine tasting and/or experiencing the attributes of a grape wine region are the prime motivating factors for visitors

(Hall, 1996) and is best seen as a specific subset of the more general concept of food tourism. Consequently, food tourism may be defined as visitation to primary and secondary food producers, food festivals, restaurants and specific locations for which food tasting and/or experiencing the attributes of specialist food production region are the primary motivating factor for travel (Hall and Mitchell, 2001a: 308). Such a definition does not mean that any trip to a restaurant is food tourism, rather the desire to experience a particular type of food or the produce of a specific region or even to taste the dishes of a particular chef must be the major motivation for such travel. Indeed, such is the need for food to be a primary factor in influencing travel behaviour and decision making that as a form of special interest travel, food tourism may possibly be regarded as an example of culinary, gastronomic, gourmet or cuisine tourism that reflects consumers for whom interest in food and wine is a form of 'serious leisure'(Hall and Mitchell, 2001; also see Wagner, 2001; Chapter 3 in this volume) (Figure 1.1).

However, as Cambourne et al. (2000) noted with respect to wine tourism, the wider region is a consideration in the attractiveness of a destination. Peters (1997) also links the concept of wine tourism to the land and suggests that when viticulture is successful, it transforms the local landscape into a combination of agriculture, industry and tourism. Peters (1997) refers to such wine regions as 'winescapes'. Similarly, Hall (2002) argues that wine, food and tourism industries rely on regional branding for market leverage and promotion and thus the appellation, or the regional 'brands' become an important source of differentiation and value added for rural regions. However, while food is an important part of regional identity and food production does have a substantial impact on the landscape it is very difficult to separate 'foodscapes' from broader concerns surrounding agricultural areas which, by their very nature, are landscapes of food production. Nevertheless, there are arguably a number of locations which, by virtue of their intensity of use for food production, including added-value processing and production, and their accessibility for visitors, including the availability of markets, farmer direct purchasing opportunities, restaurants and accommodation, are distinctive places of consumption for food tourists. Indeed, one of the critical factors in food tourism is the spatial fixity of the product. The tourists must go to the location of production in order to consume the local fare and become food tourists. This does not mean that local production is only consumed *in situ*, far from it; indeed, one of the great opportunities provided by food tourism is the potential to export to the places that the visitor comes from. Therefore, food tourism is quite literally the consumption of the local and the consumption and production of place. It is for this reason that food tourism

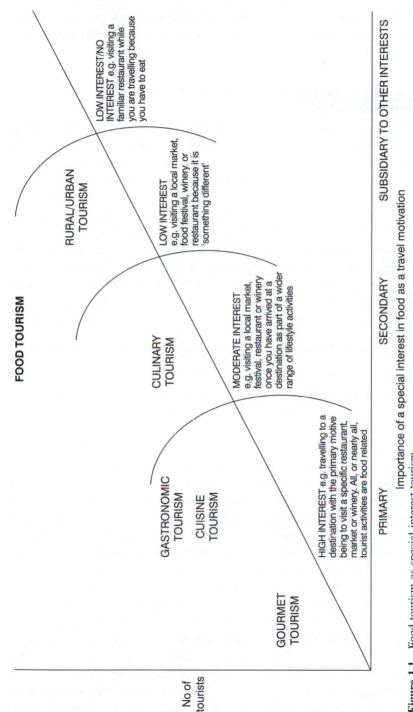

Figure 1.1 Food tourism as special interest tourism

offers so much potential to reinforce local food economies, encourage the conservation of food and biodiversity, and help sustain local identities (see Chapter 2).

Outline of book

The various chapters in the book are designed to introduce the reader to specific examples of various forms of food tourism but also to some of the general issues which surround the marketing of food tourism and its role in economic and regional development. Chapter 2 provides a general overview of food tourism's significance as a mechanism for regional development. As with many chapters and exhibits in the book the chapter places emphasis on food tourism's role in local food and economic systems. However, the chapter also uses the idea of intangible capital as a means of integrating marketing and development issues within a single management context. Chapter 3 discusses consumer behavioural issues with respect to food tourism. This includes an account not only of some demographic profiles but, more particularly, psychographic and experiential issues in food tourism. The implications and importance of social factors in influencing food tourism demand and consumption is further examined in Chapter 4 by Wan Hassan and Hall, which discusses the demand for halal food among Muslim travellers.

Chapters 5 to 11 discuss specific types of food tourism product within a range of spatial contexts. Chapter 5 by Sharples discusses the significance of European cookery school holidays while Chapter 6 by Joliffe looks at food tourism from a more international perspective in relation to a specific food product – tea. Chapter 7 examines some of the issues of product development in Papua New Guinea, a less developed country which is seeking to use indigenous foods so as to increase economic returns and maintain food diversity. In contrast, Chapter 8 looks at a very common food tourism product – the food trail – in a European country. In this chapter Meyer-Czech raises a considerable number of issues surrounding the managerial, planning and marketing of food tourism. The chapter also raises the importance of co-operation as a basis for food tourism development, a theme picked up to varying degrees in the remaining chapters in the book. For example, the study of food tourism in the Niagara Region, Canada, by Telfer and Hashimoto in Chapter 9, stresses the importance of clustering and networking as a critical factor in the success of the region for food and wine tourism. Another Canadian study by Selwood, in Chapter 10, takes on more of a destination marketing perspective, yet issues of social capital and localization as a means to attracting food orientated visitors remain important. Both Chapters 9 and 10 highlight the role of events as food tourism attractions, and this particular product is the specific focus of Rusher in Chapter 11 who also ties in issues of regional economic development, heritage and cultural commodification to food event development.

Regional issues are the focus of Chapter 12 by Sharples who examines food tourism in the Peak District National Park, England. As highlighted throughout the book, networks and relationship development have been critical for many successful developments and examples of these are presented in the Peak District, to be followed by a more analytical approach to such issues by Eastham in Chapter 13. Attitudes towards the creation of linkages in food tourism are examined in Chapters 14 and 15 which look at restaurant support for local food and wine in New Zealand and the Canberra Region in Australia respectively. Chapter 16 by Boyne and Hall reinforces the significance of many of the observations raised with respect to co-operation and networking by reflecting from their Scottish experiences on the means by which food and tourism developments can best be managed to add value for both regions and firms.

Chapter 17 by Scarpato and Daniele provides a highly significant and provocative assessment of food tourism. Much of this book emphasizes the local but, as the authors highlight, in the present era of globalization what does local really mean given that those who can afford to can, within twenty-four hours, bring in food and produce from almost anywhere in the world. Furthermore, the relationships that food tourism may create between producers and consumers at an international level may well be encouraged in order to sustain local economies, local food artisans and local food diversity. Therefore, Scarpato and Daniele provide us with a paradox with respect to our understanding of cuisine, authenticity and our sense of place. Some of these issues are taken up in the concluding chapter but, more pragmatically, the chapter also identifies a number of issues that emerge in looking at the future development of food tourism.

First course?

This chapter has provided just a brief introduction to some of the issues that surround food tourism. It is therefore only a first taste of what is to come. However, it has also provided an opportunity to consider the enormous range of concerns that emerge in any discussion of food and tourism relationships. These issues draw attention to both the production and consumption of food tourism and the very important role it plays with respect to economic development, policy, culture, heritage, identity, markets, consumers and lifestyles – issues which lie at the heart of much of the debate surrounding the future of rural places in the industrialized world as well as development issues in emerging economies.

Food is such an integral part of the travel experience that its significance has often been lost. For some it is mere fuel but for others, and arguably a growing minority, it is the prime motivation to travel. In between we have the interested and curious. This situation presents not only a challenge in the supply of food by the tourism industry (see Exhibit 1.4) but also sets a task for those who are trying to make sense out of the current situation, whether it be for academic or business reasons. Yet, in industrial society it seems that the role of food in contemporary lifestyles is undoubtedly changing. There are more cookery books sold and food programmes watched than ever before, people eat out more than they used to, and the ready-made and 'fast-food' industry also shows almost continuous growth. Yet, ironically, even though there is so much interest in food and food as a part of the tourism experience, more people than ever before do not know how to cook. It is therefore within this context that this book is written. Although this book only makes an initial contribution to understanding the tourism of taste, we hope that it is a valuable first step and will encourage others to not only study some of the issues we identify but also reflect on the practical implications of the relationship between food and tourism.

Exhibit 1.3 Portuguese food image among UK residents

Many European countries have an identifiable cuisine or, rather, key dishes that are strongly identifiable with a particular country. Tourists with only the slightest interest in food could probably identify the countries connected to pasta, tortilla, escargot, goulash, bierwurst and roast beef (Italy, Spain, France, Hungary, Germany and England, respectively). Thus these well-known food items, and others, have marketing value; they help build an image. But how many tourists could identify the country of origin of Bacalhau, Caldo Verde, Presunto, Leitao Assado, Cozido or Cataplana-based dishes – unless they had a well-developed knowledge of gastronomy or had actually spent time in various regions of Portugal? Bacalhau reputedly has 365 variations, enough to provide a different recipe for every day of the year, and Cozido is the recognized national dish so these are not obscure regional specialities and it is to be expected that visitors to Portugal will be aware of them.

A questionnaire was issued to colleagues and forty-two responses were received. The following data cannot be considered representative of UK residents as a whole as these respondents teach in a college whose primary courses involve hospitality and tourism. Though many teach business subjects and are not necessarily specialists in food or travel, it would be reasonable to assume that their combined knowledge in this area is likely to be greater than a similar number of the general public. The purpose of the questionnaire was to provide corroborative evidence to support the issue of Portuguese food image (or lack of). The findings were largely of a negative nature. This being so among these respondents, how poor may be general tourist knowledge in relation to the food of Portugal?

Table 1.2 represents the number of people, out of the forty-two respondents, who had visited selected European countries, and the total number of visits between them. It is clear that, of the European countries used in the questionnaire, Portugal was the least visited. This corresponds with general trends concerning destinations of UK residents, though Germany and Italy have exchanged places in the order. (Table 1.3 lists the European destinations of UK residents for 2000.)

Table 1.2   Respondents' visits to European countries

Country	Visited by	Total number of visits
France	41	341
Spain	38	188
Italy	31	98
Germany	25	114
Portugal	18	27

Source: Questionnaire Results (Kevin Fields, date unknown).

Table 1.3   European destinations for UK residents in 2000

Destination	UK visitors
France	11.94 million
Spain	11.15 million
Germany	2.4 million
Italy	2.32 million
Portugal	1.6 million

Source: British Tourist Authority (2001).

In both tables, Portugal is at the bottom. The population size of the other countries identified is between four and eight times greater, and the land area between three and six times greater than that of Portugal. Consequently, the difference in tourism visitors is under-standable, as fewer large cities and resorts, particularly of the mass tourism variety, exist to provide the carrying capacity of the other countries. However, 1.6 million visitors to Portugal from the UK alone indicates an extensive tourism industry. This differentiation in visitors numbers makes it understandable that knowledge of Portuguese food is less developed than for the other countries, simply because less people have been there. However, the questionnaires did not totally support this supposition.

The questionnaire asked people to identify three dishes which could be considered synonymous with each of the countries. Naturally, knowledge was greatest concerning the countries most visited and poorest for those least visited. However, many respondents demon-strated a reasonable level of food knowledge in relation to countries they had never visited, except for Portugal. Indeed, the level of food knowledge concerning countries not visited was greater than the level of food knowledge concerning Portugal demonstrated by those who had actually visited Portugal.

In general, the dishes identified for most countries involved actual names of dishes. For Portugal, what tended to be identified was specific food items (sardines, chicken, fresh fish, salt fish, and seafood) rather than dishes. One person actually identified Cataplana, which is a cooking utensil rather than the name of a dish. Nevertheless, this was an indication of significantly better knowledge than that displayed by anyone else.

Of the seventeen who had never visited Germany, thirteen managed to identify thirty-one dishes between them. Though there was a great deal of duplication of dishes, it was clear that general awareness of German food among non-visitors was quite strong.

Of the eleven who had never visited Italy, seven managed to identify twenty dishes between them. Again, there was a lot of duplication but it was also clear that knowledge of Italian food among non-visitors was quite strong. This is to be expected as many Italian dishes, particularly pizza and those that are pasta based, have become everyday staples for many in the UK. Additionally, the proliferation of Italian restaurants in the UK no doubt helps matters as well. However, the same theory cannot be used to support non-visitor knowledge of German food as few German restaurants exist in the UK and not many German food items, beyond frankfurters and Black Forest gateau, are likely to be consumed on a regular basis – at least not in comparison to pizza and pasta dishes.

In terms of Portuguese food outlets in the UK that may help build awareness of Portuguese food, the ubiquitous Nando's is the only real presence, with over fifty outlets. As the central theme of their menu is chicken with pepper sauce (chicken peri-peri), they are hardly likely to make an impact in developing awareness of Portuguese food in general.

The general lack of knowledge of the gastronomy of Portugal is all the more remarkable considering the important part that her explorers played in introducing many food items now on everyday shopping lists across Europe. The strong maritime traditions of Portugal produced Henry the Navigator and Vasco da Gama, among others. The Portuguese were reputedly the first to reach Japan and China, as well as many parts of the 'New World'. The English have the Portuguese to thank for introducing them to tea drinking. Europe, in general, has a debt of gratitude for the introduction of coriander, pepper, ginger, curry saffron, paprika, pineapples, peppers, tomatoes and potatoes (Tannahill, 1988). Indeed, some of these items are key constituents in various national dishes outside Portugal (particularly, paprika for goulash and potatoes for tortilla).

Therefore, how can Portugal have played such a crucial part in the development of European gastronomy, yet have retained so little gastronomical identity for itself? The major earthquake that Lisbon suffered in 1755 may have played a part. As well as the 15,000 lives that were lost, many books which documented traditional recipes disappeared. It is hardly credible that this is the main reason; tradition passes from generation to generation and the absence of written documentation should harm, but not destroy, this process. Recently, much of the knowledge that was considered lost has been found again. 'Fortunately just a few years ago Portuguese documents dating from the 16th century were found at Naples National Library, Italy, containing medieval recipes. In 1565 the Portuguese Princess Maria (1538–77) married the Duke of Parma. Consequently she took her personal library, including notebooks with her recipes to Italy' (www.manorhouses.com/food.htm). Modern Portugal has culinary treasures which should be as well known as others, but this appears to not be the case. How can the identity of the gastronomy of Portugal be implanted in the consciousness of potential tourists?

Building perception of Portuguese food to enhance its strength as a tourism motivator

The prospective tourist will avidly read many holiday brochures before making their choice. Even if already familiar with the destination, the brochures will be used to spark memories and build the pleasurable anticipation that is part of the holiday experience. The ready availability of publications such as *Rough Guide, Lonely Planet* and *Time Out* enables the prospective tourist to gather a great deal of information about destinations they have never visited, but these publications are more likely to be purchased after the holiday has been selected.

Kastenholz, Davis and Paul (1999) carried out research regarding the segmentation of tourism in rural areas of north and central Portugal. A survey concerning four different types of rural tourists – want-it-all, independent, traditional and environmental – produced information regarding the opportunities and activities that would most enhance their holidays. For all four categories, 'typical restaurants' came either first or second. Interestingly, 'luxurious restaurants' appeared in first and third places, in two categories, regarding the least wanted opportunities. This would appear to indicate that there is an interest in regional food, rather than 'upmarket' dining experiences.

However, the lack of familiarity that Portuguese food suffers from would be an obstacle concerning the motivation of first-time visitors. Addressing the information needs of the first-time tourist (to Portugal) would therefore appear to be a key priority. An increased level of available information would also benefit the returning tourist.

There is undoubtedly scope for developing tourism and/or enhancing the tourist experience, in Portugal, through gastronomy. The first objective would need to be the publicizing and promotion of regional and national foods in order to build awareness among prospective visitors. The most obvious vehicle for this is the World Wide Web – in terms of efficiency and cost. The type of information presented should include descriptive and specific information about Portuguese food and wine – supported by regional information in terms of restaurants and wineries, sufficiently detailed to satisfy the information search process of the most inquisitive of potential visitors.

Providing the required information is pointless unless the awareness of the availability of the information is also developed. To this end, tour operators should be encouraged to identify the uniform resource locators (URLs) for relevant sites within their brochures. All national and regional publicity materials should give prominence to the URLs and a clear indication of the information that can be obtained there. A range of initiatives to publicize Portuguese cuisine do already exist, but are most likely to be discovered by those with a specific interest in food, not those to whom it may be a secondary, but no less important, resource.

It is important that the information made available is current and updated regularly. A range of web sites, regarding Portuguese gastronomy and various destinations, were visited as part of the research for this case study. Many were clearly presenting information that had been there for some time – the 'last updated' dates were invariably one or two years ago. In reality, the information may not have needed updating as nothing has changed. But, to the visitor, the information will be viewed as unreliable and outdated if it clearly has not been altered for some time. Experienced web surfers are all too familiar with sites that have literally been abandoned, but they still have a presence on the web. The currency of the information must be obvious and beyond doubt.

None of what is proposed is going to have an overnight influence. It takes time to build an image. But, once that image is built, the effects can be self-sustaining. It is easier to sustain an image than build or change one.

Destinations in central and northern Portugal are the most likely to benefit from an enhanced gastronomical image. This is because the resorts tend to be smaller than in the south, particularly those in the Algarve. Smaller resorts tend to be less well known and prospective visitors are less likely to have preconceptions. A web site would therefore help to build an image, rather than change one. Portugal is a country with a rich history and it has made a major contribution to the development of food across Europe. Building greater awareness of its gastronomical past, and its gastronomical present, should help develop tourism in a beneficial manner.

Kevin Fields

Exhibit 1.4 Restaurants in the sky

In-flight catering is big business. The current global industry is worth in excess of US$14 billion per annum (Inflight Catering Association (IFCA), 2002) with approximately 30 per cent of this figure generated in Europe (US$4.2 billion per annum), 35 per cent in the Asia/Pacific region(US$4.9 billion per annum) and 26 per cent in North America (US$3.6 billion per annum). Latin America has a spend of US$0.4 billion per annum and the rest of the world US$0.9 billion per annum (IFCA, 2002). Despite the impacts of 11 September on consumer confidence and some airlines, the overall expansion of the air travel industry shows little signs of slowing down. Already the number of international scheduled passenger journeys stands at 550 million per annum with domestic scheduled numbers standing at 1260 million per annum (IFCA, 2002). To keep pace with this trend it is anticipated that the in-flight catering industry will see increases in turnover of approximately 2–3 per cent per annum but with some significant shifts in the way that money is allocated. It is likely that the catering spend on economy class passengers will come under increasing pressure while high-fare paying customers will expect to see an enhanced level of service and overall quality (IFCA, 2002).

All this is a far cry from the early days of 'popular' air travel in the late 1950s and 1960s when many flights offered no food at all, or merely a cup of coffee and biscuits or a sandwich. The in-flight industry today has become a complex logistical challenge where technology plays a major part in ensuring that an impressive range of hot and cold meals, snacks and drinks are prepared and served with great efficiency, and often at 'breakneck' speed, while travelling at heights of over 30 000 feet. 'Cook-freeze' and 'cook-chill' catering systems, technologies devised in the 1960s and 1970s, have provided airlines with the ability to mass produce and cook meals in advance ready for cold storage, and subsequent reheating and service from a tiny galley kitchens on board the plane. An example of this complexity was reported in the *Times Weekend* newspaper (Teeman, 2001) which discussed the case of British Airways whose individual 747 planes may carry up to 42 000 separate catering components with up to thirty items making up just one meal. Ironically, some of the budget airlines are now reverting back to the 'keep it simple' policy, in an attempt to keep prices to the minimum, offering only a minimum service or organizing their food service on a 'pay as you go' basis.

Most airlines in the Western world do not run their own catering 'in-house' but contract out to one of the specialist in-flight catering companies who look after this part of their business. The Inflight Catering Association (IFCA) lists twenty-seven in-flight companies who currently offer this type of service, ranging from a number of smaller regional companies to the giants of in-flight catering, namely LSG Sky Chef and Gate Gourmet, who currently hold about half of the total market (IFCA, 2002). Some of the airlines based in the Asia/Pacific region, for example Cathay Pacific and Malaysian Airways, prefer to maintain and manage their own in-flight catering provision.

Some in-flight caterers provide meals for up to ten separate airlines each with their own menu requirements, 'logo' crockery or packaging, and presentation and service levels, dependent on the type of market that they are serving.

To service this considerable food requirement there are approximately 600 flight kitchens throughout the world, each preparing in the region of 6000–7000 meals per day and each employing approximately 150 employees (IFCA, 2002). There are also several 'mega' operations, each capable of producing over 9 million meals annually. It is estimated that the global in-flight business directly employs in the region of 100 000 people throughout the world and a similar number indirectly, employed in associated fields such as food supply (http://www.survey.the.uk/news/release).

A number of nominated suppliers are involved in supplying food, beverages and equipment to the in-flight catering companies, all of which operate to very tight quality control criteria. Detailed dish specifications are 'worked up' each season, by the in-flight companies, after consultation with the individual airlines, in order to provide the supplier with details of the quality, ingredient profile, cost, portion size and reheating/presentation guidelines required. It is a competitive arena.

Market needs and expectations vary considerably dependent on whether the customer is flying as part of a business trip, travelling for personal reasons, perhaps to visit family or friends, or as a holidaymaker. The nature of the flight, scheduled or chartered, and the price that the client has paid for the ticket will also dictate the level of service that is required and delivered. For example, a couple embarking on a 'once in a lifetime' retirement trip travelling first class around the world will inevitably have different needs to the family with young children who are taking the advantage of a last minute cheap flight to the Costa Brava.

Caterers do not have an easy task regardless of level of service. Once on a flight, the meal takes on a certain importance in the whole proceedings, perhaps acting as a source of entertainment for those who find the whole experience of flying rather monotonous or maybe acting as a welcome distraction to travellers of a nervous disposition. Expectations run high due to the 'captive' nature of the plane – there is no alternative eating opportunity 'down the road' and the meal has been paid for in advance.

Turbulence, restricted space in which to reheat, serve and eat, passengers suffering from nausea, limited digestive capacity and reduced taste-bud sensation, and changes in 'body clocks' are just some of the concerns that the caterer has to consider when planning the menus and food-service system. Food also needs to retain its presentation, texture and taste many hours after it has been prepared and this is especially important for fresh goods, such as sandwiches, which may need to be chilled for up to twelve hours before service.

Financial restrictions are also a major limiting factor, with airlines working to an average of £3.00 cost per head for economy class, from £6.00 per head for business class and £10.00 per head for first class (Teeman, 2001). Couple this with increasingly discerning and demanding customers and the enormity of the task becomes obvious.

The cultural, religious and social mix of customers, even within one aircraft, can be enormous and this diversity presents another challenge. Caterers need to assess the types of passengers that are likely to use the airline on certain routes and cater accordingly. For example, Japanese passengers often prefer small meals, but at regular intervals of every two to three hours, adding considerably to the number of items that need to be boarded onto the plane. It would seem that the American tourist needs to eat less often, perhaps only once during a six-hour domestic flight, and Chinese passengers may require a number of snacks during a flight from Hong Kong to Shanghai. The number of customers requesting special meals such as vegetarian, vegan and restricted diets due to food intolerances is on the increase and caterers also need to be capable of providing for diets that are limited due to medical or ethnic reasons. So is this whole operation a case of mechanistic mass catering merely to provide amusement and sustenance during the flight, or should it be a memorable eating event and part of the overall holiday/travel experience?

It would appear that innovation is the name of the game. Increasingly, airlines are entering into the 'celebrity chef' market, employing big names in the catering world to advise them on their food-service provision. For example, Singapore Airlines have sought advice from Gordon Ramsey, Michel Roux has teamed up with British Airways (BA) and United Airlines are involved with American chef, Bruce Blanchard (Teeman, 2001). The creation of 'signature' dishes, specifically designed for that airline, has become a common feature of business and first class menus, and wine lists have become more interesting and comprehensive. On some airlines free drinks and wine are offered as an inclusive part of the package. In summer 2001, Singapore Airlines announced that it would be the first airline to supply free 'bubbly' to all its economy passengers (Teeman, 2001).

Peter Jones, IFCA Professor of Production and Operations Management at Surrey University, who serves on the Education and Environment committees at the IFCA, predicts that the nature of airline catering will change considerably over the next few years. At one end of the scale, airlines will seek to incorporate more relaxed styles of food service into their provision, providing customers with the opportunity of having lighter 'picnic' food, i.e. interesting sandwiches, cheese, deli items and fruit, in preference to heavier three-course meals. At the same time, some airlines will endeavour to make meals more 'individual' and exclusive by allowing customers to select their own meal choices just prior to boarding. This style of operation is already in operation with a limited number of providers. The incorporation of high-street food brands into the food-service provision, is another trend that is likely to continue (Teeman, 2001).

A glimpse into the world of airline catering reveals a multibillion-dollar industry currently demanding complex global solutions. Several questions arise. As air travel increases yet consumers become more discerning and questioning about the food that they eat, will this have an impact on the style and nature of food being offered?

In this world of McDonaldization is it important that airlines retain some cultural/local identity through the food that is being served on their planes in an attempt to incorporate the flight into the total tourism/holiday experience? Food for thought!

See http://www.inflight-catering.com/associat.htm and http://www.if-canet.com/

John Clark and Liz Sharples

2

Consuming places: the role of food, wine and tourism in regional development

C. Michael Hall, Richard Mitchell and Liz Sharples

Introduction

Industrialization, free trade (with policies of high and extensive protectionism being abandoned), widespread growth in wealth and leisure, increased environmental awareness, growing conflict among competing land use interests, ageing populations, the reduced 'tyranny of distance' in people's travel plans, inconsistent farm incomes and declining agricultural employment, and many other factors have served to change the face and structure of rural economies and the lifestyles of rural people. In addition, people's expectations of rural areas are changing as greater emphasis is given to the conservation and maintenance of natural and cultural heritage (including the rights of indigenous people). In short, economic, environmental and social developments and issues are putting increasingly varied and complex pressures on rural areas in many countries.

In this light it should therefore not be surprising that tourism and food production are seen as potentially significant sources of economic development in rural areas. Long seen as only a 'bit part' or 'minor' industry in terms of national development, tourism has now assumed centre stage as a major source of foreign income and overseas investment, and as a key component in regional development strategies (Butler, Hall and Jenkins, 1998). The reasons for the change of attitude towards tourism by politicians, business and the public are complex, but several reasons can be put forward. First, most rural areas in Western countries have suffered major recessions and concerns over foreign debt since the late 1970s. International tourism, in particular, is seen as a mechanism to help boost exports incomes. Second, economic deregulation and the impacts of globalization have affected 'traditional' employment in the manufacturing and agricultural sectors. Tourism is seen as a 'sunrise' industry that is labour intensive and therefore offers the potential to be a substantial source of employment. Finally, many rural areas in Western countries have become significant destinations for international travellers in both global and regional terms as well as domestic travellers in increasingly urbanized societies. In short, much public and private attention has been directed to tourism's economic potential (Hall and Jenkins, 1998; Jenkins, Hall and Troughton, 1998).

In the current global environment the relationship between food and tourism therefore represents a significant opportunity product development as well as a means to rural diversification. Specialized products offer the opportunity for the development of visitor product through rural tours, direct purchasing from the farm, specialized restaurant menus with an emphasis on local food, and home stays on such properties (Bessière, 1998). Indeed, in these circumstances, outsider interest in local produce may serve to stimulate local awareness and interest, and assist not only in diversification, and maintenance of plant and animal variety, but may also encourage community pride and reinforcement of local identity and culture (Wood, 2001). Therefore, it is apparent that from the seeds of globalization the development of strong local food identities and sustainable food systems have substantial potential to grow, with tourism playing an significant role in this process.

Exhibit 2.1 The Talbot

The Clift family who own and manage the Talbot at Knightwick in the UK are keen believers in the philosophy that local is beautiful. Situated on the banks of the River Teme, on the Herefordshire and Worcestershire borders, the Talbot, once a traditional coaching inn, has been in the business of offering good food and shelter to travellers since the late fourteenth century (www.the-talbot.co.uk). Today, in the hands of the Clift family, who have farmed the local land for over a century, the inn combines tradition with modern twenty-first century needs and offers a range of attractive *en suite* bedrooms, conference facilities, an award winning restaurant, and a comfortable lounge bar which is well used by both locals and visitors alike.

The family are passionate about providing a quality experience for the guests who visit and stay at the Talbot but are also passionate about being useful members of the community in which they live and work. By using locally sourced produce as a real focus for their operation, they not only provide guests with an opportunity to truly 'taste the region' but are also making a valuable contribution to food businesses in the locality.

The two sisters, Annie and Wiz, who manage the day-to-day operation of the Talbot have become experts in the art of food 'gathering'. Vegetables, herbs and soft fruits are either home-grown or come from local growers; meat, ham, milk, eggs and cheeses are provided by farms and small producers in neighbouring towns and villages and game birds, rabbits and pigeons are all obtained from local shoots. The sisters are also firm believers in the concept of 'free' food and at certain times of the year will gather wild food – nuts, berries and fruits – from the hedgerows to enhance their cuisine. The Clifts are also happy to take up the offer of surplus crops from friends' and neighbours' gardens! The only ingredient that travels any distance is fresh fish, which arrives daily from Cornwall and Wales.

Talbot food is 'honest food', without pretention, and includes many traditional favourites such as sausage and mash and steak and kidney pie, but also offers an air of excitement by the inclusion of more unusual ingredients and dishes such as stuffed breast of lamb, mutton cassoulet, confit of goose with onion marmalade, lamb kidneys in red wine marinade, potted venison and eels. Ancient recipes are often reworked with a modern twist and, wherever possible, local recipes such as treacle hollyhog, a traditional Worcestershire pudding, are included. The Talbot also has a 'make' rather than 'buy' policy and breads, raised pies, black pudding, pickles and other preserves such as jams and marmalade are all made at the inn throughout the year.

In 1997 the Clift family opened a microbrewery, the Teme Valley Brewery, at the rear of the building, so that beer and cider could be brewed in-house. The family have grown hops on their land (150 acres) for many years and this initiative seemed to be a natural step in their drive for local distinctiveness. Beer and cider are obviously served in-house but visitors can also purchase bottles and flagons to take away. In October 2001, the inn played host to the local 'Green Hop Festival'.

The Talbot has also expanded its links with the local community with the setting up of the Teme Valley Farmers' Market. On the second Sunday morning of every month the Talbot Inn car park is transformed as tourists and locals bustle among an array of stalls displaying regional food specialities and locally made crafts such as knitwear. Many of the food suppliers in attendance are also key suppliers to the Talbot operation such as the producer of Mar Goat's cheese at Great Witley. The market has proved to be such a success that in 2001 the Clifts took their 'farmers' market' to the Slow Food Show, Salone del Gusto, in Turin, Italy. They were just one of a handful of British representatives in attendance.

Events are also an important part of Talbot life, being viewed as another way of attracting business while also involving the local community. On St George's Day, for example, a mumming play and morris dancing in aid of charity takes place outside the inn.

Liz Sharples

However, as noted in Chapter 1, while the relationship between food and tourism is at first glance obvious, in productive terms the relationship needs to be integrated into a strategy for local economic development that seeks to maximize economic and social leverage between producers and the tourism industry (Centre for Environment and Society, 1999; Wood, 2001). There are several practical components to such a strategy:

- reduce economic leakage by using local renewable resources rather than external sources, e.g. use local materials for packaging, 'buy local' campaigns
- recycle financial resources within the system by buying local goods and services, e.g. hotels and restaurants need to purchase and promote local foods, produce and wine or other beverages, use local banks and credit unions
- add value to local produce before it is exported, e.g. bottle and package food locally, consider using distinctive local packaging in order to reinforce

local brand identity, use local food as an attraction to tourists thereby increasing the circulation of tourist expenditure through the local economy
- connect up local stakeholders, people and institutions to create trust, new linkages and more efficient exchanges, e.g. local farmers' and producers' co-operatives, the development of local marketing networks, 'buy local' campaigns
- attract external resources, especially finance, skills and technology where appropriate, e.g. use the Internet to connect to customers outside of the region
- emphasize local identity and authenticity in branding and promotional strategies, e.g. list the place of origin on the label and encourage consistent use of place of origin by producers
- sell direct to consumers via farm shops, direct mail, farmers' and produce markets, local events and food and wine festivals
- create a relationship between the consumer and the producer, e.g. using cellar door or farm door sales, use newsletters, web sites and the Internet to create an ongoing relationship with consumers.

The drive to create such local economic development strategies has already started in many rural regions and is increasingly being encouraged by national, regional and local government agencies (e.g. OECD, 1995; Policy Commission on the Future of Farming and Food, 2002; Scottish Food Strategy Group, 1993;). Exhibit 2.2 provides an example of such an initiative with respect to the UK Countryside Agency's Eat the View project.

Exhibit 2.2: Eat the View project

The Eat the View initiative is a project which was set up by the Countryside Agency in 2001 with the eventual aim to 'Create improved market conditions for products that originate from systems of land management which enhance or protect the countryside's landscape and character' (Countryside Agency, 2001). The project involves bringing together 'best practice' currently occurring through-out the UK with a range of activities and schemes which have a strong and sustainable focus linking food and the landscape. It is hoped that this sharing of information will encourage change by helping consumers to make the links between the products they buy and the countryside they enjoy and value.

The project has been instigated owing to the dramatic changes that have occurred in the English countryside over the last fifty years. A combination of postwar agricultural policies, designed to increase productivity, and the globalization of the food chain have had a major impact on both the character and diversity of the countryside and the methods of food production that are being employed. For example:

■ There has been a loss of local countryside 'character' and distinctiveness. Large-scale specialized farms have resulted in uniformity with a significant loss of hedgerow and woodland. This reduction in natural habitat and changes in farming practices have had a major impact on wildlife; for example, the skylark population has been drastically reduced. There is a lack of diversity among the crops that are grown and the breeds that are reared. For example, half of England's orchards have disappeared in the last fifteen years and, consequently, the range of apple varieties that are readily available has reduced.
■ More centralized and global systems of food production, processing and distribution has favoured, and been driven by, the large food retailers/supermarkets, enabling them to stock a wide range of foods at very competitive prices throughout the year. This, and other lifestyle changes, have resulted in the majority of consumers using the 'big boys' instead of local/village shops, many of which have been forced to close.
■ There has been a farming 'crisis' over the last few years particularly among small producers. Farm incomes have dropped and many farm workers have lost their jobs. This has resulted in a lack of confidence within the farming community, the industry not looking attractive to future generations and a decline in the skills and knowledge held within the sector.

Recently, however, it has been acknowledged that the establishment of a more sustainable rural policy is needed in order to prevent further decline. There are now early indicators that change is on the horizon. This has been driven and supported by several factors:

■ From the consumer perspective there has been considerable concern, over recent years, about both the quality, and the safety of food that is being sold, undoubtedly being fuelled by food scares such as the BSE crisis and the Foot and Mouth outbreak in 2001. There is also recognition, among some consumers, of the impact that long-distance food transport is having on the environment, i.e. 'food miles'. This has resulted in a small but significant, and growing, interest in organic and 'natural' produce and an awareness of ' food traceability'. Hence, a demand for more 'locally sourced' foods.

■ The maintenance of the countryside as a source of rest, relaxation and recreation is a key concern both for individuals and the industries that benefit from it. However, equally important is the maintenance of a landscape that can provide employment for the people that live there. Farmers increasingly have been forced to examine diversification into new markets and to look at ways of 'adding value' to their products in order to make a fair living.

The publication of the Policy Commission on the Future of Farming and Food's (2002a) report, *Farming & Food – a Sustainable Future*, following the Foot and Mouth crisis, highlighted the government's awareness of these issues and the need for a more integrative 'joined up' approach to rural development. The Countryside Agency through the Eat the View programme, and by working in partnership with others, list a number of outcomes that they hope to achieve namely:

■ to inform consumers about the impact of their decisions on the rural environment and economy and how they can take positive action to benefit the countryside
■ the development of systems for marketing/distributing/selling produce which will enable consumers to show support for local/ sustainable production methods
■ the development of quality standards/accreditation systems to underpin markets for local/sustainable products
■ the development of local marketing/branding initiatives which will use unique features, e.g. rare animal breeds, local customs, etc.
■ the development of new supply chain partnerships between retailers/producers which will increase the proportion of locally sourced/sustainable products
■ an increase in the proportion of produce sold through alternative markets to large retailers and bulk caterers, e.g. local collaborative arrangements
■ an increase in the number of local/community-led food initiatives creating stronger local markets for produce and strengthening links between producers and consumers (adapted from Countryside Agency, 2001).

Many of these initiatives are closely interwoven with tourism. By participating in food festivals and events, by visiting and buying from specialist food factories, by buying from farm shops and farmers' markets, and by eating at restaurants, pubs and cafés which feature local foods/dishes on their menu, the tourist connects closely with the local food culture, starts to understand the landscape that provided it and directly supports the rural economy.

The Eat the View web site (http://www.countryside.gov.uk) has details of participating projects at a local level, listed by region, with contact information enabling tourists and interested parties to access information.

See also http://www.cabinet-office.gov.uk/farming

Liz Sharples

Local food and drink networks, the development of food trails and the rediscovery of farmers' markets – often frequented by day-trippers and tourists – are testimony to the importance of the local within the global. Indeed, a key point to emerge from examining local food systems is that the problems of globalization for local food production and gastronomy present as much an opportunity as they do a threat. In addition, it should be noted that numerous places are using similar strategies, such as farmers' markets, in order to maximize the benefits of food production and tourism for rural areas. Therefore, the question must be posed as to what factors may allow rural regions effectively to differentiate themselves in the competitive economy of the twenty-first century.

Arguably, the key to maximizing the benefits of food, wine and tourism in local regional development is through understanding the nature of the global intangible economy in which we now operate.

> In the intangible economy, capital is more freely available, transaction costs are lower, and geographic barriers are dropping. These changes are . . . causing intangible capital to become more valuable, physical assets to become less valuable, and global companies to earn even higher profits. Companies are surviving if – and only if – they have privileged intangible capital. (Daley, 2001: 5)

From a regional development perspective firms survive not only if they have privileged international capital but also if the places in which they are embedded do as well. Nevertheless, it is important to recognize that the new, 'intangible' economy is not a radical break from the 'old' economy. The effects of scarce capital, transaction costs and regulatory and geographic barriers still have enormous influence. Cost-efficiency, market dynamics, and articulating a value proposition attractive to customers are as important in the 'intangible economy' as they were before (Daley, 2001). However, what is new is the growing appreciation that intangibles and globalization are important, and that no one is immune from their effects.

Critical to the success of regional business strategies is the development of intangible capital. For example, many firms and regions have intangible assets – knowledge, relationships, reputations and people. However, only some firms and regions succeed in converting these assets into intangible capital. Intangible assets only create value when captured as intellectual property, networks, brand and talent. These four intangibles are the scarce resources of the intangible economy (Daley, 2001) which also provides a basis for the success of linking food and tourism as a regional development strategy.

Intellectual property

There is a gradual recognition of the intellectual property dimensions of food, wine and tourism. This can take place at the level of individual types of food or wine product but it is also increasingly being applied to regional characteristics. Wine, food and tourism are all products which are differentiated on the basis of regional identity. For example, wine is often identified by its geographical origin, e.g. Burgundy, Champagne, Rioja, which, in many cases, have been formalized through a series of appellation controls, in turn founded on certain geographical characteristics of a place (Moran, 1993; 2000; 2001). Foods, for example cheese, are also identified by their place of origin. Similarly, tourism is also promoted by the attraction of regional or local destinations. It should therefore be of little surprise that the relationship between wine, food and tourism is extremely significant at a regional level through the contribution that regionality provides for product branding, place promotion and, through these mechanisms, economic development (Hall, 2002; Ilbery and Kneafsey, 2000a; 2000b). As Moran (1993: 266) observed:

> Burgundy gives its name to one of the best known wines in the world but at the same time the region of Burgundy becomes known because of its wine. Moreover, the little bits of it, often only a few hectares, also derive their prestige from the wines that are produced there. In Burgundy, the process has developed to the extent that in order to capitalize on the

reputation of their most famous wines many of the communes . . . have taken the name of their most famous vineyard. Corton was added to make Aloxe-Corton, Montrachet to make both Puligny-Montrachet and Chassagne-Montrachet, Romanee to make Vosne-Romanee, St Georges to make Nuits-St Georges and so on.

Relph (1996) has suggested that tourism is fundamentally about the difference of 'place'. Clearly a region's physical elements combine to define it as a 'place' and contribute to the attractiveness of a destination. Similarly, Cook and Crang (1996: 132) identify the importance of place as a means of differentiation: 'These geographical knowledges – based in the cultural meanings of places and spaces – are then deployed in order to "re-enchant" [food] commodities and to differentiate them from the derived functionality and homogeneity of standardized products and places.' Perhaps not surprisingly then, Hall (1996: 114) suggests that there is a significant overlap between the elements of *terroir* and those features that are important to regional tourism branding (e.g. landscape and climate). Hall and Mitchell (2002b: 69), for example, discuss the idea of 'touristic terroir', arguing that 'In the same way that the *terroir* of a region gives wine its distinctive regional characteristics, the unique combination of the physical, cultural and natural environment gives each region its distinctive touristic appeal – its *touristic terroir*'.

Important as this notion of *touristic terroir* is in determining the flavour of the wine and food tourism experience, it is important to note that, like wine, *terroir* is not the only influence on flavour. As the late Peter Sichel (former president of the Grand Crus de Bordeaux) suggests 'terroir determines the character of the wine, man [*sic*] its quality (cited in Halliday, 1998: 28) – the same could be said of the experience of the wine and food region. Continuing the wine and food analogy, then, *touristic terroir* may determine the character of the regional experience, but it is the influence of the tourism entrepreneur, the winery owner, restaurant manager, chef, service provider or regional tourism office that will determine the quality of the experience (as attested by the large number of visitors who cite service as the most enjoyable or important aspect of visits to wineries (Hall and Mitchell, 2002b). Similarly, just as the appreciation of wine and food is a very subjective experience that is based on individual sensory perception, experience, tastes and attitudes, the food tourist experience is shaped by the subjective nature of the individual consumer (see Chapter 3). Nevertheless, regionality is clearly important, particularly in terms of promoting the attributes of the food, wine and tourism products of a given place. For Moran (1993: 264) place allows small local producers to 'enhance their reputations and to sell directly to final demand, thus competing more effectively against large corporations'. The French have long used the term *terroir* to describe the phenomenon of the place characteristics of food products – a term which defies a literal translation into English, but which is the 'almost mystical' combination of all aspects of soil, climate and landscape present in the wine region (Halliday, 1998). Halliday (1998: 28) further suggests that *terroir* 'lies at the heart of the French appellation system, built up by a thousand years of practical experience which has led to a precisely detailed delineation of quality'. Significantly, such appellation controls have been adopted across Europe and lie at the heart of European laws regarding the regional intellectual property of wine and food.

Appellation controls have long served to act as a form of intellectual property in terms of rural space as well as product, which have international repercussions in terms of the ability – or otherwise – to copy such names. More recently, however, regional speciality food and drink products have also come to be registered as intellectual property as designated quality labels within European Union (EU) and national law (Ilbery and Kneafsey, 2000a); a process which Ilbery and Kneafsey (2000b) appropriately described within the context of globalization as 'cultural relocalization'.

In March 2002 the EU announced further amendments to Regulation (EEC) No 2081/92 in order to provide for full implementation of the World Trade Organization (WTO) agreement on the Trade-Related Aspects of Intellectual Property Rights (TRIPs) and improve protection for geographical indications. The purpose of the regulation is to protect geographical names used for products meeting certain very precisely defined requirements. The regulation provides a harmonized EU-level system protecting rights in the domain of intellectual property law and falls within the ambit of the TRIPs Agreement (1994), in terms of the protection of geographical indications. According to the EU (2002), 'By giving all WTO members the right to object to registration of these geographical names, the proposal would improve the recognition on international markets'. Franz Fischler, Commissioner for Agriculture, Fisheries and Rural Development stated, 'Better protecting [the] geographical indication [of EU foodstuffs] from pirating or unfair competition will not only help to better inform consumers world-wide. It will also encourage producers, who can be safe in the knowledge that their produce receives its legitimate world-wide recognition' (EU, 2002). From early 2002 the names of about 570 cheese, meat, fruit, vegetable and other products were registered as Protected Designation of Origin (PDO), Protected Geographical Indication (PGI) and Traditional Speciality Guaranteed (TSG) (The full list of protected names can be found on the Internet at http://europa.eu.int/qualityfood.) Examples include:

- Austria: Vorarlberger Bergkäse
- Belgium: Jambon d'Ardenne
- Denmark: Danablu
- Finland: Lapin Puikula
- France: Roquefort
- Germany: Bayerisches Bier
- Greece: Tsakoniki Melintzana Leonidiou
- Ireland: Timoleague Brown Pudding
- Italy: Prosciutto di Parma
- Luxembourg: Miel Luxembourgeois de marque nationale
- Netherlands: Noordhollandse Gouda
- Portugal: Citrinos do Algarve
- Spain: Queso Manchego
- Sweden: Svecia
- UK: Cornish clotted cream.

The amendments of March 2002 were designed to promote the EU system of denominations of origin as a model to the rest of the world. According to the EU (2002):

> The driving idea behind it is the wish to improve protection of European quality products also outside the EU. As the EU cannot force non-EU countries to do so, they would be invited to do so on a reciprocal basis. If a non-EU country introduced an equivalent system including the right of objection for the EU and the commitment to protect EU names on their territory, the EU would offer a specific procedure to register their products for the EU market.

Significantly, similar measures to reinforce the role of national brands are occurring in other jurisdictions. An act of Congress proposed in the USA early in 2002 would require US retailers to inform consumers of produce commodities' country of origin. At the time of introduction voluntary labelling guidelines were expected by 30 September 2002, and final regulations were to be put into effect on 30 September 2004. The new law would require produce retailers in the USA to inform consumers, at the final point of purchase, of the commodity's country of origin. The required information may be provided by means of a label, stamp, mark, placard or other clear and visible sign on the produce or on the package, display, holding unit or bin containing the commodity at the final point of sale. Significantly, food-service operators and suppliers are not part of the mandate. Commodities that are prepared, served, offered for sale or sold in a food-service establishment would not have to bear country of origin labelling under the proposal (American Chamber of Commerce, 2002). Although the American developments may be perceived by some as a de facto form of protection by encouraging Americans to purchase US produce it must also be recognized that the brand value of some national produce and the association of a country with quality, for example food and wine with France or New Zealand, may have positive effects for some non-American produce.

Networks

Networks and cluster relationships are also a significant part of the development of intangible capital through their role as proving the social capital which underlies much economic development. Networking refers to a wide range of co-operative behaviour between otherwise competing organizations and between organizations linked through economic and social relationships and transactions. Industry clusters exist where there is loose geographically concentrated or association of firms and organizations involved in a value chain producing goods and services, and innovating. A cluster is defined as a concentration of companies and industries in a geographic region that are interconnected by the markets they serve and the products they produce, as well as by the suppliers, trade associations and educational institutions with which they interact (Porter, 1990). Such exporting chains of firms are the primary 'drivers' of a region's economy, on whose success other businesses, construction firms for example, depend in terms of their own financial viability. An industry cluster includes companies that sell inside as well as outside the region, and also supports firms that supply raw materials, components and business services to them. These clusters form 'value chains' that are the fundamental units of competition in the modern, globalized world economy. Clusters in a region form over time and stem from the region's economic foundations, its existing companies and local demand for products and services (Waits, 2000). Firms and organizations involved in clusters are able to achieve synergies and leverage economic advantage from shared access to information and knowledge networks, supplier and distribution chains, markets and marketing intelligence, competencies and resources in a specific locality. The cluster concept focuses on the linkages and interdependencies among actors in value chains (Enright and Roberts, 2001).

Wine has been recognized as one industry in which clustering is a significant competitive factor. Indeed, Porter (1990) himself used the California wine industry as an example of successful cluster development. Similarly, Blandy (2000: 21) cites the example of the South Australian wine industry as 'the classic example of a successful industry cluster in South Australia . . . a group of competing, complementary and interdependent firms that have given strong economic drive to the State through the cluster's success in exporting its products and know-how nationally and internationally'. Marsh and Shaw (2000) have similarly commented that clustering and collaboration have been the primary reason for the success of the Australian wine industry.

Cluster formation is regarded as a significant component in the formation of positive external economies for firms, including those of the wine industry, with tourism being recognized as a significant component (Porter, 1990), while Telfer (2000a,b) has argued that cluster development has been a significant component of wine and food tourism network development in the Niagara region of Canada. Tastes of Niagara in Ontario is a Quality Food Alliance of Niagara's food producers, winemakers, chefs, restaurateurs and retailers (http://www.tourismniagara.com/tastesofniagara/index.html). Established in 1993 members have joined together to promote the uniqueness of the region's agricultural products to consumers through the development of and maintenance of high-quality regional produce, cuisine, events and service (see Chapter 9). Although one of the lessons of cluster development programmes around the world 'is that there is no precise, "right" (one size fits all) formula for developing industry clusters' (Blandy, 2000: 80), a number of factors have been recognized as significant in the development of clusters and the associated external economy which serves to reinforce the clustering process. These include:

■ the life cycle stage of innovative clusters
■ government financing and policies
■ the skills of the region's human resources
■ the technological capabilities of the region's research and development (R&D) activities
■ the quality of the region's physical, transport, information and communication infrastructure
■ the availability and expertise of capital financing in the region
■ the cost and quality of the region's tax and regulatory environment
■ the appeal of the region's lifestyle to people that can provide world-class resources and processes.

Hall (2001) identified several other factors which may be significant in cluster and network success:

■ spatial separation – the existence of substantial spatial separation of vineyards and wineries within a wine region due to physical resource factors
■ administrative separation – the existence of multiple public administrative agencies and units within a region
■ the existence of an entrepreneurial and innovative 'champion' to promote the development of a network
■ the hosting of meetings to develop relationships.

Of these factors, the role of champions as well as the involvement of the local state was regarded as especially important in the creation of wine and food tourism networks and associated new product development in the New Zealand situation (Hall, 2002; see also Henton and Walesh, 1997). Such an observation is significant as Audretsch and Feldman (1997) have argued that the generation of new economic knowledge tends to result in a greater propensity for innovative activity to cluster during the early stages of the industry life cycle, and to be more highly dispersed during the mature and declining stages of the life cycle.

The Australian Bureau of Industry Economics (BIE, 1991a; 1991b) identified four potential roles for government in the development of networks:

■ disseminating information on the opportunities created by networks
■ encouraging co-operation within industries through industry associations
■ improving existing networks between the private sector and public sector agencies involved in research and development, education and training
■ examining the effects of the existing legislative and regulatory framework on the formation, maintenance and break-up of networks relative to other forms of organization, such as markets and firms.

In the case of wine and food tourism in Australia, government has directly used the first three roles in the creation of specific organizations and/or the provision of funding for research, education, co-operative strategies and mechanisms, and information provision (Hall et al., 1998). The BIE (1991a; 1991b) considered information gaps to be a major factor in the impairment of network formation. Indeed, there are substantial negative attitudes towards tourism by wineries and some food producers, whereas tourism organizations tend to be far more positive towards the wine and food industry. This situation is reflective of Leiper's (1989) concept of tourism's partial industrialization that suggests that businesses need to perceive that they are part of the tourism industry before they will formally interact with tourism suppliers. Although New Zealand shares numerous similarities with Australia in terms of attitudes of producers towards the tourism industry, there has been virtually no national government involvement in trying to create wine and food tourism networks beyond having large producers participate in co-operative marketing and branding schemes (Hall et al., 1998). In Australia innovation and the creation of networks has occurred in great part at the regional level because of state involvement. In New Zealand, where innovation has occurred it has been because of champions and individual innovators who have been able to generate local interest and involvement.

Creating local networks

There are a number of food supply chains which have implications for local food systems and network development (Figure 2.1). The classic industrial model of the food supply chain of producer–wholesaler–retailer–consumer is often linked through transport, contractual and regulatory networks which has provided a relatively efficient means of distributing food but has substantially affected the returns that producers get as well as placing numerous intermediaries between consumers and producers. The industrial model has allowed the development of larger farm properties, reduced labour costs and has supported export industry, but it has done little to promote sustainable economic development and food systems.

One of the main influences on the development of direct sales from farmers to consumers was the extent to which intermediaries were, and still are, profiting from the industrial food supply chain. As Sommers (1980: 14) reported in his book on the rebirth of farmers' markets in the USA, 'One economist estimated that 80 per cent of the retail cost of supermarket produce goes to wholesalers, jobbers, packers and transporters' leaving only 20 per cent in the farmers' pocket'. Indeed, Jolly (1999) reported that in the USA 'the farm share of retail prices for various commodity groups range from approximately 7 per cent in the case of cereals and baked goods to 46 per cent for eggs. The average farm share is 18–21 per cent for fresh and processed fruits and vegetables' (Table 2.1).

One alternative is to create a direct relationship between producers and consumers. This can be done by direct marketing and box deliveries as well as direct farm purchase and farm stalls. In relation to tourism, an important direct relationship is the opportunity for the consumer to purchase at the farm

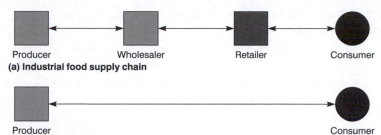

Producer   Wholesaler   Retailer   Consumer
(a) Industrial food supply chain

Producer   Consumer
(b) Farm, cellar door, pick your own, stall or direct box sales

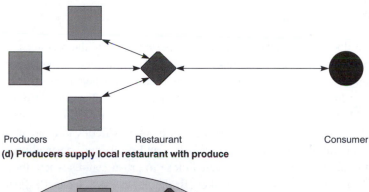

Producers   Consumer
(c) Producers cooperate in running a market and/or undertaking joint promotion campaigns

Producers   Restaurant   Consumer
(d) Producers supply local restaurant with produce

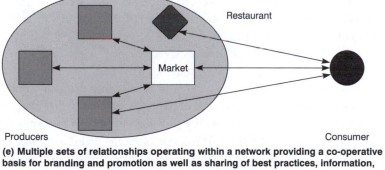

Restaurant

Market

Producers   Consumer
(e) Multiple sets of relationships operating within a network providing a co-operative basis for branding and promotion as well as sharing of best practices, information, research and development, and education and training programmes

Figure 2.1   Different supply chains and local food systems
Source: after Page and Hall (2002)

Table 2.1   Farm value as a percentage of retail price for domestically produced foods in the USA, 1987 and 1997

Items	1987 (%)	1997 (%)
Livestock products:		
Meats	47	37
Dairy	42	32
Poultry	45	41
Eggs	54	46
Crop products:		
Cereal and bakery	8	7
Fresh fruits	26	18
Fresh vegetables	31	18
Processed fruits and vegetables	24	19
Fats and oils	18	21

Source: USDA, *Agriculture Fact Book* (1998) in Jolly (1999)

or cellar door allowing the consumer to experience where the produce is from and the people that grow or make it, thereby, creating the potential for the development of long-term relationship marketing and better returns for the producer. Indeed, one of the explicit intentions of the US Farmer-to-Consumer Direct Marketing Act was to provide 'increased financial returns to farmers'. Such direct sales are extremely popular with small wineries in many parts of the world and are often used by peri-urban and rural food, horticultural and agricultural producers who are located close to urban centres where they can take advantage of the day-trip market (Bruhn et al., 1992; Connell, Beierlein and Vroomen, 1986; Jolly, 1999; Kezis et al., 1984; Leones, 1995; Leones et al., 1995; Linstrom, 1978; Lockeretz, 1986; Nayga et al., 1994; Nettleton, 1999). Nevertheless, such individual developments, while useful at the business level and adding to the overall attractiveness and diversity of a location, do not usually constitute a network relationship that can promote a region more effectively. Moreover, it also has to be recognized that many such producers do not see themselves as being in the business of tourism – even though their customers fit official definitions of tourist and day-tripper. Such an observation is significant, as previous research has indicated the difficulties that business perceptions can create in the development of networks and effective co-operative strategies (Hall et al., 1998; Hall, Johnson and Mitchell, 2000).

Co-operative relationships between producers provide the basis for the creation of a producer network that can pool resources to engage in local promotion and branding and undertaking research (Hall et al., 1998). In addition, the pooling of resources can also lead to the development of new products such as produce markets. For example, in the case of the Yarra Valley Regional Food group in Victoria, Australia, a group of small producers united their resources to run a series of farmers' markets to sell and promote their produce and that of the region. In 1999 they ran four markets. In 2000 they ran eleven and helped generate substantial publicity for the region (Halliday, 2000). Indeed, farmers' markets are one of the great success stories of food tourism in recent years. According to Hamilton (2000: 77) in the USA, 'By 1994 there were 1,755 farmers' markets nationwide, by 2000 there were 2,863'. In the UK the growth of farmers' markets has been no less dramatic. In 1997 the first farmers' market was (re)established at Bath, by 2002 there were 240 such markets (Purvis, 2002). Farmers' markets are regarded as having the potential to make a substantial contribution to the rural economy, especially for farmers seeking to maximize their returns (Table 2.2).

In a study of consumer opinions of roadside markets and farmers' markets in Ohio in the USA, Rhodus, Schwartz and Haskins (1994) found that:

- over 88 per cent of Ohio households believe they receive higher-quality produce directly from the farmer

    90 per cent of the respondents indicate a preference to buy their fresh fruits and vegetables direct from the farmer, whenever possible

    55 per cent of Ohio's households shopped at a roadside market during the survey period; 29 per cent had shopped at a farmers' market, and 40 per cent of these had shopped at this venue four or more times
- respondents perceived produce quality, produce freshness and produce prices to be better at roadside and farmers' markets than at supermarkets, but supermarkets were perceived superior in terms of convenient location to home, variety of produce, consistent supply, store promotions and convenient location to work
- for those respondents who did not shop at roadside markets, reasons included not convenient/far away (45 per cent), takes too much time (12 per cent), not open the hours I want (4 per cent), prefer supermarkets (18 per cent), raise my own vegetables (18 per cent) and too expensive (4 per cent)
- farmers' markets were perceived as not convenient by 60 per cent of the households surveyed.

    55 per cent of households would shop at roadside markets, and 58 per cent would shop at farmers' markets if they were conveniently located.

Table 2.2   Benefits of farmers' markets according to the UK National Association of Farmers' Markets

Producers

- They cut out the intermediary allowing increased financial returns through direct selling, price control, and a regular cash flow.
- They provide the producer with direct customer feedback on produce and prices.
- Transport and packaging requirements are less thus reducing the producers' costs.
- They provide a secure and regular market outlet. This is especially valuable for; new producers, producers in organic conversion, and small-scale producers who are unable to produce the quantity required by supermarkets.

Consumers

- They provide direct contact and feedback between customers and producers, so you can be sure how your vegetables are grown and meat produced.
- They help to improve diet and nutrition by providing access to fresh food.
- They play an important role in educating the consumer as to the production and origin of their food.
- They can be a source of information and inspiration on how to cook and prepare fresh ingredients.

The environment

- They help reduce food miles, thus vehicle pollution, noise and fossil fuel use.
- They help to reduce packaging.
- They encourage more environmental production practices, such as organic or pesticide free.
- They encourage farm diversification and hence biodiversity.

The community and local economy

- They help bring life into towns and cities aiding regeneration.
- They encourage social interaction, particularly between rural and urban communities.
- They stimulate local economic development by increasing employment, encouraging consumers to support local business and thus keeping the money within the local community.
- They attract business to retailers in the vicinity.
- They can encourage the unemployed and underemployed to develop new skills, self-confidence and income-generating possibilities.
- They play an important role in Local Agenda 21 and other council initiatives established to increase the environmental sustainability of government policies, local communities and businesses.

And they are fun!

Source: after UK National Association of Farmers' Markets
http://www.farmersmarkets.net/started/benefits/default.htm

Kezis et al. (1998) in their study of the Orono Farmers' market in Maine found that quality, support for local farmers and atmosphere were very significant to consumers (Table 2.3). Nearly half of weekly patrons reported spending upwards of US$10.00 per visit. Consumers also indicated a willingness to pay more for produce at the farmers' market than for similar produce at a supermarket, with 72 per cent indicating a willingness to pay an average of 17 per cent more for farmers' market produce. Similar data regarding consumer perceptions of farmers' markets was also identified in a study conducted of farmers' markets in San Diego, California (Jolly, 1999; see Chapter 3 for a more detailed discussion of consumer perceptions) (Table 2.4). In the same study, approximately equal proportions of the sample perceived prices to be higher or lower than supermarket prices. However, 73 per cent perceived quality at the farmers' markets to be superior to supermarket produce. Two-thirds of the respondents also indicated a preference to have items indicate a San Diego grown label and half stated a willingness to pay more for San Diego grown products (Jolly, 1999).

As in California, the state of Oregon has also embraced the farmers' market concept. A study of 2714 consumers at the Albany and Corvallis Saturday farmers' markets and the Wednesday farmers' market in Corvallis indicated the significant economic impacts that farmers' markets may have on a community (Novak, 1998):

Table 2.3   Most important reasons for shopping at the Orono farmers' market by non-first time consumers

Reason	Percentage
Quality of the products	72.5
Support local farmers	59.6
Friendly atmosphere	38.2
Health and food safety concerns	29.8
Convenience	13.5
Good price	10.7
Variety	8.4
Good service	5.0
Consistency	2.2

Note: N = 178 Total adds to more than 100 per cent because of the opportunity for multiple responses.

Source: Kezis et al. (1998)

Table 2.4   Factors favouring patronage of farmers' markets in San Diego County

Factor	Count	Per cent
Freshness	399	92.0
Quality	379	87.0
Taste	339	76.0
Locally grown/produced	308	71.0
Help local farmers	259	59.0
Nutritional value	211	48.0
Atmosphere	201	46.0
Best value for money	177	41.0
Convenience	164	38.0
Price	157	36.0
Know grower	62	14.0
Others	34	8.0

Note: Consumers could choose multiple responses.

Source: unpublished study of San Diego farmers' markets: consumer preferences and shopping patterns in Jolly (1999)

- Consumers at the markets bought goods from three to six vendors.
- Consumers spent an average of US$12 to US$15 a visit, with the amount increasing as more seasonal produce became available.
- Shoppers at the Wednesday market spent 30 per cent more than Saturday shoppers, with women and retired people forming a significant portion of the visitors.
- Daily revenues for vendors varied widely, from US$50 to US$2000.

88 per cent of the visitors to the Albany Saturday market and 78 per cent of the visitors to the Saturday market in Corvallis said their main reason for going downtown that morning was the farmers' market.

63 per cent of the Corvallis shoppers and 35 per cent of the Albany shoppers said they also planned to spend money at other downtown shops or restaurants after their market visit.

10 per cent of those who responded said they stopped shopping because they could not carry any more goods.
- the three markets attracted about 4500 adults and sold nearly US$37 000 during an average week, even though they were open for only thirteen hours during that time.

The benefits of farmers' markets to the surrounding regions has also been argued by farmers' markets in Ontario who state that 60 to 70 per cent of market-goers visit neighbouring businesses on their way to and from the market. On the province-wide scale the growth of farmers' markets in Ontario has had an even more marked impact. Farmers Markets Ontario (2001) estimate that in 1999 farmers' markets in the province attracted about a million shoppers a year, 90 per cent of whom came for the fresh produce. Over 25 000 people work in the markets sector with annual sales at all farmers' markets across Ontario exceed C$500 million and with an overall impact on the province's economy of over C$1.5 billion.

Another model of generating local food production is the use of a restaurant to act as the conduit by which local produce is presented to tourists. The development of local purchasing relationships by restaurants can have a substantial impact on local produce as it can assist in developing quality produce, allow producers gain a clearer understanding of how their produce is being used, as well as providing a guaranteed sales outlet for their produce. In the case of the latter, the knowledge of a guaranteed minimum income may allow producers the opportunity to expand production and find other markets for their produce. For example, in the case of both the Barossa Valley in South Australia and the Marlborough region in New Zealand, restaurant local purchasing patterns have significantly assisted the diversification of produce as well as promoted artisan foods and local wines. Similarly, in New Zealand, West Auckland restaurants have decided to support their local wine industry by offering only their products (Thompson, 2000). Studies of restaurant purchasing patterns are dealt with in more depth in Chapters 9, 14 and 15.

One major initiative with respect to the use of local foods has been the National Trust in the UK. As a major landowner within the UK, owning 245 000 hectares of countryside and working with over 2000 tenant farmers, the National Trust is keen to play its part in developing a safe future for farming and ensuring its role within the economy, the environment and society as a whole (National Trust, 2001). In 2001 the National Trust published its *Farming Forward* strategy, a vision for sustainable farming which clearly lays out its objectives for the next twenty years. The document carefully presents the National Trust's commitment to a sustainable way forward by outlining a number of 'themes' that it sees as vital and also calls for some far-reaching reforms/changes to current farming policy, for example a radical reform of the EU Common Agricultural Policy (CAP). One of the themes discussed in the document is that of 'A local food economy' where the National Trust establishes its commitment to shortening the supply chain between primary producer and consumer in order to benefit farmers economically and to improve consumer confidence. The concept of adding value to products by emphasizing local distinctiveness is also explored.

This commitment to local food is an added bonus for tourists/visitors, who visit the hundreds of National Trust properties each year, as it can enrich and add interest to their tourism experience. The National Trust has been 'wed' to the notion of local and seasonal food for some time and has already made some sound moves in embedding this focus in many of their restaurants and cafés, located on their properties throughout the country. In 2000, the National Trust described its move to make the catering provision provided in its historic properties, relevant, as far as possible, to that particular setting (Morrow-Brown, 2000). Many of the National Trust's catering operations now use vegetables and fruit picked daily from the estates' kitchen gardens, historic recipes are used to educate and delight visitors, and preserves, pickles and cordials are produced, when there is a glut of produce, to add interest to the menus. Some houses have even restored features such as their original mushroom houses in order to provide crops for the restaurant, for example Hanbury Hall in Worcestershire, UK.

In 2002, the National Trust embarked on a new venture with the opening of a farm shop at Wallington Hall in Northumberland. The 14 000 acre estate, which attracts 100 000 visitors each year, is also home to a dozen farms and has a number of other neighbouring farms from which to draw its produce (Henderson, 2002). The shop will sell meat reared to high welfare and environmental standards, free-range eggs, local cheeses and bottled goods such as chutney. The operation will act as a pilot for the National Trust, which plans to open a network of similar shops around the country. The National Trust has also explored the concept of expanding into mail and Internet ordering of meat in the future (Henderson, 2002) enabling them to 'extend' their link with visitors after they have returned home, widening their portfolio of customers and providing vital jobs for people in rural areas. In 2002, the National Trust made a public demonstration of their commitment to locally sourced food by using the theme 'From Plot to Plate' on their stand at the Chelsea Flower Show, which focused on crops from kitchen gardens and the importance of traditional fruit and vegetable varieties (National Trust, 2002).

Finally, we arrive at the ideal model of multiple sets of producer and consumer relationships operating within a formal network structure which provides for branding and promotion. In the case of Hawkes Bay in New Zealand such developments have occurred primarily because of several local champions who saw the need to promote Hawkes Bay collectively as they saw that their own individual businesses would be more successful if there was a strong brand and producer network. Indeed, following their formation in July 2000 the Hawkes Bay wine and food group have developed a food and wine trail, brochures, improved signage and have engaged in more effective joint promotion strategies, including the development of a wine and food orientated Hawke's Bay regional brand. Indeed, such has been the success of the group that local government is having to respond to the initiative and develop support structures for the group. In November 2001, Hawkes Bay hosted the second New Zealand wine and food tourism conference as part of the development of a national food and wine tourism strategy. However, unlike many of the Australian and European examples discussed above, such initiatives have come from the private sector and from the goodwill of certain individuals rather than having occurred because of initial government involvement and support (Hall, 2002).

Events also often provide a focus for network structures which integrate producer and consumer relationships. Indeed, food-related events are often an extension of previous market activities which may serve to reinforce local food traditions or may put the spotlight on important regional products. Undoubtedly, there has been a substantial increase in the number of food festivals in recent years and for many people they may provide an easy opportunity to get to know the food and drink of a particular region (Getz, 1997). A survey carried out by the Heart of England Tourist Board (2001) into the motivations and attitudes of tourists with regard to food and drink, carried out at five UK food festivals/fairs in 2001 revealed that almost one-third of visitors travelled more then 50 miles in order to reach an event and that 72 per cent of respondents were at the location specifically for the event. Indeed, such is the importance of food events and festivals to the British rural economy that, following economic impacts of the Foot and Mouth outbreak which occurred in 2001, they were one of the targets of the Department for Environment, Food and Rural Affairs Recovery Fund. Exhibit 2.3 details one of the more successful food festivals held in the UK.

Exhibit 2.3 Ludlow Marches food festival

Ludlow, a small market town nestled close to the English/Welsh border has become something of a gastronomic phenomenon over recent years. With a population of only 10 000 residents in and around the area, Ludlow has become home to more top-quality restaurants than anywhere else in the UK, with the exception of London which is home to over 7 million people. The fact that many top chefs have chosen to practise their trade in Ludlow is a reflection of the image that Ludlow has built as a 'centre of excellence' for good food. This reputation can partly be attributed to the very successful food festival that takes place in this small town each year.

The concept for holding a food festival in Ludlow was originally conceived in 1995 by the Ludlow and District Chamber of Trade and Commerce as a brave idea to boost the business image of the area. The idea of using food as a focus for the festival was initially something of a 'stab in the dark' for the organizers but, as plans progressed, the committee started to appreciate the wealth of good food and drink producers they had on their doorstep. For example, the town boasts no less then six excellent independent butchers which primarily source their meat from one of the country's remaining small abattoirs. This valuable resource acted as a catalyst for setting up a Sausage Trail, which has become one of the most popular activities at the festival each year.

The organizers also felt a certain confidence in the town's ability to host a major festival, as Ludlow has been home to a successful arts festival for nearly thirty years, and has an exceptional venue in the castle that lies at the heart of the historic town. The castle has continued to play an important part in the food festival each year, acting as a hub for the various events and competitions that take place, and by providing an ideal setting for the Food Suppliers Fair. The timing of the food festival in September was a deliberate policy to act as a balance to the arts festival, which dominates the town each May. The infrastructure enabling Ludlow to readily cater for an extra influx of visitors was already in place, with the town boasting a number of good hotels, guesthouses, restaurants and cafés to suit different budgets, and having a host of interesting specialist shops.

The festival has grown to become a significant national event and is arguably the 'number one' among rural food festivals within the UK. It was certainly one of the first food festivals of this type to have taken place within the UK and, as such, has become a model of good practice for other food-related events both in the UK and internationally. In 2001, more then 13 000 visitors were attracted to participate in the food and drink trails, sampling sessions and cookery demonstrations that were on offer at Ludlow. This was a 30 per cent increase on the previous year.

The activities during the festival are designed to create interest in 'real' food and drink but many have a fun element too. In 2001, visitors enjoyed the famous Ludlow sausage trail, a real ale trail, competitions for the best pork pie, loaf, sandwich and cake, and a waiters' race, as well as visiting and sampling at the food fair where over seventy exhibitors had stands, with the number of exhibitors predicted to increase in the future.

In the early days the organizing committee had to spend time and effort attracting suppliers to the food fair but now the suppliers view this event as one of their key promotion opportunities. Many are regulars, such as the local Hobson's Brewery who have attended since the start. A Gastronomic Celebration Dinner held in the castle on the last evening always rounds off the festival's proceedings.

The organization for the event is masterminded by John Fleming who has been involved with the festival since its humble beginnings. He chairs a committee of local representatives drawn from Ludlow's business community. The event runs strictly on a non-profit-making basis and relies almost entirely on the goodwill of a team of volunteers who help to plan and stage-manage the weekend's activities. In 2002 over eighty volunteers were involved. The only paid member of staff is a part-time employee who carries out many of the administrative and co-ordination duties.

The marketing strategy of the event is simple but effective. A well-organized web site (http://www.foodfestival.co.uk) provides information for both the exhibitor and the visitor and a leaflet campaign of approximately 40 000 leaflets is distributed to tourist information centres, hotels and libraries, in an area extending to the Manchester, Birmingham and Bristol boundaries. The event is also well served by the press, who ensure that the festival is featured extensively in both the local and national press. Visitors travel from around the UK to attend the festival, the majority coming from within a two-hour driving distance.

Sponsorship is mainly limited to local organizations and businesses, and comes from a variety of different sources including wine merchants, food retailers and hotel companies as well as some regional funding bodies such as Advantage West Midlands. Sponsorship is becoming increasingly important for the event but the majority of funding still comes from the sale of festival tickets.

Each year the festival organizers look for new ideas in order to maintain an innovative approach and in 2002, for the first time, the festival was preceded by an industry conference, which examined issues about 'real' food and drink and its impact on rural economies and tourism.

Ludlow's popularity has been boosted by an influx of top chefs over recent years, which has created an additional 'pull factor' for food lovers. Shaun Hill at The Merchant House (listed in both the Michelin and the AA guides) is probably the best known of the chefs to have chosen Ludlow as their home, but there are many other excellent restaurants in and around the town including Mr Underhills, Dinham Hall, The Cookhouse at Bromfield, The Hibiscus Restaurant, Les Marches Restaurant at Overton Grange, the Courtyard and The Roebuck at Brimfield. This wealth of good eating venues ensures that Ludlow maintains its gastronomic profile throughout the year keeping a good flow of visitors to the town even during the winter months.

See http://www.foodfestival.co.uk

Liz Sharples

Brand

The wine, food and tourism industries all rely on regional and national branding for market leverage and promotion (Hall et al., 1998). Hall (1996: 114) describes the importance of tourism place and wine appellation or region thus: 'there is a direct impact on tourism in the identification of wine regions because of the inter-relationships that may exist in the overlap of wine and destination region promotion and the accompanying set of economic and social linkages' brands become an important source of differentiation and added value for rural regions. As Daley (2001: 12) recognized:

> Brands are also increasingly recognized as the source of extraordinary profit. Companies with brands, particularly the diversified brands of companies such as Disney or Virgin, consistently generate higher returns than companies without strong brands ... Food retailers are generally integrated players, owning everything from can-making to distribution operations. Some of the most successful, such as Coke and Red Bull, have decided that the profitable part of the value chain is brand management, and have exited the other parts of the value chain, like manufacturing, where intangibles are harder to capture.

Food branding in relation to place, tourism and regional development operates at a number of different levels. Generally we can recognize difference in branding at the level of the nation, the region and of the individual firm. For a number of countries, national images become a very important part of branding strategies. In the case of Ireland, regional images operate at the national scale in the marketing of the main Irish food and tourism products (Cawley et al., 1999). However, Irish products are usually being marketed rather than Irish regions. Regional images are used to invoke the environmental images which are usually associated with Ireland: 'the clean, green environment associated with geographical position on the western edge of Europe, low levels of industrialization and relatively low-intensity methods of . . . production' (Henchion and MacIntyre, 2000: 632). Interestingly, such images are also used by a number of other countries, including Iceland and New Zealand, as a means of reinforcing national brands (see below). Nevertheless, what is significant in the Irish case is the extent to which place has become an important factor in the cross-promotion of food and tourism and the development of brand Ireland (Cawley et al., 1999; Cotter, 1992; Henchion and MacIntyre 2000). For example, in January 2002 the Irish Food Board, Bord Bia, launched its 'Pure Ireland. Pure Taste' marketing theme in the western USA. Participating companies included Nestlé Ireland Ltd, McCann's Irish Oatmeal, Irish Biscuits Ltd, Jacob's Biscuits, Barry's Tea and the Irish Dairy Board, including the Farmhouse Cheese Group. The eighteen-month campaign was designed to consolidate and leverage the marketing activities of the participating companies behind a comprehensive marketing programme aimed at achieving increased retail distribution, maximizing consumer awareness and trial, and raising the overall level of awareness of Irish produce (Just-food.com, 2002).

Similarly, the link between tourism and the development of the New Zealand wine and food industries has given rise to opportunities for the co-branding of a number of New Zealand products.

> When one product does well overseas there are spin-offs for others. As a country's trade in food and drink develops, it has an effect on tourism. Similarly, visiting a country and enjoying its products can create a market for those products elsewhere. New Zealand has used this technique to advantage with a number of products, such as wine. (Bramwell, 1994, in Mitchell and Hall, 2000)

In 1994 the New Zealand Tourism Board (NZTB) entered a joint marketing programme with Air New Zealand and Silver Fern Holidays to capitalize on the export success of New Zealand wine to Canada (New Zealand Tourism

News [NZTN], 1994). The headline of the article reporting the Canadian venture (NZTN, 1994) was 'NZ's wines attract Canadian visitors'. The NZTB combined demographic information with consumer profiles of New Zealand product sales to target key markets in urban centres through the Canadian travel magazine, *Latitudes*. The issue featured New Zealand, its wines, wine regions and wine heritage, and included a recipe insert called 'A taste of New Zealand'. Readers were offered three 'FIT [free and independent traveller] orientated wine trail tours' (NZTN 1994).

Similar campaigns have also been held in conjunction with food exporters. A 1997 NZTB marketing campaign in four of its key markets involved both tourism wholesalers and two non-tourism partners – Zespri (New Zealand kiwifruit brand) and ENZA (export division of the New Zealand Apple and Pear Marketing Board). The Australian campaign promoted a broader range of products than previously, including 'fine food and wine' (NZTN, 1997: 6). One advertisement stated 'We're not ones to brag, but our wines are winning awards, even in France' (NZTN 1997: 6).

Food, export and tourism were regarded as ideal partners for joint marketing activities because they target consumers with a high discretionary income (NZTN, 1994), use similar brand statements based on New Zealand's 'clean-green image' (Hall and Kearsley, 2001) and reflect and promote the distinctiveness of regions (Mitchell and Hall, 2000). Recognizing the importance of the relationship between images of food exports and tourism, the NZTB and *TradeNZ* now jointly market products under the 'New Zealand Way' brand and 'Fern' logo. Launched in 1993, New Zealand Way is an international branding exercise that identifies, positions and markets quality New Zealand products. It was developed after it was recognized that:

> New Zealand is not top of mind internationally and whilst generally positive images exist they lack clarity and consistency. Research showed that while New Zealand was generally regarded as a distant and friendly country, with a strong 'clean and green' association, this was usually a vague understanding and did not translate into competitive advantage. In some developing markets, customers had little or no perception of New Zealand at all. (New Zealand Way, 1998)

The 'Fern' brand and logo has been registered in forty-four countries across the globe. New Zealand Way uses a range of events, advertising, promotional activities and imaginative public relations exercises developed around themes such as 'Fresh the New Zealand Way', 'Taste the New Zealand

Way' (both associated with food and wine products) and 'Experience the New Zealand Way' (associated with tourism activities). In 1998 New Zealand Way's 170 'brand partners' jointly accounted for 20 per cent of New Zealand's foreign exchange earnings (NZ$4 billion) and represented the top 20 per cent of New Zealand companies (New Zealand Way, 1998). Some of the more well-known brand partners include, among others: AJ Hackett Bungy (Queenstown) Ltd, Helicopter Line, Air New Zealand, Quality Hotels Ltd, Corbans Wines, Steinlager (beer), ENZA (New Zealand Apple and Pear Marketing Board), Anchor (butter and dairy products), Fernleaf (dairy products) and Cervena (farmed deer) (http://www.nzway-.co.nz/brand_partners.html) More recently, the Brand New Zealand campaign has gained substantial leverage from Tourism New Zealand's 100 Per Cent Pure campaign to encourage international visitors to New Zealand, thereby reinforcing the clean, green image of New Zealand tourism and produce.

The New Zealand Way and the Pure Ireland promotions are examples of national-level advancement of the relationships between food and tourism. However, while they may work effectively at the national level and will promote broad awareness of produce, the costs of participating in these strategies is prohibitive to most small food producers and even local food producers networks may not have the financial resources to be involved, although they may still benefit from flow-on effects. For example, the Australian national wine and food tourism strategy has been substantially criticized for being steered to meet the interests of large export-orientated companies even though the majority of visitors to wineries are domestic and the large number of wineries in Australia are only small operations (Macionis and Cambourne, 2000). Nevertheless, the fact that places can become brands and hold significant brand values indicates why, as discussed above, place now has significant importance as intellectual property. Just as significantly region of origin also clearly influences consumer purchasing patterns.

According to Henchion and MacIntyre (2000) in a study of the consumer preferences in Ireland, region of origin was an important consideration for two out of three consumers when deciding to purchase quality products. Reasons as to why region of origin encourages purchase are provided in Table 2.5. However, significantly, the study went on to note that while links between regions and purchase of quality products exist, there was a relatively low level of awareness and understanding of the selected territorial/regional labels that existed for Ireland. Almost one out of every two respondents understood region of origin to mean country of origin.

Table 2.5   Reasons why region of origin encourages purchase

Reason	Percentage of respondents
Support Irish products	20
Trace back to producer	15
Ensure Irish jobs	15
Region is associated with quality	14
Loyalty to local producers	10
Keep money in local area	4
Other	6
No difference between sources	17

Source: Henchion and MacIntyre (2000: 639)

Talent

Talent and knowledge retention and management are also key elements in successful innovation and competition. In the knowledge economy it becomes vital that regions, as much as individual firms, attract, retain and develop the best of their people. Therefore, education and training programmes are important for regional development in the food and tourism area, as is the conduct of research programmes. However, many smaller businesses often have very limited budgets for research and development with the expectancy in some countries and regions that education, training and research will be undertaken or funded by government. In a study of the development of alternative enterprises on New Zealand farms Taylor and Little (1999) reported that deterrents to training included:

- time
- being rural based, away from places where training and education are usually available
- childcare or family demands
- clashes between training programmes and peak farm or enterprise times
- the unique nature of some enterprises and their skill requirements.

In the USA extension services have clearly played a major role in developing intellectual capital in rural areas with respect to food and regional development. Nevertheless, tourism may also have a significant role to play in attracting people to rural regions in terms of its contribution to the amenity values which may attract or retain people in certain areas (Galston and

Baehler, 1995; Power, 1996). Amenity values include such items as an attractive rural environment, recreational and leisure opportunities, cultural richness, reasonable costs of living, safe communities, good transport and communications access to major urban centres, and quality public services. Such amenities attract retirees, second-homers (holiday homes) and tourists, thereby creating demands for additional services and labour (Hall and Williams, 2002; Williams and Hall, 2000; 2002). In the case of Norway for example, Flognfeldt (2002) has identified second-home developments as being a significant factor in bringing entrepreneurial expertise into rural communities as well as providing trading linkages between rural areas and urban consumers. Research in the western USA also suggests that quality of life factors are major determinants of population change and employment growth (von Reichart and Rudzitis, 1992; 1994; Shumway and Otterstrom, 2001) with jobs following people, rather than people following jobs (Vas, 1999). Similarly, lifestyle entrepreneurship is a major factor in the development of a number of new food and tourism related developments in countries as diverse as Finland and New Zealand (Hall, 1992).

Conclusion

Factors leading to the rural restructuring in the developed world are related to the development of strategies to promote local food systems and economic development. Both are a result of globalization. They are interconnected because in as much various facets of globalization have affected the production and consumption of food so it is that those same dimensions can be used to promote local food-ways, identity, and economic development. Perhaps most significantly they also need to be contextualized within the notion of the development of intangible capital centred on intellectual property, networks, brand and talent. These four intangibles are the scarce resources of the intangible economy which places therefore need to maximize if they are fully to leverage the relationships between food and tourism for the purpose of place competitiveness. In addition, intellectual capital lies at the heart of the intrinsic properties of quality food products which consumers value. Four quality indicators can be identified (Henchion and MacIntyre, 2000; Ilbery and Kneafsey, 1998):

- *Attraction*: generating attraction by tapping into the wants of consumers, designs, textures, taste, freshness, price and consumer perceptions.
- *Specification*: ensuring specification of production method or use of raw materials or ownership in order to ensure authenticity.

- *Certification*: achieving certification by a professional organization, government or other accrediting body, e.g. quality marks, organic symbol, self-regulation, appellation, PDO, PGI or TSG.
- *Association*: establishing association either geographically with a place or historically with a tradition or culture, e.g. using traditional methods in the preparation of a product.

Strategies to integrate tourism and cuisine in order to promote economic development and the creation of sustainable food systems occur at national, regional, and local levels (Figure 2.2). Ideally, these levels should be integrated in order to maximize the likelihood of policy success. However, often the reality is that different levels of government and industry will undertake their own initiatives without consulting or co-operating with other levels.

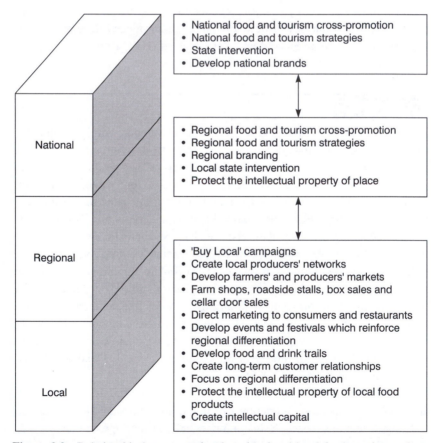

Figure 2.2 Relationship between national, regional and local food, tourism and regional development strategies

There are a number of mechanisms for promoting sustainable food systems using the relationship between food and tourism, each of which operates most effectively at particular levels. Although intervention by the national and local state will occur at all levels it is very common for the policy activities at the higher level to be implemented at the lower level in order to achieve targeted regional and local development goals. This approach has been particularly common within the EU and in federal states, such as Australia (Hall, Johnson and Mitchell, 2000).

In addition, the relationship with tourism is being used more effectively to brand national and regional foods as well as supply tourists directly in the expectation that this may create further demand when they return to their home countries. At the local level the development of networks is crucial to this task and also allows for the pooling of resources between small enterprises. The developed world is experiencing a dramatic upsurge of interest in artisan foods, food markets and promoting regions on the basis of their local produce. In the global market long-term competitive advantage will be gained by differentiation on the basis of what is unique to a place, not on the production of low-value undifferentiated product. Promotion of the interrelationships between food and tourism should therefore continue to be an essential component of the place marketing and development mix if rural places in the developed countries, as elsewhere around the world, are to thrive in the global food and tourism environment of the twenty-first century.

3

Consuming tourists: food tourism consumer behaviour

Richard Mitchell and C. Michael Hall

Food has many roles to play for consumers: it is functional (sustaining life); it plays a key role in our celebrations; it is a conduit for socializing; it is entertaining; it is sensuous and sensual; and it is a way of experiencing new cultures and countries. For many, food becomes highly experiential (i.e. much more than functional) when it is part of a travel experience, it can become sensuous and sensual, symbolic and ritualistic, and can take on new significance and meaning. Even the most basic meal can be etched in memory forever when it is eaten when surrounded by awe-inspiring scenery or at the end of a special day exploring a new city. You would expect, then, that an understanding of tourists' food consumption and experiences would be a highly studied area of hospitality and tourism studies. However, studies of food and tourism are largely limited to food safety and hygiene issues (e.g. MacLaurin, 2001, MacLaurin et al., 2000), analyses of food and wine festival attendance (e.g. Pratt, 1994), supply-side issues such as business networks (e.g. Hall and Johnson, 1998), food production and tourism (e.g. Telfer and Wall, 1996) and cross-promotion between food and tourism (Mitchell, Hall and Johnson, 2001) or the impacts of tourism on regional or national cuisine (e.g. Bessière, 1998, Hall and Mitchell, 2001). Even more established disciplines studying the 'human element' of food consumption such as anthropology, sociology or cultural studies have done little to explore the consumptive experiences of tourists. Because of the paucity of established research in this area, this chapter focuses on providing some *a priori* frameworks for consumer behaviour research in food tourism. Despite this, some details of food tourists and their behaviour are available from a disparate and largely unrelated range of sources, and this chapter also attempts to paint a picture (albeit a sketchy one) of food tourism consumer behaviour on the basis of existing research.

Mitchell, Hall and McIntosh (2000: 118)suggested that:

> consumer behaviour research is important for stakeholders in wine tourism because it can help provide important insights into who the wine tourist is, what motivates them to visit a winery, take a guided tour, attend a wine festival or purchase wine and why, thus allowing marketers and managers to effectively target and develop markets.

The same can also be said of food tourism stakeholders such as restaurant and café owners, cookery school providers, festival organizers, hotel and resort managers, bed and breakfast operators, and food producers. By understanding how tourists make their decisions to purchase and/or consume food products we will be able to gain a better understanding of when we need to intervene in their decision-making process. Appropriate intervention can, in turn, be used to persuade them to purchase 'our' food products and services.

Consumer behaviour research is the study of why people, either individually or in groups, buy the product they do and how they make their decision (Swarbrooke and Horner, 1999). Such research therefore examines a range of internal (e.g. motivation, attitudes and beliefs, learning, lifestyles and personality) and external (e.g. demographics, reference groups and culture) influences on decision making (e.g. purchase decision, choice, brand awareness and loyalty, evaluation and post-purchase decisions) and, more recently, the consumption experience (e.g. the occasion, consumption setting and benefits gained from the experience). Research on consumer behaviour is interdisciplinary, drawing on concepts and theories from such fields as psychology, sociology, social psychology, marketing, cultural anthropology, economics, media studies, cultural studies and geography (Bell and Valentine, 1997). While there appear to be few studies relating specifically to food and tourism, these disciplines have studied the consumption of food more generally and undoubtedly provide a useful basis for research into food tourism.

Consumer profiles of food tourists

It is widely recognized that tourists provide a significant proportion of the market for restaurants and cafés around the world, including empirical evidence from France (Euromonitor, 2001a), the UK (Euromonitor, 2001b), New Zealand (Restaurant Association of New Zealand, 2001a; 2001b) and the USA (National Restaurant Association, 1997; 1998; 2002). Further, some tourism authorities have undertaken research that includes eating out as an activity for various segments of the travel market. For instance, Tourism New Zealand identified that dining out is the most commonly cited activity for international visitors (54.1 per cent of visitors for the year ending June 2001), ahead of both general sightseeing (53.6 per cent) and shopping (46.2 per cent) (Tourism New Zealand, 2002). However, despite the positive contribution that tourists clearly make to restaurant profitability, there is little published research on how this market is constructed. This view is echoed in the comments of the Economic Planning Group of Canada (2001: 10), who state that, while they have been able to find a considerable amount of material on wine tourism from around the world, 'other than the research from the TAMS study . . . [conducted specifically for their purposes] . . ., there appears to be little market research on culinary tourism'.

Demographic profiles

As a result of this lack of direct research into food tourism, there are few insights into the demographic characteristics of food tourists, and those insights that do exist are largely superficial. For example, Tourism New Zealand (2001a) provide basic demographic data by segmenting the international visitor market visiting restaurants by country of origin (Table 3.1). One area in which some marketing research has been conducted is with respect to farmers' and produce markets and farm outlets. Research by the UK National Association of Farmers' Markets suggests that the typical customer falls into the AB (upper/middle class) or C1 (lower middle class) socioeconomic group – working people with high disposable incomes, 'the kind who know a good cut of Dexter beef when they see one' (Purvis, 2002). In the USA, demographic surveys at farmers' markets have indicated that patrons are predominantly white females with above average incomes, age and education (Abel, Thomson and Maretzki, 1999; Connell, Beierlein and Vroomen, 1986; Eastwood, Brooker and Gray, 1995; Govindasamy, Italia and Adelaja, 2002; Hughes and Mattson, 1995; Leones, 1995; Leones et al., 1995; Lockeretz, 1986; Thomson and Kelvin, 1994). That the majority of patrons to American farmers' markets are women should not be surprising. Women still make the bulk of all food purchases in the USA.

> A full 86% of the produce buyers surveyed for *The Packer Fresh Trends edition* were women. Women are more sensitive to price than men and are more likely to try new or unusual fruits and vegetables. The percentage of women making purchasing decisions in households with children under 18 is a whopping 99%. (Leones, 1995: 1)

However, interestingly, Leones went on to note that visits to farmer's markets tend to be more family orientated, so other members of the family tend to take a more active role in purchasing decisions. Table 3.2 provides a demographic profile of visitors to farmers' markets in the USA. Hughes and Mattson (1995) also noted that farmers' market shoppers typically patronize a greater number of food stores than non-farmers' market shoppers. They, therefore, suggest

Table 3.1 Eating out/restaurants as an activity while on holiday in New Zealand (year ending June 2001)

Nationality	Number visiting restaurants	Total visitors	% of nationality	Ranking out of all activities
UK	115 558	191 044	60.5	2
Germany	29 509	49 962	59.1	2
Hong Kong	23 159	39 484	58.7	3
USA	107 734	183 774	58.6	2
South Africa	10 362	17 924	57.8	2
Taiwan	21 399	37 348	57.3	2
Canada	21 517	37 711	57.1	2
South Korea	32 297	56 577	57.1	1
Australia	286 584	522 925	54.8	1
Singapore	18 742	34 738	53.9	2
Netherlands	12 733	24 292	52.4	6
Japan	77 000	157 465	48.9	3
Total all countries	905 164	1 672 677	54.1	1

Source: adapted from Tourism New Zealand (2001a)

Table 3.2 Demographic characteristics of US direct farm outlet customers

Characteristics	Arizona	Illinois	Wisconsin	Michigan	New York
Sample size	904	136	873	-	856
% female	55%	–	–	65%	75%
Average age	approx. 35–45	53–55	49	45	25–40
% with some college education	69%	–	60%	65%	65%
Household size	-	2.9–3.0	2–4	-	–
% first-time visitors	32%	–	–	39%	9%
% coming from within 20 miles	less than 11%	approx. 75%	80% within 40 miles	–	78%
Most common way to learn of direct farm outlet	word of mouth (45%)	word of mouth (66%)	word of mouth (55%)	word of mouth (51%)	word of mouth

Source: after Leones (1995)

that low-income consumers do not frequent farmers' markets because 'despite the price savings at farmers' markets, [they are] not inclined to make as many stops because of the extra time and gasoline involved' (Hughes and Mattson, 1995: 2).

One exception to this lack of data on the demographics of food tourists is a comprehensive study of the market potential for 'wine and culinary' tourism for Ontario, Canada (EPGC, 2001). This background report to the *Strategy for Wine and Culinary Tourism in Ontario* provides an in-depth analysis of three market segments in the USA and Canada: those with low interest, moderate interest and high interest in wine and cuisine. Exhibit 3.1 provides some of the highlights from this study.

Exhibit 3.1 High interest in wine and cuisine tourism among the US and Canadian populations

Cuisine and Wine Interest Index

The Cuisine and Wine Interest Index was developed as part of the Travel Activities and Motivation Survey (TAMS) of Americans and Canadians, which was prepared by Lang Research for an association of Canadian tourism ministries and other tourism organizations. The Index relates to the following six items from the survey associated with cuisine:

1 Pursuit of the following vacation experience during the past two years:
  (a) 'To experience the good life with fine cuisine, good wine, being pampered.'
2 Participation in the following activities during the past two years:
  (a) local outdoor cafés
  (b) restaurant dining – regional or local cooking.
3 Restaurant dining – internationally acclaimed restaurants.
4 Touring a region's wineries where you stay one or more nights.
5 Going to wineries for a day visit and tastings.
6 Indicating that the following new attraction would make them 'a lot more interested' in taking a trip to Ontario:
  (a) a wine region such as the Napa Valley or Cote d'Or in France.

Factor analysis classified respondents as either:

- low interest (below average score in the six items)
- moderate interest (average participation score in the six items)
- high interest (significantly above average score in the six items).

Market size and location

Canada: high interest respondents accounted for 14.2 per cent of respondents (extrapolated to 2.5 million individuals), while another 18.8 per cent (3.37 million) had a moderate interest. Quebec and Ontario had the highest level of interest.

USA: high interest accounted for 19.6 per cent (30.65 million) and a further 18.8 per cent exhibited a moderate interest. Interest was strongest in the Pacific/Hawaii states of California, Hawaii, Oregon, Washington, Alaska and the Southern Atlantic states of Florida, Georgia, North Carolina, South Carolina.

Demographic characteristics

In both Canada and the USA, higher levels of interest were observed among the more affluent and better educated sectors of the marketplace, particularly couples without children.

Canada: High interest demographics included:

- young couples (married or living common law, 18–35 years, no children under 21 at home)
- mature couples (married or living common law, 36–65 years, no children under 21 living at home)
- advanced university degree (21 per cent high interest)
- income levels of C$80 000 plus (24 per cent high interest).

USA: High interest demographics included:

- young couples
- mature couples
- mature singles (not married or living common law, 36–65 years, no children under 21 living at home).

Market segments

The study used a market segmentation approach known as Lifespan Demographic Segments which uses lifecycle stage, education level and household income as the basis for analysis. The Lifespan Demographic Segments that rated highly on the Cuisine and Wine Interest Index were Affluent Mature and Senior Couples:

- **Canada**: 33 per cent with high interest compared to the average of 14.2 per cent
- **USA**: 39 per cent with high interest compared to the average of 19.6 per cent.

Key characteristics:

- 3.5 per cent of the Canadian adult population
- 85 per cent mature couples (35–65 years) and 15 per cent senior couples
- average age 54.5 years
- 100 per cent university or college educated – 30.8 per cent advanced degrees
- 100 per cent household incomes over C$80 000
- average household income – C$108 600.

Also important in both markets were Affluent Young Couples, Affluent Mature Singles, Affluent Families, and Affluent Young Singles, all with above average interest levels.

Source: EPGC (2001) after Lang Research (2001)

In the absence of data for other destinations, it can be useful to make inferences about wine tourists from sources other than visitor surveys. A possible source of demographic data is readership profiles for magazines targeted at those interested in food and travel. In Australia, for instance, *Australian Gourmet Traveller* is one such magazine and its readership profile provides a rich source of demographic data (see Table 3.3).

Table 3.3 shows that readers of *Australian Gourmet Traveller* were more likely than the general population to be female, aged between 35 and 49 years, middle class (socioeconomic groups AB and C), professional or white-collar workers and earning more than A$30 000 per annum. It is perhaps too presumptuous to suggest that all food tourists have these characteristics. However, it could be suggested that, by purchasing this magazine its readers show a strong commitment to food and travel as a lifestyle choice and, as such, are likely to be those most motivated to travel because of food.

Table 3.3 *Australian Gourmet Traveller* readership profile

Profile	Magazine (%)	Population (%)
Men	34.15	49.28
Women	65.85	50.72
Age[1]		
14–17	1.23	6.89
18–24	7.69	12.2
25–34	19.69	18.72
35–49	36.31	27.72
50+	35.08	34.48
Socioeconomic[1]		
AB	47.08	20.01
C	24.62	20.0
D	16.31	20.0
E	8.31	20
FG	3.69	19.99
Personal occupation[2]		
Professional manager	45.03	30.51
Clerk/white collar	40.35	33.32
Skilled tradesman	8.77	17.12
Semi/unskilled	5.85	19.05
Personal income[2]		
Under $20 000	4.09	8.65
$20 000-$29 999	8.77	19.62
$30 000+	87.13	71.73
$40 000+	66.67	47.08
$50 000+	47.37	29.64
$60 000+	32.75	18.03

Notes:
[1] Percentages are percentage of all people.
[2] Percentages are percentage of all full-time workers.

Source: ACP

Psychographic profile

While demographics can provide the basis for simple segmentation of food tourist markets, psychographic data (such as motives, lifestyles, interests, attitudes and values) allow the researcher to add 'vitality to consumer profiles that cannot easily be captured by demographics' (Schiffman and Kanuk, 1987: 141). In the absence of any research dedicated to identifying the psychographic profile of food tourists, data relating specifically to food tourists is once again relatively scarce. A search of the existing studies, however, allows an, albeit fragmentary, picture to emerge of some of the lifestyles, attitudes and values of food tourists.

Motivation

One of the most elementary typologies of tourists that uses motivation is that proposed by Johnson (1998: 15) relating to wine tourists: *specialist* versus *general* tourist. While the general wine tourist is 'one who visits a vineyard, winery, wine festival or wine show for the purpose of recreation', Johnson suggests that the specialist wine tourist is 'one who visits a vineyard, winery, wine festival or wine show for the purpose of recreation and whose primary motivation is a specific interest in grape wine or grape wine-related phenomena'. This definition therefore excludes the tour party whose key motivation was certainly not wine per se, but the desire to have a relaxing day out (Johnson, 1998: 15). This typology can be directly applied to food tourists, with Lang Research's (2001) 'high cuisine and wine interest' tourists the most likely to be the specialist food tourist. Lang Research found that few American (19.6 per cent) or Canadian (14.2 per cent) tourists fell into this category, reflecting findings by Mitchell and Hall (2001c) in relation to specialist wine tourists (i.e. less than 10 per cent with high knowledge and interest in wine). This is also supported by other specialist/generalist distinctions within tourism (see for example Richards, 1996). An expanded discussion of this typology is discussed below.

A further insight into the motivations of wine and cuisine interested tourists is also found in the study of Ontario, Canada (EPGC, 2001, after Lang Research, 2001). Lang Research (2001) identified the vacation experiences sought during pleasure travel by the respondents and the results provide a useful perspective on what motivates those most interested in food tourism. According to the EPGC (2001: 13, after Lang Research 2001) those with a high interest in vacation activities associated with wine and cuisine were considerably more likely to also have sought out vacation experiences that fall into the following categories:

- *Personal indulgence*: 'To visit a popular, trendy place; To visit casinos and gamble; To experience the good life – fine cuisine, being pampered; To experience city life.'
- *Exploration*: 'To visit historical sites and important places in history; To see natural wonders and important natural sites.'
- *Romance and relaxation*: 'To rest, relax and recuperate; For intimacy and romance; To spend quality time with family away from home.'

69

Travel lifestyle

Lifestyle research is closely related to motivation, in that the lifestyle choices made by an individual are the manifestation of their external and internal travel motivations. The motivation profile provided by the EPGC (2001) is therefore both an insight into what motivates high-interest cuisine and wine tourists and the 'travel lifestyle' choices that they make. The EPGC (2001: 13–14) also outline a range of activities and travel product choices that give us a further insight into high interest cuisine and wine lifestyles:

Activities of high cuisine and wine interest respondents

A higher level of participation than moderate or low interest respondents in outdoor activities such as water sports. However, the association was much stronger with cultural and entertainment activities, particularly:

- Shopping and dining
- High arts e.g. ballet, opera
- Gardens and natural attractions
- Concerts, carnivals and festivals
- Gambling, horse and auto racing

Accommodations of high cuisine and wine interest respondents

More likely to stay at:

- A B&B [bed and breakfast], spa or accommodation at a gourmet restaurant
- A seaside resort
- A ski resort
- A lakeside or wilderness lodge
- A cookery or wine tasting school

These choices clearly reflect the motivations above. For example, B&Bs, spas or accommodation at a gourmet restaurant are most often associated with 'romance and relaxation' and/or 'personal indulgence'.

Tourism New Zealand's market tracking research has also provided some insight into the travel lifestyle choices and attitudes of various markets. The UK market, for instance, is 'more likely to eat out in local restaurants, go sightseeing, visit friends and family, geothermal sites, museums/galleries, beaches, the Sky Tower, the America's Cup regatta and bars and nightclubs' (Tourism New Zealand, 2001b: 5). This hints at the type of lifestyle choices that might be associated with food tourists.

Attitudes and values

An examination of the wider attitudes and values of food tourists provides invaluable information for marketers wishing to promote food tourism. Attitudes and values are critical determinants in the decision making of consumers, as these are much more enduring and engrained than motivations, which are derived from immediate need (Kotler, Bowen and Makens, 1999). Value segmentation is viewed as an important tool in the targeting of markets (Ross, 1994) and, as a result, a number of commercial tools have been developed in response to its utility (e.g. VALS, LOV, Rokeach and the Roy Morgan Value Segmentation).

Tourism Victoria (2000) have used the Roy Morgan Value Segments of visitors to Victoria (Australia) to identify value segments with (among other things) a greater propensity to be motivated by wine and food tourism. They suggest that 'Socially aware' and 'Visible achiever' visitors are most likely to be attracted by food and wine tourism products. The characteristics of these markets (Mitchell and Mitchell, 2000, after Roy Morgan Research, 1997) include:

Socially aware

- Tertiary educated
- Professional/managerial
- Public servants, politicians and researchers
- Well educated
- Attracted to things new and innovative
- 'Learning a living' rather than earning a living
- Seek education and knowledge.

Visible achievers

- Around forty years old
- Wealth creators
- Traditional values about home, work and society
- Work for financial reward and job stimulation
- Look for quality and value for money
- Direct interest in public affairs, economy and politics.

Tourism Victoria (2000) provide a further analysis that identifies subsegments (combining both demographics and values) within each of the Roy Morgan segments whose core travel activities are food and wine related. Within the 'Socially aware' segment it is 'young couples' (under forty-five years, single and with no children) and within the 'Visible Achievement' market it is 'midlife households' (forty-five to sixty-five years, single or married with children under sixteen) that have food and wine as core tourism activities. The remaining Roy Morgan segments, 'Young optimists' and 'Traditional family life', also have subsegments with a strong interest in food and wine tourism: 'young singles' and 'midlife households', respectively.

While value segmentation and an analysis of attitudes can be used to identify high interest/specialist food tourists, they can also be used to understand more about those with a lesser propensity to be motivated by food. For example, despite the high likelihood of the UK market to visit a local restaurant in New Zealand, there is evidence that some of the UK market have a very conservative attitude towards food while on vacation. An insight into this attitude comes from Tourism New Zealand (2000: 30), who cite a female potential mass-market visitor from England: 'Not that I am a racist, but I do like to see all white people together – they speak our language, they eat our food. My husband is very English and I am too, to be honest.' This conservative attitude to New Zealand food is also reflected in the sentiments of a mass-market Japanese visitor who said that 'I was worried that I would not be able to eat the food because the culture is so different' (Tourism New Zealand, n.d.). This suggests that neophobic mass-market tourists, regardless of their origin, have little desire to eat anything other than food similar to that which they eat in their home country.

An experiential view of food tourism

In the 1980s the 'experiential view' emerged in consumer behaviour research as it was recognized that the purchase and consumption of many goods and services had a hedonistic nature (e.g. Holbrook and Hirschman, 1982; Lofman, 1991). The traditional model of consumer behaviour (the information processing model [IPM]), did not recognize the special nature of products and services that have a hedonic component, such as wine, leisure activities and pleasure travel. When purchasing these products decision making is not always based on problem solving (as suggested by the IPM), rather, decisions are often the result of 'primary process thinking': 'fun, amusement, fantasy, arousal, sensory stimulation and enjoyment in much the same way that a baby seeks immediate gratification' (Holbrook and Hirshman, 1982: 135). By recognizing the significance of these primary processes, the 'experiential view' identifies the 'stream of consciousness or sensory, imaginal and affective complex that accompanies a tourist experience' (Lofman, 1991: 729). While Pitkänen (2002: n.p.), says that 'it is becoming increasingly difficult to distinguish between consumption of experiences and the experience of consumption'.

According to Pitkänen (2002: n.p.), when discussing concepts of experiential consumption put forward by Pasi Falk (Professor of Sociology at the University of Helsinki):

> Eating out is certainly an excellent example of experiential consumption. Appreciating good food and drink has always been one way of standing out from the crowd. An essential part of that is the ability to discuss the enjoyment of taste and the object to which it relates. The experience of dining has acquired an accentuatedly aesthetic nature now that food is very much meant to gratify the eye as well. 'In the visual sense, food portions at their best are like abstract art – at least in the aesthetics of nouvelle cuisine. Likewise, given that music or movies resemble dining in that they are one-off acts of consumption, we also have to wonder where the familiar borderline now runs in their cases too,' says Falk.

Further Mitchell, Hall and McIntosh (2000) have advocated an experiential perspective of wine tourism, citing the rich and diverse nature of descriptions of wine travel experiences in popular literature. They continue:

> Such mellifluous imagery suggests that there is more to wine and wine tourism than the simple consumption of a beverage or that this experience is limited to the senses and emotions associated with the wine alone. Wine tourism experiences (as with most tourism experiences) are much more than this, relying on the characteristics of the individual . . . the setting in which they occur, socialization with the personalities of wine, and interaction with other elements of the experience such as food, accommodation and other visitors. It is the sum of these elements, not each individually, that make up the winery experience. (Mitchell, Hall and McIntosh 2000: 130)

The number and range of images of food related travel in popular literature are at least equal to those of wine and, some would contend, that in fact they are much more prolific, vibrant and verbose.

Studies have found that dining out as a tourist is a different experience than when dining out for other reasons and, as a result, an examination of an experiential nature might be important to an understanding of food tourism consumer behaviour. For example, Koo, Tao, and Yeung (1999) found that individuals had different perceptions of the utility of restaurants, depending on the situation that the restaurants were used for. Focus groups of Hong Kong residents identified a range of differences between 'family meals', 'business meals' and 'tourists'. In particular they found that the perception was that tourists placed different emphasis on the location of the restaurant (urban rather than outlying island), price (more important than business and less important than family meals), if it was a famous tourist spot or if it had a Chinese cultural dance.

This difference in experience is also borne out in figures from the National Restaurant Association (USA) (2002) that suggest 'approximately 50 percent of revenues at tableservice restaurants with check sizes of $25 or more [come] from tourists . . . [while this drops to] . . . roughly 20–25 percent of revenues at tableservice restaurants with average check sizes of less than $25'. Clearly, then, tourists have a propensity to spend more than other restaurant consumers and it might be suggested that this is, at least in part, due to the experiential differences between tourist dining and other dining.

Involvement and the experience of food

One concept that might be used to explain some of the differences observed between various food consumption experiences (i.e. eating at home compared with eating out, compared with eating out while on vacation) is that of product or leisure involvement. Havitz and Dimanche (1999) define leisure involvement:

> as an unobservable state of motivation, arousal or interest toward a recreational activity or associated product . . . In other words, involvement refers to how we think about our leisure and recreation, and it affects our behavior as well. Leisure involvement has usually been treated as a multifaceted construct including attraction, sign [symbolism], centrality, and risk.

Involvement is an important concept in tourism as the decision-making process for tourism requires a high level of involvement (Swarbrooke and Horner, 1999). Further, Havitz and Dimanche (1999) found that while most 'products' score low in all areas of involvement, leisure activities always have involvement. This distinction between products and leisure activities is important for food consumption as the nature of the consumption experience determines how food and the experience of eating is viewed. Eating has a functional component (in that it provides sustenance) (Beardsworth and Keil, 1997) and in our day-to-day eating there is a tendency to treat food as a functional product. However, eating is also a very culturally ascribed function (Beardsworth and Keil, 1997), rich in symbolism and meaning (Trossolöv,

1995). The higher the level of involvement in food and eating (and sometimes cooking), the greater the symbolism and the deeper the meaning.

Eating out, for example, in certain circumstances has more symbolic aspects than eating in. It can transform emotions into commodities which are sold back to use (Beardsworth and Keil, 1997), i.e. a romantic dinner for two or a celebratory dinner, while restaurants are a 'place ballet' where both the provider and the consumer act in a highly choreographed and symbolic manner (Bell and Valentine, 1997). When on vacation the meaning of eating is further intensified as the very nature of the travel experience heightens our sensory awareness and imagination, and the high level of involvement tends to lead to greater symbolic significance (e.g. Urry's 1990 'tourist gaze'). Indeed, the sensory awareness of place is now being used by marketing agencies in a further attempt to build both a relationship with potential customers and differentiate places in a crowded tourism destination marketplace. For example, in South Africa's KwaZulu-Natal (KZN) province, the provincial tourism marketing authority undertook a series of focus groups with holidaymakers from Gauteng (their major domestic source of visitors) regarding their perceptions of KZN in terms of taste, objects, colour, sound, touch and smell. In terms of taste the items most associated with KZN were meat, pap, beer and fruit (interestingly, no foods were associated with KZN in terms of smell) (Tourism KwaZulu-Natal, 2002). Indeed, arguably there is now a wide realm of tourism experiences identified by what may be appropriately described as the 'tourism of taste'. This includes not only the realms of wine and food tourism but also beer and spirits. For example, the successful development of whisky trails in Scotland and whiskey trails in Ireland is testimony to the tourism potential of being able to taste products *in situ*. Moreover, taste, along with freshness of produce, is frequently cited as a reason for visiting farmers' markets. Taste test studies have shown that consumers typically prefer produce sold at farmers' markets to that from other sources (Hughes and Mattson, 1995). Consumers frequently cite freshness, taste, flavour, appearance and nutritional value as reasons for preferring farmers' market produce (Kezis et al., 1984; Sommer, Stumpf and Bennett, 1984; Connell, Beierlein and Vroomen, 1986; Bruhn et al., 1992; Thomson and Kelvin, 1994; Hughes and Mattson, 1995; Leones, 1995; Abel, Thompson and Maretzki, 1999; Govindasamy, Italia and Adelaja, 2002).

Of course, food consumption with high involvement may not be limited to eating out and/or eating out while on vacation. Special occasions at home (such as birthday parties, dinner parties, anniversaries and family reunions) can also have high levels of involvement. Further, Bell and Valentine (1997) have suggested that 'kitchen table tourism' has replaced 'armchair tourism' as a form of vicarious exploration, where eating at ethnic restaurants, cooking from ethnic cook books and watching food and travel television shows (often sponsored by local and national tourism organizations) allows us to travel without leaving our home, town or city. Vicarious exploration means that we can have the same emotional and symbolic experience of a vacation before leaving home or after returning from a vacation (Fridgen, 1984). For example, Zelinsky (1987) suggests that:

> The diners at ethnic restaurants don't go just for the food. They also hunger for an exotic dining experience. Ethnic restaurants offer an effortless journey to a distant land where the waiter recites a menu of alien delights in charmingly accented English. The patrons of ethnic restaurants are gastronomic tourists.

While the above discussion suggests that the occasion is critical in determining the level of involvement related to food consumption, involvement clearly also varies between individuals. An example of this variability is manifest in the three levels of cuisine and wine tourism identified by Lang Research (2001) (see Exhibit 3.1).

Involvement, risk, neophilia and neophobia

One of the key measures of involvement is risk (Havitz and Dimanche, 1999) and risk is also an important concept when discussing the individual differences observed in relation to the experience of food, wine and tourism. In tourism, the notion of risk is related to one of the key motivating factors for pleasure travel – novelty seeking (Bello and Etzel, 1985; Crompton, 1979; Lee and Crompton, 1992; Mitchell, 1998). High risk-takers (and therefore those with high degrees of involvement) seek extremely novel environments and situations. Plog (in Ross, 1994) has suggested that this behaviour can be closely related to personality type, proposing that allocentrics seek more novel/new environments and psychocentrics seek familiar and less threatening vacation settings. The work of Plog (in Ross 1994) then, suggests that allocentrics are naturally neophilic (literally they 'love new/novel' phenomena), while psychocentrics are neophobic ('fear of new/novel').

In food and wine, risk is also closely related to the concepts of neophilia and neophobia. In wine, for example, Dodd (1997) and Mitchell (in progress), suggest that there are neophilic tendencies within individuals with an advanced level of wine knowledge that mean that are constantly seeking new wine experiences (i.e. visiting new wineries, tasting new wines and matching wines with different foods). Neophilia is also widely discussed within food literature, where it is suggested that human omnivorous behaviour is a paradox between neophilic *and* neophobic tendencies (Beardsworth and Keil, 1997; Bell and Valentine, 1997). This paradox occurs at three levels: pleasure versus displeasure (seeking new flavours but the fear of unpalatable flavours), health versus illness (ensuring a varied healthy diet without encountering toxins), and life versus death (to maintain our life other organisms must die) (Beardsworth and Keil, 1997). Tuorila et al. (1994) suggest that neophobia in food consumption results in those with neophobic tendencies disliking novel looking, smelling and tasting foods. In contrast, Bell and Valentine (1997) have suggested that the development of 'new cuisines' and the globalization of national cuisines around the world has relied on neophilic tendencies and that travel has long involved food neophilia as an important motivator (e.g. Grand Tours).

Neophilia and involvement are, therefore, important concepts in the discussion of the food tourism experience. They provide an insight into some of the experiential differences observed in food tourism consumer behaviour. The following typology of food tourists attempts to conceptualize some of the behaviour that can be observed over a range of different market segments using these concepts.

A typology of food tourists

Adapting the 'phases of the travel experience' framework discussed by Fridgen (1984) (anticipation, travel to, on-site experience, travel from and reminiscence) and applied to wine tourism by Mitchell, Hall and McIntosh (2000) to the food tourism experience allows for a detailed typology of the behaviour of various food tourism segments. The phases of the food tourism experience conceptualized here are:

- eating at home (pre-travel)
- eating out (pre-travel) – advocated above as a form of vicarious exploration that is different to eating at home
- food at the destination
- vacation experiences at the destination – advocated by Mitchell, Hall and McIntosh (2000) as important influence on the on-site visit, in this case food tourism experiences]
- food (post-travel).

Table 3.4 combines these phases with the level of involvement, neophilia/neophobia and the level of cuisine and wine tourism interest indicated in the

Table 3.4 A typology of food tourist behaviour

			Phase of food tourism experience	Neophiles/allocentrics ←	
Category	*Eating at home (pre-travel)*	*Eating out (pre-travel)*	*Food at destination*	*Vacation experiences*[1]	*Eating (post-travel)*
			Neophiles/allocentrics		
Gastronomes (high interest/ involvement)	Extensive research of foods at destination Eat a wide range of cuisines Member of food society/group Hobby related to food May be a food professional High commitment to farmers' markets in order to be able to learn about produce	Eat a wide range of cuisines Many different restaurants frequented Eating out occurs on a regular and frequent basis	Cooking schools Food education 'High' cuisine and 'rustic food' Food markets, with emphasis on farmers' markets are a very significant food attraction Local growers and suppliers	Personal indulgence Exploration Romance and relaxation	Search for new food experiences Use learned techniques and cuisines to develop own recipes 'Fusion' with existing knowledge Ongoing high commitment to farmers' markets
Indigenous foodies (high and moderate interest/involvement)	Research local culture at destination Cook a range of styles of food at home Interested in foods at public markets and farmers' markets	Usually eat at ethnic restaurants Relatively high level of eating out	Cooking schools 'Local restaurants' 'Rustic food' Food markets an attraction because of produce, with no substantial differentiation between farmers' and public markets	Personal indulgence Exploration Romance and relaxation	Cook food from destination Adopt new ingredients Regularly frequent restaurants and public markets

Neophobes/psychocentrics →

Neophobes/psychocentrics

'Tourist' foodies (low interest/involvement)	FIT destination planning Cook some pre-prepared ethnic foods at home Occasional purchaser from public markets	Eat at a range of mainstream restaurants Eating out less frequent but more than just special occasions	'Tourist' menus 'Westernized' hotel/ resort food International chains Food market as a component of local colour food not an attraction in its own right	Sports, hobbies and learning Socializing	Talk about 'wonderful' food at hotel/resort May seek mainstream restaurant with cuisine from destination
Familiar foods (low interest/involvement)	Package tour planning only 'Meat and three veg' at home	Rarely eat out Fast foods	Package tour food International fast-food chains	Sports, hobbies and learning Socializing	No change to pre-visit behaviour

Note: [1] Vacation experiences sought drawn from Lang Research's (2001) are as follows:

Exploration: to visit historical sites and important places in history; to see natural wonders and important natural sites; to experience different cultures and ways of life; to experience unspoiled nature.

Personal indulgence: to visit a popular, trendy place; to visit casinos and gamble; to experience 'the good life' – fine cuisine, being pampered; to experience city life (e.g. nightlife, shopping, museums).

Romance and relaxation: To rest, relax and recuperate; for intimacy and romance; to spend quality time with the family away for home.

Sports, hobbies and learning: to participate in a hobby or sport (e.g. golf, fishing, photography); to participate in a hands-on learning experience (e.g. archaeological digs, cooking courses).

Socializing: to visit friends or relatives who live in another city or country; to spend time with a group of good friends; to be somewhere that feels familiar and safe.

Source: high, moderate and low interest relate to Lang Research's (2001a) Cuisine and Wine Interest Index (refer to Exhibit 3.1) and relate to the level of involvement of the individual.

study by Lang Research (2001). Four segments have been identified to reflect high to low interest and involvement and neophilic to neophobic tendencies. The behaviour of these segments has been described to give an indication of how the food tourism experience might unfold for individuals within each segment. The segments identified are 'Gastronomes', 'Indigenous foodies', 'Tourist foodies' and 'Familiar foods', but the framework allows for the addition of further segments should they be identified.

Conclusion

Studies of consumer behaviour in the area of food tourism are rare and, as a result, the picture we have of the food tourist is, at best, sketchy. This chapter has attempted to provide an analysis of the research currently available and has proposed a typology of food tourist that uses the concepts of neophilia/neophobia, psychocentrism/allocentrism and involvement in an attempt to explain some of the behaviour of various food tourism sectors. It is clear, however, that a considerable amount of research is required more effectively to understand food tourism consumer behaviour.

To date the material that does exist has been borrowed from more general tourism studies or has been inferred from studies not directly related to tourism. At their most basic then, studies should be specifically targeted at food tourists that explore their demographics, psychographics and experiences. Key areas of research should include segmentation of food tourists that do not include wine (as even specialist food tourists may not necessarily be interested in wine), analyses of the motivations of the specialist and general food tourists, measurement of the degree of neophilic tendencies and involvement among these segments, and the importance of occasion in the consumption of food (e.g. eating at home, celebrations, eating out compared with tourist experiences).

4

The demand for halal food among Muslim travellers in New Zealand

Melissa Wan Hassan and C. Michael Hall

About 80 per cent of sheep and 50 per cent of cattle in New Zealand are slaughtered 'halal', in accordance with the shariah laws of Islam. This figure may seem surprising to some readers but viewed from an economic perspective, it is not hard to see why halal foods are extremely crucial for New Zealand. The Middle East is now an essential market for major exporters of New Zealand meat and dairy products (Buang, 2001), with the growth in halal food exports testimony to the importance of Muslim customers' demands.

The tourism sector in New Zealand has also recently taken an interest in the demand for halal food. Since Tourism New Zealand (TNZ) began marketing in the Middle East, they have become more aware of the needs and sensitivities of Muslim travellers (Sulaiman, 2001). Muslims are prohibited from pork and alcohol and can only eat the meat of animals that are slaughtered according to the manner prescribed in Islam. Tourism New Zealand Chief Executive, George Hickton, believes that New Zealand can be promoted as an attractive destination for Muslim travellers due to the high volume of meat that is slaughtered halal in the country (Sulaiman, 2001). Promoting New Zealand as a major producer of halal meat, however, can lead to an undesirable dilemma in tourism. Through export promotions, tourists are initially led to believe that it is easy to find halal food in New Zealand. However, once they arrive in New Zealand the tourists will then be provided with the opportunity to judge first hand whether or not this image is valid.

It has been observed that while the supply of halal slaughtered meat is high in New Zealand, local Muslims have actually found it difficult to find halal food while travelling within the country (Sulaiman, 2001), with many often unaware of the availability of halal food during their travels and only coming across halal restaurants by chance. While outlets selling halal food are few and often obscure, the problem is exacerbated because halal signage and labelling is often lacking. In addition, many Muslim travellers in New Zealand are concerned not only about the availability of halal food but also the increasing number of halal claims, by restaurants and food companies, that were not being verified by a recognized Muslim authority in New Zealand.

This chapter therefore provides an overview of some of the issues facing Muslim travellers in New Zealand in both a domestic and international context. The chapter also discusses halal food traditions and the significance of halal food in a tourism setting. In addition, the chapter presents the results of a study of travellers within New Zealand and the issues they face with respect to halal food availability.

International inbound Muslim travellers in New Zealand

According to the New Zealand International Visitors Survey, it is believed that the Muslim inbound market in New Zealand is mainly from the Middle East (especially Saudi Arabia and the United Arab Emirates), and from Malaysia and Indonesia (NZTB, 2001). However, the exact number of Muslims travelling to New Zealand is unknown since visitors are not asked to declare their religion on the New Zealand visitor arrival card (NZTB, 2001).

The Middle Eastern inbound market to New Zealand has been described as an emerging 'hot new' market that 'holds potential' (Meikle, 2001: 10). The Arabian Gulf provides an outbound travel market of approximately 5 million people who are affluent and frequent international travellers. Visitors from this part of the world spend well above the average, stay far longer than other visitors, prefer travelling in groups and show a high percentage of repeat visitation (Meikle, 2001).

A majority of visitors from the Middle East also undertake long-haul travel in the months of June, July and August during their hot, humid summer and school holidays. This is a period that coincides with a time when the number of international visitor arrivals in New Zealand is at its lowest (Hall and Kearsley, 2001; Tourism Strategy Group, 2001). Statistics show that, in the last few years, seasonality patterns have changed very little in New Zealand although the percentage of visitors has increased (Tourism Strategy Group, 2001). Therefore, the growth of the Middle Eastern market is welcomed because it can strategically optimize New Zealand's visitor yield and assist in smoothing out seasonality.

Domestic Muslim travellers in New Zealand

In order to reduce the effects of seasonality, domestic travellers should also be included in tourism marketing strategies (Tourism Strategy Group, 2001). Apart from being a source of revenue, domestic travellers provide a foundation for the development of tourism infrastructure and are an important element in the tourism mix. For the purposes of the present chapter, domestic Muslim travellers are those with any one of the following: New Zealand citizenship, a New Zealand residence visa or a New Zealand work visa.

The New Zealand domestic Muslim population is a small minority and has sometimes been described as an 'invisible society'. They are growing in number; official figures show that Muslims account for only about 0.5 per cent of New Zealand's population (*Al Mujaddid*, 2001), and this figure is rapidly increasing. The 2001 census revealed that Muslims increased by 74 per cent since the 1996 census from 13 548 to 23 631 people (Statistics New Zealand, 2001). In the 1996 census, the male Muslim population (7323) was slightly higher than the female (6042). The majority of Muslims were between the ages of thirty and thirty-nine (2943) followed by the twenty to twenty-nine (2745) and five to fourteen (2595) age groups (FIANZ, 2001). By regional distribution, 12 000–15 000 Muslims lived in Auckland, 3000 in Wellington, 1500 in Hamilton and between 3000 and 5000 throughout the rest of New Zealand (FIANZ, 2001).

In terms of ethnic groups, it is clear that the Muslim population in New Zealand is of diverse ethnic and cultural backgrounds. Muslims in New Zealand are mainly Indian, either from the Indian subcontinent or Fiji, followed by other groups including Arab, Turkish, Persian, those from the

Balkan states (Bosnia, Kosovar and Albania), as well as Asiatic people such as Malays, Indonesians and Cambodians (Krogt, 1996). The cultures and societies of the Muslim people are indeed diverse but despite such differences, Muslims are united by their religion and belief in Islam.

Halal food

Halal is one of the most important aspects of Islamic life. Although it is a standard that Muslims around the world live by, many non-Muslims are still unaware of halal food and its significance for the Muslim community. As Riaz (2001: 1) observed, 'Most Americans and Europeans have at least a rough idea that kosher refers to Jewish dietary laws. But almost unknown to Americans and Europeans is the meaning of halal – the Islamic counterpart of kosher'.

The halal food market exists where there are Muslim consumers with tastes and preferences that are governed by halal rules on food and beverages. Despite Blackler's (2002: 32) observation, that 'Halal meat is a special kind of food which in theory ought to have disappeared with the secularization of Islam', the demand for halal foods grows in relation to the growth of Islam. In 1996, the United Nations estimated the world population of Muslims to be at 1.482 billion (World Muslim Population, 2001). Over the last few years, however, the number of Muslims has increased up to nearly 1.6 billion, making one in every four people in the world today a Muslim (World Muslim Population, 2001).

Islam is the world's second largest religion and the majority of Muslims can be found in Asian countries as well as the Middle East and North Africa. The halal food market, estimated to be worth US$150 billion per year, therefore presents great opportunities for multinational food corporations, food retailers and food-service providers around the world (Chaudry, 2001).

Halal food and drinks must conform to Islamic dietary laws as specified in the Koran, the Hadith (sayings) and Sunna (tradition) of the Prophet Muhammad (peace be upon him), as well as in the *fiqh* (teachings) of the four Islamic Jurists: Hanafi, Shafi'ie, Maliki and Hambali. Other sources of laws are the *Ijma'* (collective approval) and *Qiyas* (syllogy) of Islamic scholars (El Mouelhy, 1997).

Halal and haram are the two major terms used in Islamic dietary laws. While halal means 'Permitted, allowed, authorized, approved, sanctioned, lawful, legal, legitimate or licit' for Muslim consumption, haram, on the other hand, means: 'Not permitted, not allowed, unauthorized, unapproved, unsanctioned, unlawful, illegal, illegitimate or illicit' (El Mouelhy, 1997: 1).

Several criteria must be met before food products can be certified as halal. First, the product must be free from any substance or ingredient taken or extracted from a haram animal or ingredient (Twaigery and Spillman, 1989). Halal products are made from naturally halal animals, such as cattle, goat, sheep and chicken that are slaughtered according to the manner prescribed in Islam. Second, halal products should also be 'processed, produced, manufactured and/or stored by using utensils, equipments and/or machineries that have been cleansed according to Islamic law' (Twaigery and Spillman, 1989: 89). The main idea behind this is that manufactured products should be free of contamination and must not come into contact with haram substances during its preparation, production and/or storage. In addition, halal ingredients should also not be mixed with objectionable or haram ingredients like enzymes and emulsifiers of porcine origin or other non-halal animals. Any other groups of food, like cheese and meat, may be combined together, as long as no haram or prohibited foods are included in the mixture.

Prohibited foods in the Koran

Islam places a very strong emphasis on cleanliness in everything, especially in the context of food and drink. In Islam, eating is regarded as a matter of worship, like prayer and other religious activities. So, just as Muslims perform the ablution as a means of cleansing themselves before their daily prayers, they must also ensure that the food they consume is clean and prepared in the correct manner, starting with the avoidance of items that are prohibited in Islamic dietary laws. The Koran clearly prohibits Muslims from consuming the following categories of food: carrion, flowing blood, pork, animals that have been slaughtered with the invocation of a name other than the name of God, and alcohol.

Carrion or animals that are killed by strangulation, by a blow, by a fall, by being gored, or that are partly eaten by wild animals are forbidden as food for Muslims. The eating of carrion or 'dead animal' is regarded as contrary to human dignity and harmful to one's health. Islam prescribes that an (halal) animal should first be slaughtered before its consumption, in order to get rid of the blood. The Islamic method of slaughtering an animal is to cut its throat to enable as much blood to run out and not congeal in the veins. The incision is 'made in the neck just below the glottis, cutting the throat and oesophagus, the jugular vein and the carotid artery' (Erbil, 2001: 1). This is done *without* cutting the spinal cord or severing the head from the body. The animal must also be completely dead before the skinning and dismembering of its body takes place (Sami'ullah, 2001).

Flowing blood, which is similar to the Jewish as well as 'the Noachian, Levitical and early Christian prohibitions of blood as a food' is also prohibited (Mickler, 2000: 2). The consumption of blood is forbidden because, apart from being distasteful, it is also regarded as harmful for human beings. Blood carries organisms that are responsible for diseases although their clinical symptoms may not be present when they are still in the animal's healthy living body (Erbil, 2001). Separated from its body, however, these disease-carrying organisms are harmful (Erbil, 2001).

Pork is often associated with harm and disease in Middle Eastern societies and religions (Harris, 1974; 1985). In the Middle Eastern context pigs may be regarded as both harmful to the environment and a carrier of disease from swine to humans, particularly parasite infestations like those of the *Trichinella spiralis*, *Echinococcus granulosis* and the *Taenia Solium* tapeworm. Muslims in general are convinced that there is a good reason for the prohibition of pork and would regard its consumption as undesirable.

Animals that have been slaughtered with the invocation of a name other than the name of God are prohibited apart from carrion, blood and pork. This type of food is associated with the practice of idolatry that Islam strictly opposes to. This prohibition also addresses the issue of halal slaughtering, in which pronouncing the name of God is a required condition while slaughtering an animal (al Qaradawi, 1995).

Alcohol, whether in food or beverages, is clearly forbidden in the Koran. Islam takes an uncompromising stand in the prohibition of intoxicants and stipulates that whatever intoxicates people in large amounts is haram and forbidden in any amount, even in minute quantities (al Qaradawi, 1995).

Other prohibited foods

All the categories of forbidden food discussed above are those that have been clearly mentioned in the Koran. There are, however, other prohibitions that have arisen either according to the *(fiqh)* teachings of Islamic jurists or based on the (Hadith) sayings and (Sunna) tradition of the Prophet Muhammad (peace be upon him). These prohibitions include the consumption of *all beasts of prey and birds of prey*, such as dogs, lions, tigers, owls, eagles and other carnivores. *Amphibians* like frogs, crocodiles, and turtles; *undesirable insects* such as worms, flies, and cockroaches; *vermin* or poisonous animals like rats, snakes, centipedes and scorpions also come under the category of forbidden foods (El Mouelhy, 1997, Mickler, 2000). In addition, Muslims are strictly prohibited from eating the '*meat that has been cut from a live animal* such as limbs, tails' (El Mouelhy, 1997). This is based on a Hadith of the Prophet Muhammad condemning those who carried out this barbaric practice during the period of *Jahiliyyah*, before the advent of Islam (al Qaradawi, 1995).

The exemption of seafood and locusts

According to Islamic law, fish and other sea creatures are exempted from the category of 'dead animals' (al Qaradawi, 1995). All marine animals are therefore halal and can be eaten without the requirement of slaughtering and bleeding (al Qaradawi, 1995). Human beings are permitted to catch seafood in any manner they like, using methods that are as humane as possible (al Qaradawi, 1995). It also matters not whether seafood comes out of the water dead or alive, as a whole or in pieces, or caught by a Muslim or a non-Muslim (al Qaradawi, 1995).

Although seafood is generally regarded as halal, there are some disagreements among Islamic school of thought concerning animals like shrimps, crabs and lobsters as they live both inside *and* outside water (Mickler, 2000). While jurists of the Shafie school of thought regard crustaceans and molluscs as halal, other Islamic schools of thought, like Hambali, Hanafi and Maliki, have a more conservative view of these sea creatures.

In addition to seafood, locusts are also exempt from the category of 'dead animals'. Ibn Abu Awfa related: 'We went with the Prophet (peace be upon him) on seven expeditions and we ate locusts with him' (al Qaradawi, 1995: 48). Muslims are thus permitted to eat dead locusts and like seafood, the issue of slaughtering does not arise.

The situation of halal food in New Zealand

The tourism industry in New Zealand stands to gain from the thriving meat trade that New Zealand has with Muslim countries. New Zealand exports between 50 000 and 60 000 tonnes of meat to the Middle East annually, of which approximately 40 000 to 50 000 tonnes are lamb (Meat NZ, 2002). The Middle East has, in fact, been an essential market for all major New Zealand meat exporters since 1979 when halal first became a key factor in New Zealand–Middle East trade relations (Chun, 1987).

New Zealand has also become the biggest exporter of dairy products in the Middle East and is the first country of preference for dairy product imports in both Saudi Arabia and the United Arab Emirates (Christchurch Press, in Buang, 2001: 15). A study by Sydney research firm, BIS Shrapnel, states that at present, 'New Zealand dairy products is about 14 per cent of the total food market in the Middle East valued at US $11.46 billion' (Buang, 2001: 15). Interestingly, New Zealand's success story in the Middle East has been attributed to its 'good repute' in that part of the world, along with 'the advantages of offering halal products' (Christchurch Press, in Buang, 2001: 15).

The success of New Zealand's export products in the Middle East has provided encouragement to TNZ. As mentioned above, TNZ believes that New Zealand can be promoted as a destination for Muslim travellers because of the high volume of halal slaughtered meat in the country (Sulaiman, 2001). However, this assumption does not take into account the various issues involved in the production of halal food. For example, under Muslim law meat is regarded as haram or non-permissible once it comes into contact with non-halal meat, through storage, during distribution or by using the same utensils to cook it. While restaurants in New Zealand may be able to offer halal meat on their menu, they can present an ambiguous situation for Muslims if they also serve pork and alcohol on their premises (Sulaiman, 2001). Caution is also required of restaurants when using manufactured foods like cheese, yoghurt, ice cream, jelly and various other instant or canned foods, as they may contain animal-based ingredients such as gelatine and emulsifiers that are non-halal.

Considering the above factors, it would not be surprising if many restaurants in New Zealand find it hard to strictly observe halal guidelines in food preparation. Restaurants preparing halal and haram food in the same area, with the same kitchen utensils are especially prone to having 'accidents', even during the preparation of vegetarian meals. Such was the case for a Pizza Haven company in Hastings that was in trouble for delivering a Muslim customer two vegetarian pizzas with bacon pieces in them (*Otago Daily Times*, 2001). In addition, many restaurants are still oblivious to the various reasons that lie behind vegetarianism. Few understand that vegetarian meals can sometimes be the only option for customers like vegans, Hindus, Buddhists, Seventh Day Adventists and Jews, apart from Muslims.

Halal food and the need for statutory control

To address the issue of halal food, the Federation of Islamic Associations of New Zealand (FIANZ) has written to the Minister of Consumer Affairs, the Honourable Philida Bunkle, asking the Ministry to 'consider investigating some means of officially defining halal food in order to protect Muslim consumers' (*Al Mujaddid*, 2001: 9). Currently, there are no statutory regulations or guidelines pertaining to the issue of halal in New Zealand (*Al Mujaddid*, 2001). As a result, any individual or business proprietor in New Zealand will not be liable in the court of law should they falsely and fraudulently use the claim of halal. Manufacturers and business operators in New Zealand can freely claim their products or restaurants to be halal without having to seek any form of endorsement or verification. This has often caused problems for Muslim consumers, especially in cases of fraud where the onus would be on consumers to prove that such individuals or businesses were selling non-halal. By then of course, it would have been a case of 'a little too late' since many Muslims would have consumed the product.

Therefore, Muslims in New Zealand are concerned about the increasing number of reports regarding businesses that claim and label non-halal food as halal (*Al Mujaddid*, 2001). Those proprietors who want to gain extra customers succeed at what they do because many Muslims are not vigilant in ensuring that the food they purchase is genuinely halal. There are also many Muslim immigrants as well as Muslim tourists who are unaware of the absence of any laws in New Zealand regulating halal food.

Halal certification and labelling

To enhance the confidence of Muslim consumers and ensure the authenticity of their halal products, businesses are encouraged to apply for halal certification. In many countries, halal certification is widely accepted not only for export but also for products meant for domestic consumption (Chaudry, 2001). Halal supervision is taken on by a company in order to expand its market opportunities and is a business investment, which like any other investment should be examined critically.

In New Zealand, there are currently two agencies that produce halal certificates – FIANZ and a private Muslim company called the New Zealand Islamic Meat Management (Buang, 2001). These two organizations mainly issue halal certificates for meat. At present, there seems to be more focus on halal meat certification in New Zealand because it is recognized as an important and valuable marketing tool, especially for export trading. The certification of halal meat includes regular supervision and the inspection of abattoirs. Certain guidelines pertaining to halal meat slaughter are also provided to companies operating halal meat exports (Buang, 2001).

Apart from the meat industry, New Zealand restaurants serving halal meat were also previously endorsed by FIANZ and issued with halal certificates (Sulaiman, 2001). According to Drury, however, FIANZ has stopped doing this because the certificates issued to restaurants and outlets previously did not have any expiry dates on them. There have since been cases where, for example, restaurants changed ownership and stopped serving halal meat. For unscrupulous reasons, there were also many restaurants that 'operated under the pretext of being halal due to its non-expiry halal certificate being indiscriminately issued' (Sulaiman, 2001: 9).

The halal certification of restaurants and manufactured foods is undoubtedly a huge task. Sufficient personnel and funding is needed to cope with the massive workload envisaged by such a system. As with any certification system involving consumers, the confidence of the consumer is of prime importance. Halal, being a religious issue, would be more demanding since any mistake or lapse on the part of the people implementing the system would have dire consequences. Although FIANZ is currently expanding its services to include the halal certification of processed foods (Buang, 2001), its main focus at present remains on certifying halal slaughtered meat, especially beef and lamb. Until the problems and complexities of halal certification are solved and managed, it is hoped that manufacturers and businesses providing halal food to the Muslim community in New Zealand will continue doing so on the basis of good faith.

Survey on Muslim travellers and their access to halal food in New Zealand

In early 2002 a survey was undertaken of halal food and Muslim travel in New Zealand. A primary objective of the survey was to investigate the level of access that Muslims have to halal food while travelling in New Zealand, as well as to determine whether or not Muslim travellers strictly follow halal guidelines. The project employed both quantitative and qualitative methods. Apart from questionnaires, the *participant observation* method was used, in which the researcher participated as one of the domestic Muslim travellers in New Zealand, while travelling from Auckland to Dunedin. During this journey, observation was done to see, for example, how the restaurants promoted themselves as 'halal' and how Muslim consumers, in turn, determined that the food they purchased was genuinely halal. Interviews were conducted on the proprietors of halal restaurants in Dunedin, Christchurch, Wellington, Auckland and Queenstown regarding their experience in selling halal food and some of the difficulties they faced as halal food-service operators. Additionally, selected individual Muslim consumers were also interviewed regarding their perception of halal food businesses and their access to halal food as travellers in New Zealand.

Although qualitative interviews provided a 'rich' source of information, a questionnaire was also administered to the Muslim population. Owing to insufficient information regarding the Muslim population as well as the difficulty of contacting them through a conventional probability sampling technique, a *purposive sampling* technique was instead used to select potential participants. This involved administering questionnaires through selected representatives at mosques and Islamic centres.

A total of 2000 questionnaires were posted to twelve mosques and Islamic centres in major cities across New Zealand: Auckland, Christchurch, Wellington, Dunedin, Hamilton and Palmerston North. Favourable factors for selecting these sites included the relatively high number of Muslims at mosques and Islamic centres, especially on Fridays (during the Friday congregational prayer). The above mentioned cities were also chosen because they are areas with the highest Muslim population (FIANZ, 2001).

The purposive sampling technique unfortunately resulted in a relatively low response rate, possibly as the result of concerns following the answering of surveys in the aftermath of the events of 11 September 2001. Due to the general difficulty of locating Muslims in situations other than the Friday congregational prayer event, the researcher was then compelled to use another non-probability sampling technique called *snowball sampling*. This procedure involved extracting data from a few members of the target population who then provide the information needed to locate and network with other members of that population. The fieldwork and data collection period took place from 13 March 2002 to 10 April 2002. Data collected from completed questionnaires was then keyed into SPSS (Statistical Package for the Social Sciences) for further analysis.

Results: key findings and discussion

From the research methodologies employed, a sample size of 371 Muslim travellers was acquired. Of the total sample, 54.2 per cent were male and 44.2 per cent were female. Table 4.1 indicates that the respondents were also typically young with the majority aged between eighteen and twenty-four years (22.4 per cent), followed by those aged thirty-five to forty-four years (21.8 percent) and twenty-five to thirty-four years (20.8 per cent).

The ethnic mix of the sample population was extremely cosmopolitan, comprising thirty-four different ethnic groups (see Table 4.2 for original breakdown of ethnic groups). Although English was by far the most spoken language, only 41.2 per cent of research participants felt they were able to 'have a conversation about a lot of everyday things' in English. Arabic (11.8

Table 4.1   Participants by age group

Age cohort	Frequency	%
< 18 years	50	13.5
18–24	83	22.4
25–34	77	20.8
35–44	81	21.8
45–54	54	14.6
55–64	13	3.5
65 years and above	10	2.7
No response	3	0.8

per cent) was the second most spoken language, followed by Malay (10.3 per cent), Urdu (8.7 per cent), Hindi (8.3 per cent), Somali (5.6 per cent) and other languages. In total, there were thirty-eight languages spoken by the participants (see Table 4.3).

The sample population was predominantly domestic Muslim travellers. Seventy-two per cent of respondents claimed New Zealand as the country they had last lived in for twelve months or more. Table 4.4 shows that nearly half of the respondents (48.2 per cent) were New Zealand citizens, while 21.8 per cent were permanent residents. The majority of international inbound Muslim travellers, on the other hand, who were holders of a New Zealand student visa (13.2 per cent), nearly doubled the number of New Zealand visit/holiday visa holders (7 per cent).

Students formed the majority of respondents. As illustrated in Table 4.5, university students alone (28.6 per cent) nearly equalled that of wage or salary earners who stood at a figure of 29.6 per cent. Other student segments include polytechnic students (1.6 per cent) and secondary school students (7.8 per cent). Since the percentage of tertiary students (university and polytechnic combined) was 30.2 per cent, it was not surprising that 29.1 per cent of respondents identified 'secondary school' as their highest level of education. For the majority of respondents, tertiary qualifications were the highest level of educational achievement, with 25.9 per cent having at least attained a bachelor degree and 17.8 per cent a postgraduate degree. A significant number of respondents (22.1 per cent) declined to inform their level of annual income. Nevertheless, the average annual income of those who did respond fell within the NZ$15 000–NZ$20 000 range. Of the sample, 39.3 per cent had an annual income below NZ$10 000, while 12.9 per cent received an annual income above NZ$40 000.

Table 4.2   Participants by ethnic groups

Ethnic group	Frequency	%
Indian	78	20.2
Malay	51	13.2
Somali	44	11.4
Arab/Middle-Eastern	38	9.8
Other	26	6.7
New Zealand European	23	6.0
Pakistani	21	5.4
Indonesian	15	3.9
Egyptian	11	2.8
Bangladeshi	9	2.3
African	8	2.1
Sri Lankan	8	2.1
Afghan	7	1.8
Palestinian	7	1.8
Iraqi	5	1.3
Cambodian	5	1.3
Maori	4	1.0
Omani	3	0.8
Chinese	3	0.8
Saudi	3	0.8
British/English	3	0.8
Samoan	2	0.5
Tongan	1	0.3
Australian	1	0.3
Jordanian	1	0.3
South-East Asian	1	0.3
Kuwaiti	1	0.3
Japanese	1	0.3
Ethiopian	1	0.3
Sudanese	1	0.3
Turkish	1	0.3
South African	1	0.3
Danish	1	0.3
Moroccan	1	0.3
Total	386	100

Only thirty-eight responses were received from inbound Muslim travellers. Out of this proportion, a majority group of 31.6 per cent listed 'visiting friends and relatives' (VFR) as their main reason for travelling to New Zealand. It is possible that the survey had greater access to VFR travellers because of the

Table 4.3 Languages spoken by participants

Language	Frequency	%
English	331	41.2
Arabic	95	11.8
Malay	83	10.3
Urdu	70	8.7
Hindi	67	8.3
Somali	45	5.6
Bengali	10	1.2
Tamil	10	1.2
Fijian	10	1.2
Indonesian	10	1.2
Pashto	9	1.1
French	9	1.1
Sinhalese	8	1.0
Japanese	6	0.7
Punjabi	4	0.5
Gujarati	4	0.5
Italian	3	0.4
German	3	0.4
Dari	3	0.4
Samoan	2	0.2
Malayalam	2	0.2
Khmer	2	0.2
Champ	2	0.2
Swahili	2	0.2
Persian	1	0.1
Hausa	1	0.1
Filipino	1	0.1
Dutch	1	0.1
Polish	1	0.1
Turkish	1	0.1
Czech	1	0.1
Pigin	1	0.1
Afrikaan	1	0.1
Oromic	1	0.1
Mandarin	1	0.1
Zulu	1	0.1
Maori	1	0.1

Table 4.4 Type of traveller: domestic vs international inbound

	Frequency	%
NZ citizenship	179	48.2
NZ resident visa	81	21.8
NZ work visa only	15	4.0
NZ visit/holiday visa	26	7.0
NZ student visa	49	13.2
Other	9	2.4
No response	12	3.2

Table 4.5 Number of participants by current position

Current situation	Frequency	%
Wage/salary earner	110	29.6
University student	106	28.6
House person/non-employed	47	12.7
Self-employed	38	10.2
Secondary school student	29	7.8
Other	18	4.9
Retired	9	2.4
Polytechnic student	6	1.6
No response	8	2.2

snowball sampling technique used for the distribution of questionnaires. The question targeting domestic Muslim travellers, on the other hand, received the highest rate of non-responses with 29.4 per cent of the sample population choosing *not* to answer a question regarding purpose of travel. However, most of the 262 participants who did respond travelled mainly for leisure or holidays (38.2 per cent). The second largest group was the VFR market, totalling 25.6 per cent of respondents. As the majority of research participants were students, it was not surprising that 'education/study' was the third most popular reason for travel among domestic Muslim travellers (16.8 per cent). The majority of responses came from Wellington with a count of 111 (29.9 per cent). The second largest number of responses came from Christchurch (20.2 per cent) followed by Dunedin (17.3 per cent), Auckland (13.7 per cent), Palmerston North (10.2 per cent) and Hamilton (8.1 per cent).

Muslims who participated in the study were asked to indicate how easy or difficult it was for them to find halal food while travelling in New Zealand. The results, in Table 4.6, show that only 12.4 per cent of the sample population found it easy, while 62.8 per cent of the participants said it was difficult to find halal food. The acquirement of such a substantial percentage of those saying it was difficult can be used to reject the assumption claiming that it would be easy for Muslims to find halal food while travelling in New Zealand.

Table 4.6   How easy or difficult is it to find halal food while travelling in New Zealand?

	frequency	*%*
Easy	46	12.4
Unsure	79	21.3
Difficult	233	62.8

Respondents were also asked to compare New Zealand to other non-Muslim countries, in terms of their ability to find halal food. The results, in Table 4.7, indicate that a slight majority of 50.9 per cent of the sample population felt that it was 'more difficult' while a significant 34.2 per cent of the sample was 'unsure'. The remaining 14.8 per cent of respondents said that it was 'easier' to find halal food in New Zealand compared to other non-Muslim countries.

Table 4.7   In terms of your ability to find halal food, how would you rate New Zealand in comparison to Muslim and other non-Muslim countries?

	Compared to Muslim countries		*Compared to non-Muslim countries*	
	Frequency	*%*	*Frequency*	*%*
More difficult in New Zealand	283	76.3	189	50.9
Unsure	52	14.0	127	34.2
Easier in New Zealand	36	9.7	55	14.8

Through cross-tabulation, the results from this question were also used to determine the general perception of Middle Eastern Muslims regarding their access to halal food in New Zealand. Travellers from the Middle East are generally assumed to be 'relatively discerning' and 'easily accommodated', having travelled to Europe and other Western countries before their visit to New Zealand (NZTB, 2001: 1). The results from this research indicate that while 38.6 per cent of Middle Eastern Muslim travellers found it 'more difficult' to find halal food in New Zealand compared with other non-Muslim countries, a significant 35.1 per cent was 'unsure' whether it was 'easier' or 'more difficult'. Only 26.3 per cent said that it was 'easier' to find halal food in New Zealand compared with other non-Muslim countries. The results therefore do not support the notion that Middle Eastern Muslims are more 'easily accommodated' compared to other Muslims in their observation of halal guidelines.

Table 4.8 indicates that a significant percentage of survey participants (36.6 per cent) reported that they *always* prepared their own meals while travelling in New Zealand. These respondents represent the numerous Muslims who have found it hard to dine in restaurants or buy food from takeaway outlets in New Zealand. Many Muslims are not willing to buy food from restaurants that also serve pork or alcohol on their premises, as is often the case in New Zealand, because, as noted above, under Islamic food laws what is halal becomes haram or non-permissible once it comes into contact with any non-halal items 'either through storage, during distribution or by using the same utensils to cook it' (Sulaiman, 2001: 9). Muslim consumers with a high degree of religious commitment are usually not risk-takers in food purchase and consumption (Saleh, 1996). Therefore they often shy away from ambiguous

Table 4.8 How do you manage your meals while travelling in New Zealand?

	I prepare my own meals		I buy fast food takeaways		I dine at restaurants	
	Frequency	%	Frequency	%	Frequency	%
Never	24	6.5	63	17.0	102	27.5
Seldom	24	6.5	83	22.4	102	27.5
Sometimes	66	17.8	102	27.5	61	16.4
Often	87	23.5	47	12.7	25	6.7
Always	147	39.6	17	4.6	6	1.6
No response	23	6.2	59	15.9	75	20.2

situations and are cautious about trying out food in restaurants that have not been halal certified by a credible Islamic authority (Saleh, 1996). Unfortunately, there are currently few halal certified restaurants in New Zealand.

While halal certification was lacking, it was also observed during the research fieldwork that halal food was generally not to be found in great variety, especially in places that were not mainly frequented by Muslims. The halal food outlets found by the researcher while travelling from Auckland to Dunedin were mainly kebab restaurants. Sometimes the food available in such outlets was not particularly appetizing and was far from pandering to the palates of jaded travellers. The travellers interviewed in this research expressed their desire to taste a variety of good food, especially Western food such as Italian and Mexican. Asian travellers, in particular, especially those accustomed to having more variety and spice, also found it quite difficult to not have available their staple diet, rice, alongside other meat and salad dishes. After a few days of eating kebab or fish and chips in New Zealand, Muslims interviewed admitted that they were not able to resist preparing their own meals. Fortunately for them, New Zealand's motels are usually equipped with full cooking facilities.

There are several sources from which Muslim travellers can locate and obtain halal food in New Zealand. Of the total sample, 81.7 per cent said they had taken halal food from friends and relatives while travelling in New Zealand, making friends and relatives the most popular source of halal food in New Zealand. The second most popular was mosques or Islamic centres, with 73.8 per cent of the sample having found or purchased halal food from this source. Specialist food stores, such as Asian food shops came in third, with 73.6 per cent of the sample having found halal food in these outlets while travelling in New Zealand. Other sources of halal food include supermarkets (61.0 per cent), restaurants (59.3 per cent) and dairy or other food shops (56.3 per cent).

Apart from sources from which they found or purchased halal food, respondents were also asked to rate the sources from which they obtained information regarding halal food. This was to measure the awareness that Muslim travellers had towards the availability of halal food in New Zealand. Awareness is the first important stage in any adoption process (Kotler et al., 1999). Before consumers adopt any goods, service or ideas, they must first become aware of it through a variety of sources such as the media and word of mouth.

Results showed that word of mouth was by far the most common method of obtaining information regarding halal food in New Zealand, with 90 per cent

Table 4.9   While travelling in New Zealand, I always look for halal food

	Frequency	%
Agree	305	82.2
Unsure	30	8.1
Disagree	36	9.7
No response	7	1.9

of the sample having obtained information on halal food via this media. Just over half of the sample population (51.2 per cent) said that they had learned about halal food in New Zealand from newsletters, while 50.9 per cent of the population had also referred to brochures/pamphlets. Other types of media such as the Internet, newspapers, radio, magazines and television only provided Muslims with very limited information regarding halal food in New Zealand.

Having examined the level of access that Muslim travellers have to halal food, this research also tried to determine how strictly Muslim travellers observe halal guidelines in New Zealand. In April 2001, the National Animal Welfare Advisory Committee (NAWAC) published a discussion paper that questioned the appropriateness of halal slaughter in light of a new law pertaining to animal welfare (Buang, 2001). The paper also mentioned that while Muslims represented only 0.39 per cent of New Zealand's population in 1996, it was unknown how many of them adhered strictly to the religion, especially with regards to the consumption of halal food (NAWAC, 2001). This research has therefore provided empirical evidence showing that the majority of Muslims in New Zealand adhere to halal guidelines. Results in Table 4.9 indicate that at least 82 per cent of the sample population *always* look for halal food while travelling in New Zealand.

Conclusions

Muslim consumers in New Zealand are today in urgent need of statutory or legislative regulations and stronger guidelines pertaining to the issue of halal food. There is also a need to establish and implement an effective halal certification system that is standard throughout the country. Awareness is one of the prerequisites to having more halal food outlets all around New Zealand. Owners of restaurants and food outlets may not know of the potential customers who live around them, or the availability of halal products including beef 'bacon', turkey 'ham', beef salami, luncheon meat, frankfurters and various types of sausages that only contain halal beef and chicken (El-Mouelhy, 2001). Non-Muslim customers may also have unfounded reservations about eating at halal food outlets. The commercial advantage of developing halal certainly exists for both domestic and international travellers, although many potential entrepreneurs may not be aware of them. Companies that have been issued with a halal certificate are not only likely to gain the confidence of Muslim consumers, but also enhance their products' marketability, especially if they are exporting to Muslim countries.

Due to the significant link between food and relationships in many cultures, the availability of halal food also brings more than mere economic profit. Businesses need to realize that offering halal food attracts not only Muslims but also their non-Muslim friends and relatives. In a multi-racial and multi-religious society such as New Zealand, it is important that people understand each other's sensitivities so that they can live in harmony. As Saleh (1996: 44) asserts, 'Halal food and certification plays a significant role in the social interaction of the various ethnic and religious groups as it enables Muslims and non-Muslims to share the same food and eat at the same table'. Food businesses that can help enhance social integration among the different communities may also help build a more harmonious and stable multi-religious society (Saleh 1996).

The results from the survey discussed in this chapter have indicated that businesses provide limited information to consumers regarding the availability of halal food in New Zealand. However, further research is required to find out why many halal food proprietors in New Zealand are reluctant to apply for certification and put halal labels or signage on their products or shops. Advertising is the key to marketing and sales. In a multi-religious society where Muslims are a minority, halal labels are important because they would not only attract, but also inform members of the Muslim community regarding the halal status of food products.

Further research should also look into the perception of non-Muslims regarding halal food and any reservations that may exist about consuming halal food. For example, in the case of Singapore the non-Muslim majority showed no resistance to the establishment of halal fast-food restaurants such as McDonald's. According to Rasheed (1992: 2) the majority of Singaporeans were not upset or disappointed about 'the prospect of losing bacon or pork sausages for breakfast at McDonald's'. On the contrary, they accepted halal food and welcomed it as a step towards social integration in Singapore (Saleh, 1996).

Although the issue of halal food is undoubtedly important for Muslims, academic literature and research regarding the topic, especially in relation to hospitality and tourism, is extremely sparse. This is perhaps surprising given that countries such as New Zealand have started to target Islamic regions as a source of inbound tourism. Nevertheless, it also perhaps reveals the cultural blindness that may exist in many Western countries not only with respect to the sacredness of food for many visitors and those in the community, but also the overall significance of food within the tourism experience and as a means of providing a secure environment in which to travel. However, if the tourism and hospitality industry is aiming to attract Islamic tourists, then they also need to identify the design features that may be a component of ensuring confidence in the halal product with respect to kitchens, dining rooms and serving areas for example. Given the need to understand both the supply of and demand for halal foods as part of the tourism experience it is therefore not surprising that countries which are more culturally aware of the needs of Muslim travellers, such as Malaysia and Singapore, are become increasingly attractive as tourist destinations for travellers from the Middle East and other Islamic countries.

5

The world of cookery-school holidays

Liz Sharples

Introduction

For some people, the idea of spending precious time on holiday, sporting a stripey apron while chopping, filleting, mashing and stirring would fill them with horror. For others, this would be gastronomic bliss.

For a certain group of people there appears to be a need to explore the fascinating world of food. To learn how to make a perfect béchamel sauce, to appreciate the difference between a cold pressed extra virgin olive oil and a sunflower oil, to get to grips with the dressing of a crab or to grasp the fundamentals of a whisked sponge cake. A culinary holiday is far more than this of course. Add all of this 'grind' in the kitchen to the chance of tasting mouthwatering food, accompanied by a glass or two of the local vino, possibly set in a breathtaking rural setting and suddenly the concept becomes quite palatable. Presented in this way, the concept of learning to cook while on holiday appears to be an attractive one, made up of a number of exciting ingredients, carefully presented for its invited guests. But who comes on these holidays and why? How much do they cost and who are the providers? And where, if at all, does the cookery school experience fit into the whole spectrum of holidays already provided within the tourism sector?

This chapter takes a look at the tempting world of cookery-school holidays in an attempt to answer some of these questions. It is designed to provide a brief introduction to this interesting culinary phenomenon, whose market appears to be expanding year by year. Initially, the chapter examines the complex blend of elements that combine to make up the cookery school experience. It then suggests some of the reasons why an increasing number of people, both male and female, of all ages, make the decision to embark on a food learning experience during part of their leisure time. This is done by examining some of the social and cultural influences which appear to be bringing about a need, or desire, to learn more about food and cooking skills.

The chapter then explores the range and nature of holidays/day courses that are currently provided by some of the cookery schools/specialist centres in Europe. This is not an exhaustive study of every provider but is sufficiently detailed to give the reader an overview of the scale and nature of the sector. The section includes a simple categorization of the types of holiday on offer, a detailed analysis of the experiences provided by twelve European cookery schools and a discussion about the techniques used by the companies to promote these experiences to their target market. Schools used in this section have been specifically selected to show the diversity of the sector, which extends from experiences based on a single commodity, for example bread, fish or mushrooms, to courses that offer an opportunity to acquire more generic skills.

The chapter also includes more in-depth case studies of three cookery schools which specialize in culinary holidays. These nicely illustrate the individual companyies aims and objectives, their pattern of growth and development, and the factors that have influenced their success. Data to inform these cases was obtained from telephone interviews with key members of staff from the organizations, web-based research and literature searches. The chapter concludes with an examination of the future and impacts of this growing market sector.

The cookery-school holiday: where does it fit in?

The question of where the cookery-school holiday fits into the whole spectrum of experiences on offer within the tourism sector, is an interesting one. It is a multifaceted product, crossing the boundaries of several tourism 'typologies' and brushing on the edges of neighbouring disciplines such as leisure, hospitality and gastronomy, and cannot therefore be readily categorized, labelled or defined. The debate of how, and where, this type of holiday should be studied and debated, from both the demand and the supply dimensions, is therefore somewhat complex. The following section attempts to illustrate this. The discussion also highlights the fact that a culinary holiday is capable of providing a number of 'different things to different people' dependent on the aspects of the package that the consumer decides to buy in to.

The rural dimension

The cookery-school product often, but not always, has a strong rural element. Many of the holidays on offer, as can be seen from the cases in this chapter, take place in attractive rural locations, such as Tuscany, Provence or the Highlands of Scotland, but with the food element playing a key role. However, with regard to customer demand, in certain situations the food aspect may be merely an 'added extra', to an already planned vacation to a particular destination, i.e. the location may be the key attraction. At other times, the food element may be major 'pull' factor and the location will adopt a secondary role.

As far as the 'supply' element is concerned a cookery school situated in the country or in a coastal setting is, by its nature, a rural business (English Tourism Council, 2001; Page and Getz, 1997). An examination of the case studies reveal that many cookery school businesses have been established as a diversification of an already established business, which is a characteristic of much rural tourism entrepreneurship (Butler, 1998; Ilbery, 1998). For example, at rurally located hotels or restaurants, such as Ballymaloe House and Le Manoir, or at a rural food producers, such as the Village Bakery.

Exhibit 5.1 Ballymaloe Cookery School

Ballymaloe is one of Europe's foremost cookery schools, and has attracted students from around the globe since its opening in 1983. The school is situated in one of the most scenic areas of Ireland, East Cork, surrounded by beautiful rolling countryside and only half a mile from the sea. Despite its quiet location, it is easily accessible by good road links and Cork Airport is just 25 miles away. The venue has much to offer the visitor. In addition to the cookery school, there are a number of excellent beaches, cliff-top walks, craft shops, heritage centres and historic buildings all within easy distance.

The school is run by Darina and Tim Allen, both well-known cooks in their own right, who keep the culinary style pioneered by Myrtle Allen, from the nearby Ballymaloe House (http://www.ballymaloe.com/), at the heart of their operation. This well-loved award-winning country house hotel and restaurant, situated 2 miles from the cookery school, has helped to establish Ireland's rightful place on the international culinary circuit, with its tireless commitment to the use of excellent fresh local ingredients on its menus. Darina and Tim have also adopted this ethos and this is demonstrated by the school's approach to food supply. The cookery school obtains most of its vegetables and herbs from the Allens' own organic gardens, free-range eggs are collected daily from their chickens and fish is bought daily from Ballycotton harbour nearby. Fresh meat and farmhouse cheeses are all purchased from local suppliers.

The school attracts students of all ages and abilities. Some are complete novices, while others are more experienced cooks, keen to improve their skills and expand their culinary horizons. Many of the students in attendance enrol purely to have a 'fun' experience but the school also offers intensive twelve-week certificate courses designed for those who wish to embark on a career within the hospitality industry. Many of the courses on offer are booked up well in advance and have waiting lists, a clear demonstration of the school's popularity.

The courses range from simple one- to two-day courses, based on a certain theme, for example baking, entertaining, salads or pasta dishes, to more lengthy week-long courses which are designed to establish a foundation of culinary skills. The teaching style is relaxed and friendly, and at lunch times students and tutors sit down together to enjoy the fruits of their labour over a leisurely lunch. The school's facilities are excellent and while some sessions are taught by the owners the school also calls upon the expertise of a number of guest tutors. The school even offers a number of cookery demonstration afternoons for those people who are too busy to embark on a day's course. The school has also recently added a number of com-plementary courses to its portfolio, for example in foraging, gardening and wine tasting.

Visitors can choose whether they wish to stay in one of the school's well-equipped self-catering cottages adjacent to the Allens' Regency home, stay at the nearby Ballymaloe Hotel or make their own accommodation arrangements. The school's web site is a good point of contact for both prospective and past students (http://www.cook-ingisfun.re/school/) as it includes a useful job section, recipe ideas, past student news and other local tourism links.

Liz Sharples

The cultural dimension

This type of holiday also has a strong cultural dimension. Many of the experiences on offer concern themselves with an exploration of national or regional food ingredients and dishes, which have their roots deeply embedded in the geography of the area. For example, schools such as Vallicorte in Italy has a focus on the preparation of traditional Tuscan dishes, while others such as Stein's school at Padstow celebrates a specific ingredient, in this case the local fish and fishing tradition, that is an important part of Cornish culture. This cultural aspect can play an important part in the learning experience as local or appropriate wines/drinks can be used to accompany the dishes, traditional food-service traditions can be observed and local food events and customs that have their roots in that region can be showcased (Bode, 1994; Tannahill, 1998; Wood, 2001).

Other schools adopt a wider approach to their learning by offering a range of culinary opportunities for their visitors rather than concentrating on one particular style of cuisine. These courses may reflect the changing seasons, for example Christmas entertaining, or cover the latest food trends, such as fusion food. Again, culture plays an important part as modern food culture and fashions can be discussed and demonstrated in the use of 'new' ingredients or food presentation styles.

A school's approach is likely to be dictated by a number of factors but inevitably will reflect the particular interest and specialist knowledge of the owner and team involved in teaching the courses.

Exhibit 5.2 The Padstow Seafood School, Cornwall

If you want to learn more about fish this is the place, or 'plaice', to go! The school is owned and operated by the renowned seafood chef, Rick

Stein, who has become something of a household celebrity in recent years. This man has a passion for fish and appears to have made it his personal mission to inform and inspire the public about the delights of seafood. His extremely successful television series and host of cookery books have been designed to educate his audience about the simple 'fishy' facts, like the difference between a cod and a haddock, but also to entice his followers to experiment with, and enjoy, fish as often as possible. There is no doubt that Stein has been partially responsible for the resurgence of interest in fish around the UK not only in the home, but also on the restaurant menu.

The Seafood School is just part of Stein's portfolio of business activity in Padstow. The village also boasts a very popular and successful Seafood Restaurant, opened over twenty-five years ago, St Petroc's Hotel and Bistro, a small hotel known as St Edmund's House, Rick Stein's café, which also offers bed and breakfast, Steins, an up-market gift, art and wine shop, and a Seafood Deli. The Padstow Seafood School (http://www.rickstein.com/school_course) opened in 2000 and experienced instant success with cookery courses already showing an average 95 per cent occupancy rate.

Guests can select from a wide range of courses. The most popular choice is the one-day 'taster' course based around the preparation of several fish dishes and includes the preparation of a delicious lunch which clients can then enjoy with colleagues accompanied by a glass or two of suitable wine. For clients wanting a more in-depth experience, two-day, two-night and four-day, five-night residential courses are available, whose fees includes all tuition, accommodation, meals, wine and course materials. Generally speaking, the one-day courses run during the high season, when participants can enjoy the experience as a special part of their pre-planned holiday to Cornwall. The longer courses take place during the quieter times of the year when the accommodation is more readily available. The school also offers a series of specialist two-day, two-night courses based on a particular style of fish cuisine. For example, Thai and Chinese Fish cookery, French and Italian cookery and Shellfish cookery. The school even offers half-day courses for children.

Many of the courses held by the cookery school are sold to people wanting either to 'treat' themselves or as a present to a partner, relative or friend for some sort of special celebration. For example, a wife may buy a husband a one-day course as a fortieth birthday present. The school provides gift and Christmas vouchers for this purpose and participates in the 'Red Letter' scheme. Partners are welcome to accompany guests on their courses and the school will go out of its away to arrange/suggest alternative activities for them to be involved in while their partner is in the kitchen. Cornwall has a lot to offer the visitor including the recently opened Eden Project and the Gardens of Heligan.

Course participants predominantly come from around the UK but the school also attracts a number of European and a few Australian visitors, where the Rick Stein television series have also proven popular. The school is currently less popular with the American market possibly due to its 'out of the way' location, which is not on American tourists' usual UK circuit. The school is looking to expand this market, however, with the help of an agent who specializes in gourmet tours. The school is also in the process of arranging a number of courses for the Japanese market, which will be taught with simultaneous translation.

All the courses are taught in an informative but relaxed way in a specially designed modern kitchen, complete with the latest equipment. A huge emphasis is placed on the quality of ingredients and Stein's sets the standard by taking its fish straight off the trawlers which fish out of Padstow.

The school still has the potential to expand into new markets. A number of businesses are now looking into the possibility of using the Seafood School as an incentive package and the school is recognizing the potential of using the premises for private functions and events.

Liz Sharples

The educational dimension

It is important to make a distinction between the accredited diploma/degree catering courses taught worldwide at colleges, hotel schools and universities, which are specifically aimed at training professionals for employment in the hotel and catering industry, and recreational courses taught at cookery schools which are primarily aimed at the leisure market. Of course, the two products are somewhat blurred due to the educational culinary element of both types of courses. For some hobbyists embarking on a cookery holiday this 'learning' element may be very important as there may be a desire to return home with a package of new or improved culinary skills, which can be used to impress their family and dinner guests. This newly acquired knowledge may even act as a catalyst and push the participant towards a career working with food. For other clients the hedonistic element is more important – they simply want to have a good time surrounded by good food and wine.

Some of the cookery schools covered in this chapter are capable of providing opportunities at both the 'fun' and the 'skill' level, and some are even capable of preparing students for specialist catering positions, for example as chalet cooks in ski resorts or as cooks on board a chartered boat.

The special interest dimension

The cookery school holiday also has a strong hobby or special interest factor (Hall and Mitchell, 2001). Many of the people deciding to enrol for this type of holiday will already have a passion for food and may see the holiday as an opportunity to share information, cook and eat with other like-minded 'foodies'. In special interest tourism the activity becomes the main attraction or motivating factor for travel as opposed to more general interest tourism where the destination is the major pull factor (Brotherton and Himmetoglu, 1997). Building on the work of Culligan (1992), Brotherton and Himmetoglu (1997: 16) argue that 'as the tourist's level of experience and confidence rises there will be a movement away from the "safer" and more limited type of holiday-taking characteristic of the novice tourist towards progressively more adventurous forms of travel and holiday-taking'. They observed that as a tourist's affluence and experience grows over time so does their need or desire for more exciting tourism experiences that have a high prestige/ego enhancement element. However, they also highlight the relative decrease in the number of tourists that have the opportunity to partake in this type of holiday compared with a holiday where the destination is the key focus. In certain situations the special interest market can be an exclusive one due to the fact that the holidaymaker is not purely paying for the journey and the hospitality elements, but is also paying for a chance to belong to a special 'club' during the duration of their stay. A look at the cookery-school market suggests that this is the case in much of this sector. With day courses ranging from £50 to £200 per day for tuition and food and week-long courses including food and accommodation costing from £500 to £2000, this is not a last minute bargain type of holiday. It is more of a treat that is carefully planned and saved for.

Brotherton and Himmetoglu (1997) also note the link that exists between the leisure pursuit enjoyed at home and the special interest holiday. They suggest that many of the people who decide to embark on a specialist holiday are those holidaymakers who already have an interest in a specific activity as a 'dabbler', an 'enthusiast', an 'expert' or a 'fanatic'.

The temptations of a culinary holiday

As can be seen from the previous section, the elements that make up a cookery school holiday are complex. As such, the motivations that lie behind an individual's decision to spend a day, a weekend or longer on holiday with a mission to learn more about food are also complex. The following discussion outlines just a few of the reasons that may play an important part in the decision-making process to become a 'food-explorer'.

Linking food with the countryside

The natural connections that once existed between our food, and the land it was grown or reared on, have largely been eroded (Kuzenof, Tregear and Moxey, 1997). The nature of the food supply chain, certainly within the Western world, has shifted dramatically over the last 200 years and these changes have formed the subject of considerable debate by many academics and researchers. The crux of the debate has been the move from a local system of food supply, where many foods were produced or sourced close to home, to a global system where many foods travel vast distances from 'field to plate' (Beardsworth and Keil, 1997; Montanari, 1994; Oddy, 1990).

One of the most recent aspects of this ongoing discussion has been the issue of 'traceability' within the food supply chain. Although many consumers remain blissfully unaware of the source of the milk they are pouring onto their breakfast cereal, or the tomatoes they are chopping to go into their salad, an increasing number of consumers are not fully convinced about the safety of our current methods of food supply. A variety of complex factors have been influential in this growing uneasiness but it is fair to assume that food scares such as BSE in the 1990s and more recently the Foot and Mouth crisis in 2001 have had an obvious impact at an international level.

Within the UK the publication of reports such as the landmark *Food Miles Report* (Paxton, 1994) which questioned the environmental impact of long-distance food-sourcing strategies and, more recently, a far-reaching government report, which was the result of an inquiry into the future of food and farming in the UK (Policy Commission, 2002) have also heightened public awareness. This latest inquiry has called for a total 'reconnection' along the food chain, between all of the key stakeholders, in an attempt to assure the sustainability of our food and farming industries in the future.

The interest and desire for 'real' or 'authentic' food is now gathering pace and some consumers are actively seeking out opportunities to reconnect with the origins of the food that they and their families are consuming by 'buying local' whenever possible. This has been demonstrated by the growing popularity of outlets such as farmers' markets and farm shops over recent years (see Chapter 2). The concept, therefore, of a culinary holiday where dishes are prepared using local foods from the surrounding region may therefore be appealing to this sector of the market.

There also appears to be a need among some consumers to reconnect with the countryside as a source of recreation and relaxation, and the number of people who are now making trips 'out of town' in search of peace, solitude, fresh air and wide open spaces is on the increase (Butler, 1998; Butler et al., 1998; Page and Getz, 1997). For some people this search for a rural 'dream' appears to be the one thing that sustains them during their weekly stint at the urban office. Whether this dream exists in reality or whether this rural 'idyll' is purely a myth is seriously open to question, but nonetheless the vision and promise of an uncomplicated life free from the strains of modern living continues to attract visitors to the countryside (Bramwell, 1994; Cloke, 1993; Lane, 1994) and as the pace of urban life appears to quicken in Western society it is likely that this trend will continue.

Put these two factors together and you have the raw material that cookery holidays are made of. Consumers anxious about searching out real food combined with a need to escape to a peaceful rural setting. Many of the cookery holidays on offer can offer these two magic ingredients while also allowing individuals to really get a sense of connection. For example, at Rick Stein's idyllically located cookery school in Cornwall the fish is brought straight from the harbour, and at Raymond Blanc's school at the impressive building of Le Manoir a huge emphasis is placed on the fresh vegetables and herbs he uses from his extensive garden.

Exhibit 5.3 Le Manoir Ecole de Cuisine

The cookery school at Le Manoir aux Quat' Saisons (http://www.goodfood.co.uk/le-manoir-ecole-de-cuisine.htm) is currently in its tenth year of operation and advertises itself as the only 'school' in the world where the guests have the opportunity of watching and learning in the kitchens of a two Michelin Star restaurant.

Le Manoir, owned and managed by its expert chef patron, Raymond Blanc, is one of the UK's premier restaurants and, as such, attracts visitors from around the world in search of excellent cuisine. The restaurant is situated in the sleepy village of Great Milton, just outside Oxford, but is within travelling distance of London, several international airports and good road and rail links.

The cookery school is devoted to involving its clients with some of the fundamental techniques of cookery so that they leave knowing a little more about how to use food creatively, without always having to stick religiously to a recipe. Course numbers are deliberately kept small, usually no more than ten people at a time, to ensure an intimate experience.

Courses are run throughout the year, with the exception of July and August, and clients can choose from a one-day, two-day or a week-long course. Currently the one-day courses, which are the most popular, focus on dinner parties, fusion cuisine or nutrition, and the two-day courses cover fish and shellfish or vegetarian dishes. The weekly courses are aimed at people who wish to improve their skill levels and often attract guests who have already enjoyed a short course there. To enable progression they operate under a Stage 1, 2 and 3 system. Guests enrolled on the one-day course prepare dishes that can be shared with fellow students at lunch time and the students embarking on the week's course have the opportunity of dining in the main restaurant each evening.

Students are supervised by chef Stephen Blanc, the school's director, who carried out his apprenticeship at Le Manoir under the watchful eye of Monsieur Blanc. It is never difficult to fill the spaces on the courses at the school. In fact, a waiting list operates for most of the year and courses get booked up well in advance. Clients come to the school from around the UK and, indeed, internationally, the school being particularly popular with American visitors. Its easy access to London is a key selling point.

The school relies heavily on word of mouth for its advertising but the web site is another useful and effective method of promotion (http://www.goodfood.co.uk/le-manoir-ecole-de-cuisine) The school also regularly places advertisements in high-end magazines and journals, such as the *Tatler*.

Liz Sharples

Food as a lifestyle issue

Food is now a 'hot' topic on the streets, on prime time television, in the popular press and on the radio. At least in Western society it is no longer purely an element in human survival or a part of one's culture, it is wrapped up with status, part of fashion and plays an important part in determining who you are and how you interact with society.

At one time the whole subject of food was simple, food was primarily fuel and, occasionally, at special events and festivals, it played an important part in celebration. Now the role that food plays in society is far more complex and it has become the subject of considerable debate by sociologists, anthropologists, health professionals, marketing gurus and economists, to name a few. The food industry has become a massive global multibillion pound industry and we are all affected by it, whether we choose to be or not. You do not need to look far to find evidence to support these rather bold statements, although the wealth of literature regarding food and lifestyle is so extensive that it is impossible to examine all this vast subject within the context of this chapter.

One particularly interesting and relevant angle, however, is the influence of the media on food consumers, and the arrival of the 'celebrity chef' on the television screen is just one example of this. A vast array of cookery programmes, for example, *Ready Steady Cook*, *Master Chef* and *Cooking with Delia* fill our screens on a daily basis, and in some ways they have become one of the most fashionable ways to learn about food. People are now exposed to a startling amount of information about international cooking styles and ingredients, and the programmes have even had an influence on food purchasing patterns as devotees rush to buy the latest trendy ingredients from the supermarket (Wood, 2001).

Food 'experts' such as Delia Smith, Nigella Lawson, Gary Rhodes, Jamie Oliver and many others have all become celebrity household names with their own television series, best selling cookery books and some even have their own web sites. For example, see Delia Smith's site at http://www.deliaonline.com. However, the media competition has become so intense that one recent article in the hospitality trade press warned chefs that it may be time to return to their kitchens rather than chase media glory (Harmer, 2000).

The number of magazines that have food and lifestyle as a focus is another useful indicator of this growing fascination with the culinary arts. Publications such as *Waitrose's Food Illustrated*; *Food and Travel* and the *Observer Food Monthly* are all recent additions to the wealth of food publications that can be found in any high street newsagents.

The mere fact that food is a subject right at the forefront of discussion in society is bound to have an impact on how we, as individuals, feel about it and the part that it plays in our lives. In some people this has created a fascination and curiosity with the subject and a need, or desire, to know more. Despite the fact that many people appear now to spend less time in the kitchen, due to the rise of ready-meals, and proportionately spend less of their income on 'basic' food, than they did fifty years ago, the topic of food has become sufficiently interesting that many people are choosing to pursue it as part of a leisure experience.

The search for skills

One interesting, and in some ways quite worrying, factor is that some people reach adulthood with very few, even basic cooking skills. Traditionally, cooking skills have been automatically passed down the female line of the family, from grandmother to mother to daughter, and UK-based research shows that, with some class and educational variations, the mother is still the one who primarily shoulders responsibility for this important task (Caraher et al., 1999). Cooking classes in school were cited as the next most important source of learning about cooking skills by the majority of correspondents. However, the study also reveals that the UK population, as a whole, lacks confidence in the kitchen:

> What emerges is a population unsure of specific cooking techniques and lacking confidence to apply techniques and cook certain foods. Women still bear the burden of cooking for the household, with four out of five women respondents cooking on most or every day, compared with one in five men. This may be related to the large number of men who claim to have no cooking skills (one in five). (Caraher et al., 1999: 590)

Significantly, the study also shows the importance of partners as a source of information about food, particularly in the case of women passing on knowledge to men, and the fact that cookery books and cookery programmes on the media play a small but significant role in the process.

The debate of how this situation is changing, and will change in the future, is an interesting one. As more women enter the workplace, particularly in Western society, and their traditional role as 'homemaker ' changes, will there be less time and energy to spend on educating children, and men, about food? An article in *The Times* (Lee, 2002) highlights this very problem and the 'Focus on Food' campaign which has an aim to promote cookery teaching in schools to encourage children to appreciate food and its preparation (http://www.waitrose.com/focusonfood). Will future generations have to rely on the media and other external methods of education, either at school or later in life to pick up these basic skills? Are cookery-school, and other food-based holidays, starting to fill a gap in some people's lives?

The cookery-school product

The range of cookery school holidays now on offer within Europe is extensive and includes a number of innovative experiences for the food enthusiast. At one end of the scale are the holidays that have a strong countryside element, where the emphasis is on food gathering rather than food skills. This type of holiday is likely to be a short break or a day course spent at a rural destination. An opportunity for cooking and tasting is likely to be included but much of the work will be spent in the field. For example, Sue Webster (2001) in the *Sunday Telegraph* travel section describes a holiday in the Elan valley in Wales organized by Daniel Butler's Fungi Forays (http://www.raptor-rambles.co.uk) where the central theme is gathering the mushrooms in delightful countryside before a cookery demonstration and mushroom feast. Other fungal expeditions are organized by a number of different companies, for example, Mycologue, a mushroom lovers network (http://www.mycologue.co.uk) who offer three-night breaks in Brittany, and the UK Vegetarian Society who feature Fungal weekends in the parkland and woods near to their headquarters.

Other holidays concentrate less on the gathering of food in a rural setting but have a mission to search out good food in an urban setting. One such holiday is the Promenades Gourmandes, a guided gastronomic walk around the specialist food shops, markets and butchers of Paris in search of delicious ingredients. The day concludes with the cooking of the bought produce in the guide's kitchen followed by a gourmet meal accompanied by suitable wines (Gerrard, 1999) (see Gourmet on Tour at http://www.gourmet on tour.com).

At the other end of the scale is the more intensive type of cookery holiday, which has a strong emphasis on skills. The quality of ingredients will, of course, be vital to the success of the experience but the instructor will be keen to send the students home armed with a 'tool kit' which will enable them to replicate practised dishes. Le Manoir and Le Marmiton are two such schools but there are many others, several owned and run by celebrity chefs, e.g. Nairn's and many long-established schools, such as Leith's in London founded in the 1970s (http://www.leiths.co.uk), and the Tante Marie School of Cookery in Surrey, founded in the 1950s. (http://www.tantemarie.co.uk).

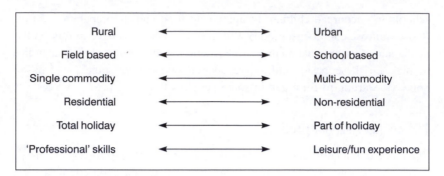

Rural		Urban
Field based		School based
Single commodity		Multi-commodity
Residential		Non-residential
Total holiday		Part of holiday
'Professional' skills		Leisure/fun experience

Figure 5.1   Cookery holiday spectrum

From the discussion above it is possible to produce a simple figure that illustrates the continuum of components that make up cookery school holidays (Figure 5.1). The majority of culinary experiences on offer within the marketplace can be placed somewhere within these component ranges and it is then possible to classify the product more readily. For example, a bread-baking course may be:

■ aimed at the leisure market who may have an interest in flour and a love of bread
■ set in a rural location
■ just one day in duration
■ aimed at the tourist who is already planning to stay in the region
■ reasonably priced
■ non-residential.

This simple positioning could help the tourist, who may be planning to embark on a culinary holiday, to identify the nature and aims of his or her trip. More importantly, it helps to focus the mind of the organizer when deciding upon the type of product that he or she plans to provide and the market that is being targeted.

Building on this analysis, Table 5.1 describes a number of holidays that are currently available in Europe. The list is not extensive but provides a flavour of the type of products available in the marketplace. Several of the holidays are explored in more depth in the exhibits. Please note that prices are not included for two reasons, first, because some schools were not happy to openly publish their rates and, second, because of timing – prices change annually.

Table 5.1 Analysis of selected European cookery schools

Name of school	Web address	Location	Focus	Day course	2–3 day course	Week course	Residential or non-residential	Owner/director/tutors	Special features
ENGLAND									
Le Manoir de Ecole de Cuisine	http://www.goodfood.co.uk/le-manoir-de-ecole-de-cuisine.htm	Great Milton, Oxford	Classic culinary skills and creativity; nutrition.	Yes	Yes	Yes	Yes – for longer courses	Owner – Raymond Blanc	See Exhibit 5.1
The Seafood School	http://www.rickstein.com/school	Padstow, Cornwall	Fish cuisine – classic and modern	Yes	Yes	Yes (4 days)	Yes – for longer courses	Owner – Rick Stein	See Exhibit 5.2
The Cordon Vert Cookery School	http://www.vegsoc.org/cordonvert	Altrincham, Cheshire	Vegetarian cuisine – basic to advanced; themed days	Yes	No	Yes	Yes – for longer courses	Director – Lynn Weller	This is the cookery school based at the long established UK Vegetarian Society
The Village Bakery	http://www.village-bakery.com	Melmerby, Cumbria, Lake District	Bread-making courses	Yes	Yes	Yes	Can be organized	Owner – Andrew Whitley	Courses are taught at this organic bakery which bakes using wood fired ovens
SCOTLAND									
Naim's Cookery School	http://www.nairnscookschool.com	Lake of Menteith, Stirling, Scotland	Modern Scottish cuisine – classic skills.	Yes	No	Yes	Can be organized	Owner – Nick Nairn	A purpose-built school which showcases the best of Scottish ingredients
IRELAND									
Ballymaloe	http://www.cookingisfun.re/school	Co. Cork, Ireland	A range of courses from bread baking to entertaining	Yes	Yes	Yes and 12 week	Can be residential or non-residential	Owners – Darina and Tim Allen	See Exhibit 5.3

Table 5.1 Continued

Name of school	Web address	Location	Focus	Day course	2–3 day course	Week course	Residential or non-residential	Owner/director/tutors	Special features
FRANCE									
Ecole des Trois Ponts	http://3ponts.edu/	Roanne, near Lyon, France	French Country Cooking courses	No	No	Yes and 2–4 week	Residential	Owners	Set in an eighteenth-century chateau this school also teaches language courses
Le Marmiton	http://www.avignon-et-provence.com/seminaires/marmiton	Avignon, France	Provencal French cuisine	Yes	Yes	Yes	Can be residential or non-residential	Guest tutor – Daniel Hebet	Taught in the nineteenth-century kitchens of the Hotel La Mirande
ITALY									
Vallicorte	http://www.vallicorte.com	Lucca, Tuscany, Italy	Tuscan food and wine	No	4 days	7 day	Residential	Owners – John and Berenice Bonallack	Relaxed courses taught by Ursula Ferrigno in a restored Tuscan farmhouse
Villa Ravida	http://www.tastingplaces.com/html/ravida.html	Menfi, Sicily	Sicilian cookery	No	No	Yes	Residential	Guest tutor – Maxine Clark	Taught at the eighteenth-century villa; the family farm produces award-winning olive oil
PORTUGAL									
Refugio da Vila	http://www.refugiodavila.com	Portel nr Evora, Portugal	Portuguese cookery	No	No	Yes	Residential	Head Chef – Miguel Amaral	A cookery school based at a rural manor house hotel set in the Alentejo region
SPAIN									
Finca Buen Vino	http://www.buenvino.com/cookery_courses.html	Andalucia, Spain	Traditional Spanish cookery	No	No	Yes	Residential	Owners – Sam and Jeannie Chesterton	A relaxed cookery course set in a family home in the Sierra mountains

Analysis of European cookery schools

The question of whether the cookery-school holiday should be promoted/ advertised through its very obvious geographical and cultural dimensions, or through the food and skills element of the product that the holiday incorporates, is a complex one. The marketing networks and mechanisms that *are* used by the cookery schools, however, appear to be working well. Despite the price of enrolling on many of the courses, which puts them at the luxury end of the tourism market, demand is high, with all three of the schools interviewed reporting rapid take-up of courses and waiting lists necessary for many of the more popular courses. A check on the web sites of the other schools shown in Table 5.1 reveals a similar picture with many courses being filled several months in advance.

Specialist tour operators, offering a range of gastronomic holidays, play a major role in promoting this type of holiday via their web sites and literature. Many of these companies advertise regularly in quality food and travel magazines, in addition to weekend newspaper supplements, and, although the number of operators is now vast, several established companies still dominate the market:

■ Arblaster and Clarke (http://www.arblasterandclarke.com) a company who specialize in wine tours, continue to hold their place as one of the top travel companies in this field offering gourmet tours to Italy and France and cookery courses in Northern Italy as well as other locations such as Bali in Indonesia.
■ Tasting Places (http://www.tastingplaces.com/) also offers a comprehensive service providing courses in Italy, Greece and Thailand as well as master classes in London with some of the capital's top chefs.
■ Patanegra (http://www.patanegra.net/home.html) is well established as one of the leading providers for Spanish cookery courses particularly in the Andalucian region.
■ Gourmet on Tour (http://www.gourmetontour.com) offers culinary holidays world-wide including experiences in France, Italy, UK, Ireland, Asia and Australia.

Conclusion

Indications are that the market for cookery school and culinary holidays in Europe is likely to increase. At the time of writing, articles in the press and on the World Wide Web, such as 'Top ten cookery schools in Europe' (http:/ /www.supanet.com/lifestyle/food/topstory.htm, 2002) and '12 Best Foodie holidays' (*Independent on Sunday*, 2001) reflect the current excitement about this new type of leisure experience in some markets.

The reasons behind this predicted growth are complex but increased leisure time, more disposable income among some consumer groups and a desire in some markets to have good food and wine, and its associated culture, as an indicator of status, identity and health are possible factors. The size of the market will always be restricted to those consumers who can afford to pay relatively high prices for an exclusive leisure activity but at the moment the market is buoyant with new providers still entering the market and consumers 'lining up' to get places on courses.

So what will be the impact, if any, of all this culinary self-improvement on cooking patterns within the home? Will cookery holiday graduates return to their homes and families keen to share knowledge and 'up' the general standard of food that they eat on a day-to-day basis as well as become more committed supporters of the local food economy? Or will their new-found skills be carefully tucked away and only brought out for dinner parties and festive occasions? And what about the men? As more men learn how to cook the Sunday lunch with ease could this ultimately lead to a total shift in the balance of power in the kitchen? Unlikely, but a delicious thought!

6

The lure of tea: history, traditions and attractions

Lee Joliffe

The word 'tea' has a number of connotations. It can refer to a plant, a beverage, a meal service, an agricultural product, an export, an industry, an art, a religion or a dedicated pastime. Tea, the plant, had its origins in China and its subsequent introduction to other countries and adoption as a beverage around the world has romantic connections to travel to exotic places. Tea as a beverage has been adopted in different cultures, and many countries have evolved their own tea traditions or assumed those of others. Tea has developed as a dedicated meal service in food-service establishments such as hotels where tea services reflecting the tea traditions of their location are offered. Tea is also an agricultural product and for many countries an important export product. Tea as an industry consists of tea associations, tea farmers and producers, tea brokers, tea auctions, tea blenders and tasters, tea distributors, tea-service establishments, tea retailers and tea consumers. A peripheral industry built up around tea focuses on the production of goods for a tea-loving public, including books on tea, tea accessories and a variety of tea-themed giftwares. Tea blending has developed as an art (Shalleck, 1972) and in some societies, such as Japan, as a religion. For many, the romance and history of tea and the experience of consuming tea is a pastime (Pratt, 1982). This pursuit includes collecting, either associated to the purchase of tea and related items such as teacups and teapots, or the seeking out and amassing of tea experiences, independently or as part of an organized tea tour.

It is in the areas of tea services, tea attractions, tea tours and tea destinations that tea is clearly directly connected to tourism, as contemporary tourists seek out unique and authentic experiences related to the consumption and appreciation of the beverage called tea. For the tea industry, tourism related to tea encourages both the consumption of tea and the development of relationships with potential customers. Tourism clearly has the potential to enhance the brand image and marketing of tea-producing destinations such as Assam and Ooty in India. In Canada the tea industry has promoted the proper brewing and serving of tea in food service establishments serving tourists, and has extolled the health benefits of tea to a sympathetic public (Tea Council of Canada). In Sri Lanka tourism related to tea has been recognized as a potential strategy for the diversification of tea plantations and the encouragement of sustainable development in tea-producing regions (Tourism Concern, 2001). In India regional governments in tea-producing regions such as Assam are sponsoring tea festivals as both a way of nurturing relationships with potential customers and encouraging the development of tourism in their areas. These examples demonstrate the rich connections between tea histories, traditions and travel as well the relationship of tea to tourism that is explored and discussed in this chapter.

Researching tea and tourism

A review of the literature on tea provides a context for the examination of tea and its connection to tourism. This diverse literature consists of classic works on tea – for example Lu Yu's reprinted (Carpenter, 1974) eighth-century *The Classic of Tea* as well as books on the tea industry such as C.R. Harler's *The Culture and Marketing of Tea*, first published in 1933 and reprinted in 1956. There are also newspaper articles reporting on the popularity and attractiveness of tea destinations such as the tea producing village of Ping Lin, Taiwan (www.sld.gov.tw/english/Pinglintea.htm). A number of books chronicle the history of both tea companies and the individuals who have been instrumental in these companies, for instance Alec Waugh's, *The Lipton Story* published in 1950 and Stephen Twining's *The House of Twining, 1706–1956* published in honour of the company's two hundred and fiftieth anniversary in 1956. The many books on tea as a pastime include *Michael Smith's Afternoon Tea* published in 1986. Books on the occupation of taking tea include Dalton King's *Tea Time* published in 1993. This latter type of book usually also includes recipes for afternoon tea or teatime. There are also numerous Internet references to the various segments of the tea industry, such as the Tea Council of Canada's web site (www.tea.ca) that provides information about the serving of tea and its health benefits. Other web sites promote the appreciation and consumption of tea, as well as the phenomenon of tea as a social pastime as reflected in afternoon teas, tea tours and magazines and books about tea. Several students have done papers relating to tea and tourism, for example at the University of New Brunswick Saint John a student examined the existence of tea tourism and inventoried the resources for developing such tourism in Saint John (Cong, 2001). However, there is little to be found in any published literature source about tea and tourism and this chapter aims to address this gap by exploring the nature and occurrence of tea-related tourism.

The information reviewed on the tea industry, traditions and products for tourism provides a context for discussing the development of tea as a tourist activity. An inventory and analysis of resources for tea tourism includes the identification of examples of a number of types of unique tea attractions and tea destinations. This review culminates in a discussion of the emergence of 'tea tourism' as a niche area of culinary tourism. This chapter explores the nature of tea tourism with a number of limitations. It does not deal with the story of herbal teas, beverages brewed from herbs, but deals with the beverage of tea brewed from the leaves of the tea plant (*Cameillia sinesis*) and with the associated traditions that have developed around its cultivation, processing, manufacturing and consumption. It considers the history and origins of tea only as a context for examining the role of tea in tourism. There are many other volumes that treat the history of tea in detail. This chapter also only highlights examples of tea attractions and destinations. Data on the characteristics of the tea tourist have been derived from the interpretation of secondary sources. These are both areas for future more detailed investigation.

The nature and origins of tea

Tea is produced from the young leaves and unopened leaf buds of the tea plant, *Camellia sinesis* (Harler, 1956). The plant is an evergreen shrub native to the hillsides of China, India, Ceylon (Sri Lanka), Malaysia and Indonesia.

This native plant has been introduced to other countries with suitable growing conditions for tea. The climate should be relatively warm and the rainfall should be evenly distributed throughout the season (Shalleck, 1972). Tea is grown in both terraced hillsides and open fields. The tea is harvested by picking the bud and the two terminal leaves from each shoot. This is referred to as the 'flush' (Weinreich 1980). Since the difference between the three main types of tea – green, oolong and black – is in the processing, it is possible for these types of tea to come from the same bush. In processing the tea, green tea is unfermented, oolong tea is partially fermented and black tea is completely fermented before being fired or dried. After firing, some teas are scented with a variety of flowers, including jasmine, gardenia and rose petals. Tea is graded and sorted and differences in varieties and grading terminologies between countries and types of tea, as well as the location of tea production, account for the wide variance in the types and names of teas. For example, Ceylon teas grown in Sri Lanka are marketed as high-grown, medium-grown and low-grown; black Ceylon teas are graded as broken orange pekoe, broken pekoe, orange pekoe, pekoe, pekoe souchong, souchong, fannings and dust. After grading, tea is packed in aluminum-lined foil chests and sent to auctions located in important tea shipping areas, such as Calcutta and Cochin, in India, and also in Amsterdam, Hamburg and London. At these tea auctions tasters who represent buyers take samples and decide which teas should be purchased (Shalleck, 1972).

In addition to the classification of teas by country, market name, type of tea and grade, teas are recognized by the individual tea garden where they were produced. This system of identifying tea reflects the many venues in which tea is grown and produced, resulting in a multitude of types of tea available to the consumer. There are over 4000 tea gardens in India and more than 2000 of such gardens in Sri Lanka (Shapira, 1975). Pratt (1982) refers to there being well over 6000 tea estates outside China. As an agricultural product the quality of a particular type of tea from a specific tea garden can also vary from crop to crop and from year to year. Most tea available at the retail level is blended from different grades of tea to achieve a consistent taste. This is also the job of the tea taster. Shalleck (1972: 208) refers to tea tasting as an art form, the domain of a few expert buyers, blenders and government officials: 'Tea is judged by appearance and smell of the dried leaf, color and odor of a weak infusion, and the flavour characteristics of the drinking infusion.'

It is common for tea companies to have signature blends, for example Twining's English Breakfast Blend or Bigelow's Constant Comment. As many as twenty or thirty different teas can go into a popular blend of tea as Michael Smith (1986: 32) notes: 'The taster's blend must match up with previous blends in order to achieve a continuity of flavor, almost in the same way that a blended wine must have no recognizable difference from its predecessor.'

There are many legends surrounding the beginnings of the adoption of tea as a beverage. It is believed that tea was first cultivated and the leaf brewed as a beverage in China. However, historians do not agree on the validity of China's tea history, both written and oral, and much of the tea history relating to China that we read today might be considered as myths (Shalleck, 1972). This is because it is difficult to substantiate the early stories about tea. In AD 780 Lu Yu wrote a three-volume, ten-part work, *The Classic of Tea*. This was the largest and most complete treatise produced on tea (Carpenter, 1974). It included sections on the pleasure of tea drinking, the preparation of tea, tea varieties, tea utensils and tea history. This work also created a system for the critical evaluation of tea drinking, a Code of Tea, and is acknowledged to have elevated tea drinking to an art (Shalleck, 1972). Tea spread from China to Japan where in the fifteenth century the Japanese created the Tea Ceremony. This ceremony elevated the drinking of tea from a social pastime into an aesthetic cult (Shalleck, 1972). Through trading, tea was introduced to Europe and then later to America. Tea has played an important role in American culture and customs. The Boston Tea Party, protesting the British tea tax, was one of the protests that led to the Revolutionary war. In the twentieth century America contributed to tea history with two innovations, the creation of iced tea at the World's Fair in Saint Louis in 1904 and the development of the tea bag by a New York tea merchant in 1908.

The traditions surrounding the consumption of tea are closely related to the history of tea and in most cases have taken centuries to develop. Each country that has adopted tea as a beverage has developed its own customs related to the blending, brewing and serving of tea. In a number of instances the traditions of one country have influenced that of another, as the ritual and traditions related to tea consumption are imported from other cultures. Shapira (1975: 233) acknowledges that: 'Ceremonies, customs and rituals that have grown up around the practice of tea drinking are an integral part of the life and culture of many societies.'

In China, referred to as the 'homeland of tea' (Pratt, 1982) there are rich tea traditions. In Japan, green tea is favoured and it is customary to serve sencha green tea to visitors at home or in the workplace. Shapira (1975: 150) describes the Japanese tea ceremony as 'an aesthetic experience, evoking a relaxation of spirit and a worship of purity, beauty and serenity'.

In England a number of traditions have grown up around the concept of afternoon tea, a late afternoon meal service occurring after lunch and before dinner. Michael Smith (1986) documents the history and development of afternoon tea as well as related events, such as At Home Teas, Tennis Teas, Nursery Teas and Tea Dances. In Sri Lanka it is reported that tea boutiques, identified by a bunch of bananas over their door (Pratt, 1982; Shapira, 1975) are popular. They function as a place for visiting friends over a cup of tea.

The tea industry

Today, the beverage of tea is consumed, either as a hot or a cold beverage, by approximately half of the world's population (Walker, 2001). As a beverage tea is second in popularity only to water. While tea is cultivated in forty countries around the world, most of the world's tea crop is consumed in tea-producing countries. In most of the countries in which it is cultivated tea is a significant economic force. For example, in India, the leading tea producing country, tea accounts for 1 per cent of exports (Rasmussen and Rhinehart, 1999). In terms of the number of cups of beverage prepared the annual world tea production of 2.8 billion kilograms for 1.4 trillion cups of tea exceeds the annual world coffee production of 6 billion kilograms for 0.6 trillion cups of coffee (Fockler, 2002). The consumer industry surrounding the consumption of tea in individual countries is also substantial. In Canada, the Tea Council of Canada reports that Canadians drink over 7 billion cups of tea each year (*Coffee and Beverage*, 2002).

The tea industry consists of a layering of producers, dealers or brokers, distributors and retailers. This section discusses the role of these various players and identifies their connection to tourism. Tea is now grown mainly in China, India, Sri Lanka, Malaysia and Indonesia, Japan, Africa, South America and the former Russian states (Weinreich, 1980). Tea requires a climate suitable for its growth and production. Tea may be grown in small tea gardens or in larger tea plantations and processed in small production units or larger factories. Shapira (1975: 222) indicates that, 'tea is born on the bush but must be made in the factory'.

The factory must thus transform the tea leaf picked in the field through processing into the raw material for consumption. This is done by inducing chemical and physical changes in the leaf so the tea is manufactured resulting in green, oolong or black tea. As mentioned previously, green tea is not fermented, oolong tea is partially fermented and black tea is fully fermented. Green tea is steamed, rolled and fired (dried) in the manufacturing process. The steps in the processing of oolong tea are; a slight withering, fermentation, firing, rolling, briefly fermented again, rolled again and re-fired. The steps in the processing of black tea are; withering, rolling, roll breaking, fermentation and firing. The finished leaf is the material necessary for tea blending (Shapira, 1975). There are several interesting by-products of the tea-manufacturing process, some of which have a historical connection with travel and trade. Brick tea, made in China, was historically used by the Chinese as a form of currency in trading with Tibet and Mongolia (Pratt, 1982; Shapira, 1975). Tea is compressed into flat bricks. To brew tea a small amount of tea is shaved from the tea brick, pulverized and combined with boiling water. Tea bricks are still made in China, in one uniform design, manufactured from tea dust hydraulically pressed into 1-kilogram bricks scored on the back. Cake tea, made in China from bitter leaves steamed into 8-inch circles, is believed to be the oldest form of tea manufacture as mentioned by Lu Yu in AD 780. Tablet tea is pill sized wafers of fine-quality tea, ground and formed into small tablets under pressure. Shapria (1975) indicates that these tablets are popular with backpackers and travellers.

In the history of tea, a number of individuals and their companies have influenced the adoption of tea as a beverage and the development of related traditions. An example is that of Thomas Lipton, who made tea more popular by making an inexpensive blend of tea available to the public (Lipton, 1930; Waugh, 1950). He did this partly by purchasing his own tea gardens in Ceylon, thus eliminating the intermediary. He was then able to make available to the public a reasonably priced Lipton's blend sold through his chain of Lipton's Markets. Lipton also played a role in introducing reasonably priced tea to America. A number of contemporary tea companies are encouraging the consumption of tea and the development of tea-related activities for the public. For example, a Red Rose Maritime Tea Tour circulating to festivals and events in the maritime provinces of Atlantic Canada (New Brunswick, Nova Scotia, Prince Edward Island) during the summer of 2001 served samples of the Red Rose tea blend from a booth that featured a silver Volkswagen Beetle dressed up as a tea pot. The Red Rose Tea brand is now marketed by Brooke Bond, one of the world's largest tea companies (Pratt, 1982) is, of course, a part of the maritime tea tradition, having been originated in Saint John, New Brunswick, by T.H. Estrabrooks Company. Red Rose is reported to be the best selling tea in Canada. Red Rose has also produced a Heritage Inns calendar, encouraging visitation to inns where their tea blend is served.

Tea and travel

With its colourful history and unique cultural traditions in different societies tea is a natural focus for travel. The histories and traditions of tea entice both the independent and the group traveller. In a publication for student travellers, Hamel (2001) suggests a tea-related itinerary in his article 'Tea: a silk road odyssey'. In this article the author describes his trip to China, Tibet, Mongolia and Iran as well as the accompanying tea traditions experienced in those countries. Group travellers can take a special tea tour offered by a number of operators. The Carmelian Rose Tea Company offers a Tea Time Tour in the Land of Shires and Spires. This tour has a focus on the history of tea in England and includes a lecture on the History of Tea in England as well as a visit to Sally Lunn's at Bath for tea, taking tea at Studley Priory, the Orchards in Grantchester, the Orangery at Kensington Palace (Teatime Travel to England, 2000). Tourists attracted by this tea travel might be referred to as tea tourists. Such tourists could be described as 'tourists experiencing the history, culture and traditions related to the consumption of tea'. These so-called tea tourists could be classified as either accidental or intentional tourists. Accidental tea tourists may be tourists who experience a traditional English afternoon tea service during their visit to England. The intentional tea tourist may be the tourist who not only experiences the afternoon tea but also seeks out other tea experiences, by visiting tea attractions such as museums and by shopping for tea-related consumer goods. There is little concrete information available on the nature of the tourist motivated by an interest in tea. However, a wide range of products is available for the tourist who is motivated by this interest. This includes experiencing the various types of tea services, such as an English afternoon tea or the Japanese tea ceremony, as well as shopping for speciality tea blends and related tea accessories reflecting the area visited.

Tea services are offered in hotels as well as in tea rooms and tea shops offering food services that focus on tea. For example, in England a brochure on

Table 6.1 Tearooms on farms – Leicestershire, England

Name	Location	Services
Halstead House Farm	Tilton	Teas served
Jacqui's Tea Room	Saddington	Cream teas
Our Little Farm	Vale of Belvoir	Homemade fare
Seldom Seen Farm	Billesdon	Teas served
Stonehurst Farm	Mountsorrel	Cream teas
Whatoff Country Lodge Walk	Loughborough	Farmhouse teas

Source: Leistershire Farm Tourism Association (1993)

Leicestershire Farms lists seven tearooms on farms, inviting visitors with country appetites to spoil themselves in farm-based tearooms and cafes. These tearooms usually serve cream teas, afternoon teas and lunch (Table 6.1) with tearoom offerings complementing the activities offered by farm centres, farm trails and museums. While the nature of these tearooms reflects Leicestershire's rural and pastoral nature, tearooms in other areas also take on the character of their region. For instance, tearooms with historical connections in Avon include both The Pump Room and Sally Lunn's House, Bath. Throughout England tearooms such as these and many others form an important attraction for and compliment to tea tourism.

Tea and cuisine

There is considerable evidence of a developing interest in culinary tourism. In Canada, an industry conference highlighted the tourism industry interest (Canadian Tourism Commission, 2001) in developing culinary tourism as a special-interest type of tourism. Tea, as a beverage, with its varying types, grades and blends as well as national, regional and local traditions in serving has a natural role to play in culinary tourism. The potential for the appreciation of tea as a beverage is immense. With its many different qualities and areas of origin there is a lot for the potential tea connoisseur to learn about tea. From the perspective of tourism, experiencing these different tea qualities and traditions in addition has the potential to be an integral part of culinary tourism.

Tea experts describe some blends in the same way that a wine connoisseur would, for example in describing a Darjeeling from India, Shapira (1975: 208) indicates that, 'The rich golden-red liquor of a fine Darjeeling and its exquisite, penetrating aroma foreshadow a truly unique tea-drinking experience.' The cultivation and harvesting of tea is also somewhat of an art akin to the making of wine with the tea farmer overseeing his tea garden with similar care to that of the vintner overseeing his vineyard. The making of oolong teas in Taiwan is thus regarded as an art which takes generations to master. In Taiwan the production of oolong is described: 'From the nursing of the seedling, to planting, to nourishing the bushes, to properly selecting the best time to pluck the leaves, the husbandry of the tea farmer is a legacy passed down from generation to generation' (Rasmussen and Rhinehart, 1999).

There is also considerable discussion in the literature about tea on 'brewing a good cup of tea' that has relevance for those hospitality establishments wishing to serve tea to the public. King (1993: 6) describes the method:

To brew a perfect pot of tea, boil fresh, cold tap water in a kettle. While the water is boiling, warm the teapot with hot water. Once the teapot is warmed, pour out the water and put in the tea. Use one teaspoon of leaves or one tea bag per cup of tea. Once the water is boiling bring the teapot over to it and pour in the boiling water. Let the tea brew three to five minutes. Serve hot.

The brewing of a good cup of tea is an important attraction for tea shops and other food-service entities serving tea. Seeking out an authentic tea service may require the visitor to seek out local food service establishments including tearooms and tea shops where tea is served in a manner traditional to the locality. One example of a local tea experience is found in the distinctive culinary tradition that has evolved around the English afternoon tea. This is a meal service that usually consists of tea accompanied by sandwiches and sweets. In the south of England traditional cream teas are served. Christine Taylor, the owner of Periwinkle Cottage Tea Rooms in the village of Selworthy, England, reports, 'On a summer weekend we probably serve around three hundred cream teas. Each cream tea consists of two scones, a bowl of clotted cream, strawberry or loganberry jam and a pot of tea' (Rivers 1995: 45).

In some cultures, tea also plays another role in cuisine, either as a dish on its own or as a flavouring for local dishes. In some regions of Taiwan a dish featuring fried tea leaves is a local culinary speciality. In Ping Lin, Taiwan there are four tea restaurants (Ju-Ping, 2001). These restaurants specialize in tea cuisine and feature dishes where tea is used as a flavouring or ingredient. In Scotland's Isle of Skye, China tea is used as flavouring in the preparation of local tea bread (MacDonald, 1987). (Tea is used to flavour Irish soda bread too!) In Japan a ceremonial tea ice cream is made using the green powdered ceremonial tea, Mattcha (Shapira, 1975).

An extension of the culinary experience with tea lies in the area of tea retailing. Shopping is a popular tourist activity and the tea tourist has a special interest in purchasing speciality teas, accessories and tea-themed gifts. It is often suggested that providers of tea services can supplement revenues by adding a retail aspect. A retail aspect is thus found in many tearooms, shops and inns that focus on offering tea services. Elmwood Inn Fine Teas located in Perryville, Kentucky, USA, operates two retail tea gift shops in conjunction with afternoon teas offered at the Elmwood Inn. Anne's Tea Party in Charlottetown, Prince Edward Island, operates a retail component and is located adjacent to the Anne Store. Both enterprises play on the characterization of island author L.M. Montgomery's fictional character, Anne of

Green Gables. A number of other tea companies have built up lucrative wholesale, retail and/or mail-order businesses around the provision of tea blends attractively packaged for different geographical markets. For example, the Metropolitan Tea Company has developed a Lighthouse Tea blend for the eastern Canadian and US market and a Maple Tea blend for the Canadian market. In many localities local tea companies and tea shops will have their own special blends of tea available for purchase. In Prince Edward Island the Prince Edward Preserves Company retails a line of tea under the name of New Glasgow Tea Merchants and the Island Chocolate Company also retails a line of tea blends under its own name.

Tea attractions

A number of popular tourist activities are thus related to tea. For the tourist this includes attendance at a variety of tea attractions (museums, exhibits, festivals and events). In these situations a complementary activity is the experience of tea services and the purchasing of tea-related goods. All of these activities are often bundled together to form another attraction, the packaged tea tour, where participants have a number of tea experiences and learn more about the rich history and culture of tea. There are therefore a number of types of attractions that focus on tea (Table 6.2). Some of these attractions, such as tea gardens and plantations, were not originally built to attract tourists but, nonetheless, will be of interest to visitors wanting to learn about the cultivation and production of tea. In some situations visitors will be able to pluck their own tea and participate in processing it. Tea history and traditions can also be employed to develop purpose-built tea-themed attractions. Such attractions play an important role in preserving local tea histories and are also

Table 6.2 Typology of tea attractions

Category	Example
Human-made – not originally designed to attract visitors	Tea gardens, tea plantations, tea factories
Human-made – purpose-built to attract visitors	Tea museums, tea exhibits
Special events	Tea tours, tea tourism festivals

Source: based on Swarbrooke (1995)

important in attracting the tourist interested in tea. Attractions have therefore been built specifically to attract the tourist, for example, museums that focus on tea or special exhibits within museums that develop various aspects of the history and traditions of tea. Another type of attraction is the festival or special event with a tea focus designed to attract visitors.

There is considerable evidence that tea gardens, tea plantations and tea factories, while not developed for tourism, function as tea attractions. In India, visits and/or tours to tea gardens or plantations are an integral part of a number of emerging tea festivals, for example the Teesta Tea and Tourism Festival. Tea museums are very often built in tea-producing regions and visits to small local tea gardens and factories can form an adjunct to the museum visit. Visits to tea gardens and plantations are also an important component of organized tea tours, for example the China Tea and Culture Tour organized by the Imperial Tea Court in San Francisco includes visits to tea plantations in China where participants are able to pluck, fire, brew and drink their own tea (Pratt, 1982). In his typology of heritage attractions, Prentice (1993) includes both 'attractions concerned with primary production' and 'attractions concerned with manufacturing industry'.

There are a number of tea museums around the world (Table 6.3). These museums have developed around tea-producing, tea-manufacturing or tea-importing areas. It is of note that many of these museums have been established and opened in the last decade. This could be evidence of increased interest in the establishment of such museums, to preserve and interpret tea histories as well as to attract visitors. A number of major tea-producing localities – Japan, China and Taiwan – have consequently developed tea museums.

The China Tea Museum, opened in 1991, located in Hangzhou, China, profiles the rich traditional tea-growing areas south of the Yangtze River. This museum is said to be the first of this kind of tea museum (Ju-Ping, 2001). The Ping Lin

Table 6.3 Tea museums

Name	Location	Opened
China Tea Museum	Hangzhou, China	1991
Ping Lin Tea Museum	Ping Lin, Taiwan	1997
The Tea Museum	Japan	1998
Bramah Coffee and Tea Museum	London, England	n/a

Tea Museum opened in 1997, is located in Ping Lin, a town in northern Taiwan that cultivates and produces Formosa Oolong, considered to the champagne of tea (Pratt, n.d.: 139). The latter is referred to as the 'world's largest tea museum'. In Japan, The Tea Museum opened in 1998 in the Shizuoka prefecture, one of the leading tea-producing areas in Japan. The museum profiles the history of drinking and making tea in Japan and explains the processing of the local green tea, sencha. A historical teahouse on the museum grounds, built in the sixteenth century by a prominent tea taster, has been restored.

Other museums, while not focusing purely on tea, have individual galleries and/or exhibits that feature tea or tea-related artefacts. For instance, in Norwich. England. the Norwich Castle Museum houses the Twining Teapot Collection of nearly 3000 teapots dating from around 1720 to the present. With support from the R. Twining and Company Limited, this museum has also developed a travelling version of this exhibit, 'Traditions in Elegance: 100 Teapots from the Norwich Castle Museum'. This exhibition explores the custom of tea preparation and tea drinking in England through the history of the teapot. This particular exhibit was featured at the Concord Museum in Concord, Massachusetts, from 25 January 2002 to 27 May 2002.

Another form of tea attraction is the organized tea tour, a thematic tour with a focus around experiencing tea services, visiting tea attractions and in general learning more about tea. Its clientele normally consists of tea enthusiasts and intentional tea tourists. The tea tour usually has a focus on a destination with a rich history and tradition of tea and related tea traditions, for example both England and China are the subject of a number of these tours. James Norwood Pratt, author of *The Tea Lover's Treasury* (1982: 69) describes the cultural and culinary aspects of China Tea Tour organized by the Imperial Tea Court in San Francisco:

> This is not simply a tea tour or tour for tea lovers only, but tea is the thread we will follow through all the aspects of Chinese culture we experience, just as wine runs through Mediterranean culture from agriculture, cuisine and custom to recreation and worship. This tour includes visits to tea plantations where participants pluck their own tea in a classic Dragon Well garden and then are tutored in firing it.

Tea festivals are becoming another type of tea attraction. A number of these festivals have emerged in the tea-producing areas of India and China (Table 6.4). Organizers of these festivals, usually local and regional governments and the tea industries are interested in raising the profile of their own areas

Table 6.4   Tea tourism festivals

Name	Location	Activities
Teesta Tea and Tourism Festival	West Bengal, India	Tours of tea gardens, cultural programme
Tea Tourism Festival	Jorhat District, Assam, India	Visits to tea gardens, entertainment
Tea and Tourism Festival	Ooty and Coonoor, India	Tea exhibits, cultural performances

through tourism and also in developing relationships with potential buyers. It is thus clear that the festivals are not only developed for the purposes of tourism. These festivals take a number of years to develop and will evolve during their history. A spokesperson from the West Bengal government indicates that while there has been a good response to the Teesta Tea and Tourism Festival over the first two years there are plans to commercialize the event and to promote it through government tourist offices abroad. It was also noted that it would take five to six years to establish the event on a commercial basis (*Express Travel and Tourism*, 2000).

Tea destinations

A thematic approach is very often used in regional tourism development (Heath and Wall, 1992). Tea offers potential as a theme for such development. There are a number of existing destinations which, because of their history and development in relation to tea, might be considered as tea destinations. Examples are presented along with an indication of the resources available for tea tourist visitation at these locations (Table 6.5). Many other destinations with tea history have the potential to develop as tea destinations. To develop in this manner a locality should exhibit a number of the following general characteristics related to tea:

- tea history
- tea traditions
- tea ceremonies
- tea cultivation and production
- tea manufacturing
- tea attractions

Table 6.5   Examples of tea destinations

Name	Location	Resources
London	England	Tea history; tea attractions – Bramah Tea and Coffee Museums, the *Cutty Sark*; tea service in hotels and teashops; tea retail outlets
Boston	USA	Tea history; tea attractions – Boston Tea Party Ship and Museum; tea services

- tea services
- tea festivals and events
- tea retailing.

Even locations without a history of tea but with the setting for developing traditional tea services can be developed as tea destinations. An example is that of the small (year-round population of 800) historic town of Perryville, Kentucky. The town is home to the Elmwood Inn Fine Teas and Gourmet Foods, the Elmwood Inn Tea Room (which serves traditional afternoon tea) and two Elmwood Inn tea gift shops. Shelley and Bruce Richardson, owners of these businesses, also host an annual seminar 'Tea Room 101: The Art of Owning a Tea Room'. For destinations with a minimum of tea history, resources and traditions tea is a potential tool for tourism development. Local and regional tourism organizations have an important role to play in developing initiatives concerning tea and tourism. The tea theme can be used to develop focused attractions such as museums and events or it can be used to tie together existing attractions. An illustration is the introduction of a 'tea trail' that links tourist locations featuring tea into one tea experience. Sometimes tea companies are involved in the development of these trails, for example the Brooke Bond series of regional Teapot Trail publications produced in the UK feature local tearooms and tea shops along with their signature recipes. Tourism can also be used to diversify existing tea industries, such as tea gardens and tea plantations. An example of such development has been documented by the British organization, Tourism Concern, a non-governmental organization that works to protect communities and to ensure fair trade in tourism (Page et al., 2001). In Sri Lanka this organization has worked with a women's group in Bandarawela to use tourism to diversify local tea gardens. Tea Concern indicates that this women's group coined the term 'tea tourism' years ago. It also reports: 'The Green Field tea plantation at Haputale has made tea tourism a central component of their diversification project' (Tourism Concern, 2001). There is also promise for strategic partnerships between neighbouring tea-producing regions in developing tea tourism. An example of this potential is that in India the regional government in Ooly has indicated an interest in future partnerships in this area with nearby Bhutan and Bengal.

The emergence of tea tourism

This chapter identified a gap in the tourism literature in the area of the connection between tea and tourism. However, despite this disparity there is a diverse body of literature on the various aspects of tea as well as substantial evidence that the history and traditions of tea are being employed to develop tourism products for the public. Many of these products, such as dedicated tea museums and specialized tea tours, have emerged in concert with the growing interest in, and demand for, authentic tourism experiences. The recent development of tea attractions and tea cuisine documented in this chapter reflects a growing interest in culinary tourism. These factors serve as indicators of the emergence of tea tourism as a special-interest form of culinary tourism.

The findings of this chapter can frame further research. For instance a definition of tea tourism, derived from observations regarding the nature and occurrence of such tourism, can delineate the area of study for future research. For these purposes tea tourism can be defined as, 'tourism that is motivated by an interest in the history, traditions and consumption of the beverage, tea'. Further research is needed to fully define the scope of tea tourism and to identify the motivations and preferences of the tea tourist. The suggested typology of tea attractions (Table 6.2) can be used as a foundation for the identification and analysis of the nature of the attractions available for tea-related culinary tourism. There is also a need to understand the development and marketing of the tea tourism product and to gain further insights into the use of tea as a tourism development tool. For the potential researcher there are many areas of tea tourism to explore and to experience at first hand.

Acknowledgements

The author thanks Yan Cong for her research efforts on tea and tourism and Noni Regan for reading and commenting on the text.

7

Food and tourism in Papua New Guinea

Geoffrey Le Grys and Peter Van Fleet

Introduction

Papua New Guinea's (PNG's) potential as a tourism destination is intimately linked to its natural, environmental and cultural resources including its flora and fauna, aquatic resources, especially diving, bush walking and its diversity of art, dance and personal adornment. Individuals participating in such speciality activities will often have an expectation that food service should reflect these activities. Food supply in PNG is characterized by an agricultural industry producing a wide range of interesting and nutritious tropical and semi-tropical foods, especially fruit, root and leaf vegetables and home-produced poultry and pork. In most cases these foods are prepared by smallholders using traditional low-input (organic) agricultural practices. The supply chain for many of these foods will be short and as such these foods are characterized by being harvested at their prime and very fresh. If one adds to these the fish resources in coastal and island areas, one can identify foods that will, in principle, satisfy the needs and expectations of many speciality tourists. On the other hand, cereal-based foods and products derived from them will often be imported and these, together with wines and locally produced beers and soft drinks, will be familiar to many international tourists although 'organic' origin is no longer guaranteed and there may be an extended supply chain. Cuisine in major urban hotels is international although supplemented by products from the local cuisine. Local supply of many raw materials, especially seafood, is a characteristic of many offerings. However, in remoter areas, cuisine would be based on 'availability;' with a concentration on fresh materials and often cooked on flavoursome wood-burning stoves, or for larger groups based on a traditional 'mumu'. This chapter commences with an introduction to the geographic context of PNG before discussing the nature of its tourism resources. The chapter then goes on to examine the relationship between food and tourism with specific reference to the nature of the food chain. The chapter concludes with reference to the significance of food and tourism for sustainable development of the PNG tourism product as well as of the country itself.

Geographical, historical and demographic background

Papua New Guinea, located to the north of Queensland, Australia, between the Equator and 12° latitude, consists of the eastern half of the New Guinea island together with the associated islands making up the Bismark Archipelago (New Britain, New Ireland and Manus), the North Solomons and various small islands (Figure 7.1). The variety of geographical landforms is diverse with elements made up high mountains, fertile high-altitude valleys, lowland wetlands and plains, and coral islands. On the whole, communications are poor with a reliance on air transport, particularly to the remoter locations. Transfer between the capital, Port Moresby, and Lae, the second largest city on the New Guinea island, a distance of less than 200 miles can still only be made by air. However, Lae has a major metalled road artery leading to the relatively densely populated areas of the Highland provinces and the cities of Goroka, Kundiawa, Mount Hagen, Mendi and Wabag. The larger islands of the Bismark Archipelago have effectively similar geographic forms, while many of the smaller islands have a continental landform and many are coral atolls with associated low-lying landform, vegetation and reliance on aquatic resources.

The high mountains, which include Mount Wilhelm (4509 m) and its location in the tropics results in extremely high annual rainfall with average

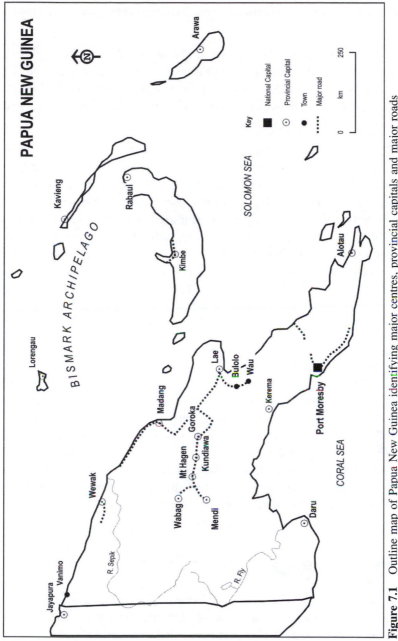

Figure 7.1 Outline map of Papua New Guinea identifying major centres, provincial capitals and major roads

annual rainfall of 2000 mm and some areas experiencing inundation in excess of 8000 mm per year. The capital, Port Moresby, lying in a rain shadow, however, is exceptional, often experiencing drought and some water shortages.

The total land area is 462 840 sq km of which some 9980 sq km is inland lakes (CIA, 2001). It shares one common land border with the Indonesian province of Irian Jaya, although this for the most part is in the remoter and higher (Star Mountains) parts of the country and transfer is by one short air hop from Jayapura (Irian Jaya) to Vanimo (PNG).

The peoples of PNG, estimated at just over 5 million (CIA, 2001) are characterized by a diversity in culture and ethnicity but, particularly, in language. It is routinely stated that PNG has in excess of 700 indigenous languages (not dialects). Smith (2002) reports that the Summer Institute of Linguistics has identified 862 different languages, while CIA (2001) suggests 715. Given this diversity it is not surprising that other languages take on the role of lingua francas. These are now English, Hiri Motu – a creole arising in the Port Moresby area of the country – and Tok Pisin – a creole spoken almost universally throughout the country often being the first language for children of a 'mixed' marriage (a mixed marriage in PNG would entail a marriage between partners from a different tribe or province).

Papua New Guinea is now an independent state, a member of the British Commonwealth with the Queen as Head of State, having gained independence from Australia as the colonial power in 1976. Its early history reflecting, initially, its acquisition by Britain and Germany and subsequent period are described by Hudson (1971). In spite of early control by the colonial powers, only the coastal areas were explored and brought under control. Much of the interior was not explored until the 1930s and control of these regions was only established after the Second World War. There are several popular reports of these early stages in the development of the interior, however, perhaps the most authoritative can be found in the original reports of patrol officers or from *Taim Bilong Masta* (Nelson, 1990).

Tourism resources

Tourism activity in PNG has developed slowly, perhaps reflecting a variety of factors including especially the expense of international travel, the difficulty of internal travel, issues of law and order within the country and the lack of significant tourism infrastructure able to cater for mass tourism. At many levels this might be expressed as a good thing. Basu (2000: 910) suggests it is a 'grossly under-exploited economic activity in PNG' and then continues 'however, its widely diversified geographical terrain within a small region, innumerable unique and vibrant cultures, and traditional life-styles of its people can conveniently make it a major tourism destination for several groups of visitors such as mature travellers, special interest tourists, soft adventurers and so on'. Indeed, the PNG Tourism Promotion Authority is not seeking to establish large-scale urban-orientated tourism. Rather, conservation of its ecosystems and traditional culture is key to developing a vibrant and sustainable tourism industry. Papua New Guinea tourism is entirely dependent on natural, environmental and cultural resources (PNG Tourism Promotion Authority, 1995). If this is the stated aim then one might expect food resources and agriculture to have some link to ensuring that food and food service satisfies this specialist traveller.

Various advertising and recent promotion schemes have emphasized the diversity and cultural aspects of PNG's tourism products. Air Niugini, the national airline, has images of nationals punting up river in a hollowed-out canoe and suggests 'The kind of travel experience you thought disappeared ten thousand years ago', while other agencies such as Trans Niugini Tours and Coral Seas resorts continue to market the wild and unusual experience tempered with the availability of first-class accommodation and international cuisine in their hotels and on board their cruises undertaken by the MV *Sepik Spirit* and MTS *Discoverer*. Tourism in PNG is focused on a number of speciality travel attractions.

Flora and fauna

Papua New Guinea's extensive biological resources make it a must for anyone with a keen interest in natural history and the exotic. New Guinea is home to over 700 species of birds of which 269 are endemic with the birds of paradise being the most sought after. Of the forty-three known species of birds of paradise in the world, thirty-three are indigenous to Papua New Guinea (Coates, 1977). The wealth of avifauna and the experience to be gained from a systematic visit can be judged from the report by Vermeulin (1998) who identified 310 species and twenty-two birds of paradise during a twelve-day trip. Nightingale (1992) along with other authors (Attenborough, 1960; MacKay, 1976) also emphasize the wealth and diversity of the biological resources in PNG. These include:

■ butterflies including Queen Alexandra's birdwing with a wing span of nearly a third of a metre

- the cassowary, a flightless bird growing to 2 metres in height and weighing 50–60 kg and highly valued for it its ceremonial food value
- the leatherback turtle weighing over half a ton and growing to 3 metres in length with a major nesting site close to Lae in Morobe Province
- a wide range of marsupials including tree kangaroos, possums and quolls
- some 2500 species of orchids
- crocodiles, both farmed and in the wild, the former often being available on the 'menu'.

Ultimately access to areas rich in flora and fauna will involve walking, although limited viewing can sometimes be possible via four-wheeled access to the emerging National Parks. In many parts of the country access is limited to flying or walking. Access to the bush is not recommended undertaken alone but with a guide or sometimes with one of the bush-walking clubs operating from the major cities. There are several major classic routes including the Kokoda Trail (the wartime Japanese supply route from Popondetta to the ridge above Port Moresby – five to seven days), Mount Wilhelm (the highest mountain in PNG – three to four days), Wau to Salamaua (the supply route from the coast to the PNG gold field in Wau and Bulolo – three days) and Nipa to Lake Kutubu (a major lake in the Southern Highlands and now the site of one of PNG's oilfields – three to four days). Lipscomb et al. (1998) suggests that, given the nature of the terrain – rugged, forested mountains and wild rivers – that it is surprising that bush-walking has not developed to the extent that trekking has elsewhere.

Diving

As would be expected, given its location in the South Pacific, the number of coral reefs and the remnants from the war in the Pacific has resulted in PNG being a significant dive location. The nature of the aquatic resources has been described by Halstead (1996) and includes an identification of dive operators/charters, major reefs and wrecks. This notwithstanding, local operators will often have a recently discovered site which has yet to be described in the guidebooks. The absence of mass tourism means that individuals can still dive pristine virgin coral or wrecks that are seldom visited. Although some coastal hotels such as the Madang Resort Hotel, Jais Aben (Madang) and Walindi Plantation operate close to urban areas, many of the more remote sites can be accessed via dive charters operating from Port Moresby, Lae, Madang and Rabaul. The live-in nature of these charters means that food is often relatively basic. However, it is almost always be supplemented with fresh tuna or other fish trolled earlier in the day or crustaceans found during the dive.

Culture and artefacts

Papua New Guinea culture is more than '700 ways of dressing up' (Mills, 1991) although self-adornment is a key characteristic of many of its peoples (see, for example, Timmer, 2000). It encompasses people able to work in harmony with their environment, an oral tradition of storytelling, a traditional sustainable architecture epitomized by the *haus tambaran* or spirit house of the Sepik and arts, crafts and wood carving (Miller, 1988). Arts, crafts and Sepik architecture can be accessed through the luxury of the specialist cruises on the MV *Sepik Spirit* or MTS *Discoverer* or by a more traditional approach via canoe organized locally or through one of the larger tourist companies. Silverman (2000) discusses the tourism on the Sepik River and its economic consequences and role in enacting cultural change.

Ultimately, culture exists within the peoples of PNG and, perhaps, this is most admirably demonstrated at the agricultural or cultural shows held annually in several regions of the country. These include:

- Mount Hagen Cultural Show – late August
- Goroka Cultural Show – mid-September
- Enga Cultural Show – late July
- Lae Agricultural Show – October/November
- Hiri Moale in Port Moresby in September.

One aspect of the shows is the competition held to identify the best traditional dance and attired group with significant cash prizes being available. Although such shows or *sing-sings* are of tremendous interest to the international tourist, such tourists are few and far between, the major audience being Papua New Guineans. However, that is not to underestimate the tourism potential of such shows which are a visual and olfactory experience second to none. These shows encourage the preservation of traditional ways and values, yet are still agents of change where 'new materials' are finding their places alongside old.

Tourism statistics

It has already been suggested that tourism in Papua New Guinea is developing slowly if at all. Published statistics show a variable performance. The number of visitor arrivals to PNG increased from 37 000 in 1991 to 67 000 in 1998

(Hamal and Yomapsi, 2001), while the PNG Tourism Promotion Authority identified figures of 58 448 in 2000 falling to 54 235 in 2001. They attributed this drop to a variety of factors including student unrest together with the consequent curfew and travel alerts issued by foreign missions to PNG; these continue to highlight the continuing law and order problems which plague the country, particularly the urban areas.

In interpreting these figures it is important to note that they involve international arrivals. Basu (2000) suggests that, perhaps, only 25 per cent are 'genuine tourists' the majority being business visitors or families and children visiting expatriate workers who still work in the private sector. The intermittent arrival of a cruise liner, although significantly affecting arrival statistics, would have only a minor impact on service providers at the arrival port.

The hospitality sector

Papua New Guinea has a range of hotels from those boasting an international 4/5 star status and associated dining and fine wines, to some limited budget accommodation. The formal hospitality sector has some 160 hotels (Douglas, 1998) with approximately 2640 rooms throughout the whole country (Bar-On, 2001). The major urban areas, particularly Port Moresby, Lae, Madang and Rabaul, have several alternatives especially at the top end of the range. Some of these, being part of a larger group, will offer a full range of tourism services including diving, Sepik and Trobiand Islands cruises, bush-walking and canoeing ventures.

Alternative accommodation in the remoter areas can be found in guesthouses associated with missions and individual villages. Some of these have been described by Lipscomb et al. (1998). Village guesthouses are the epitomy of 'ecotourism' with basic accommodation and food based on local raw materials cooked by traditional methods, supplemented with the occasional warm beer. For tourists intent of seeking out the flora, fauna and culture of the remoter areas there are several specialist lodges catering for these needs such as:

- Bensbach Wildlife Lodge (virtually sea level) near Daru in Western Province, with fishing and hunting for deer
- Haus Poroman (6200 ft) near Mount Hagen in Western Highlands Province, with 'mumu' dining
- Karawawi Lodge near Mount Hagen in the Western Highlands, with an emphasis on artwork, river lakes and jungle and local fresh foods

- Ambua Lodge (7000 ft) in the Tari Gap in the Southern Highlands, with an emphasis on trekking and bird watching and a diet of local foods
- Kaiap Orchid Lodge (8000 ft) near Wabag in Enga Province, offering trekking, access to flora and bird watching with food cooked in a wood-burning stove.

In virtually all cases the hospitality sector emphasizes the use of locally supplied foods; those in the coastal regions having access to a variety of seafood including barramundi, crayfish, mud crabs and tuna, and menus are adapted for seasonality and the vagaries of daily changes in supply.

For the independent traveller wishing to dine away from the hotel sector the options are relatively limited. Local food tends to be associated with take-away or kai bars or, in the larger urban areas, independent ethnic restaurants, particularly Chinese; although Port Moresby does have one excellent Japanese Steak House. The local yacht club or golf club will often offer a wholesome alternative, although hours and days of opening can be variable.

Food provision and service

The food supply chain in PNG is characterized by three strands. First, a supply of fresh foods including meat, fish, fruit and vegetables. In many cases these are produced by smallholders, although there are some large-scale estate production. Smallholder production employs some 85 per cent of the population with much of it being based on traditional agricultural practice of rotation and mixed systems (World Bank, 1997). Fresh fruit and vegetables can be purchased in small amounts at any of the local markets operating in the mornings, weekdays and Saturdays in most urban areas. The products will usually be extremely fresh being harvested earlier in the day by smallholder-owners. Cooked delicacies wrapped in banana leaves based on an individual 'mumu' with meat, often a lamb flap, and vegetables can also be bought. Second is a manufacturing sector based on larger-scale production of commodities many of which are exported. Some parts of the manufacturing sector are using imported raw materials to produce such foods as bread and biscuits, snack products, beer, UHT milk and small goods. Third, an imported food sector consisting of 'Western' processed foods including dairy products, cereal products, large quantities of lamb, feed for chicken growers, cereals for downstream processing and reimported, locally grown coffee (Le Grys, 1988; 1991).

Locally produced foods have been considered in depth by May (1984) who addresses both the nature and variety of foods, and their nutritional values

Table 7.1 Major foods in Papua New Guinea

Class	Common name	Botanical or zoological name
Roots and tubers	Sweet potato	*Ipomoea batatas*
	Taro	*Araceae spp.*
	Yam	*Dioscorea spp.*
	Cassava	*Manihot esculentus*
Green leaves	Aibika	*Abelmoschus manihot*
	Water kaukau or swamp cabbage	*Ipomoea aquatica*
	New Guinea asparagus or pitpit	*Setaria palmifolia*
	Pumpkin leaves	*Curcurbita pepo*
	Taro leaves	*Araceae spp.*
	Sweet potato leaves	*Ipomoea batatas*
	Pawpaw leaves	*Carica papaya*
Legumes and other vegetables	Pumpkin	*Curcurbita pepo*
	Gourd	*Laganaria siceraria; Trichsanthes spp.*
	Cucumber	*Cucurnis sativus*
	Peanuts	*Arachis hypogaea*
Nuts and fruits	Coconut	*Cocas nucifera*
	Pandanus	*Pandanus spp.*
	Galip	*Canarium spp.*
	Banana and plantains	*Musa spp.*
	Bread fruit	*Artocarpus atilis; A. incisus*
	Pawpaw papaya	*Carica papaya*
	Mango	*Mangifera spp.*
	Guava	*Psidium guajava*
	Star fruit	*Averrhoa carambola*
	Passion fruit	*Passiflora spp.*
Flesh	Pig	*Sus saceacofia*
	Flying fox (fruit bat)	*Dobsonia moluccensis*
	Wallaby	*Thylogale bruijini and others*
	Cuscus	*Phalanger spp.*
	Sea turtles and their eggs	*Chelonia mydas; Dermochelys cori and others*
	Crocodile	*Crocodilus spp.*
	Cassowary	*Casuarius spp.*

Source: adapted from May (1984)

together with suggested recipes. This text discusses the role of food in traditional society, including agricultural practice, cooking methods, socio-logical aspects and ceremony. In addition, two resource books published by the LikLik Buk Information Centre (Bergmann, 1982; Twohig, 1988) describe many traditional foods, the range of products available and their low input growing methods. The major foods of PNG are outlined in Table 7.1.

May (1984) and the series of leaflets published by the South Pacific Commission (1983a; 1983b; 1985a; 1985b; 1986) suggest a variety of dishes based on South Pacific foods. Such dishes will often find their way on to the menus of hotels and include pumpkin soup, barramundi in red wine sauce, baked breadfruit, pork marita, kaukau casserole, taro cakes, grilled pitpit, chicken taro and vegetables, chicken in mango sauce, pumpkin bread and banana bread. Thompson (1989) in Air Niugini's in-flight magazine, *Paradise*, discusses some of the foods of the Sepik region of PNG. Descriptions of foods prepared from the sago palm include sago starch used to make a pancake and sago grubs as a source high in protein. These grubs, some 10 cm in length can be eaten raw, although May (1984) suggests removing the heads, steaming them and then grilling them, accompanied with a saté sauce.

In considering local protein sources, it is important to understand the special role that pigs and cassowaries take in ceremony and social interactions. Pigs are killed, often in large numbers, for community or village celebrations. They and cassowaries are used in bridal exchange and for settling disputes.

Another potential protein source is crocodile. Papua New Guinea is home to one of the largest crocodile farms in the world, together with others interspersed in the lowland regions of the country. Although grown for their skins (Van Fleet, 1988), the tails will often be found on the menu of the local restaurant where their tender flesh and flavour between chicken and white fish is highly valued.

Perhaps the classic Papua New Guinean dish is the 'mumu' which uses indigenous raw materials, particularly pork, together with a traditional pit-oven cooking method. It is often associated with communal activities and celebration. Actual recipes vary according to the region and availability of meat and vegetables, but essentially preparation consists of (Sopade, 1997) heating stones in an open fire in a circular pit which are then covered with layers of banana leaves to form a large pot shaped pit. The 'pot' is then filled with a variety of starch-based materials including plantains, sweet potato and taro or cassava. Roughly butchered fatty pork (often a whole carcass) is added and then finished off with green vegetables. The pot is closed with banana leaves and then covered with earth to seal it. After a period of four to six hours the mumu is opened up and everyone tucks in. Sopade et al. (1998) and Sopade (2000) discuss safety both from consideration of temperature distributions and their effectiveness at reducing microbial load and ensuring adequate cooking of the pork and reduction of cyanogenic content of cassava doughs.

Discussion and conclusions

Food service and tourist expectation are seldom deciding factors in the selection of tourism products (Nield et al., 2000). This is particularly likely to be the case in PNG, where the tourism product is centred on diving and access to its unique biological and cultural resources. The business tourist and those seeking the more luxurious resort or specialist cruise are unlikely to have serious issues unless they have special dietary needs. However, the foods available for the diver, trekker, ornithologist or amateur anthropologist will, on the whole, enhance the tourism experience.

Whether this will continue is debatable. Basu (2000) identifies conflicts with other development needs of the country, in particular agriculture, fisheries and forestry. Dynamite fishing can produce quick returns but has major impacts on the marine resources, while overfishing by foreign-owned vessels is affecting the ecological balance. Sustainability of the environmental resources is key to the current stated tourism policy in PNG.

The debate on sustainability of cultural resources is likely to be keener where the exposure of indigenous people to tourists continues. Sillitoe (2000) quotes the report in the *Post Courier* (16 October 1996) of the statement of the then Minister of Tourism and Culture: 'Cultures of PNG are a gold mine.' If this 'mining' is to be developed then tourism will lead to greater exposure of the indigenous culture to tourists. Ultimately, this exposure will result in change; the issue then becomes a sense of one's culture and the need to preserve it. As has already been stated, the highland cultural shows are a method of demonstrating pride in the culture and continuing tradition but, although not primarily activities designed for the foreign tourist, the shows themselves are an agent for change. The message for the tourism activities in PNG is not one of resisting change, be it environmental, agricultural, food supply or cultural, but of ensuring the resource is valued by the community as a whole, the best is retained and change is embraced.

8

Food trails in Austria

Kim Meyer-Czech

There are numerous examples of co-operation between agriculture and tourism at the local and the regional level in Austria. These include direct marketing of agri-tourism products, the formation of producer and marketing associations, co-operation with gastronomic, hospitality and accommodation providers, and mechanisms of quality assurance. All these fields of co-operation have occurred with respect to the development of tourist trails with a significant food component. However, only rarely do such initiatives takes place under a certain food theme. Nevertheless, there are over fifty theme trails in Austria, almost two-thirds are based on products of the region – the majority are wine roads (twenty-one) – and the remaining theme trails are based on various cultural or heritage dimensions of the regions they run through. Yet the separation between culture and food with respect to the naming of trails often occurs for marketing reasons, because in many cultural or heritage trails regional food is an integral part of the tourist product. For example, the Iron Trail's gastronomy includes regional specialities under the theme 'Eating like the blacksmiths'!

This chapter aims to provide a brief overview of food trails in Austria. First, it details examples of some of the food orientated trails and their products, including wine roads, apple cider and oil trails, as well as those trails for which food is a minor though significant component. Second, it discusses some of the management and marketing issues associated with such trails. Finally, it provides an outlook on the potential future of food trails in Austria.

Wine roads

Austria is divided into sixteen wine regions, mainly for purposes of advertising the produced wines on a regional level. Wine roads can be found in three Austrian provinces: in Styria with 3280 ha of viticultural land, the Burgenland (14 500 ha) and Lower Austria (33 500 ha). Aside from the differences of the grown wines due to climate and geology the wine roads reflect certain characteristics in each province.

In Styria wine roads have had the longest tradition and are therefore the most popular. The South Styrian Wine Road (Südsteirische Weinstraße), built and opened in 1955, is by far the oldest theme trail in Austria. It was built to encourage the further development of this then structurally and economically weak frontier region. The original intention was to improve the accessibility of the vineyards for the farmers but at the same time a basis for the development of leisure and tourist activities was established because of the increased accessibility of the wine region to tourists. To promote the wine road, farmers established 'Heurigen', a typically Austrian form of direct marketing, a type of restaurant where farmers can serve drinks and foods that they produce. Further wine roads (there are now eight in total) were established more than three decades later, in the late 1980s and beginning of the 1990s, the last one being signposted and opened in 1999.

Due to the attractive characteristics of the viticultural landscape and the very high quality of wines, Styrian wine roads have been able to position themselves successfully even though five of them lack underlying organizational structures at the regional level. Instead, they only have the local associations of wine farmers, as has every wine village in Austria, which organize wine tastings and festivals. The other three wine roads are based on regional associations either of local wine associations or of wine enterprises. The local and regional tourist boards promote the wine roads, with the regional agricultural boards being responsible for giving technical support to the wine farmers.

Lower Austria is the only province where there are efforts on the part of the provincial government to harmonize the offer of wine roads and to make them more professional. In 2000 the consortium, Wine Road Lower Austria, was founded, consisting of the eight wine regions of Lower Austria and their ten suborganizations, i.e. ten wine roads. It includes about 1200 enterprises (700 of them are wine enterprises) and 150 municipalities, and is headed by the provincial tourist board. Criteria for joining the Wine Road Lower Austria were developed for the wine road itself, the wine villages and for every member category, including wineries, heurige, wine restaurants and bed and breakfast establishments.

Except for one wine road which was already established in 1999, the formation of the consortium was the trigger for the founding of the remaining nine wine roads in 2001 and 2002. There had been efforts to establish wine roads in the late 1980s and the beginning of the 1990s but, due to lack of personal and financial resources, these efforts did not go beyond the production of a map and/or the signposting of the road. Today the associations which underlie the wine roads include wineries and heurige, gastronomy and accommodation, and sometimes the retail trade. They see their main tasks as the co-ordination and promotion of tourist activities such as festivals and wine tastings, which have always existed but are only promoted on a local level, on the one hand, and in organizing seminars for continuing education for the wine farmers, on the other.

The Burgenland is the province where wine roads are the least visible. Here the market profile of the four wine regions dominates the four corresponding wine roads, except for Austria's smallest wine region, the South Burgenland (4269 ha), whose wine road is more visible. There the participation in the EU's LEADER II programme helped to realize projects such as the establishment of a college of continuing education for wine farmers. The provincial agricultural board and the Austrian Wine Marketing Board are focusing their support strategy on regional promotion and brands, with the expression 'road' not being very popular in the Burgenland because of common associations with traffic jams and long queues at the border with Hungary. Instead, the wine regions have come up with their own regional and local brands, e.g. 'Blaufraenkisch Land' (Blaufraenkisch is the name of a red wine), usually linked to an association whose main task is quality assurance.

Apple, cider, oil and cheese trails

Aside from the wine roads there are a few other food trails in Austria: the oldest is the Styrian Apple Trail which was established in 1986, followed in the 1990s by the Styrian Oil Trail, an initiative based on pumpkin, pumpkinseed oil and health. In addition, there are the Cider Trail Lower Austria and the Cheese Trail Bregenzerwald in the province of Vorarlberg. The latter is an initiative whose central elements are the landscape of alpine pastures, creameries and, of course, cheese – from the pitchfork to the dinner fork. All these trails started as producer and marketing associations that tried to find links with tourism and then developed a tourist product around an existing agricultural product of the region. These include events (e.g. blossom or pumpkin festivals) and guided tours, for example of creameries or oil mills. More recent offerings include treatments with pumpkin cosmetics in the oil trail and whey cosmetics in the cheese trail (whey used to be a waste product in this region), and the 'Apple Men', a group of schnapps distillers, in the Apple Trail.

The members of the associations which support the food trails come from various sectors: agriculture (e.g. dairy and fruit farmers, tillers, creameries, heurigen, oil mills), tourism (e.g. gastronomy and accommodation), trade (e.g. joineries) and culture (e.g. museums and artists). Municipalities also are paying members. The apple and oil trails have voluntary management structures. The cider trail's management is taken care of by two existing institutions: the regional union (regional unions are offices supported by the province that initiate, co-ordinate and accompany regional development projects) and the regional tourist board. The cheese trail is managed by a limited company which was founded in the course of a LEADER II programme and which is owned by the Regional Planning Congregation, a voluntary regional parliament consisting of mayors and other political leaders of the region. The company implements projects on the advice of the Cheese Trail Association.

In addition to designated food trails, there are a number of other instances in which food becomes a component of trails or regional tourism products:

- The trail is only visible on a map that is produced by the regional agricultural board
- a region is branded using a typical agricultural product of the region, but there is no food trail.
- A thematic round trip organized by the regional tourist board, e.g. the 'Beer Trip' to several breweries in Upper Austria.
- Instructional paths based on a product of the region.
- Trails that are not merely based on food, e.g. the Via Iulia Augusta, an international (Austria and Italy) regional development initiative along an ancient Roman trade route. Aside from typical regional foods and

traditional dishes, regional arts and crafts are an important part of the tourist offering and the brand Via Iulia Augusta.

■ Theme villages: a successful example of a theme village is the Poppy Village in Lower Austria. Even though it is only a local initiative, it very clearly demonstrates two basic principles of rural food trails: cross-sectoral co-operation (agriculture and gastronomy) and staging of a theme (e.g. one festival to celebrate the blossoming of the poppy fields and one on Thanksgiving Day with different poppy products such as food, poppy oil, decoration and cosmetics).

■ Culinarium Oesterreich: this is an initiative that started in 1999, supported by state and EU funds, that aims to develop regional profiles based on typical foods and drinks of the region. On the one hand, the sale of agricultural products should be increased while, on the other, tourist offerings based on food should be developed. Co-operation should be established at a cross-sectoral level as well as between the national tourist board and the regions. A successful example for interregional marketing support and co-operation is the collaboration of the Cheese Trail Bregenzerwald and a wine road in Lower Austria, where their respective cheeses and wines are offered together to visitors in both regions.

Management and marketing issues

One of the main challenges for the management of food trails is that the administration and organizational units in tourism as well as agriculture are very small in Austria. Austria is a federal state with nine provinces, the smallest of which, the Burgenland, has only 280 000 inhabitants. Local government is also organized on a small scale. There are 2355 municipalities, 97 per cent of which have less than 10 000 inhabitants. The majority of municipalities (38 per cent) have between 1000 and 2000 inhabitants. Every municipality has its local tourist board. If it is a wine village it also has a local wine farmers' association, while there are corresponding institutions at the regional and provincial level. A variety of institutions (agricultural board, tourist board, regional management) therefore claim responsibilities for food trails. With respect to the ownership structures of businesses which are part of food trails, small and medium-sized enterprises (SMEs) dominate: 70 per cent of the accommodation facilities are privately run, while 70 per cent of the farms are smaller than 30 ha. This situation could be viewed as an advantage as it results in a large diversity of tourist product, but it is also a great challenge in terms of management. These observations show how these problem have been best met:

- An overall organizational structure and some sort of 'manager' who co-ordinates and ensures that the trails rules are kept by participants is necessary right from the start. This position might even be undertaken by a volunteer.
- As long as financial support is granted by the state or the EU, food trails initiatives are often implemented, but when the support ends such initiatives often fall apart. It is difficult to find volunteers, but often teachers or successful farmers take on the role of the manager. Some trails make use of existing institutions, e.g. a regional tourist board, while others ask for membership fees that are high enough to employ a manager. The latter is usually the best solution from the perspective of members.
- Involving key individuals from politics and public administration can be of assistance. Yet party politics can be very strong in Austria, so if the organization managing the trail does not tend to any political party, some institutional support might not be forthcoming.
- When small-sized farms co-operate in supplying agricultural produce they might not be able to deliver their products on a regular basis with the security a gastronomic trail needs. This problem is often solved by producer associations that can provide assured amounts more easily.

Some trails seemingly remain stuck in the very early stages of development in that all they have done is put up signs and/or have a tourist concept developed by a consultant. Yet successful food trails need to be filled with life, accompanied by professional staging of the theme, hosting related themed events such as festivals or sports events such as marathons, and providing a diversified product offering. Nevertheless, it is also important that food trails do not overexpand and exceed the capacities of the members and of the market. For example, on the one hand, tourist services have to be co-ordinated and the theme visible but, on the other, too much of the same type of product weakens the market attractiveness of the trail and leads to unwanted competition between the member communities or enterprises of the food trail. To avoid this some trails are very strict in admitting new members. The Styrian Oil Trail, for instance, only permits one new municipality per year to join on condition that it contributes something new, although still related to pumpkins, to the overall offering.

Food trails need to position themselves appropriately, develop a common tourist offer and build up a marketing network. Yet most trails have not gone beyond the early stages of product development and mutual sales promotion, e.g. creating a brochure. Often the question of actual value added for the region and its enterprises is not answered sufficiently and marketing efforts are usually underdeveloped. Significantly, since increasing the number of day tourists and of buses is not sufficiently beneficial on a long-term basis, several trails are starting to develop strategies to increase the length of stay of visitors and are creating packages and co-operating with tour operators. They are also trying to increase the length of the tourist season.

Most trails have established a set of strict quality standards that have to be fulfilled in order to qualify for membership. Quality assurance concerning the agricultural products is well organized, e.g. associations that are responsible for ensuring the quality of wine in Austria are long-standing and their role is accepted by wine producers. However, with respect to additional criteria in which there is not a similar history, for example providing minimum sanitary standards for restaurants or serving wine in good-quality glasses, there is often a lack of quality controls. Adding to the problem is the structure of the accommodation industry, which also lacks professionalism. Potential responses to quality assurance issues include continuing qualification of the members and supervision of quality standards by persons or institutions from outside the region (e.g. organized by an umbrella organization or conducted by a mystery guest from another region).

Benefits also have to be clear for the members of the trail, i.e. financial, social and emotional benefits, and results have to be clearly visible, which includes physically tangible results (e.g. project outputs) and well-structured meetings. If the benefits are not clear or if there is a feeling that they are lacking altogether, then initiatives usually fall apart. Members have to realize that they have to actively contribute to the positive outcome and be interested in creating a product offer together. They also have to realize that the problem of free-riders and of too high expectations cannot always be solved.

When a food trail is established not all existing institutions who are in pursuit of targets that fit into the overall goal want to join. For instance, in the cider region there are several organizations which are not members of the Cider Trail Association, such as marketing organizations, the agricultural college or the renowned 'Cider Gallery', an exquisite shop where cider tastings take place and a prize-winning cider is sold. Significantly, this kind of competition can have positive effects as it means constant innovation, particularly an increase in the range of products offered.

Most importantly, the personal relationships underlying the organization of food trails are a crucial factor for the trail's success or failure. Many co-operative ventures, including the expansion of food-trail networks to national or even international associations, are started on the informal level and enabled by friendships and good acquaintances.

The outlook for food trails in Austria

Establishing a food trail offers a wide range of opportunities and it often means that the available resources of the region are being used in a positive way. Trails can help to position and brand a region and to create a feeling of togetherness among its inhabitants. Strategic partnerships are formed, farmers can sell more products, and gastronomy and accommodation benefit by increasing numbers of tourists. Changing holiday patterns will likely bring new perspectives for food trails. In Austria, rural destinations without lakes are rapidly losing their attractiveness as summer holiday destinations while short-term stays are becoming more popular. Theme trails are trying to position themselves as an ideal location for a weekend getaway. Another trend trails can profit from is an increasing demand for authentic tourist products, which food trails can often satisfy as authenticity is usually an integral part of their image.

Looking back at the food trails in Austria it is obvious that, starting from the late 1980s until today, the establishment of these trails has become popular. However, if too many trails continue to be created then they will lose their competitive advantage compared to other rural areas and there will be increased competition between trails, particularly if they become too similar. This will lead to a devaluation of food trails, especially if there are still no standard procedures or guidelines for the establishment of theme trails. Currently, every association developing a trail can define their own membership and quality assurance criteria. Co-ordinated efforts at provincial level, e.g. the Wine Road Lower Austria consortium, to provide minimum quality standards are rare. Aside from a set of quality standards there is also a lack of standards for a minimum of various elements the trail should contain. For example, the national tourist board promotes several so-called 'holiday specialists' – groups of hotels with a specialized offer for a certain target group, e.g. 'fishing ground Austria' or 'farm holidays in Austria'. These specialists have set standards for quality and entertainment.

Asking for more professionalism, on the one hand, and maintaining the authenticity of food trails, on the other, might be like walking a tightrope, yet there are successful examples such as the Cheese Trail Bregenzerwald that have even managed to gain a high profile on the international level. Nevertheless, a problem many theme trails have to face is the short tourist season, i.e. usually weekends in the summer or for the wine roads in the autumn – if the weather is good – and the fact that they mainly attract day tourists, which means that most of the time they cannot operate at full capacity.

Finally, we should note that the establishment of trails leads to very specialized forms of co-operation, which have the potential to help overcome the disadvantages that SMEs have to face compared with larger enterprises. Austria clearly has the resources available for the development of successful food trails. However, to a large extent the likelihood of success of these co-operative ventures depends not on its raw resources, but on whether or not an effective management strategy can be developed and implemented between the wide range of stakeholders that have an interest in such trails.

Web sites

Austrian Tourist Board: http://www.austria-tourism.at/index_e.html

Cheese Trail Bregenzerwald: http://www.kaesestrasse.at/

Wine Road Weinviertel in Lower Austria: http://www.weinstrasse.co.at/

Wine roads in Styria: http://www.rebenland.at/dasrebenland/weinstrasse.htm

Weinidylle Südburgenland (brand name of the wine region South Burgenland): http://www.weinidylle.at/index.htm

Oil trail: http://www.oelspur.net/

Apple trail: http://land.heim.at/podersdorf/220210/apfelstr.htm

Cider trail: http://www.most-strasse.at/de/index.html

Via Iulia Augusta: http://ns.iulia-augusta.com/home_t.html

Poppy Village: http://www.mohndorf.at/

Culinarium Oesterreich: http://www.culinarium.at/

9

Food tourism in the Niagara Region: the development of a nouvelle cuisine

David J. Telfer and Atsuko Hashimoto

Introduction

Examining food in history, Tannahill (1973) describes the Grand Tour in the eighteenth century where intrepid travellers in Europe had begun to make pilgrimages to the shrines of established culture. No matter which route they took, these tourists inevitably ended up in Rome admiring the architecture and antiquities of the classical world while at the same time complaining bitterly about the food. 'There might be raw ham, Bologna sausage, figs and melons, but there was nothing of substance. No boiled leg of pork and pease pudding' lamented one traveller. 'No bubble and squeak' (Tannahill, 1973: 277). The 'Gastronomic Grand Tour' was missed by many and as Tannahill (1973) suggests, a really enterprising traveller could have made their trip more stimulating if they had been interested in food and were prepared to look into the previous two centuries. They would have discovered that most major countries had their own 'national cuisines' and their own distinctive modes of cooking or foods, which would be recognizable as 'characteristic'. Today, greater attention is being placed on cuisine as part of the tourism product and it is being incorporated into the marketing plans of national tourism boards which, of course, hope that visitors do not return home 'complaining bitterly about the food' as their predecessors did. As Ferguson (2000: 9) suggests the 'food ways of every country are a direct reflection of everything else about the country – its geography, history, culture, people', and hence provide a special sensory window into the culture of a country for tourists who are willing to taste.

While national cuisines of the Old World may have more history behind them and perhaps are more readily recognizable than the cuisines of the New World, countries such as Canada are incorporating cuisine into their national tourism product. The Canadian Tourism Commission has 'identified that culinary tourism is emerging as an important component of the rapidly growing cultural tourism market. An increasingly significant number of travellers are stating that food is a key aspect of the travel experience and that they believe experiencing a country's food is essential to understanding its culture' (MacDonald, 2001: 1). However, Canada is a country that covers some 8000 kilometres, encompassing dramatically different regions and a history which is influenced by wave after wave of new flavours from immigrants from all over the world (Ferguson, 2000). As a result, regional differences are becoming important. Bell and Valentine (1997: 149) note that 'as regions seek to market themselves while simultaneously protecting themselves from the homogenizing forces of globalization, regional identity becomes enshrined in bottles of wine and hunks of cheese'.

The Niagara Region is one of the regions leading the way in Canada, hoping to capitalize on culinary developments and market itself as a destination for food and wine tourism. Niagara Falls has long dominated tourism in the Niagara Region, however, the tourism product is diversifying, and leading this process is the food and wine industry. Regional grape, wine and food festivals and the Niagara Wine Route continue to grow in popularity as the Niagara Region establishes itself as the home of regional wine country cuisine. Known as part of the fruit belt of Canada, being a temperate zone, the region is able to produce a wide range of products including peaches, plums, cherries, grapes, apples, apricots, nectarines, kiwi and a wide range of vegetables. Focusing on local products, area chefs have begun to develop Niagara cuisine recently featured in *Maclean's*, a Canadian weekly news magazine, as well as

Gourmet, an international food magazine (Ferretti, 1999). One of the leading organizations in the push to develop regional Niagara cuisine is 'Tastes of Niagara'. This organization is a strategic alliance of the region's food producers, processors, distributors, hotels, wineries, restaurants and chefs who have the desire to use and or promote local agricultural products in the tourism industry. Wineries along the Niagara Wine Route are opening restaurants with Niagara dishes on the menu, while hands-on cooking schools are offering a culinary experience for the traveller. Local tour operators have also developed specific agricultural tours visiting area farms and vineyards. The purpose of this chapter is to highlight the nature of a new evolving tourism product, Niagara cuisine. The chapter will first identify the nature of the link between food and tourism followed by an examination of the concepts of national and regional cuisines. The chapter will then focus on efforts under way in the Niagara Region to develop this new regional cuisine tourism product.

Food and wine tourism

In previous centuries when travelling was only for a privileged few, inns and taverns offered a very limited catering service to travellers. However, it is argued that inns, taverns, pubs, coffee houses and cafés all played a significant role in the development of commercial hospitality and the formation of a 'well informed and knowledgeable eating pubic' (Mennell, Murcott and Van Otterloo, 1992: 83). Food for the traveller has gone from an age when the traveller had to provision themselves (Tannahill, 1973) to a situation influenced by agricultural technologies, worldwide transportation networks, supermarkets, pre-cooked meals, food processors, microwave ovens and fast-food restaurants which has completely changed the notion of the practice of food. The processes of globalization, immigration and the worldwide media have exposed people to a wide variety of cuisines and dining out has become more commonplace in many countries. 'Eating out' often bears positive emotional meanings such as a sense of occasion (Finkelstein, 1989). It is also argued that choice of restaurants is charged with a sense of luxury and self-indulgence (Beardsworth and Keil, 1997) and bourgeois sensibility of self (Finkelstein, 1989). With food representing approximately one-third of tourist expenditures (Belisle, 1983), developments in tourism have led to the demand for a variety of eating establishments for people while they are away from home (Beardsworth and Keil, 1997).

The growing numbers of food, wine and travel magazines appearing on store shelves along with the popularity of twenty-four-hour food network television channels in some countries demonstrate the growing interest in culinary experiences. Bell and Valentine (1997: 6) go as far as to suggest that professional and amateur chefs have become household names bringing haute cuisine into our living rooms and kitchens via the television, and food writers, critics and broadcasters are not only showing us 'how to cook but also tell us what, when, where, how – and even why – to eat and drink'. Curiosity in novelty in food practices is encouraged and reinforced by the food-related mass media and 'sensation-seeking' activities are a natural consequence. In terms of cultural tourism, Robinson (1999: 1) suggests, 'the desire to make contact with one's own culture, in all its forms and the search for experiences of other cultures is very much at the heart of tourism'. Food is an important part of culture or identity and there has been an increased interest in food and wine tourism. The 'Gastronomic Grand Tour' referred to by Tannahill (1973) is alive and well with people travelling to visit wine routes, dine in restaurants and to attend food festivals both in the 'New' and 'Old' worlds. As Telfer and Wall (1996) suggest, there can also be a symbiotic relationship between tourism and agriculture, with the farm providing food inputs into the tourism system as well as acting as an attraction and providing positive externalities in the form of attractive landscapes. The chapter now turns to examine the links between national and regional cuisine and tourism before focusing on efforts under way in the Niagara Region to capitalize on the increased interest in culinary tourism.

National cuisine

The link between food and national identity has been explored by a number of authors, however, Bell and Valentine (1997) raise the question as to what can one do in a nation without a clearly marketable culinary heritage? They examine the case of Australia, which has had to face this question. Parallels can be drawn between Canada and Australia, as there is difficulty in identifying what Canadian cuisine is or what the Australian national dish is. Similarly in New Zealand, Taylor (1996) acknowledges that the country has no particular cuisine, nonetheless, that has made the country more open to a wide range of flavours and influences from around the world. She goes on to argue that what is exciting in New Zealand restaurants today is not authentic but is innovative which, as will be illustrated later, is what is occurring in Niagara. Stewart (2000: 13) attempts to define the nature of Canadian cuisine:

Canadian cuisine is about celebrating our magnificent differences, our roots and our ethnicity. It's about possibilities and how as a people we continue to welcome immigrants from all over the world and in doing so permanently enrich our food ways. It's about creating the best from our local ingredients, then selling it to the world. It's about branding ourselves Canadian and giving our producers an unmistakable edge that no other nation can emulate.

Another food writer, Ferguson (1995: 3) comments on the longstanding dilemma of defining Canadian cooking:

What do you call the cuisine of a country that spans some 8000 kilometres and encompasses a dozen dramatically different regions and three centuries of culinary traditions? A cuisine as modest as shortcakes baked up by a rural church group for a strawberry social and as spicy as the jerk chicken at a Toronto Jamaican jump-up? As traditional as fish-and brewis in Newfoundland and as innovative as steamed goose-neck barnacles at Sooke Harbour House? You call it Canadian that's what. Canadian cooking is defined by its diversity. We're country style cosy and city-street sassy. We're butter tarts, Nanaimo bars, chili sauce, and figgy duff. We're poutine and perogies and pasta. We're curries and tacos and tiramisu. And the revolution continues.

Ferguson (1995) argues that Canada has not become a melting pot but, rather, distinct regions across the country have their own culinary personality which reflects the climate and local ingredients along with the varied background of the people who have immigrated there. Not to omit the First Nations people, the Internet web page for Nunavut Tourism (www.nunatour.nt.ca/BUS/BUS5a_1.htm) promotes Northern Cuisine, which includes caribou, muskox, Arctic char, scallops, turbot, and a northern appetizer called *maktaaq*, i.e. the outer layer of the skin of a whale served raw.

With the rich diversity across the country, Canadian cuisine has come to be focused on local products. In hopes of further developing culinary tourism, the Canadian Tourism Commission (CTC) hosted eight Regional Round Tables on Culinary Tourism across Canada between October 1999 and May 2001 (MacDonald, 2001). The round tables were held in the following locations – St John's (Newfoundland), Charlottetown (Prince Edward Island), Vancouver (British Columbia), Niagara Falls (Ontario), Saskatoon (Saskatchewan), Winnipeg (Manitoba), Edmonton (Alberta) and Montreal (Quebec). The objectives of the round tables were to bring together representatives from the food and travel industry on a regional scale to share information and to explore the possibilities of further developing Canada's food and wine tourism

Table 9.1   Selected success stories in culinary tourism in Canada

Associations
Tastes of Nova Scotia
Tastes of Niagara

Gastronomical routes
La Route des Saveurs in Charlevoix, Quebec
The Gourmet Trail of First Island Tours, British Columbia
The Niagara Wine Route

Culinary and wine festivals and events
The 'SAQ Culinary Arts' of the Montreal Highlights Festival, Quebec
The Okanagan Wine Festival, British Columbia
The Arctic Food Celebration, Nunavut
The Niagara Grape and Wine Festival, Ontario

Culinary destinations and historical attractions (interpreting culinary flavours and
food preparation techniques of other eras)
The Acadian Historical Village in Caraquet, New Brunswick
Fortress Louisbourg National historic Site, Nova Scotia
Le Village Québécois d'antan à Drummondville, Quebec

CTC product clubs related to culinary tourism
Country Roads Agri-Tourism Product Club, Manitoba
Cuisine, Wine and Culture Product Club, Ontario

Source: MacDonald (2001)

sector. A National Tourism and Cuisine Forum was then held in Halifax, Nova
Scotia, in June of 2001 with the idea of moving into strategic business
planning on a national scale for culinary tourism. During the round tables a
number of success stories in culinary tourism in Canada were identified and
these are presented in Table 9.1.

The National Forum explored a number of different elements of culinary
tourism including defining culinary tourism and the distinguishing characteristics of cuisine in Canada, branding and standards, defining the market,
product development, promotion, education and training, and communication
and collaboration. Out of the forum, three main strategies were identified,
which included the creation of a National Task Force on Culinary Tourism,
examination of the feasibility of developing national standards, and the
development of a national tourism and cuisine database accessible over the
Internet (MacDonald, 2001). The database comprises people and organizations that are actively promoting and developing Canadian cuisine. The list of
organizations includes influential chefs and restaurants who have received

acclaim through the use of indigenous products; exceptional and distinct beer, wine and food producers; national, provincial/territorial and regional organizations that market Canada as a culinary destination based on the notion that local food is an integral part of any tourist experience; festival organizers highlighting local products; tour operators incorporating regional cuisine into tour packages; influential food writers advocating Canadian cuisine; identification of the awards Canadian cuisine has received; and, finally, relevant web sites (CTC, 2000).

One of the main questions surrounding culinary tourism is where the markets are for these products and which demographic profile is the most likely to respond to this development. An association of Canadian Tourism Ministries and organizations collaborated to conduct surveys to assess travel motivations of pleasure travel among Canadian and Americans. The Travel Activities and Motivation Survey (TAMS) was conducted between September 1999 and April 2000 by means of a telephone survey to 28 397 individuals in the USA and 18 385 individuals in Canada. Respondents who had travelled in the previous two years or expressed an interest in travelling in the next two years were also sent a mail-back questionnaire. The questionnaire was returned by 5490 Canadians and 6405 Americans. Using the TAMS, Lang Research (2001) examined interest in travel activities associated with cuisine (e.g. fine dining) and wine (e.g. tours of wineries). A few of the findings of the study are reported here as they relate to culinary tourism. In terms of location, in Canada, residents from the provinces of Quebec, Ontario, Alberta and British Columbia were shown to have higher interests in vacation activities associated with cuisine. In the USA, these individuals tended to be from the Pacific Region (e.g. California, Oregon, Washington, Hawaii), the South Atlantic (Florida, Georgia, North and South Carolina) and the Middle Atlantic (e.g. Pennsylvania, New York, New Jersey) (Lang Research, 2001). It was found that affluence had an impact on who is interested in cuisine. The market most likely to be interested in cuisine when travelling was found to be Affluent Mature and Senior Couples. Other potential secondary markets, which showed above average interest in cuisine, were Affluent Young Singles, Affluent Couples, Affluent Families and Affluent Mature Couples. It was also found that those who were interested in vacation activities connected with wine and cuisine were more likely to have sought out vacation experiences that were associated with exploration (e.g. visiting historical sites, natural wonders), personal indulgence (e.g. experience the good life, visiting a casino, experience city nightlife) and romance and relaxation (e.g. experience intimacy and romance, relax and recuperate). It was suggested from the results of the study that advertising and marketing materials for cuisine and wine should focus on cultural, entertainment and romantic images of the destination. In fact there should be a hedonistic quality to the promotions (Lang Research, 2001). Participation in activities related to culture and entertainment while on a trip is more closely linked to those who are interested in wine and cuisine than participation in outdoor activities. This association was found to be very strong for those who shopped or dined, attended high performance art (e.g. ballet, opera), attended concerts, carnivals or fairs, visited botanical gardens or visited casinos (Lang Research, 2001). Those with an interest in cuisine and wine were also more likely to have participated in certain types of outdoor activities while on a trip and especially water sports, fitness activities, swimming and sunbathing, team sports, natural sightseeing and golfing. Finally, those with an interest in wine and cuisine are more likely to consult a large number of information sources including newspapers and magazines, travel guides, travel agents, travel information offices and the Internet (Lang Research, 2001).

The market profile outlined above is the one being pursued to a certain extent in the development of culinary tourism in the Niagara Region. Before focusing on the developments in the Niagara Region, the chapter turns briefly to examine concepts related to regional cuisine.

Regional cuisine

The questions central to this chapter are 'what regional cuisine is?' and, in the case of Niagara, 'how has it developed into a new tourism product?' The previous section highlighted the nature of national cuisine. There are, of course, examples where regional food has been elevated to represent national cuisine. In the case of Canada, for example, maple syrup is often noted as a national product when in fact it is mainly produced in certain provinces such as Ontario and Quebec. Telfer (2002) has pointed out the difficulty of identifying the nature of a region. The different perspectives of a region highlighted by Malecki (1997) are relevant to the discussion here. The different perspectives include:

- the relations of production in a given space and time
- regions defined by a local culture
- the region as a setting for social interactions of all types.

As Bell and Valentine (1997) observe, a region is a product both of human and of physical processes: a natural landscape and a peopled landscaped. The concept of a food region can vary in scale from international regions such as the Mediterranean to the area covered by Tastes of Niagara. The larger the scale, the more unique differences within nations are lost.

Drawing on the work of Crang (1995), who stated that regional cuisines are invented traditions, Bell and Valentine (1997) argue regional cuisines are invested and reinvested with meaning, and often with vehement local patriotism. Indeed, cultural practices such as food preparation and consumption are important in marking regional identity (Bell and Valentine, 1997). Food products are identified by the region, with the region becoming the brand. The wine region is one example of how the rhetoric of the region is pulled together to stress uniqueness and how the human and the physical landscapes produce that uniqueness. The concept of appellations represent wine from a specific region where particular environmental conditions and the skill of the wine maker come together to produce a distinct character for wine identity (Bell and Valentine, 1997). There is now a movement to protect regional food products. As Bell and Valentine (1997: 153) argue, 'legal demarcation of vineyards and wine regions through appellations and other similar markers thus creates a series of monopolies on who can produce which wines, and where – more fiercely guarded than ever in today's global wine market'. Hall (2002b) also notes that this protectionist movement has moved to the area of regional speciality food and drink products within the EU (see also, Ilbery and Kneafsey, 2000b). Bottled water and cheese are other examples of products that can be tied to a specific region.

If regional cuisines are to some extent, invented traditions, the question for this chapter is what has been invented in the Niagara Region. Known for the Niagara Falls, the region is rapidly developing a reputation as a centre for fine dining based on regional cuisine. As outlined above, Canadian cuisine is based on locally available products. The remainder of the chapter explores the initiatives in the Niagara Region that have helped to develop culinary tourism.

Niagara cuisine

In order to understand the nature of Niagara culinary tourism, it is necessary to examine the agricultural resource base in Niagara. Niagara has a moderate climate compared with the rest of the province of Ontario. The Niagara Peninsula is bordered by water on three sides – Lake Ontario to the north, Lake Erie to the south and the Niagara River to the east. Running through the region is the Niagara Escarpment, which is part of the contributing factor to the presence of micro-climates. The area to the north of the Niagara Escarpment has a frost-free period ten to twenty days longer than the area to the south of the escarpment, which is important for tender fruit production (Chapman, 1994). With these favourable growing conditions, Niagara is known as part of the Fruit Belt of Canada and it has received considerable attention for its specialized tender fruit and grape production. There is also diversity in Niagara's agricultural industry, so, in addition to fruit and grape farming, there are greenhouses, intensive livestock operations and a variety of field crops (Chapman, 1994). The agricultural industry has developed not only on indigenous products, but also some farmers have imported products and raised them successfully here. One interesting example of this is Lake Land Meats which raises a wide variety of game animals such as deer and wild boar. Drawing on the concepts of Bell and Valentine (1997), Niagara is a geographic region but it also a human region where entrepreneurs with the assistance of the government have helped to build or invent the overall region. One of the tender fruit crops that has been drawing the most attention is the wine industry. The wine industry has gone through a tremendous number of changes over the last twenty years and there are now over fifty wineries along the Niagara Wine Route with many of them being open to tourists (see Telfer, 2001a, for a detailed historical account). The industry has increased the quality of the wines produced by switching to *vitis vinifera* varieties. Along with this has been the development of the Vintner's Quality Alliance (VQA) which is the appellation system covering the quality of the wine produced in the region. The Niagara Wine Route has quickly developed into a tourism attraction with two main clusters of wineries. The first cluster is in the east located near the historic tourist town of Niagara-on-the-Lake while the second cluster of wineries is located towards the west in the Niagara Peninsula (Telfer, 2001b). To a large extent, it has been the development of wine tourism in Niagara, which is helping to lead the drive to culinary tourism in Canada. As will be illustrated later, many of the wineries have started to open restaurants which focus on using high-quality local products.

In order to help facilitate the development of culinary tourism in the region, the Provincial Government of Ontario and the tourism industry have been working to develop a wine strategy with organizations such as the Wine Council of Ontario, the Ontario Grape Growers' Marketing Board, the Liquor Control Board of Ontario and the VQA to develop a wine strategy. The overall goal of the strategy is to have the region recognized as one of the best wine producing regions in the world and to achieve C$1.5 billion in sales by 2020. The Ontario Wine Strategy is made up of three documents:

■ *Poised for Greatness: A Strategic Framework for Ontario's Wine Industry*

- *Wine of Ontario: Sales and Marketing Plan*
- *Wine and Culinary Tourism in Ontario Strategy.*

The first document establishes a twenty-year vision for the grape and wine industry. The vision includes statements such as the wine industry will be a C$1.5 billion business that employs 13 500 people contributing C$1 billion to the economy of Ontario annually. In addition, Ontario red and white wine will make up 60 per cent of the premium wine purchased by Ontario consumers and over 90 per cent of the grapes grown in Ontario will be used to make VQA wines. The objectives to achieve these goals include focusing on premium quality and the varieties that Ontario excels in, investing in the VQA, nurturing wine tourism, making Ontario wine broadly available and, finally, forging partnerships with the grape and wine industry.

The second document focuses on sales and marketing plan. The five-year strategy is designed to increase market share in the home market from 42 per cent to 50 per cent. In order to achieve this, Ontario wine will be marketed as source of pride for all Ontarians. It is anticipated that 1000 new direct and indirect jobs will result through the marketing strategy (Ontario Government, 2002).

The third document is of the most relevance to this chapter. *The Wine and Culinary Tourism in Ontario Strategy* document has a vision which states that Ontario should be established as a quality wine and culinary tourism destination in both domestic and international markets. As illustrated in the overall strategy below, Niagara and Toronto have been identified as being the primary culinary destinations:

- Establish compelling high-quality experiences for visitors targeting high-yield visitors for whom wine and culinary experiences are a lifestyle choice, and who have a high propensity to travel for such experiences. Different strategies will be employed for the Ontario market, the cross-border US market and the longer-haul Canadian and international markets.
- Build on the world-class wine-making, agricultural and culinary capabilities of the Niagara region, on the diverse and multicultural dining opportunities available in Toronto and on the unique cultural and culinary offerings of selected communities and destinations in the province.
- Build upon the many complementary tourism attractions and visitor appeals in these areas of the province (EPG, 2002).

It is argued that both Niagara and Toronto have a strong base from which to build, they are located close together and they are both close to cross-border

Table 9.2   Recommended wine and culinary strategy for the Niagara Region

Establish an internationally recognized 'signature event' to raise Niagara's profile as an international quality wine destination and to attract high-yield visitors to the region for a wine and culinary experience

Enhance the Wine Route experience
- Establish Wine Country Signs on the QEW (highway)
- Develop two sub-brands under the Wine Route brand – one for 'Niagara-on-the-Lake', the other for 'Escarpment'
- Add additional wine route signs, develop a guidebook and improve the wine route map

Develop packages and itineraries:
- Wine and Culinary Adventures in Niagara – half-day to multi-day experiences in a mix and match modular format
- Wine and Culinary Vacations in Niagara, two- to seven-day destination vacation packages

Establish selected communities as hubs for wine and culinary experiences, and the primary focus for the development of accommodation and other services

Encourage the private sector to establish more accommodation in the region, particularly quality inns and character properties and particularly in the western part of the region

Develop a diverse mix of wine and culinary-based learning packages to cater to short-term leisure visitors as well as multi-day destination markets

Develop experiences targeting the corporate and group markets as well as incentive travel markets

Focus on a smaller number of quality events that will attract visitors, with a focus on the early spring and late fall periods

Undertake a detailed feasibility on the wine discovery centre concept

Pursue proposals for a new mid-peninsula highway as well as other transportation modes that can provide improved access to the Niagara Region for wine and culinary tourists

Establish a number of quality standards programmes, initially including a basic market-readiness standards programme for wineries, along with an 'Awards of Distinction' programme for restaurants, and an award for outstanding customer service for front-line personnel

Introduce a 'tourism strategies outreach programme' for the management of wineries, restaurants, cooking schools and other stakeholders to assist them in developing a better understanding of tourism success strategies and their benefits

Increase the level of training of front-line staff through the tourism sector, in customer service and in their knowledge of the Niagara Region. Introduce a more in-depth wine knowledge and customer-service training programme for winery staff

Undertake a special study to identify models for 'sustainable' tourism related development on protected lands (e.g. the Niagara Escarpment and agricultural lands) addressing issues such as environmental quality standards, viable business models and appropriate limits and guidelines for approving development on protected land

Source: EPG (2002)

traffic. The strategy for Niagara is listed in Table 9.2. In terms of regional branding, one of the recommendations in Table 9.2 is to create two sub-brands within the overall Wine Route brand. The two brands represent two different geographic areas – one for Niagara-on-the-Lake which is at the eastern end of the wine route and the other is the escarpment which is at the western end of the wine route.

In order to structure the remainder of the chapter, the organization, Tastes of Niagara, will be used to highlight the development of regional cuisine in Niagara. This organization is a strategic alliance among the region's food producers, processors, distributors, hotels, wineries, restaurants and chefs who have the desire to use and or promote local agricultural products in the tourism industry. This movement to focus on local products is highlighted by de Selincourt (1997: 6) who argues: 'buying delicious, wholesome, locally produced food sounds attractive to almost everyone'. Using vegetables, for example, de Selincourt (1997) argues that freshness is a very important measure in the quality of most food and if one wants the food to be fresh it has to be harvested less than twenty-four hours ago. This then means that to obtain fresh food one needs to go direct to the farm, pick it oneself or buy it from a greengrocer who collects daily from local growers. In order to help link chefs to local producers one of the initiatives of Tastes of Niagara is the *Agri-Hospitality Resource Guide* which lists producers and the types of crops they produce. Niagara cuisine is built then on the premise of locally available Niagara products.

One of the recent initiatives of Tastes of Niagara is the creation of a web site. The slogan on the web site is 'Niagara – where New World creativity sparks Old World tradition'. The description of the area reads as follows:

> Picturesque Niagara-on-the-Lake, the verdant Niagara Escarpment, and, of course, the magnificent Niagara Falls. From the heart of this romantic landscape springs not only food and wine to please the most discriminating palate, but also a convivial atmosphere in which to enjoy them. Delicious innovative cuisine prepared from fresh local produce. Award-winning wines made from only the finest *vinifera* grapes. Talented chefs and memorable restaurants where North American flair meets European sophistication. Exciting. Exceptional. Outstanding theatre and colourful festivals enhance Niagara's cultural experience. When you explore Niagara, you discover more than a place. You discover an adventure. (www.tastesofniagara.com/index.cfm)

The website also tempts the reader with some of the products available locally:

When it comes to the creation of outstanding cuisine and fine wines, fresh, high-quality ingredients are essential, and Niagara – located on the same latitude band as Provence and Tuscany – has them. Moderate winters, cool springs, and the protection from strong winds, offered by the Niagara Escarpment result in ideal growing conditions. These, in turn, yield bountiful orchards, lush vineyards, and centuries-old farms boasting a rich array of colourful produce. Looking for crisp apples, juicy peaches, luscious cherries? Delectable apricots, perhaps? Or how about quail eggs? A Gewurztraminer ice wine? Edible flowers or a fillet of ostrich? Niagara's diverse offerings continue to amaze – and once you've tried them, you'll be back for more. Arouse your palate. Pleasure your senses. Taste Niagara, and savour the experience. (www.tastesofniagara.-com/index.cfm)

The web site also contains a few seasonal recipes from chefs, which are dedicated to the regional cuisine movement of Niagara. The recipes are presented along with comments from the chefs. There is also a list of area festivals and events. In the summer of 2002, Tastes of Niagara hosted its eighth Annual Summer Showcase, which is a one-day event from 3 p.m. to 8 p.m. in August. For C$75, visitors have unlimited food tastings, twelve (one-ounce) wine tastings and a commemorative wine glass. There is a limit of 750 tickets, which in the past have sold out in advance of the event. In the brochure advertising the event, celebrity chefs from the area's restaurants are listed along with a sample list of the food prepared for the previous year's event. This list includes: ice wine and mustard marinated venison striploin; brioche toast and apricot chutney; and panko crusted crab cake with Wyndym Farms beet fennel gazpacho and tossed chopsticks greens (Tastes of Niagara, 2002). Table 9.3 is a sample of some of the dishes prepared for the 2000 showcase along with the names of the Niagara restaurants and producers.

One of the other recent initiatives of Tastes of Niagara is a twelve-page brochure on the Niagara fruit stands and markets. There are forty-five entries in the guide listed by geographic area and containing information on the produce they have, directions, hours of operation, if pick-your-own is available and, finally, if they have any other types of products. In the introduction to the guide, visitors are encouraged to 'Travel throughout our beautiful region and taste the freshness and quality of our produce. Look for the Tastes of Niagara logo – it is the symbol of local produce' (Tastes of Niagara, n.d.).

Table 9.3   Dishes, restaurants and producers for the 2002 Tastes of Niagara Showcase

Dish	Niagara restaurant	Niagara producer
Veal tonnato with three pepper coulis	Casa Mia	Doughert's Meats
Bison salami with fruit berry chutney	Hillebrand Vineyard Cafe	Century Game Farm
Orange pistachio and black olive biscotti with maple smoked chicken	Kristen's Fine Cuisine and Catering	Niagara Presents
Smoked tamarind quail	Casino Niagara	Speck Farms
Grilled Cumbrae Farms beef medallions	Niagara Falls Marriot Fallsview	Cumbrae Farms
Four pepper berry spiced rainbow trout	Niagara Parks Commission	Kats Okashimo
Terrine of quail	On the Twenty	Speck Farms
Potted duck and Red Haven peach butter	Pillar and Post	Jay Dee Ducks
Szechuan chili rubbed pork tenderloin with Wyndym Farms tomatoes	Queen's Landing	Wyndym Farms
Seared leg of venison	Vineland Estates	Lake Land Meats
Betheny Farms Red Curry Chicken	Niagara College	Bethany Meats
Cedar Plank Short Hills trout	Sweeney Todd's	Niagara Aqua Culture
Black bean and roasted bell pepper cake, Niagara Herb Farm Savoury Herbs	Wild Flower	Niagara Herb Farms
The famous Capri eggplant Parmesan	Capri Restaurant	Lococo's Fruits and Vegetables

Source: Tastes of Niagara (2000)

Profiles of Tastes of Niagara members

To better illustrate the nature of the evolving culinary tourism developments in Niagara, a series of short profiles are presented of members of Tastes of Niagara. Table 9.4 indicates the number of members in the organization

Table 9.4   Tastes of Niagara membership

Member category	Number of organizations
Fruit and vegetable grower and producers	31
Meat and poultry producers and processors	14
Fish producers and processors	2
Other products, processors and services	11
Farm markets and distributors	6
Restaurants (chefs) and caterers	29
Cooking schools	4
Wineries	25
Tour operators	3
Culture groups	9

Source: Tastes of Niagara web site at www.tastesofniagara.com/index.cfm

according to various categories from their Internet web page. The largest membership categories include 'Fruit and vegetable growers and producers' (thirty-one), 'Restaurants (chefs) and caterers' (twenty-nine) and 'Wineries' (twenty-five). With any alliance, the membership can change over time. According to the 1998 *Agri-Hospitality Resource Guide* for the organization there were 148 members with the largest category being the 'Fruit and vegetable growers and producers' of which there were fifty (Telfer, 2000). There has, however, been growth in the 'Restaurants/chefs caterers and cooking schools' moving from twenty-three in 1998 to thirty-two in 2002 according to the membership list on the Internet (www.tastesofniagara.com/index.cfm). An interesting addition to the list of categories has been the inclusion of the 'Tour operator' category and the 'Culture group'. This clearly indicates that a number of related industries that perhaps are after a similar market segment have decided to join Tastes of Niagara.

Tour operators

There are three tour operators listed in the Tastes of Niagara membership guide. Niagara Peninsula Agri-Tours features grower-guided tours of Niagara's agriculture, food and wine bounty. They have specifically targeted 'high-end, custom designed, authentic educational tours, offering first-hand insights into the Niagara Peninsula's unique agriculture, and regional cuisine'. The tours also are designed to point out how the region fits into the 'big picture' of Canada's agri-food industry (www.tastesofniagara.com). Wine Country Tours offers a number of tour packages directly connected to culinary tourism. Besides offering a number of tours to wineries, they offer day tours with titles such as 'Wine and Agriculture Tour', 'Wine Agriculture and Picnic Tour' and 'Wine Culinary and Agriculture Tour'. The 'Wine and Food Education Tour' involves learning about gourmet cooking at the Niagara Culinary Centre, a wine education seminar which involves matching food with wine, and a tour of a VQA winery (www.winecountrytours.ca). Finally, Phantom Trolley Tours are centred in Niagara-on-the-Lake and they offer a variety of tours including ghost tours. Their link to culinary tourism is that they offer a four-course guided wine and food tour pairing regional cuisine entrées with Inniskillin VQA wines (www.tastesofniagara.com).

Restaurants

There are an increasing number of restaurants opening at wineries, which are one of the driving forces behind the development of Niagara cuisine. Vineland Estates is one of these wineries featuring regional Niagara cuisine. The winery has 350 acres and offers a boutique, tours and links to bed and breakfast establishments in the area. The chef at Vineland Estates was interviewed to get an idea of how he sees the development of culinary tourism in Niagara. The chef is one of the local celebrity chefs who is starting to be recognized at international level and has done guest cooking in Quebec, Italy, France, Hawaii and Seattle. The focus of the winery is on premium wines and food experiences. The chef has a strong commitment to Tastes of Niagara, being a charter member, and makes every effort to incorporate local products into the menu. The chef often puts the name of the local grower/producer on the menu. In fact, very few items are purchased from outside the Niagara Region. When asked what Niagara cuisine is, the chef responded that it is the sourcing and cultivating of Canadian and Niagara products and it involves the modification of dishes to suit the area. The chef indicated that the restaurant prepares many of its own products. All bread is made in the restaurant. They clean and bone their own fish, butcher their own meat, have an extensive preserves cellar, make their own vinegars and hard cider, smoke their own salmon, age cheeses and they have their own private vegetable garden. Besides using the Tastes of Niagara network, they also contact suppliers/producers that they do not know and visit farms and invite them for lunch. In terms of their customers, it is believed that customers are becoming more discriminating, more sophisti-cated and more demanding. Cooking classes have also been offered on the premises and Vineland Estates has participated in numerous local wine and food festivals. One of the other initiatives that the winery was attempting to move forward was the development of a culinary centre. However, this has been put on hold as there are regulations regarding further development of the

Niagara Escarpment. Finally, it was suggested that the profile of Niagara cuisine could be raised by the increasing awareness of the region as a whole and by placing more emphasis on the mandate of Tastes of Niagara.

A second winery restaurant, Bench Bistro at EastDell Estates winery, also focuses on local products. On their menu, they state that wherever possible, the chef 'works with local farmers and suppliers in creating dishes that showcase rustic wine-country cooking at its seasonal best'. As indicated in Table 9.4, there are twenty-nine restaurants, chefs and caterers in Tastes of Niagara indicating many other non-winery restaurants are trying to incorporate local products into their menus. For example, the Wildflower Restaurant offers regional, continental and Mediterranean cuisine. It also offers 100 per cent VQA Niagara wines and beer. The Wildflower Restaurant states that in the winter, 60 per cent of their products are regional and in the summer 70 per cent regional products are used. With more and more restaurants opening with innovative chefs highlighting Niagara cuisine, the region is starting to be noticed as a new culinary tourism destination.

Cooking schools

Related to the movement in the restaurants is the development of cooking schools. There are four cooking schools in Tastes of Niagara and two are briefly profiled here. Korchok (2002: L2) states that 'The Good Earth Cooking School in Beamsville and Wine Country Cooking School in Niagara-on-the-Lake have stirred up some savoury programmes that combine southern Ontario's regional cuisine with top chefs, amazing recipes and complementary Niagara Wines'. The Wine Country Cooking School is located as part of the Strewn Winery Complex in Niagara-on-the-Lake, which also includes a restaurant. The growing links the cooking school has to tourism is evident by its membership in the Culinary Vacation Alliance, which is a group of six cooking resorts and schools in Ontario that share information and occasionally host a celebrity chef (Stimmell, 2002). The advertisement below from the Cooking School's web page, illustrates the services it offers along with a definition of Niagara regional cuisine.

> The Wine Country Cooking School celebrates Niagara's culinary and viticultural heritage. Our focus is on Niagara regional cuisine – local grown and raised products, recipes which change with the season, and the pairing of food and wine. Cabernets risotto with wild mushrooms, maple glazed pork tenderloin with rhubarb chutney, roast squash soup with red pepper puree, and peach melba shortcake are examples of our wine country cuisine. The Wine Country Cooking School is located at Strewn

175

winery in a beautifully restored and rebuilt 1930s fruit cannery. Light, bright and with a friendly elegance describe the school. The demonstration kitchen has a teaching island with gas stove and grill, wall ovens, overhead mirror and state-of-the-art sound system. Comfortable tables and chairs make it a pleasure to follow the classes. The hands-on kitchen has four maple-top work areas with gas cooking units and grills. After an instruction class, the maximum of sixteen students will roll up their sleeves and prepare a meal. A private patio, dining room and herb garden complete the school facilities (www.winecountrycooking.com/about.html).

The operator of the Wine Country Cooking School was also interviewed in order to obtain a better understanding of the nature of the school and Niagara cuisine. When asked to clarify the essence of Niagara cuisine, the response was that Niagara cuisine is dishes that incorporate local products in season. It reflects the culinary background of the region and the culinary background of the chefs. Cuisine is based on product. Chefs bring the influence of their background, Italian, French, Indian, etc. and adapt to those ingredients that are available locally. The cooking school and the winery are marketed as a destination bringing food and wine together. The cooking school uses 100 per cent regional and seasonal food and they participate in many local food and wine festivals. The Tastes of Niagara guidebook has been useful to the school in locating local growers. However, they would like it if Tastes of Niagara could also help facilitate distribution of local products. The school and winery benefit from the clustering of wineries as many of their visitors are day-trip people. They do, however, work closely with bed and breakfasts for those staying for a longer period of time. It was also recognized that while the region has a lot to offer, wine and in particular culinary tourism is still in its infancy. There is a great deal of potential for growth but a more integrated, co-operative and focused policy needs to be adopted with more networking between different private and government bodies.

The Good Earth Cooking School is another leading cooking school in the region, located on a 55-acre fruit farm in Beamsville. They offer cooking classes for up to twelve taught by either the resident chef or a guest chef brought in from an area restaurant. The cost of the classes is C$125 for each three-hour cooking class. The philosophy behind the school is to focus on the bounty of local farms. The classes highlight local fruit and vegetables in season (www.goodearthcooking.com.). Their brochure states: 'Come and experience Niagara cuisine in our special place among our orchards of sweet cherries, sun-ripened peaches, and dew kissed pears and plums. We invite you to linger and discover for yourself what makes Niagara the centre of Canada's food and wine revolution' (Good Earth Cooking School. n.d.).

Conclusion

As food practices have changed over time, dining out in travel destinations has become more than just a necessity and is an extra 'tourist experience' that can affect the overall evaluation of the travel experience. Many countries in the Old World such as France and Italy have a long-established reputation based on their national cuisines (e.g. French wine and cheese and Italian pasta variations). New World nations also see the potential of culinary tourism products and are trying to establish their countries as culinary destinations by inventing New World national cuisines.

The Niagara Region has successfully started down the path of wine and culinary tourism. As the Niagara Region is part of the 'New World', there are fewer easily recognizable national or regional cuisine dishes/products compared with countries from the 'Old World'. The question is: what is Niagara Cuisine? In a sense, Niagara regional cuisine has been invented and reinvented based on the local products available and the background and innovation of area chefs. The historical introduction of immigrants and products from all over the world has created a fusion cuisine rich in diversity. Change has come quickly over the last twenty years and the developments in regional cuisine in Niagara have been led to a certain extent by the wineries. As more winery and non-winery restaurants open, wine country cuisine is becoming more readily recognized.

With current trends in tourism, tourists are looking to experience the local culture and food, which means investigating local agricultural products. The 'Gastronomic Grand Tour' (Tannahill, 1973) of the Niagara Region now offers over fifty wineries, restaurants, cooking schools and agricultural tours. With help from partnerships at provincial and national levels, various strategies have been put in place to further help put Niagara on the map for culinary tourism. One of the main recommendations of the Niagara Culinary Strategy (Table 9.2) is the development of a signature wine and food event internationally to raise the profile of Niagara as a culinary destination. Initial steps have also been taken to better understand the nature of this higher end market so that the industry can meet their demands. The Niagara Region is rapidly developing a new tourism product which has shifted the focus away from Niagara Falls and on to making Niagara a food and wine destination.

10

The lure of food: food as an attraction in destination marketing in Manitoba, Canada

John Selwood

Introduction

Food is one of the most important attractions sought out by tourists in their craving for new and unforgettable experiences. However, food is a very much overlooked and unsung component of the tourism literature. Typically, food is lumped together with accommodation in compilations of tourism statistics, partly perhaps because of it being almost always part of another attraction, and also because of it being a necessary element of survival no matter where a person is located. Dining out is one of the most popular activities undertaken by Canadian tourists and the practice is rapidly growing (Coopers and Lybrand Consulting, 1996; Wilton, 1997). Furthermore, the contribution of food to the tourism economy is of very considerable importance and, because of their intensive use of labour, food preparation and services also contribute very heavily to the tourism employment sector. In Canada, nearly a million people work in the food-service industry, and according to Statistics Canada, 21 per cent of a tourist's budget is spent on food and drink (Statistics Canada, 1998: 144). Manitoba statistics show an even higher percentage of the tourist dollar being spent in this way, with more than 28 per cent being spent on food and drink by intra-provincial travellers (Statistics Canada, 1997). The promotion of regional cuisine is therefore an effective way of supporting local economies and agricultural production. This chapter provides an overview of the relevance of food to Manitoba's tourism industry.

Manitoba's food attractions command scant attention from international food guides such as the *Michelin Guide,* nor do they receive much notice from Canadian productions featuring restaurant fare. As examples, Air Canada's in-flight magazine, *En Route* typically contains only a handful of entries for Manitoba, and a feature article, Haute Canuck', in *Maclean's* magazine, Canada's leading weekly news magazine, barely mentioned Manitoba's contribution to Canada's haute cuisine (Chidley, 1998). How-ever, as the statistics indicate, revenues from the sale of food are a very large component of the total amount of tourism product sold. Fine dining is important in Manitoba, and as a survey undertaken in 1995 demonstrated, more than 50 per cent of travellers to Manitoba were motivated in part by the desire to try different foods (Travel Manitoba, 1995). Manitoba restaurants boast a number of top-ranked chefs who have developed a distinctive 'Manitoba Regional Cuisine,' carrying off gold medals from the World Culinary Olympics and other international competitions (Tourism Winnipeg, 1999a: 1999b). The Manitoba Restaurant Association is more than fifty years old, has more than 500 members, and takes an active role in promoting the province's food-service industry. The association sponsors an annual trade fair, the Food and Beverage Expo, while some thirty of its more upmarket restaurants are featured at the Manitoba Food Fair, one of the more popular of Winnipeg's annual visitor attractions (Manitoba Restaurant Association, 2000). But as the statistics also show, most food expenditures are for more mundane dietary needs. As with world tourism, it is the largely unsung domestic tourist who consumes the bulk of the food and contributes most to the food tourism total. Thus, at the lower end of the hierarchy of culinary cuisine, there is a wealth of foods consumed by the local tourist and only to a lesser extent by the traveller from more distant parts, even though the latter may be critical to the success of the food outlets available.

Winnipeg festivals

Nowhere is the above relationship between domestic and international tourism more readily visible than at Folklorama, Manitoba's largest festival and most important annual tourist attraction. Begun in 1970 in celebration of Manitoba's centennial, Folklorama originally took place over a single weekend and was a totally volunteer-run operation comprising a mere handful of cultural groups. However, it became an instant success with the local population and is now a firmly established event in Winnipeg's calendar, normally spanning a two-week period in midsummer and consisting of around forty 'pavilions' scattered through the city, each representing one of Winnipeg's diverse cultural groups. The pavilions present displays, crafts, dances and, most important, a sampling of distinctive foods which, along with drinks, generate substantial revenues for the festival and its participant groups. In 1998, the festival attracted more than 425 000 visits to its pavilions, serving up 600 000 meals and 1 million beverages (Folklorama, 2000). According to Tourism Winnipeg's research, Folklorama in 1996 contributed C\$7.2 million to Manitoba's gross domestic product, more than twice as much as any other annually recurring event. With this growth, the character of the event has changed significantly.

Although volunteers and the ethno-cultural mosaic remain at the heart of the operation, there are now strong corporate and commercial interests involved. Folklorama is presently organized by the Folk Arts Council of Winnipeg, a non-profit corporation with a board of directors and a dozen permanent staff, including four marketing personnel. Their efforts are supplemented by the activities of Travel Manitoba and Tourism Winnipeg, both of which feature Folklorama in their promotional work. More than 20 000 people still volunteer their time to the festival, frequently giving up part of their holidays to the event. Others spend weeks and months in advance preparations. However, the large scale of current operations has meant that the bigger pavilions now contract out their food preparation to professional caterers and have to rent space for their activities. In 1998, only six pavilions failed to earn a profit, while twenty made over C\$6000 (Folk Arts Council of Winnipeg, 1998: 14). There are guidelines in place which seek to prevent profiteering, keep prices in line and ensure that the spirit of Folklorama is retained. However, participating organizations do use the event as a money-making venture to support their other activities and the event has now become very much a commercial operation. According to some, new volunteers are becoming more difficult to recruit and there are dark suggestions that 'money is being made on the backs of the babas', the dedicated, but ageing ladies who still spend countless hours of their time preparing foodstuffs for the occasion.

The Ukrainian Lviv Pavilion, one of the mid-sized pavilions operating out of the Ukrainian Labour Temple, still relies almost entirely on volunteer help. Its culinary crew meets in the spring to review past years' orders and begins purchasing bulk foods in May. Food preparation starts in early June, over a month before the festival opens. A fifteen-person team spends a total of 260 hours making, packaging and freezing more than 8000 pyrohi, a potato and cheese filled dumpling; another 150 hours is spent producing about 4000 holuptsi, or cabbage rolls; 60 hours making khrustyky, a light pastry dessert, along with the labour required to shred 100 lbs of beets and 500 lbs of cabbage for borscht and sauerkraut. These staple items are supported by freshly produced nalysnyky (cheese filled crepes), kapusta (baked sauerkraut, onions and cabbage) and kasha (buckwheat). Purchased headcheese, garlic sausage, bread, pastries and beverages round out the meal. Revenues from Folklorama net the Lviv Pavilion around C$12 000 with about 60 per cent of that coming from food and most of the remainder from entry passes. Clearly, the food component is central to the operation.

Tourists make a considerable contribution to the revenues. Many former Winnipeggers use Folklorama as an opportunity to visit with friends and relatives. Even if their visit is coincidental in time, they are inevitably invited to take in some of the activities. There are also special, major efforts to attract tourists to the event. The Folk Arts Council attends trade shows and arranges familiarization (FAM) tours for tour operators and travel agents across the USA and Canada. Their efforts have led to Folklorama being recognized as an 'Internationally Known Super Event' and the 'Number One Event' in Canada by the American Bus Association. The festival organizers claim that '30 per cent of attendees are from outside of Winnipeg, some travelling from as far as Australia, Korea and Paraguay' (Folklorama, 2000). Between 70 and 110 busloads of tourists take in the festival, most of them from the USA. The tour buses stay in Winnipeg between one and three days, are supplied with local guides and transported between pre-designated pavilions. Typically, the visitors are served an appetizer at the first site, a meal and a show at the principal stop, and possibly a dessert at their third destination. Although food is only one component of the total Folklorama package, it is an essential ingredient, not only as an attraction, but also as a supplementary revenue producer for the participant groups.

Winnipeg's two other major festivals operate along similar lines to Folklorama. However, there is less emphasis on food. The Festival du Voyageur, a ten-day event held in the French quarter of St Boniface, is Western Canada's largest annual winter festival and one of the three biggest Canadian winter festivals. As with Folklorama, Festival du Voyageur consists of a number of pavilions scattered through the community that are operated by sundry groups which offer entertainment and food services to their visitors. These highlight their French-Canadian, Metis, and fur-trading heritage, featuring favourites such as tortiere, pea soup, pork and beans, bannock and the like. Beaver tails, maple syrup and poutine have been more recent additions to the selections. The third largest festival, Winnipeg's own week-long version of 'Oktoberfest,' is billed as the world's third largest, and is essentially an excuse for swilling beer. However, it also features an interesting blend of delicacies such as 'Oktoberfest sausage on a bun with 4 perogies,' 'Knackwurst pizza' and sundry other innovative, but hardly 'authentic' dishes, which contribute to the event's revenues.

The previously mentioned Taste of Manitoba festival is held on the July long weekend, also in Winnipeg. More than thirty of 'Manitoba's great restaurants' attract in excess of 50 000 visitors (Manitoba Restaurant Association, 2000). Not only is the festival a major attraction in its own right, but it also lures people to the participating restaurants. For example, because of its participation in the food fair, the Roblin Inn succeeded in bringing the 1991 Canadian Association of Geographers' Prairie Division conference to Russell, in rural Manitoba.

Another interesting development in Winnipeg has been the generation of street festivals with a neighbourhood focus that feature the distinctive foods of the district and which attract the so-called intra-urban tourist. These are people who seldom, if ever, visit 'foreign' parts of their city unless attracted to do so by some tourism-like promotion. Two such festivals come to mind. The first, the Corydon Avenue's Days of Wine and Roses street festival was sponsored by the local Italian community and the speciality Italian restaurants along the Corydon commercial strip. What began as a local event promoting Italian culture and foods became so overwhelmingly popular, especially with the addition of huge bars pushing beer sales, that the whole scheme was eventually abandoned. As with some other tourist events, the festival's success in attracting massive numbers of visitors brought about its own destruction (Spina, 1998). Another street festival has recently been initiated in the inner city's Wolseley district. This residential enclave, known as Winnipeg's 'granola/muesli belt', has been experiencing a degree of gentrification, with its festival featuring 'veggie' burgers and carrot sticks, as well as the more conventional hamburgers and wieners.

An even less conventional festival featuring food, although not in the usual sense, is the Winnipeg Banana Festival. Not included in the mainstream tourism publicity and promotions of Travel Manitoba and Tourism Winnipeg, the

Banana Festival is an annual week-long event held in March and sponsored by 'Teasers', Winnipeg's principal burlesque house located in St Boniface. This event, dreamt up a decade ago by the proprietor, Sabino, began as a publicity stunt wherein patrons/exotic dancers participated in a simple banana-eating contest. Now, nearly a decade after its inception, the banana-eating contest has evolved into its current format. The showroom, decked out in a variety of bananas, inflated and plastic, some of them up to six feet in length, form a backdrop suspended around the room. Bunches of real bananas hang from the ceiling around the stage, ready at hand for the exotic dancers. These are plucked by the dancers and incorporated into their dances. Dancers also feast on the bananas with gusto with all the lascivious gestures and mannerisms reminiscent of the classic feast scene in the movie *Tom Jones,* urged on by the heavy beat and reverberation of the music, the deafening encouragement of the disc jockey, and the shouts and hooting of the patrons. The Banana Festival is advertised through mid-western cable television channels 8 and 4. Channel 8's primary market is Winnipeg, but it is also readily available to American audiences in Grand Forks, Fargo and the like in North Dakota and Minnesota. Channel 4 WDAZ, based in Fargo/Grand Forks, serves a similar region and also penetrates further south into the cities of Minneapolis and St Paul, reaching a potential total audience of several million people.

The American pornographic magazine, *Cheri*, which dubs itself 'the world's most explicit sex mag!' frequently features a multi-paged spread of Teasers' strippers, and in doing so, also promotes them as a north-of-the border tourist attraction. To quote from a recent issue:

> Winnipeg, Manitoba, has been called 'the dullest city in Canada, and therefore the world.' Of course that was *before* CHERI Magazine showed up. We went to this medium-sized city in Canada's 'wheat belt' to look for the finest flesh that the sleeping giant to the north has to offer . . . They searched – and they found . . . Maybe Winnipeg ain't so boring after all! Any town with a hopping strip joint like Teasers within its borders can't all be bad . . . And for anyone who thinks that Canadians are uptight or (pardon the pun) *provincial*, consider that even a farm town like Winnipeg permits bottomless dancing in establishments with liquor licenses – at a time when some clubs in New York can't even show *topless*. Kind of makes us here at CHERI want to apply for Canadian passports. (Anonymous, 1999)

Cheri's reporters showed up at Teasers' first Banana Festival in 1991 and have continued to promote the burlesque palace since then (Anonymous, 1991). Sabino, the former proprietor, claims that the festival attracts visitors from as far away as Toronto, Vancouver and other major Canadian cities, as well as from the USA. He estimates that the festival attracts around 60 per cent of its audience from south of the border. Furthermore, Teasers is locally owned and most of the strippers are from Winnipeg, resulting in there being very little leakage from the community.

Rural events

Food tourism is very important to the rural areas of Manitoba where there are literally dozens of festivals featuring food as their principal attraction. Virtually every Manitoba community of any size continues to put on its annual agricultural fair, an event dating back to the early days of settlement. Even more widespread and frequent are the harvest, fall/fowl suppers that take place around the province. These are concentrated in the autumn months, complementing the summer fairs and less frequent winter festivals and spring celebrations. The rural fairs and suppers feature local food specialities that include indigenous produce such as berries and fish, foods representative of ethnic concentrations of population, and agricultural produce special to the different regions. These differences are particularly noticeable in the south central part of the province with its higher population, rich chernozem soils, warmer climate and longer growing season that have encouraged the production of a wide range of speciality crops.

Among the larger rural summer festivals featuring food is the Morden Corn and Apple Festival celebrated at the end of August. Formerly a two-day event, it now extends over three days and attracts 40 000 to 50 000 visitors each year. Although the festival boasts a wide variety of attractions that include a midway, live stage entertainment, parade and a hundred or more booths and street displays, important lures are the free hot buttered corn on the cob and apple cider drink 'giveaways'. During the 1999 festival weekend some 32 000 corn cobs and 34 000 ciders were dispensed to the crowds. The Morden festival attracts numerous day visitors, including two busloads from Winnipeg, just over 100 kilometres away. However, many visitors stay over the weekend at the 100-unit local beach permanent campgrounds or the 135-unit temporary campground in the school yard.

At nearby Altona, the town's Sunflower Festival emphasizes the importance of sunflower and vegetable oil production to the local farm economy. Altona's Rhineland Agricultural Fair Day dates back at least to the 1930s and the Sunflower Festival, inaugurated in 1965, originally ran independently of the older fair (Town of Altona, 1999). The two operations have now been amalgamated and the two-day festival is celebrated at the beginning of

August. Whereas the fair focused on the more traditional agriculturally based activities such as farm implement displays, livestock and produce shows, the July festival features a more popular range of attractions and entertainment that include motocross races and a demolition derby. Distinctive food attractions have Mennonite origins, including 'rollkuchen', a pastry rolled out and deep fat fried, as well as sunflower ice cream. However, the festival's organizers determined that they would not boost their budget to compete with other localities for outside visitors, but should instead concentrate on providing the local community with some summer fun. Nevertheless, they are still concerned to attract tourists and are promoting the festival more widely. In contrast, Winkler, like Morden, has built its Harvest Festival and Exhibition into a major three-day attraction with a wide variety of entertainment and bus tours laid on from Winnipeg. The event still includes the Municipality of Stanley's traditional Agricultural Society Exhibits and Horse Show, but it also incorporates a parade, rodeo, fireworks, midway, Low German Theatre Festival, victory ball, queen pageant, Hutterite colony choir, Ukrainian dance ensemble, skateboard demonstration teams, square dancing, heritage fashion show, dog team performances, classic car show, and 'exciting live entertainment all weekend long'. Other highlights are free pancake breakfasts and a free barbecue with 'lots of Great Mennonite Food' (Town of Winkler, 2000). Clearly, these events, although still featuring agricultural produce, rely on other inducements to attract their visitors.

Further north, in the cooler, mixed farming area near Riding Mountain, the town of Russell celebrates its Beef and Barley Festival and Rodeo in October. Further east, at Ste Rose du Lac, the self-styled 'Cattle Capital of Manitoba', puts on its Hoof and Holler Days in the same month. These events feature 'western style' foods such as pancake breakfasts and a beef barbecue. Autumn events, and the prospect of Halloween, feature the pumpkin. An example is Teulon's Pumpkin Fest with its competition for the 'largest pumpkin, most perfect, most unusual and best carved pumpkin', along with its farmers' market and food booths. And then there is Roland's Pumpkin Fair featuring the giant pumpkin weigh-off and 'pumpkin desserts in the Pumpkin Patch Tea Room' (Travel Manitoba, 1999a).

Other small towns base their festivals on natural resources, for example, the Garland's Blueberry Festival, the St Pierre Jolys' La Cabane a Sucre and Selkirk's Manitoba Catfish Festival. These events have evolved as the different communities have sought to reposition themselves and lend uniqueness to their otherwise conventional summer festival fare. Then there are the more people-orientated celebrations: Brandon has its Children's Country Picnic, there's the Mother's Day Tea at Piney and the Father's Day

Smorg at Steep Rock. There is even recognition given to expatriate Maritimers with the Manitoba Maritimers Lobsterfest Picnic at Bird's Hill.

These events, as with most other Manitoba attractions, are largely directed at the local market. However, they have become essential ingredients in the drive to flesh out the menu of Manitoba's tourism offerings directed at Canadian and international guests. For Manitoba, one of the most effective ways of increasing tourism revenues is to persuade visitors to stay longer than they are otherwise prone to do. The promotion of food-based fairs and festivals is part of this strategy. Similarly, small-town Manitoba hopes to cash in on the wider market and to encourage visiting friends and relatives to return for perhaps an overnight stay.

The fall supper

Along similar lines, the fall, or fowl supper, is a Manitoban institution that appears to be undergoing a renewal despite the continuing depopulation of the countryside. Literally hundreds of these events occur each year, sponsored by church and community groups as a means of raising funds for a variety of purposes. Most suppers attract only a local clientele consisting of church members and neighbours, but many have risen in importance to attract 'out-of-towners' in large numbers. They are an important incentive to former residents and relatives of rural townspeople and the surrounding countryside to return for a visit to their roots. As Lucille Chappellez says of the St Claude fowl supper: 'People come from far and wide to attend this event which doubles as a reunion/gathering of old friends and family. People who have moved away from St. Claude will often return on this occasion to visit with their loved ones'. However, the fall supper is also an increasingly important mechanism for attracting the excursionist or para-tourist, particularly Winnipeggers out for a drive into the country.

The fall supper has its origins far back in time. They have evolved from being a purely local and primarily religious celebration of the harvest to that of a major fund-raising event. Nowadays, organized church support groups or secular institutions such as the chamber of commerce sponsor the fall supper. There are carefully worked out marketing plans designed, not just to notify, but to attract visitors from far afield, increasingly from metropolitan Winnipeg, the principal population centre. The season starts in September and runs through virtually to the end of the year when Christmas suppers take over.

The suppers are widely and intensively advertised locally using district newspapers, church announcements, posters and the like. However, to a growing degree, Winnipeg's principal newspapers and radio stations are asked to publicize the events. Last fall, the number of requests to the Canadian Broadcasting Corporation's Winnipeg regional network for inclusion of fall supper dates in its public service announcements reached such proportions that they could no longer be accommodated 'on air'. Fall suppers are also now being listed by Travel Manitoba in its *Events Guide*. The 2000 season's guide listed more than thirty suppers in its columns, more than doubling the previous year's entries (Travel Manitoba, 1999b: 2000). Countless more suppers rely solely on local advertising and word of mouth.

The popularity of the fall supper is quite immense, with the larger events drawing more than a 1000 people to share in the bounty of a single supper. In addition, many towns have several suppers in a single season. For example, Pilot Mound, some 200 kilometres from Winnipeg, hosts two fall suppers on consecutive weekends in October. Pilot Mound began its suppers back in 1963 to pay for the then recently built community hall. From that time, the institution burgeoned to the point where more than 1000 people were being served at each of the suppers. However, since the early 1990s, competition has increased so that a turnout of 600 or so is the norm. The suppers are advertised over a radius of approximately 100 kilometres, although some people are drawn from as far away as Winnipeg. Pilot Mound's suppers are operated by the chamber of commerce, which puts on four fund-raising smorgasbords a year, two in the spring and two in the fall. The town also hosts a United Church fall supper and the legion puts on a steak barbecue. Competition between communities is kept to a minimum by staggering the events among towns in the immediate vicinity of each other. Nevertheless, the district's local radio station at Portage-la-Prairie announced fifteen other suppers to be held on the same weekend as Pilot Mound's.

Part of the attraction of the fall supper excursion lies with the multicultural structure of Manitoba's communities, which lend diversity to the meals. Pilot Mound, in the south-west of the province, an area substantially pioneered by British migrants. Their fall supper menu is therefore relatively conventional and representative of the majority of the population: roast ham, roast beef, baked chicken, a variety of salads, aspics and pickles, followed by pies and other desserts, washed down with tea and coffee. However, at St Claude, a French Canadian community 100 or so kilometres to the east, essentially the same menu is slightly more flavourful. As an added touch, the very attractive table centrepieces of wheat ears, miniature squash and corn enhance the presentation of the meal. Further east again, at St Joseph, the flavour is even more distinctively French Canadian. There, tortiere is featured, along with hominy corn, bean pie and sugar pie. Wine is also available. At Dufrost, some

80 kilometres south of Winnipeg, there is a mixture of French Canadian and Ukrainian food on the menu. As a result, perogies, holuptsi and home-baked beans appear on the menu, along with the ubiquitous meats, salads, pies and desserts. Dufrost, with only a handful of local people, is a much more 'homespun' affair, although it does feed about 450 people over the course of the meal. Its suppers are held in a small hall that was formerly a church, creating a very different ambience from the much more spacious and more recently built community halls of the larger communities. It is interesting to note that many of these halls are being paid for by the proceeds from fall suppers.

It has not been possible to obtain conclusive data on the total number of fall suppers prepared during a season, but there can be no doubt that the numbers are high. Using a rough estimate of 300 people per supper, ten suppers per weekend, and a twelve-week season, this would suggest that in the order of 36 000 meals are served. With current prices now at around C$8.00 per plate, this would generate in the order of C$288 000 a year. Given the much higher numbers generated by some of the larger suppers, this is a very conservative estimate. With these numbers, it is obvious that the suppers perform valuable services to the host communities and to those who patronize them. For smaller communities they are a 'mini-mega' event, providing them with revenues to support a wide variety of facilities and services. These range from general support for community infrastructure to special projects such as the purchase of a wheelchair for a needy invalid. They foster community spirit in giving a sense of pride and purpose to residents in presenting the suppers. They also offer excellent value for money to the patrons who also enjoy the opportunity to socialize and to take advantage of these occasions to get out and enjoy the fall countryside. Weather conditions and the pressures of farm work can have a considerable effect on visitor numbers. Finer weather brings out more people, except farmers, who take the opportunity to work their fields. Adverse conditions reduce turnout. However, many people attend several suppers during the course of the season, often travelling much further than necessary because they 'enjoy the ride', or go out of their way to take in a supper destination more renowned for its cuisine than one that is available closer to home.

These numbers have brought changes to the manner of food preparation, although almost everywhere the emphasis is on local volunteer contributions. In Pilot Mound, one of the more 'commercial' operations, major food items are purchased from local suppliers and cooked in the town bakery rented for the occasion. These include four whole hams of about 80 lbs each, a hip roast of beef of about 100 lbs, and 1200 pieces of chicken. Initially, volunteers would start peeling potatoes at five in the morning for the dinner, but now powdered mix is used. However, volunteers still prepare the salads, pies and other desserts, with the country ladies producing them for one of the suppers and the town ladies for the other. The women slave over the dishes in the kitchen down in the basement, while the men serve the meals. The school's student council is given C$100 for providing clean-up assistance. Because the hall seats only 250 people, clean-up is continuous throughout the meal period. As elsewhere, it is becoming increasingly difficult to find the necessary volunteers to meet the demand (Krotz, 1993; Simon, 1999). Pilot Mound used to have fifty or so men to call on; now there are forty volunteers altogether. The declining rural population, changing demographic structure and reduced volunteerism are taking their toll. Nevertheless, net proceeds from Pilot Mound's two suppers amount to between C$7000 andC$8000 a year – a profit similar to that produced by the St Claude supper.

Because of these potential profits, many communities are now aggressively marketing their suppers and developing new initiatives. St Claude, for example, advertises in six district newspapers as well as notifying the Winnipeg press; five television stations are notified; posters are displayed in all towns within a 40-mile radius of St Claude, and larger billboards are placed on Highway No.2, which passes the town. St Claude is also involved with the Gathering of Nations Festival, an annual rotating festival including St Claude, Trhearne, Swan Lake, Somerset and Pilot Mound. Other communities have learned the benefits of cross-marketing their supper with other events. Eriksdale, for example, now schedules its fall supper to coincide with the town's Cream of the Crop horse sale, an important regional attraction in the Interlake. Some communities, like Miami, St Joseph and Cook's Creek have also attracted organized bus tours out of Winnipeg (Fehr, 2000). Smaller communities are also benefiting from one-off tours by special interest groups such as the Manitoba Historical Society and geographical associations which for years has led groups of their members and other interested parties on trips around the province. These tours rely very heavily for their success on the dining component of the trip. Itineraries are built around places that are able to offer the trippers a 'unique' dining experience offering 'authentic' recipes prepared in the traditional manner, and often served up in a relatively rustic setting.

Discussion and conclusion

Food is fundamental to survival. Eating is an acknowledged part of the tourist experience and is featured in a significant amount of tourism promotion. The tourist is necessarily eating away from home, but food is also a strong motive for travel. To many, dining out is relaxing and an opportunity to relieve the cook from the drudgery of everyday living. While eating away from home is enjoying a massive following, so combining it with and element of travel and a more exotic location is also growing in popularity. Food is a reminder of one's roots, a window into the identity of other cultures, and a pleasurable experience. For the tourist, therefore, the consumption of food is likely to be a central part of the travel experience.

Although much of what has been discussed in this chapter pertains to the excursionist and therefore is not tourism in the strictest sense, the events described are nevertheless taking on the trappings of mass tourism and pushing local organizers to larger-scale production to cater for the growing demand. To the small community it is immaterial as to whether the visitor is from Timbuktu or from another town. The small town, or community-based organization, is putting on its fowl supper as a revenue-producing device and it is of no consequence that at a regional level the money redistribution amounts to a zero-sum game. The local sees it as a means of obtaining visitor dollars to finance and help support the local parish or community facility. To the extent that the smaller communities can attract people from Winnipeg to their events, it is a reversal of the normal pattern of money flows and a worthwhile strategy in the struggle to maintain the health of the rural economy.

As postmodernists have observed, the world today is full of contradictions and counter-movements. The same can be said of the lure of food and current trends in food tourism. Globalization has led to homogeneity. Cuisine has been internationalized, food has become genetically modified, allowing it to be shipped worldwide, uniform in shape and taste, and lasting for ever. To even the most unsophisticated palate, the loss of taste, texture and flavour is conspicuous. Food is beautiful in appearance, even aroma, but in the eating a disappointment. It tastes the same. There is shape over substance. For mass marketing, these characteristics are accept-able and also desirable to many consumers. However, this leads to the counter-revolution. The jaded palate, recalling the succulence, juiciness, sweetness and variety of the taste experience, searches for the 'authentic'. There is a growing demand for organic farming, maintenance of the foodstuff gene pool, and the restoration of food varieties. This counter-movement expresses a desire for uniqueness, distinctiveness and the taste of authentic foods prepared in the traditional manner. Food fairs and festivals attempt to service both demands, appealing to those who want the convenience of eating out, and offering distinctive tastes to those who are seeking something different. However, in catering to these contrasting wants, compromises in preparation become necessary. Menus lose some of their authenticity by being produced in large quantities for a diversity of tastes. Just as with most other tourism attractions, as food becomes commodified, it is adapted to satisfy tourism demands.

11

The Bluff Oyster Festival and regional economic development: festivals as culture commodified

Kristy Rusher

Why, then the world's mine oyster

Which I with sword will open.

(William Shakespeare, *The Merry Wives of Windsor*, in Line, 1995: 60)

Introduction

For human societies food is 'the sense of identity which is at the core of human autonomy. The biological need for food and the social act of eating combine to give . . . a particular meaning, a kind of cultural power' (Simpson, 1999: 6). In the postmodern era, festivals and events have provided communities with an effective means of affirming their cultural and regional values and identities. Food as a central element of cultural values and regional identity is a popular theme and central focus of New Zealand events and festivals. However, the audience for such festivals and events is much greater than its immediate regional community. Increasingly, such festivals and events have attracted tourists from other parts of New Zealand, and have also included participation by international tourists to the region. Host communities have leveraged this attention to derive commercial benefits from the media coverage, tourism and economic activity generated by these events. These efforts have been so successful that using festivals and events as instruments of regional development is a strategy now frequently employed by New Zealand's rural and peripheral regions. Food and wine are therefore important elements in regional development due to their role in the commercialization of New Zealand's regional identities at festivals and events.

This chapter describes the social and cultural significance of oysters in New Zealand society, and how these values have been leveraged to create the Bluff Oyster Festival, an entertainment commodity central to the economic development of the Invercargill City and Bluff communities.

Oysters and culture

When oysters first became a part of New Zealanders' diet has never been recorded. However, it is likely the practice began as a continuation of the dietary heritage of the main cultural groups of Pacific Island, Asian and European origins who settled in New Zealand. Eating oysters 'unites us with all our ancestors – [it is] the dish you consume in what is recognizably the way people have encountered nourishment since the first emergence of our species' (Fernandez-Armesto, 2001: 2). Oysters have been a part of the human diet and hence human society and culture since neolithic times. Middens of ancient peoples, which contain remnants of oyster shells, reveal that the oysters were a significant component of early human diets, most probably because they did not require cooking.

In neolithic times this type of food source would have been particularly important to those cultural groups with nomadic or migratory behaviours. Subsequently, oysters also became an important commodity, cultivated and transported across vast distances to sate the palates of settled societies.

Regional variations in oysters caused by minor differences in location, and tide movements affect the flavour, size and shape of any oyster (Line, 1995). 'An experienced person can often tell from the shape and appearance of the shell from what bed any particular oyster has come' (Younge, 1960). These differences are reflected in great variations in the commercial value of oysters. As a result, even in ancient times, traders went to extraordinary lengths to satisfy demand for oysters from particular regions. The Chinese, Greek and Roman cultures have all been recorded as cultivating oysters in pre-Christian times due to the healthy commercial returns for a product which could be supplied more reliably and with lower harvesting and transportation costs. Oysters collected from as far away as the English Channel were rapidly transported in barrels of snow over the Alps to be delivered live to Rome's markets. These oysters sold for their weight in gold (Line, 1995: 17).

In America, oysters grew on mangrove tree roots, as well as the sea floor. Native Americans are the only cultural group that have been recorded as collecting and cooking 'tree' oysters and are therefore also credited with creating oyster stew (Williams and Warner, 1990). However, the new settlers continued their cultural legacy by damaging the newly discovered oyster beds in the same way as the European beds had been – by over-harvesting and later poisoning the oyster beds from effluent dumped by the cities built on the oyster estuary shores.

As well as being a culinary delicacy, oysters also have a history of use for other purposes. The ancient Chinese primarily used oysters as a medicinal cure for minor ailments and impotence. Oysters were dried before eating to cure skin problems such as acne and freckles. The use of oysters for medicinal and health purposes was also documented in eighteenth-century England. 'In Wales it was believed that pale young women would improve if they were fed oysters' (Williams and Warner, 1990: 41).

Settlers of European and Asian origin have a long-documented cultural heritage associated with the eating of oysters, which were imported along with other cultural artefacts to their new Antipodean homes. However, the origin and cultural significance of oysters within the Pacific Island cultures which settled in New Zealand prior to the European and Asian groups, is less clear.

'Captain Cook on arrival in New Zealand found that the local people ate mainly oysters, mussels and cockles which they collected from the rocks and mud banks of the seashore' (Coupe, 1991: 107). As Maori society was a solely oral culture, the observations and documentation of their cultural and social practices begins during these early and infrequent contacts preceding colonization. Each tribe had their own independent identity and culture, so it cannot be inferred from Cook's observations that oysters were a significant component of Maori culture and diet throughout New Zealand. However, it may be more valid to conclude that there was a high degree of awareness of this food product throughout the various tribes, given that Maori language differentiates between oyster varieties using the names tio, tio para, tio repe, for both the rock oyster (*Crassastrea glomerate*) and the deep water oyster (*Ostrea angasi*) (Fuller 1978).

Oysters and society

The choice and use of foods has historically differentiated social groups within a community. 'Those groups in society who are better able to create notions of "good taste" – legitimate the forms of consumption to which they have more access. They are able to define their bodies, their lifestyles, and, in this case, their preferred food choices as superior, worthy of respect, and "classier"' (Crotty, in Germov and Williams, 1999: 144).

Despite the oyster's status as a delicacy in Europe during the Middle Ages, due to the scarce supply as a result of overfishing, and the shrinking of their breeding grounds (Fernandez-Armesto, 2001), European settlers in New Zealand perceived oysters as a food for the poor. 'Dickens, in the Pickwick Papers has Sam Weller remark that oysters and poverty always seem to go together' (Coupe, 1991: 107).

New Zealand's abundant supply of oysters in harbours throughout the country, and the availability of other sources of protein meant that this inherited attitude persisted until relatively recently. Initially, a social statement was made in terms of excluding the oyster from the diet of the more socially prestigious households, but this attitude later softened when social status became differentiated by *how* food was prepared and served rather than *what* food was prepared and served. 'Instead of the differences in the use of single foods, social classes . . . differ in the way they talk about food, set their tables and combine their foods into dishes and meals' (Crotty, in Germov and Williams, 1999: 145).

Due to the abundant supply of oysters, differences in social structure were not reflected in terms of access to this food product during this period. Instead, social structure was reflected in how oysters were gathered and served. Low-status social groups typically ate deep-fried battered oysters, while higher-status social groups served oysters raw with lemon juice, reflecting their modern ideas about food brought back from their travels on the 'Big OE' (overseas experience) in Europe and Australia. In the diet of New Zealanders in the 1940s, when retired fish retailer David Fairweather was a child, oysters were a staple food. 'They were eaten by everyone in those days. They were an ordinary man's meal . . . Families would have a feed of oysters and chips two or three times a week' (personal communication). David Fairweather describes a time when oysters were sufficiently prolific to be harvested without catch restrictions.

The food experience of the generation following David Fairweather was vastly different. Oysters' social status as a food product climbed dramatically. Although there is no written record of this rapid transformation, the change can be explained as the result of a combination of several factors. Commercial fishing became a heavily regulated industry and recreational harvesting of oysters from some areas became prohibited. The oyster industry also suffered when disease and over-harvesting dramatically affected the size of harvests taken from many oyster beds, including those of the Bluff oyster discussed in this chapter. This reduced the number of oysters available on the market and social groups with low purchasing power were unable to continue eating oysters as a major part of their diet. More stringent health regulations meant that oysters had to arrive at markets quicker and be delivered using refrigerated transport. This increased processing costs, further escalating retail oyster prices. Also, as a result of government-initiated health campaigns, New Zealanders were encouraged to adopt healthier eating practices. These campaigns discouraged the Friday night tradition of purchasing deep-fried fish and chips. The success of the campaign, combined with an increase in alternative takeaway foods and the subsequent decline in fish and chip shops has resulted in a corresponding decline in the number of retail outlets for householders to buy oysters. National retailers take extraordinary steps to be the first to stock the Bluff oyster, due to its status as a delicacy, but the majority of oysters are purchased from restaurant menus, although small quantities are often found at supermarkets and some of the few remaining fishmongers that have survived the growth of the mass food retail industry.

The Bluff oyster and Foveaux fishing industry

The Bluff oyster (*Tiostrea Chilensis*, formerly known as *Ostrea lutaria*) is named after the small town of Bluff located at the bottom of New Zealand's South Island. This species of oyster is found in other parts of New Zealand, but only grow in sufficient numbers to make it commercially viable to harvest them in the Foveaux Strait, between the bottom of the South Island of New Zealand and Stewart Island, New Zealand's third largest island. The Bluff oyster is famous for having a superior flavour, which is highly distinctive from those oysters grown in other parts of New Zealand. Experts attribute the flavour difference to the water purity and tidal movements of Foveaux Strait.

The development of the Bluff oyster industry has been turbulent, but is currently worth approximately NZ$30 million to the Bluff and Invercargill region. The industry began when the first commercial oysters were taken on Stewart Island in the 1860s, but such was the exploitation that the oyster had become so small as to be of little market value and fishing there virtually ceased.

As a result of several other oyster beds being overfished in the region, the New Zealand government began to regulate the fishing industry. A harvesting season of seven months was imposed. By 1969, the industry harvest size had been restricted to 170 000 sacks of oysters (approximately 10 200 000 dozen oysters) each season and the season was cut back to six months. However, between 1993 and 1995 the Bluff oyster industry closed as there was no harvest due to an outbreak of the Bonamia parasite in the oyster beds. The parasite invasion decimated the oyster population, causing concern that the species would become extinct. Less than 10 per cent of the oyster population survived the outbreak. As a result, the oyster season now opens for approximately five months and the harvest is restricted to approximately 20 000 sacks of oysters (1 250 000 dozen oysters) to allow the oyster beds to recover.

The local fishing industry has also been affected by the fishing quota system that the government introduced in 1988 to better manage fish reserves. Under the quota management system, only fishing companies can commercially harvest oysters in Foveaux Strait. Each oyster boat was allocated a specific number of oysters they could harvest. These quotas had to be reorganized among the oyster-boat owners when the government transferred ownership of 10 per cent of the quota to Ngai Tahu (the local Maori *iwi* or tribe), in settlement of Treaty of Waitangi grievances.

External factors can also intervene and interfere with the supply of the oysters. Bad weather can prevent the oysters from being harvested, leading to long interruptions in supplying oysters to restaurants. The amount of phytoplankton carried by the tide can also affect the size of the oyster, causing significant variations in quality.

Continuing restrictions on harvesting, difficulties in ensuring a regular supply of a consistent product, and the intense demand on this regional food product means that its status as an elite food product continues to grow. This further enhances the value that the community place on the product and the social status associated with consuming it, and reinforces the status of the Bluff oyster as not only a highly prized regional food product, but also an icon of cultural and regional identity.

Symbolic consumption of cultural icons: wine and food festivals as entertainment commodities

Festivals and events are 'specific rituals, presentations, performances or celebrations that are consciously planned & created to mark a special occasion or to achieve particular social, cultural, or corporate goals & objectives' (McDonnell, Allen and O'Toole, 1999: 10). Modern food and wine festivals are derived from the practice of holding feasts in medieval times.

> Many occasions [for feasts] were regarded as suitable: religious festivals such as Christmas or the end of Lent; or secular ones such as the end of harvest or sheep shearing. The main purpose of a feast was a celebration, and a formal feast was part of all ceremonies, such as coronations and receptions. These feasts demonstrated the wealth and taste of the host and reaffirmed his place in the social hierarchy. (Hammond, 1993: 216)

Similar to the medieval feasts, the essence of the food and wine festival is an affirmation and celebration of common cultural values. However, in this style of event the nature of celebration is staged, and is devised specifically to display local culture to attract and entertain a large audience, rather than mark a significant community milestone. Such festivals raise awareness of the host community and region, repositioning or reaffirming the region in the minds of festival attendees. It is therefore not surprising that the Bluff oyster is the subject and theme of a wine and food festival. For the host community, the oyster symbolizes their regional identity and, given the social status of oysters in the New Zealand diet, the event also provides the opportunity for festival attendees to indulge in consuming gourmet food items.

Consumption at food and wine festivals is largely symbolic as people consume for pleasure rather than survival, and engage in eating practices different to their normal food habits. The social norms of consuming food at a food festival are vastly different to those concerning food behaviour and habits in other contexts. Examining the motivation for behaviour provides one explanation for why social norms differ between consumption contexts. Maslow's hierarchy of needs provides a useful framework for examining such motivations. In situations outside the festival environment, eating is first concerned with satisfying survival needs. Depending on the consumption context other needs will also be satisfied. 'Eating for survival evolves into eating to satisfy needs for security then for belongingness then for self-esteem, and finally for self-actualisation' (Ikeda, 1999: 150). The relative importance of meeting these needs is determined by the consumption context. This influences the individual's behaviour in terms of the choices that are made regarding food selection, quantity consumed and to what degree the individual will comply with the social norms that regulate the food habits and behaviours within that context.

Food festivals are a unique context where usually strict social norms regulating consumption habits and food behaviour are relaxed. Relaxation of social norms creates a socially endorsed hedonistic environment in which individuals can express self-actualizing consumption behaviour. For some individuals, self-actualization is the creation or deepening of new social relationships or affirmation of their position within the community. Such individuals attend and consume at festivals in order to 'be seen'. Other individuals express their self-actualizing behaviour by taking full advantage of socially endorsed hedonism to indulge in consumption by imbibing quantities of food or drink in excess of their typical habits, or in consuming food and drink which they would not select in usual circumstances. Self-actualizing consumption is 'a medium for social relationships [where] satisfaction of the most individual needs becomes a means of creating community' (Visser, 1991: ix).

The Bluff oyster as the regional food product is the symbol of the values and culture of the Invercargill and Bluff communities. Individual and community attitudes and values have formed as a result of the style of work involved with the harvesting and selling of the Bluff oyster. In fulfilling their need for self-actualization, the festival attendees are also endorsing the cultural values of the community by purchasing food and wine products symbolic of the region.

Community support as an essential ingredient in the success of the Bluff Oyster and Southland Seafood Festival

The Bluff Oyster and Southland Seafood Festival has its origins in a small community festival, organized as a fund-raising event for local schools and other community organizations. The event had run successfully for several years, with attendances growing. In 1996, The Bluff Promotions Committee approached the Invercargill City Council for assistance in developing the event further. At the same time, the Invercargill community was discussing the possibility of designing a festival around the region's seafood industry. In 1997, the Bluff Oyster Festival was amalgamated into the first Bluff Oyster and Southland Seafood Festival. While the festival was still held in Bluff, reflecting its origins, the organization and administration of the event was transferred to the Invercargill City Council, causing resentment among some sectors of the Bluff community who felt that this conflicted with Bluff community ownership and involvement in the event.

The Bluff Oyster and Southland Seafood Festival is a six-hour event that has attracted a peak attendance of more than 3000 people. A small entrance fee is charged, and event attendees purchase food and wine. The festival provides all-day entertainment, with two small stage areas. One stage is devoted to competitions such as the Oyster Sack Fashion Parade, where competitors make clothes and wearable art out of the sacks used to collect and store oysters. Other popular competitions, which capture media attention, are the oyster-opening competition and the oyster-eating competition. Audience members are invited to pit their skills against Southland's best. Winners are awarded a small trophy and cash prize, or three dozen oysters. The second stage is dedicated to live music and performances from performing arts students, community groups and professional entertainers from the local community. All the entertainment is sourced from the talent base of the local community, which is also involved in organizing the entertainment and competition programmes.

The festival has run successfully since 1996. However, despite the intensive planning for the 2002 Bluff Oyster and Southland Seafood Festival, it was almost cancelled. As Julie Paterson, Venture Southland Promotions and Events Manager, stated:

> Never in my wildest nightmares had I ever dreamed the weather would be as bad as it was. We've had periods of rain (close to the festival day) and I used to think, oh I wouldn't mind if it rained – as long as it's coming straight down or, I wouldn't mind if it's an overcast day just as long as it's not too cold. Never did I think that it would be hurricane type weather.

The festival's outdoor marquee was torn apart by high winds just two days before the event was to be held and the bad weather was forecast to continue over the festival weekend. This meant that a new indoor venue had to be found in less than twenty-four hours. The community rallied to ensure the festival went ahead. A major agricultural company made their Invercargill wool store available as an alternative venue. Despite the extra work that was required in setting up the festival in an indoor venue, the residents of Invercargill and Bluff pitched in.

> On Friday we had to set the whole venue up and they (Invercargill and Bluff residents) were all there with their husbands and kids and dogs and

the whole ten yards and everybody did everything that they could because at the end of the day it was about the festival, and about the festival being really good and Southland and Seafood and Bluff Oysters and all those sorts of things being shown in a really positive light and they could see that.

The exceptionally rough weather had also prevented oysters from being harvested for sale at the festival. The day before the festival, one boat owner braved the atrocious conditions to get oysters for the festival. 'In the future I think we would try to dredge oysters ahead of time and keep them underwater for the festival'. An oyster-processing factory deferred their normal process-ing schedule in order to prepare the oysters in time for the festival opening. However, the demand for the oysters was so great that within fifteen minutes all the oysters had been sold.

The weather conditions did not improve on the day of the festival. Surface flooding on the major highways into Invercargill, deterred many people from attending from outside the Southland region. Despite the rough weather, the lack of oysters and difficulties of advertising a last minute venue change, attendance at the festival was only slightly less than the highest ever attendance figures.

The success of the 2002 festival in overcoming the threat of cancellation was ultimately due to the support of the Bluff and Invercargill residents for the Festival. The extra effort that residents put in to stage the festival, and the high degree of participation and effort made to provide food and entertainment illustrate the value and importance the community places on the festival as a means of promoting their community values and the region. This form of support is essential for the success of this kind of event.

Exhibit 11.1 Risk management planning: insurance, regulations, licences and permits

There are myriad risks involved in organizing a food festival. The foundation of an effective risk management strategy is applying three key principles. First, identify all the potential risks. Second, identify the probability of the risk occurring. Third, minimize the risk by using planning techniques to eliminate as far as possible the likelihood of the risk eventuating and to control the impact if should it occur.

Serving food and wine is an area in which risks are commonly identified, as public health can easily be compromised at this style of event. The Bluff Oyster and Southland Seafood Festival involves barbecue-style outdoor cooking and serving raw foods. There is a risk of food becoming contaminated at the festival due to food-handling practices that have to be adapted to an environment with limited water, limited working space and limited ability to clean food equipment. Food handling within the festival environment is therefore very different to that of a restaurant where food contamination risks are easier to control.

Responsibility for managing public health and food safety at the Bluff Oyster and Southland Seafood Festival lies with the Environmental Health Department of the Invercargill City Council. The department controls this risk by issuing stallholders with licences to sell food at the festival. The stallholders must satisfy the department that they are equipped to comply with the food safety and handling standards outlined in brochures included within the festival's stallholder registration pack. However, despite intensive planning, it is not possible to minimize the likelihood of some risks eventuating. Instead, it is the impact of these risks that must be managed. Weather is an example of this type of risk.

The weather had a considerable impact on the 2002 Bluff Oyster and Southland Seafood Festival, almost forcing the cancellation of the event. Hurricane-type weather decimated the festival site, damaging the marquees and other equipment that had been set up two days before the opening of the event. A new indoor venue had to be found and lost set-up time recovered before the scheduled opening of the festival in less than thirty-six hours. The impact of the weather on the success of the festival was minimized by the extra effort that Bluff and Invercargill residents and businesses made to relocate and set up the festival.

Arranging the correct insurance cover is also an important element of a risk management strategy. The Bluff Oyster and Southland Seafood Festival has insurance arrangements made by its organizers, the Invercargill City Council. The council arranges public liability insurance for the event, and further insurance for damage to property or the event site. Festival suppliers must have their own prearranged insurance before they are contracted to work at the festival.

Legal and regulatory compliance is also an important issue for a risk management strategy to address. Local authorities such as the Invercargill City Council are responsible for issuing licences for the sale of alcohol. The festival organizing committee arranges for a general liquor licence for the festival site, and stallholders are required to arrange their own licences if they intend to sell alcohol. The organizing committee also arranges for security services to have an obvious presence at the festival to manage any disruptive behaviour, and to ensure that the cash on the premises is secure.

Developing a comprehensive risk management strategy involves acting to minimize the probability of anything going wrong. It also involves making arrangements for complying with the laws and regulations of the local authority, especially in relation to liquor licensing issues. Contingencies must also be planned so that should any problem occur, the event is not threatened with cancellation.

Kristy Rusher

The Bluff Oyster and Southland Seafood Festival and economic development

Invercargill and Bluff are small communities with just 49 600 residents combined. Invercargill was founded as a port city to service New Zealand's growing agricultural base. The port was established in 1855 to import stock and farming products from Australia. Today, the city still acts as a hub to service the rural community of Southland. Half of all employment in Southland is based in the agricultural sector (Southland Spirit of a Nation, 2002), illustrating the dependence of the region on one industry for economic stability.

Economic success is an important value within the Bluff and Invercargill communities. The city has constantly struggled to diversify its industrial base, and dwindling returns from the agricultural sector before the turn of the century meant that the city became economically marginalized. The construction of the Tiwai Point aluminium smelter slightly revitalized the economy. However, changes to the management of the commercial fishing industry and the 1987 share market crash led to the closure of major employers such as the Bluff Ocean Beach Freezing Works, instigating a second and more prolonged economic downturn.

In response to the economic downturn, Southland District Council launched a major economic and community development campaign, 'Venture Southland' aimed at attracting new businesses and industries to the region to diversify the economic structure of the community. An economic revival of the city has begun due to these economic development initiatives and also improving returns from the dairy industry.

The Bluff Oyster and Southland Seafood Festival is an overt symbol of the value that the Southland community places on community and economic development. Generating economic success has been an important theme and feature of the community's history, and has therefore become a central value in the community's social identity. The Bluff Oyster and Southland Seafood Festival was designed as an innovative way of raising awareness and creating a positive image of Southland, to encourage further commercial investment. A further objective of the festival was to stimulate economic activity from planning and staging the event, and also to inject more money into the region from tourist spending. This strategy has attracted a growing number of visitors from outside the Southland region. In years prior to 2002 between 30 per cent and 50 per cent of festival attendees lived outside the Southland region.

The major commercial benefit of the festival is the media attention it attracts for the Southland region. As television coverage is expensive, and beyond the promotional budget of the region, the national news report covering the festival is a free, national profile of the region. Increasingly, the event has also been attracting international media attention.

Surprisingly, this media profile has little or no effect on the sales of Bluff oysters. Processing factories do not report a spike in demand immediately before or after the festival. Instead, the oyster industry reports that the main benefit from the festival is creating awareness that the oyster season is open, and Bluff oysters are available on the market. This initially seems to be a surprising result, but industry experts think that in such a tightly regulated market, the Bluff oyster has such a strong brand presence that the additional awareness is likely to intensify existing competition to be the first to stock the product, rather than increase the size of the market demand for the oysters.

The Bluff Oyster and Southland Seafood Festival also has an important social function, in transferring values between successive generations. Due to the luxury status of Bluff oysters, and the three-year harvest hiatus, young New Zealanders outside the Southland region have low awareness of the Bluff oyster and its social and cultural significance. The festival communicates the importance and value of this product to this emerging market, ensuring the Bluff oyster's icon and social status continues.

Conclusion

The significance of the Bluff Oyster and Southland Seafood Festival is greater than providing a community with a means expressing and affirming its values and regional identity with a wider audience. The festival is the result of the community undergoing a continual process of transforming the essence of its values into a commercially viable entertainment product. In designing such a product, the host community is inviting visitors to place a commercial value on the host's regional identity and cultural values, particularly when the cultural significance is derived from the social status of a regional food product such as the Bluff oyster. In return, the host community can leverage the economic activity generated by staging the festival into commercial benefits to further their economic development objectives.

The Bluff Oyster and Southland Seafood Festival as an entertainment commodity created to celebrate a regional identity and food product, has made a significant contribution to the regional development of the Invercargill and Bluff communities by transferring cultural values to future generations and enhancing the effectiveness of the region's economic development strategy.

12

Food tourism in the Peak District National Park, England

Liz Sharples

There is now a growing recognition, in many parts of the world, of the importance of food to the overall tourism experience. There is also an acceptance that food is not always a mere supporting act in the tourism product. Sometimes it can, and does, play a starring role. Indeed, in certain situations around the globe, the promise of an exciting food and drink culture, or experience, can be the driving force that motivates and enthuses people to visit certain holiday destinations.

The linkages that exist between food, the landscape or place that the food has strong associations with, and tourism have started to form the basis of an interesting academic debate in recent years (see Chapter 1). For example, Reynolds (1993) discusses the importance of preserving traditional foods as an essential part of sustainable tourism, Telfer and Wall (1996) comment on the linkages that exist between tourism and food production, Hall and Mitchell (2000) debate the role of cuisine as a factor in globalization and localization and Hjalager and Corigliano (2000), examine the development of food standards for tourists. There are many others.

Part of this important debate is the concept that 'local' food can form an essential and innovative part of a regional tourism marketing strategy and this argument is now gaining ground. There are a growing number of public and private initiatives that demonstrate a commitment to this idea. Examples of this include, the Countryside Agency's recent 'Eat the View' campaign, aimed at promoting sustainable local products within specific regions (Countryside Agency, 2001) and a joint publication between the Countryside Agency and the English Tourism Council (English Tourism Council, 2001) which makes recommendations about the use of local produce as a vehicle for enriching the rural tourism experience (see also Chapter 2).

This chapter discusses the way in which food tourism initiatives are now starting to be used as a vehicle to benefit both the tourism and the food/ agricultural industries within the English Peak District. The study brings together information derived from a number of secondary and primary sources. Key literature provides a useful theoretical background, while data collected during a series of interviews and observational sessions, held in four key food/tourism organisations in The Peak District, forms the basis for a number of case studies. The four cases (Exhibits 12.1, 12.2, 12.3 and 12.4) , namely, the Chatsworth Farm Shop, the Old Original Bakewell Pudding Shop, the Hartington Cheese Shop and Caudwell's Mill, demonstrate the diversity of food tourism approaches currently on offer to visitors travelling to, and within, the Peak District. They also enable the reader to reflect on the current situation with regards to regional food tourism policy in the UK.

The chapter concludes with a discussion about a number of pilot projects, based around food tourism, which have taken place in the Peak District during 1999–2002. With a focus on the promotion and use of 'local' foods, it is hoped that these schemes will act as a catalyst, and provide a framework for, strong and sustainable development of the food tourism product in this area.

Tourism in the Peak District National Park

The county of Derbyshire lies in the centre of England, approximately 180 miles to the North of London, and surrounded by no less than six other counties – South and West Yorkshire to the north, Lancashire, Cheshire and

Staffordshire to the west and Nottinghamshire to the east and south. The county is also encircled by a number of large industrial cities and densely populated areas including Manchester, Sheffield, Nottingham and Derby. The terms Derbyshire and the Peak District are commonly used as one, although this is not strictly accurate. About three-quarters of the National Park's 555 square miles lie within the county of Derbyshire but the park also includes small parts of some of the surrounding counties. The area known as the Peak District actually involves seven local authorities, four regions and six counties, and yet it has a strongly defined geographical identity (Prince, 2002).

The Peak National Park was set up in 1951 in an attempt to 'protect and enhance this precious landscape and to provide quiet, open-air recreational opportunities for visitors' (http://www.derbyshire.gov.uk). It was Britain's first National Park. The Peak District Authority plays a delicate balancing act in attempting to meet both conservation and recreational aims as well as looking after the livelihoods and lifestyles of the 38 000 people who live and work within its boundaries.

The managing authority has two statutory purposes:

- To conserve and enhance the natural beauty, wildlife and cultural heritage of the area.
- To promote opportunities for the understanding and enjoyment of the Park's special qualities by the public (http://www.peakdistrict.org).

Any development in the Park must bear these objectives in mind.

This is a county of extreme geographical contrasts, the harsh dramatic 'Dark Peak' moors and gritstone edges balanced against the gentler, more sheltered 'White Peak' limestone dales which lie to the centre and the south of the region. It is this unique landscape that is the main 'pull' factor for the region, but the park also boasts a fascinating history and culture. The Peak District National Park currently attracts 22 million visitors annually, making it the most heavily used National Park in Britain and the second most visited National Park in the world (http://www.derbyshire.gov.uk; Prince, 2002).

In particular, the county attracts 'adventurers'. Walkers, climbers, cyclists, cavers and other outdoor enthusiasts, of all abilities, are drawn to the region, which has features such as the 2088 ft Kinder Scout, a number of interesting walking and cycling routes including the Tissington, High Peak and Monsal trails, an impressive collection of caves in the Castleton area and extensive gritstone edges and limestone walls (http://www.derbyshire.gov.uk). More 'sedentary' visitors can find interest in a number of stunning historical buildings such as Chatsworth House, Haddon and Hardwick Halls, a host of museums and attractions based around the county's industrial past, such as Cromford Mill, and in the attractive towns such as Bakewell, Buxton and Matlock.

Exhibit 12.1 The Chatsworth Farm Shop

The Chatsworth Estate, home to the Duke and Duchess of Devonshire, is one of Derbyshire's best known tourist destinations, attracting thousands of visitors a year from across the globe. The 14 000 hectare estate extends over 30 miles, 2500 hectares of which are farmed 'in hand' with the grasslands surrounding the house being used to farm deer, sheep, dairy and beef cattle as well as providing an extensive area for public recreation. The estate contains a number of different visitor 'experiences' including the house itself, which is open to the public for much of the year, the formal gardens, an adventure playground, a children's farm, garden centre, several gift shops and a restaurant and bar situated in the original stable block.

The Chatsworth Farm Shop is another 'success story' in the Chatsworth portfolio. Located in the village of Pilsley on the Chatsworth Estate, the shop is housed in the corner of what was the Estate Shire Horse Stud, originally built in 1910 for the breeding of heavy horses.

At its opening in 1977, the shop had just one clear objective: as a direct outlet for the sale of large 'freezer-style' packs of the estate's beef and lamb and the pork from one of the estate's tenant farmers. It quickly gained a reputation as being a provider of good quality meat at a fair price. The sale of the estate's pedigree Jersey herd in 1982, which had occupied part of the stable block, allowed the shop to expand and, therefore, extend its product range. The butchery started to offer a wider range of retail meat cuts and a small kitchen was introduced to bake bread, cakes and cooked meats and pâtés. At the same time the remaining part of the building was converted to workshop space for local craftspeople. This pattern of use remains today with several outlets being occupied by gift shops, artists and textile/knitwear manufacturers.

Since that time there has been a steady growth of the farm shop business, both in the range of products that the shop now offers, but also in the way that the products are developed, marketed and sold. In 1991 the shop space was completely gutted, extended and refitted in order to comply with, and keep ahead of, the latest hygiene legislation, and in 1999 new kitchens were built to streamline the production of 'in-house' products.

The shop has now become one of the top speciality food shops within the country and has won a string of awards including; the 'Best Farm Shop in Britain' by Henrietta Green's *Food Lovers Guide to Great Britain* in 1977 and was awarded the title of 'Best Speciality Food Retailer' by the *BBC Good Food Magazine*. In 2001 the *Independent* newspaper listed Chatsworth in their top ten of speciality food shops within the UK. Since 1992, the shop has also been listed as a Q-Guild butcher putting it among the top 150 butchery shops in the UK.

The product range is now extensive including fresh produce – meat, fish, vegetables, fruit, herbs, and dairy products; delicatessen items such as cooked meats, pâtés, cheeses and savoury pies, bakery items such as home-made cakes, biscuits and breads, and provisions such as preserves, tea, coffee, chocolates, beer, cider and fruit wines. The shop also offers the 'Duchess of Devonshire' brand of speciality foods which is exclusive to the shop and is a reflection of the energy and enthusiasm that the family still devotes to the organization and management of the shop.

Mail order is another important part of the business, allowing visitors the opportunity of maintaining their connection with the shop once they have returned home and also providing the mechanism for sending exclusive gifts to friends and family. Mail order is available for simple provisions such as meat and cakes and the shop offers an extensive 'hamper' list with prices ranging from £30 to £150.

Despite the growth, the Chatsworth team remain loyal to their original 'food-sourcing' philosophy with a focus on the sale of fresh produce obtained from its own farms and also products that have been manufactured on the premises. The remaining lines are bought in from either local suppliers, i.e. from within a 40-mile radius or from top-quality British producers. The Chatsworth shop also aims to stock those products that are not readily available in the high street supermarkets, thus retaining some exclusivity.

The Derbyshire shop has undergone changes over the last year and in 2001 the coffee shop that is housed in one of the stable units was refitted to form the Stud Farm Pantry, serving an extended menu including hot lunches prepared with Chatsworth produce each day.

Source: interview with Mr Andre Birkett, Manager of the Chatsworth Farm Shop, data collected from their web site (http://www.chatsworth.org) and in-house publicity material.

Liz Sharples

Food tourism and regional identity

As noted in Chapters 1 and 3, in some countries and regions of the world the existence of a very strong food and drink culture, that is actively protected and promoted, as part of an overall tourism product, is both assumed and expected. In certain regions of the UK there have been recent attempts to rekindle interest in local food and drink products and traditions that have a strong identity/link with a specific geographical area (see Chapter 5 in this volume). Several areas have undertaken a partnership approach to the development of regional food policy and identity. One such region is the North East of England, where academics from the University of Newcastle's Centre for Rural Economy (http://www.ncl.ac.uk/cre/abou) have worked alongside the Countryside Agency and other partners to see how the 'Eat the View' project (Countryside Agency, 2001) and other regional food initiatives could be developed in the North East. To date, the centre has been involved with the launch of a new regional speciality food group, Northumbria Larder, and the organization of the region's biggest ever food festival, held on the banks of the River Tyne, in spring 2002 (Henderson, 2002). The team has also been working on a feasibility study to inform the National Trust about the viability of opening a farm shop on the Wallington Estate (Henderson, 2002). Research carried out by the Newcastle team in the late 1990s (Kuzenof, Tregear and Moxey, 1997; Tregear, Kuzenof and Moxey, 1998) has undoubtedly been useful sources of information for these projects. However, in other parts of the UK, and indeed the world, despite sometimes the existence of strong agricultural traditions and an availability of unique and interesting food and drink products, there has been less of a commitment to the development of regional food policy linked to tourism. As the Enteleca report (Enteleca

211

Research and Consultancy, 2001: 2) comments: 'In other countries or regions tourists have little recognition of this element in the culture of the region. Concerted marketing efforts will be required to raise the profile of local products and influence consumer attitudes.'

The following section contains a simple analysis of the four case studies contained in the chapter, which provides an insight into the range of food tourism opportunities on offer in the Peak District and a reflection on the strength of its regional food identity.

Food tourism in the Peak District : analysis and reflection

It could be argued that a food tourism 'experience', either at an individual site or at a regional level, is made up of a number of key elements which, together, form a unique package for the visitor to interact with. The relative success of a food tourism initiative will be determined and influenced by a number of internal and external factors, which may vary over time. Before embarking on any new venture an honest assessment of the market that the initiative is hoping to attract/interact with is required, together with a realistic assessment of what the venture can sensibly offer to this market. This needs to be followed by a careful 'putting together' of the key elements, in order to present an innovative, yet cohesive, offering. For the purpose of the research leading to this chapter it was decided to summarize and analyse the data collected under four main elements in order to assess the food tourism experience that is currently being offered in the Peak District:

- food and product
- place and landscape
- people and market
- promotion and packaging.

Food and product

- The region has a simple, well-established, agricultural heritage focused on sheep, beef and dairy cattle, which the farming community and the Peak District authorities are keen to maintain. The direct linkages between locally produced food and the landscape are therefore easily demonstrated to the visitor. For example, at farm shops, farmers' markets and on menus in local hospitality outlets.

- The Peak District has a strong historical background, and has already demonstrated its ability to promote this type of tourism. This knowledge could support future development of events/attractions based on the historical/cultural aspects of food, e.g. food events based on a particular period in history.
- There are a number of good stories and myths linked to food held in the region. For example, the history of the Bakewell pudding. These stories can add interest and authenticity, and can be used as a promotional tool.
- The businesses visited all offered a range of 'added value' opportunities. For example, cafés, craft shops, food gifts and books. This enhances and lengthens the stay time by the visitor and can increase average spend.
- The National park is home to one of the 'top' farm shops in the country (Chatsworth). This is a good example of best practice for other businesses to learn from and is a popular attraction in its own right.
- The county of Derbyshire is one of only three counties in the world that is registered to make Stilton cheese. The county produces four protected destination of origin (PDO) cheeses (see Exhibit 12.2), more than any other county in the UK.
- The food sourcing strategies used by the businesses are not wholly consistent, however. Some are committed to the idea of local sourcing, for others it is less of an issue.

Exhibit 12.2 The Hartington Cheese Shop

The picturesque village of Hartington in Derbyshire is one of the most important centres for Stilton cheese production in the UK. The village itself is situated in the south-west of the county, close to the spa town of Buxton, in the heart of limestone country. The attractive valleys of Dovedale, Berisford Dale and the Manifold Valley are close by, and the area is particularly popular with walkers and cyclists, being close to several of the Peak District's long-distance walking and cycling routes. Hartington has therefore become an important centre for visitors who are drawn to the beautiful scenery that this area has to offer and it contains a number of good guesthouses, pubs, cafés and gift shops neatly located around the village green.

The Hartington Creamery was established over 100 years ago, by the Duke of Devonshire, purely to manufacture Stilton due to the plentiful supply of milk that is produced by the dairy herds which thrive in these valleys. Originally, the creamery struggled as a business but in 1900 it was bought by Thomas Nuttall of Beeby, in Leicester, and since then has gradually gone from strength to strength. In 1962, the creamery was sold to the Milk Marketing Board, and it became a division of Dairy Crest in 1982. The factory now employs in the region of 200 staff and has won numerous awards for the excellent cheeses that it produces.

The dairy manufactures a number of cheeses under the 'Hartington' brand but the speciality cheeses that the centre is best known for are Blue Stilton, White Stilton, Dovedale Blue and Buxton Blue. Blue Stilton is probably the most widely recognized of these and has earned itself the title of the 'King of English Cheeses'. All four of these cheeses are protected by a certificated trade mark, the PDO, which is a European Community Council regulation (Reg. 2081/92) which prevents other producers from copying the cheeses and also sets a standard about how and where the cheeses can be made (http://www.defra.gov.uk/foodrin/foodnamePFNames) (see Chapter 3). Stilton, for example, can only be made in the three counties of Derbyshire, Leicestershire and Nottinghamshire and is currently made in just twelve dairies. The sources of milk for the production of the cheeses are also restricted by the PDO and, as such, the majority comes from within the Derbyshire boundary. Hartington is by far the largest of the Stilton producers and currently makes over 50 per cent of the total UK production.

In the mid-1980s a shop was established in Hartington to retail a selection of cheeses both to locals and visitors to the town. Conveniently sited close to the factory but facing on to the village green this tiny shop has become a tourist attraction in its own right. The shop is housed in an eighteenth-century outhouse, which at one time was part of the creamery manager's house. After falling into disrepair, the building has been completely refurbished, in a traditional style, in keeping with its village setting.

The shop stocks in the region of thirty cheeses, primarily good quality English varieties, but with an emphasis on the cheeses produced at the factory. The shop also stocks a limited amount of complementary gift ideas such as cheese boards, knives, tea towels, books and postcards.

The employees who work in the shop are well informed about the cheeses they are selling and are happy to share this knowledge with visitors who may be buying a particular cheese for the first time.

The majority of visitors come from within a 50–60 mile radius but the shop also welcomes visitors from around the globe who have included the Peak District in their itinerary. American and Canadian visitors are particularly well represented.

The shop is open seven days a week throughout the year in order to capture the weekend tourist business and also to provide a service for the local customers. The business is particularly busy at Christmas time due to the high demand for Stilton-based gifts and hampers which are particularly popular at this time of the year.

An informative web site is used to promote the shop and includes a number of 'added-value' opportunities for the cheese lover. The site offers an online shop, a wealth of information about the cheeses sold, a range of cheese recipes, information about suitable wines to accompany particular cheeses and details of how to join their Cheese Club. The site also contains useful information about Hartington and the surrounding area.

The concept of opening a visitor centre at the factory, has been discussed but at present the company has decided that the idea is not feasible.

Source: an interview held with Mr Alan Salt, Dairy Consultant for Dairy Crest and from the shop web site http://www.hartingtoncheese-.co.uk/creamery/shop.

Liz Sharples

Place and landscape

- There is a strong commitment in the region to the notion of 'sustainability', as demonstrated through National Park statutory agreements. The promotion therefore of a more localized food economy linked to the conservation of the countryside through good farming practices could support this. This policy could then be used to educate and inform visitors to the region.
- The region already has a good infrastructure in place, with regards to transportation links, accommodation and hospitality outlets, which will support future tourism development.

- The park has an interesting industrial archaeology, including a unique working roller mill (Caudwell's Mill). This, and other historical buildings, such as old farm buildings and stables, can effectively be used to showcase food initiatives and are strong attractions in their own right.
- Many of the businesses visited are located in attractive rural settings which can enhance/extend the visit.

Exhibit 12.3 Caudwell's Mill

Standing next to the River Wye in the hamlet of Rowsley, near Matlock, Caudwell's Mill is a unique Grade II listed water-powered roller flour-mill. There has been a mill on the site for at least 400 years but the present mill was built in 1874 by John Caudwell and ran as a family business for over a century. E. Caudwell (Rowsley) Limited, which worked the mill until 1978, claimed at the time that it was the smallest commercial flour miller in the country. After its closure as a commercial enterprise it was bought and restored by the Caudwell's Mill Trust Limited, which now manages the day-to-day running of the site.

The mill has become an important tourist attraction offering a number of different experiences for the visitor. The complex machinery needed to grind the flour is situated in the fascinating four-floor mill building, which is powered by two water turbines, driven by the adjacent river. The mill machinery runs daily and visitors can pay a small admission charge to tour the building. There are numerous displays, hands-on models, and information cards designed to make the visit as enjoyable and informative as possible. The mill has become a popular attraction for school parties and groups who can book a private tour, but is also visited by a steady stream of individual visitors. They are drawn, undoubtedly, by the 'magic' of the milling process but also by the simple product that is produced as a result, good quality flour.

The small mill shop sells a range of different flours and supplies a host of free recipe sheets designed to tempt visitors to make a purchase. The range of flours includes the classic strong wholemeal flour, the mill's 'core' product, but also strong white flour, malted flake flour, rye flour and a number of 'speciality' flours including pizza base, French, pastry and white cake self-raising. Oat flour and quick oats are also available. The flours are packaged in uncomplicated paper sacks in a range of sizes from the usual 1.5 kg bag up to a 32 kg sack, designed for catering purposes. The arrival of the bread machine in many people's homes has had a major impact on the popularity of the flour and has been an influential factor in the expansion of the product range. Ironically, and quite sadly, the mill is no longer able to mill all the flour required. The running of a mill at a commercial level takes time, effort and finance to be able to service and clean down the machinery and, although the trust has the expertise, it does not have the personnel to facilitate this. Some of the flour is still milled in-house but some is now supplied in bulk by another local mill, which still operates on a commercial basis. However, all Caudwell's flour is packaged at the mill. This fact is not hidden from the visitors, which does not appear to deter them from making a purchase.

The buildings surrounding the mill have also been put to good use. One houses a busy café, which has an emphasis on whole-food and vegetarian dishes made from natural ingredients, including the mill flour; an ideal opportunity for visitors to taste the product. The old mill stables have now been converted into a number of craft workshops and include a blacksmith making traditional wrought metalwork, a glass-maker, an artist and a ceramics producer. At the other end of the site there is a large craft/gift shop selling an extensive range of books, pottery, glassware, jewellery, clothes, children's toys and ornaments, many with a local emphasis.

Source: informal interviews with staff from the Caudwell's Mill Trust, a range of in-house publicity material and the Arkwright Society leaflet (1993).

Liz Sharples

People and market

- The region already has a ready-made market due to its unique geography and National Park status. Some of its visitors will be keen to learn more about the local food culture.
- The thousands of visitors that visit the park each year need feeding. There is an enormous potential here to showcase local recipes and ingredients through the many hospitality providers.
- A number of skills associated with food are held in the region, e.g. cheese making and flour milling. These can be used to add value to and enhance the visitor experience.

- Owing to the decline in agriculture in the National Park there is a potential workforce who could become involved in the tourism sector.

Promotion and packaging

- Most of the businesses visited have a useful web site based around its own activities, but only one of the sites was accessible via an 'official' Peak District web site. This was the Old Original Bakewell Pudding Shop, accessible through the Derbyshire County Council site (http://www.derbyshire.gov.uk). This site, coincidentally, has a small section devoted to some of the local delicacies, e.g. Stilton cheese and Ashbourne biscuits but, unfortunately, fails to give detailed information on where to source them.
- Each business has been proactive in developing good publicity material focused on its own facilities and activities but there was little evidence of 'joint purpose', i.e. relationship marketing. For example, despite the fact that two of the food products, Stilton and Caudwell's flour are supplied to the Chatsworth Farm Shop, they do not appear to stock each other's literature.
- The production of local food directories within the region that list key food producers is valuable, e.g. the 'Savour the Flavour' leaflet (Peak District Foods for Tourism, 2002), the 'Taste of Derbyshire and the Peak District' (Women's Food and Farming Union, 2002), both described later in the chapter, and the East Midlands Food Directory (Speciality Food from Britain). Several of the businesses visited, however, were not aware of their own inclusion in the directories and therefore did not stock/promote the publication.
- Promotion of the businesses tends to be carried out on an individual basis. This could make it difficult for the tourist who wishes to access an 'overall picture' of regional food or for the visitor who wishes to access information prior to the holiday, perhaps via a tourist web site. A visit to several of the other key Peak District web sites, used to promote the area to potential visitors, confirms this. The official Peak District National park web site (http://www.peakdistrict.org) contains a wealth of useful information for the visitor, but food and dining out in the Peak District are hardly mentioned. Likewise, two other web sites, (http://www.peakdistrict-nationalpark.com) and (http://ww.cressbrook.co.uk,) are useful general sources but contain little information for those visitors interested in seeking out good food.
- Several of the businesses visited had postal shopping/online shopping facilities for personal purchases or gift sending. This is a highly effective promotional tool as it can build up an effective database, which can extend the market and generate repeat sales.

Exhibit 12.4 The Old Original Bakewell Pudding Shop

Situated in the centre of the picturesque market town of Bakewell, the Old Original Bakewell Pudding shop has been in existence since the 1860s when Mrs Wilson, wife of a local candle maker started the successful business from her cottage, where the shop stands today. The history of the Bakewell pudding, proudly recorded on both the shop's web site and on free leaflets available in the shop, is an essential part of the product. This is what gives the puddings some authenticity, some strong connection with the past, a feeling of tradition derived from the fact that the recipe has been passed down over the generations and is still made according to the original recipe. The story tells us that Bakewell puddings were first made by accident at the nearby White Horse Inn when there was something of a misunderstanding between the innkeeper, Mrs Graves and the cook. Important visitors to the inn had requested strawberry tart but the cook reputedly spread the egg mixture on top of the jam rather than adding it to the pastry as instructed and hence Bakewell puddings were discovered. Mrs Wilson managed to obtain the recipe around this time and hence the business was born. The recipe remains a company secret and has a protected trade mark.

Since this time, Bakewell puddings and tarts have been made and served throughout the UK and the dish has become a national favourite. The popularity of the dish has been given a boost in recent years due to the fact that traditional puddings, such as the Bakewell pudding, have enjoyed a revival, thanks to the efforts of celebrity chefs such as Gary Rhodes, who have brought regional food firmly back onto the food agenda. The business, ideally located on Bakewell's main street, has now become something of a tourist attraction in its own right, and has gradually expanded its product range in an attempt to maximize visitor impact.

On the ground floor there is a bakery offering a wide selection of breads and baked goods to both locals and visitors, but with a strong focus on their range of Bakewell puddings, offered in three sizes with prices ranging from 99p to £3.30. The puddings are still handmade on the premises with some of the ingredients being acquired locally, although this is not a specific company policy. The shop extends throughout the ground floor offering a range of speciality food products, gifts and handmade chocolates.

Upstairs there is a restaurant, serving drinks, cakes and hot and cold lunches where the emphasis is on simple home cooked food at 'value for money' prices. The restaurant provides the business with the ideal opportunity of allowing visitors to sample the famous Bakewell pudding before buying one to take home.

A new venture is the opportunity to participate in an evening Bakehouse Tour, which includes a 'hands-on' bakery session, where visitors have the chance to make their own Bakewell pudding, followed by a meal in the restaurant. Participants can then take their own pudding home.

The Bakewell Pudding shop also offers a successful mail order service. Boxed Bakewell puddings can be sent throughout the world, carefully boxed with a personal message, and this service has proved to be very popular as a novel gift idea. The shop can even organize a monthly pudding delivery to a named recipient. The shop also produces a mail order catalogue, which offers a range of food hampers, speciality foods and gift ideas. In 2001, over 9000 catalogues were mailed out to customers.

In 2002 the shop was acquired by the Holland family, local farmers from the area, who also run a successful bed and breakfast business. They are in the process of extending and improving the product range sold through the shop in an attempt to keep at the 'cutting edge' of customer demand.

Source: interview with Gill Salmon, Shop Manager of the Old Original Pudding Shop, the website (http://www.bakewellpuddingshop.co.uk) and in-house publicity material.

Liz Sharples

These exhibits highlight the fact that initiatives linking food and tourism can stem from a range of different 'starting points', each with it's own unique focus, business objectives, product type and target market, which they hope to attract. While providing the visitor with variety and interest, this diversity of approach can present a challenge to regional bodies when attempting to market the destination as a whole.

In the case of the Peak District, the exhibits reveal a rich heritage attached to local food production, and capable of providing the visitor with a number of different and exciting food-centred opportunities. However, the success of these businesses appears to have come about by individual effort, rather than by a co-ordinated approach championed by the various Peak District authorities.

To the outside world the Peak District remains known as a place of great beauty and as a playground for recreational pursuits but fails to have a strong presence with regard to its food heritage. Its culinary delights have not, as yet, been actively used as a tool for promoting the area and therefore food does not appear to be a key motivator that would tempt visitors to make specific forays to, and within, the region. The following sections examine a shift in approach, which is gradually, and deservedly, bringing Peak District food into the spotlight.

The Peak District: a new awareness

The situation in the Peak District has recently started to change with a growing recognition of the need to use and promote the local food resource more successfully. It is now acknowledged that 'local' food could be used to enhance/add value to the Peak District tourism experience while also securing a future for the farmers and small food producers who work and live in the National Park.

This new awareness has been stimulated by a number of national and regional factors. For example, food production within the UK rural economy is changing. The publication of the enquiry led by Sir Don Curry, following the recent Foot and Mouth crisis, reveals a farming and food industry that is unsustainable in the long term (Policy Commission on the Future of Food and Farming (PCFFF), 2002). One of the key themes of the report is a call for 'reconnection' between all the stakeholders along the food supply chain. One of the ways of achieving this is a move towards more localized food economies. The report notes 'We think the time has come for locality food marketing to become mainstream in Britain as it already has in France and elsewhere' (PCFFF: 119).

Agriculture within the Peak District is in decline whilst tourism has grown in importance (Prince, 2002). This echoes the national trend. Tourism in the UK is now worth 4 per cent of the gross domestic product (English Tourism Council, 2001), while agriculture accounts for 1 per cent (DEFRA, 2002). Farm incomes have dropped by 60 per cent in the last five years (English Tourism Council, 2001). This shift has resulted in some farmers looking at ways of diversification into new markets, e.g. bed and breakfast businesses or the conversion of farm buildings into self-catering accommodation (see http://www.peakdistrict farmhols.co.uk but there is still a need to maximize the income that comes from more limited farming operations. It has been identified that if the local food resource is promoted and sold within the region, for example through farmers' markets or by local food businesses, this could improve profitability by shortening the food chain.

In UK rural areas, the proportion of visitor spending retained locally averages only 30 per cent in accommodation, 20 per cent in catering and attractions and 5 per cent in retail businesses (English Tourism Council, 2001). This trend is also evident in the Peak District. Prince (2002) reports on a study carried out by the Peak District National Park Authority in 2001 showing that 45 per cent of the total expenditure by visitors (day and overnight) is spent on eating and drinking. The study showed that 63 per cent of spending on supplies and services by the tourism businesses to provide this service went to businesses outside the study area. This dilemma is discussed in more depth in Chapter 13.

A number of factors including the recent BSE and Foot and Mouth outbreaks have resulted in many UK consumers looking for some reassurance about the quality of the food that they purchase. The growth in the organic food sector has been significant (Soil Association, 2002) and 'traceability' has become a key issue for some people who now actively seek out 'local' food. These food scares have created tension within the farming community but also provide farmers and small food producers with an ideal opportunity of 'reaching out' directly to the consumer with the offer of good quality, traceable produce. The notion of incorporating local food as part of the tourist product is therefore a sound one as many consumers are already receptive to, or actively seeking, this concept. As the recent Policy Commission on the Future of Farming and Food report (2002: 119) suggests: 'One of the greatest opportunities for farmers to add value and retain a bigger slice of retail value is to build on the public's increasing enthusiasm for local food, or food with a clear regional provenance.'

There is also a growing identification of the need to preserve and celebrate regional food skills, traditions and cuisine within the UK, and this initiative has been brought to the public's attention by a number of different stakeholders. For example, the message has been delivered by a number of celebrity chefs and television personalities, such as Gary Rhodes, who has dedicated a cookery series to regional British dishes, and Rick Stein and Monty Don, who have toured Britain in search of local food excellence. In March 2002, the BBC Radio 4 Food programme (www.bbc.co.uk) discussed how regional foods and dishes could be used to promote a region. Organizations such as Common Ground (http://www.commonground.co.uk) continue to emphasize the importance of preserving local distinctiveness within communities. More recently a number of government and other national reports (e.g. English Tourism Council, 2001; Policy Commission on the Future of Farming and Food, 2002) acknowledge the importance of retaining these local food traditions and also recognize that these can be an attractive vehicle for marketing an area to visitors.

Making the link: a new way forward

In the Peak District there have been several recent moves that have demonstrated the region's interest in investigating the linkages that exist between local food and tourism. For example, in 1999 a project was set up in conjunction with Middle England Fine Foods (MEFF), one of the local food marketing networks operating under the 'Food from Britain' banner, to encourage the sale of local foods both in shops and in hospitality operations. It was envisaged that this initiative would be of benefit both to local consumers and to tourists visiting the area. The project has had a number of outcomes including the widening of the MEFF membership, the organization of several events designed to showcase local produce, a joint venture with the Peak District Farm Holiday group to inform tourists about local food suppliers and the launch of a local specialist food directory containing details of all MEFF members. This Leader II project was partly funded by the European Agricultural Guidance and Guarantee Fund and the Ministry for Agriculture, Forestry and Fishing (MAFF).

More recently has been the emergence of a national 'Food and Drink in Tourism' project, a three-year pilot project, which has been led by the Heart of England Tourist Board. A number of associated schemes/initiatives have been set up under this remit with a plan to 'roll out' best practice/models learnt from the work throughout the country (http://www.hetb.co.uk/non-member/research-and-dev/food-and-drink.asp).

This major project, has received funding from a number of different organizations including: the English Tourism Council, the East Midlands Development Agency, Advantage West Midlands and the Countryside Agency, and supported by Heart Of England Fine foods, the Department for Environment, Food and Rural Affairs, the Royal Agricultural Society of England, East Midlands Producers, Farm Stay UK and various local authorities. The project encompasses the Heart of England Tourist Board area, with Derbyshire and Staffordshire, two of the Peak District counties, being involved. The aim of the project is to develop the distinctiveness of the Heart of England through its food and drink culture. The project involves:

> working in partnership with the farming, speciality food, food-processing and tourism industries to enhance the region's products by:
>
> ■ strengthening the links between the food and tourism sectors
> ■ encouraging tourism businesses to source food locally and to use seasonal produce
> ■ creating and developing locally distinctive cuisine
> ■ creating added value for leisure and business visitors and increased visitor spend
> ■ celebrating excellence through an awards scheme.
>
> (http://www.hetb.co.uk/non-member/research-and-dev/food-and-drink.asp)

This project has provided financial and advisory support for a number of schemes that clearly demonstrate the links between food and tourism.

Linking producer and consumer

In March 2002 a directory and web site (www.peakdistricts.co.uk) of small food producers, farm shops and farmers' markets in the Peak District was produced. It is envisaged that the contacts made during the preparation of this directory will help to form a strong network of local suppliers. The publication *A Taste of Derbyshire and the Peak District* contains information about approximately forty suppliers. The work has been co-ordinated by the Women's Food and Farming Union, but has been supported by a number of different funding organizations. It is hoped to link this web site with all of the other key Peak District sites.

New Environmental Economy Programme

The objective of this programme (see details on the Peak District Authority web site – http://www.peakdistrict.org) is to work with small businesses in the Peak District with the aim of encouraging the generation of new products and services which use the environmental assets of the area as a key ingredient. Local food could be defined as one of these assets. A number of interrelated projects have been set up under this banner which will draw funding from a number of different funding agencies. The Heart of England Food and Drink Tourism project has collaborated on three of these projects and funded one of them:

1 *Peak District Food and Tourism*: this is an important project led by the University of Derby exploring the links between the local food industry and tourism industries. For those businesses involved with food it aims to develop new food products and markets through the tourism sector. For tourism businesses it hopes to create distinctiveness on menus in local hospitality outlets. This project has been funded by the Heart of England Food and Drink Project, the Peak District Rural Development Programme, the Peak District National Park Authority, the North East Staffordshire Single Regeneration Budget and the Regional Enterprise and Development Office (RED) at the University of Derby.

2 *Peak District Environmental Quality mark*: this is a national pilot scheme being driven by the National Park Authority. The project has an aim to develop a new accreditation scheme for products and services, which make a contribution to environmental conservation. Food, tourism and craft businesses will be involved. It is envisaged that this quality mark will be used as a marketing tool in the generation of new business. This project relies upon funding from a number of agencies including the Countryside Agency, the East Midlands Development Agency and English Nature.

3 *Making the Most of your Milk*: this is a project aiming to encourage local dairy farmers to look at the possibility of developing new businesses based on the milk that is currently being produced. Local cheeses, yoghurts and ice cream are obvious ideas that could be produced on either a small 'farmhouse' scale or at a factory level. Funding for this project comes from a number of sources including the Department of the Environment, Transport and Regions.

The New Environmental Economy Programme is also involved with a number of other projects, funded by other agencies, that have a strong food tourism link. These include the expansion of produce/farmers' markets throughout the region supported by Derbyshire Dales District Council and the High Peak Borough Council in collaboration with the University of Derby Catering Training Department with the aim of developing a 'Peak Cuisine' concept for the region. This would encourage caterers to use locally sourced ingredients on their menus.

The Peak District Food and Tourism project, carried out over just five months, has been a particularly fruitful scheme and has produced a number of very useful outcomes. Sue Prince, a Derbyshire-based organic dairy farmer, who also runs a successful bed and breakfast and holiday cottage business from her farm, has been the driving force behind its success.

Prince has carried out some very useful research, outlined in a project report (Prince, 2002) and been responsible for some very positive actions including:

- the production of two new publications, one aimed at visitors entitled *Savour the Flavour of the Peak District* which lists local food producers, farmers' markets, special food shops, and Women's Institute country markets and, the other, *Peak District Food News*, a simple leaflet designed to provide a link for local food/tourism businesses
- the establishment of an embryonic collaborative network, Peak District Foods, linking food producers with other food producers in the area
- the development of two new food products aimed specifically at the tourist market, Peak Eats Ready Meals and Wakes Cakes (see Chapter 13 for more details).

The National Food and Drink in Tourism project has also been responsible for the setting up of several award schemes designed to award hospitality operations which demonstrate a commitment to the use of local food on their menus. Derbyshire and Staffordshire have an involvement in this scheme which they co-ordinate at regional level.

Conclusion

Until recently, the food available to the Peak District tourist has been viewed as a given (Hall and Mitchell, 2000) and has arguably been seen as having a secondary role compared with the host of other activities and opportunities that are on offer in this unique National Park. Despite the fact that many of the food-related businesses have been individually successful, the park authorities have just started to recognize the importance of food to the tourism product, and the role that local food *could* play, in the overall marketing of the region.

Future plans are dependent on harnessing the energy and enthusiasm of a number of key stakeholders, from both the food/agricultural and tourism sectors, in order to drive forward, and build on, the good work that has already been started. Initially, it is likely that any schemes and projects will be reliant on a certain amount of external funding but it is hoped, in time, that these initiatives will become self-financing. The co-ordination of any activities across the region will be a key factor and the appointment of an officer to take a holistic approach to the problem may be a way forward. The region contains a complex set of geographical and political boundaries, which could prevent easy communication and decision making.

A comment made in the report, researched and written as part of the Peak District Food Tourism Project (Prince, 2002) is revealing in that in the Peak District Local Authorities' (2002) tourism literature no food-related events or stories are listed. This is because when they went to press no food-related events had been planned in the Peak District. Hopefully, this situation is starting to change and the region's food will begin to reap the acclaim that it rightly deserves.

13

Valorizing through tourism in rural areas: moving towards regional partnerships

Jane F. Eastham

Introduction

In declining agricultural/rural areas, tourism is often promoted as an alternative economic activity and a means of stemming the decline of peripheral regions (e.g. Saeter, 1998; Smith, 1988). Tourists are attracted to the countryside in order to live, for whatever period of time, the 'ideal life' inherent in the Western conception of rural life. Global and local economic climates of overproduction and competition have encouraged governments, farmers and other interest groups to seek alternative uses for the areas of land traditionally used to grow food. Tourism has been identified by many Western societies as a solution. Yet many suggest that the extent to which tourism provides real value to a community

(Dwyer et al., 2000; Frechtling and Horvarth, 1999) depends on the level to which it may support existing economic activity. This chapter examines how local economic growth from tourism is dependent upon the endogenization of the multiplier effect through the recoupling of the food production and supply system. The chapter then goes on to explore different models which have, in part, or wholly recoupled the supply chain in given rural areas and discusses the relative merits of these models.

The changing countryside and food chain

In the UK there has been a continual change in the structure of agricultural businesses. Between 1975 and 1990 the numbers of farms declined (Gardner, 1996) by some 400 000. These were principally smallholdings found on marginal land in remoter rural areas. These figures hide much complexity. While there was a total decline in the number of farms in the UK, there was also an increase in the number of larger holdings, from 5000 to 20 000, although figures have not been static in recent times due to the BSE and Foot and Mouth epidemics. During the years that followed BSE, farmers in marginal areas either sold out, or supplemented a marginal income through diversification or outside employment. A recent report indicated that more women than ever have been forced to leave their farms to find additional work, e.g. as teachers or secretaries (Francis, 2001).

While figures may be currently changing, Eurostat (2000) indicates that only 1.7 per cent of the population work on the land, many of whom run their farms single-handedly or as a small family team. Contrary to common belief, for many ex-farmers the loss of their farms will not constitute an enormous financial loss. Indeed, Rowe (2000) reports that an average-sized UK farm in the year 2000 could draw only £8000 per annum as opposed to £80 000 five years ago.

Causal factors

There are a number of factors, which have been identified as key to the changes in the structure of employment and response to restructuring within rural areas:

- intensification of farming methods
- deregulation of global markets
- decline in tenancies and a move towards farmer ownership
- fuel prices
- non-membership of the euro

- competition between food businesses within a mature market
- consolidation within the food supply structures
- increased power assymetrics on the part of the food retailers
- consumer and social trends.

The intensification of farming, particularly in the UK, has been a long-continued development since the eighteenth century. The agricultural revolution, the move from mixed to non-mixed farming, and intervention by the British government and, indeed, the Common Agricultural Policy (CAP) can be seen to have contributed towards the change in the manner in which rural economies operate.

Under the European CAP agricultural production in the EU has increased by 6 per cent per year (Gardner, 1996). Even in the UK where earlier industrialization of farming resulted in less change, intensification of farming methods ensured that output grew by 25 per cent between 1970 and 1980 (Gardner, 1996). In the EU, intervention pricing protected the larger UK farmers against the impact of global prices and cheaper imports. This was supported by a system of import levies which were based on the differences between the minimum EU price and the world price. Furthermore, export subsidies compensated those wholesalers or traders who sold surpluses to the world market. In many respects intervention had proved successful. Farmers did find that they benefited from intervention pricing, but this was disproportionately in the favour of larger farms, while smaller farms have increasingly sought alternative sources of income.

The CAP was substantially reformed in 1992 with a move towards direct payments to farmers, but the key changes to European policy stemmed from the Uruguay General Agreement on Tariffs and Trade/World Trade Organization (GATT/ WTO) round and the Agriculture Agreement, negotiated between 1986 and 1994. These included an agreement to cut the base level for tariffs before 1995, which was implemented with a view to reducing the distortion to trade (Goodman and Watts, 1997).

A deregulated market has had an effect on the viability of farms at two levels. It appears that on one hand, open markets have resulted in price slumps, particularly given the fact they are subject to fluctuating exchange rates. On the other, the high rate of the pound against the dollar and euro made UK produce prices uncompetitively high which has resulted in a number of farmers selling up or making further staff reductions.

In recent years the media has emphasized the crisis in the agricultural sectors (Jackson, 2000; Walker, 2000) and reports of farm failures and bankruptcies make a periodic but regular appearance on national news. At a regional level, the government has brought agricultural and rural regeneration under the Department of Transport, Local Government and the Regions (DTLR) and focused regeneration support through regional development agencies, designed to support the regeneration activities of urban areas.

Impact of supermarkets on farming and intermediaries

There are other changes which have had a negative impact on farming and rural economies. The dominance of multiple retailers in the food sector after the dismantling of the Retail Prices Act in 1964 (the dismantling of the Retail Price Mechanism enabled supermarkets to pass on savings on operating costs brought about through the format to consumers), has eventually led to the loss of many of the traditional supply chain players within the food sector. The increased competition between retailers battling for market share in an increasingly mature marketplace has resulted in the demise of many of the intermediaries, and hence led to job losses, within the supply chain, e.g. wholesale markets (Allen, 2001). Many small abattoirs have also been closed, although changes in legislation have also been a contributory factor (Beer, 2001).

The central distribution and purchasing systems established in the 1980s have bypassed the intermediates between the farmer and retailer, further reducing operating costs for the multiple retailers. This has had serious implications for farmers, who have found that with the loss of many of the traditional supply chains, access to the marketplace has been limited. For many, alternative land uses have proved to be a solution, for others there has been a need to expand, while for some there has been a necessity to downsize, particularly labour, with significant impacts on employment within rural areas. Furthermore, while current measures, e.g. the recently established 'Race to the top' project (Burns, 2002) and local sourcing policies of supermarkets, might do much to eliminate this trend, supermarkets have been continuously accused of forcing down prices at the farm gate as a means of reducing the overall cost of food to the consumer. This has had a significant impact on the viability of farms.

Large retailers have impacted on employment in other ways. Over thirty-five years, the growth in market share of supermarket chains has led to the loss of general stores in villages and between 1991 and 1997 a total of 4000 food shops closed in rural areas (Department of Environment, Food and Rural Affairs, 2000). Similarly, larger market towns have seen the decline of food outlets and thus jobs. While supermarkets are employers, one of their key economies of scale relates to the staff to customer ratio. In the Macdonald and Swales (1991) study of the impact of hypermarkets on local multipliers, they determined that while hypermarkets offered lower retail prices and some employment opportunities, the number of jobs displaced had a net negative impact on local real income.

In essence, the emergence of retailers has significantly constrained job opportunities throughout the supply chain within rural and semi-rural areas. Furthermore, key beneficiaries from the sales transactions will tend to be found without the rural region, i.e. shareholders, chief executives, head office workers, etc. The proportion of public enterprises within a rural region represents a corresponding flow of income generated out of the region.

Tourism as an economic activity in rural areas

United Kingdom policy makers continue to adhere to the idea that among other options, tourism will replace traditional industries within rural communities. Tourism is seen as one of the fastest growing industries over the second half of the twentieth century (Font and Ahjem, 1999) and a key element for growth in rural areas. In 1999, tourism represented 14 per cent of the gross domestic product and 14.5 per cent of employment. Total expenditure on tourism in Britain increased by 58 per cent from £18.26 billion to £28.8 billion between 1990 and 1999, although there was a decline due to the impact of the Foot and Mouth crisis and the 11 September 2001 terrorist attacks (Mintel, 2001). However, it was predicted that 2002 would witness a return to high levels of tourism within the UK, in particular from the domestic short-break market (Mintel, 2002).

The 'standard view' (Dwyer et al., 2000) is that tourism is a mechanism of stemming the decline of rural and urban areas. Tourism is said to have direct and induced effects on host destinations. Consumers from high disposable income areas are imported to rural areas with a net effect of generating direct demand for tourism providers and a 'flow on' to other businesses, including food providers and their suppliers. This in turn increases the income of local residents, increases demand for other businesses within an area, thus creating jobs, and increases the region's domestic product and local multiplier (Saeter, 1998).

The concept of the multiplier is based on the premise that one firm within an economy is selling to other firms within the same economy. The sectors of the economy are thus interdependent. Injections of additional revenue from direct sales through catering facilities, holiday camps, holiday cottages and other related services will thus have a corresponding injection of revenue into producers of products throughout the supply chain within the region, e.g. food wholesalers, food manufacturers, abattoirs and farmers. Induced effects will emerge in the form of higher levels of incomes for businesses within the community, higher family income levels, job security and higher levels of disposable income from local residents resulting in higher expenditure on added-value products and so forth. Thus, additional demand presented by tourism will generate businesses for a whole plethora of non-core and augmented community and service providers for both residents and tourists alike, e.g. entertainment, construction, public services, as well as for tourism (Hjalager, 1996; Smith, 1988). This model, however, assumes a high level of linkages between parts of the local economy in which the tourism industry is developed. It also suggests that businesses involved within the provision of tourism be, in fact, embedded in the local community (Dwyer et al., 2000).

Many have expressed concern (Butler and Clark, 1992; Frechtling and Horvarth, 1999; Hummelbrunner and Miglbauer, 1994) that income leakage due to a number of factors including outside ownership of businesses, imported resources, i.e. labour, money, materials and machines, can significantly reduce the economic impact of tourism on a region.

An illustration of the problem

In an attempt to identify the significance of the business and employment generated by core activities such as accommodation providers, tourism attractions and catering facilities, and non-core activities, a small survey was conducted. An identical questionnaire was sent to a sample of:

■ *core activities*: tourism attractions, bed and breakfast establishments, hotels, caterers
■ *non-core activities*: rural shops, small manufacturers and farms who had diversified into tourism/leisure and food production.

Three main areas of the UK were selected for the survey – south-west Wales, north Yorkshire and Nottinghamshire – in an attempt to examine a cross-section of both remote/less remote areas. While the response rate was extremely low at 32 per cent and the results by no means significant, the survey raised some interesting issues as illustrated in Table 13.1.

From the results in Table 13.1 it is apparent that those who have focused on the issues surrounding local produce, e.g. farm shops, and the value of

Table 13.1   Local sourcing survey results

	Customer base	Sources of supply	Employees
Farmers diversified into tourism	Predominantly local	Some local supply, more often either cash and carry – some supermarket supply	On average 3 employees
Farmers diversified into food production	Predominantly local particularly those with lower numbers of employees	Predominantly home grown with one or two exceptions. A jam maker even had fruit given	Ranged from 0 to 9 employees
Specialist retailers and farm shops	Predominantly local	Some home grown, a significant amount locally sourced but also national outlets such as cash and carries	Varied. Farm shops where apparent that pluri-strategy, no additional employment indicated
Main stream traditional retailers/ wholesalers	Virtually all local	National suppliers. Some additional revenue generated through some local sourcing	Significant employer
Bed and breakfast	Virtually all national or international	Did not sell food?	None/minimal
Self-catering cottages	National/international	Do not sell food	Minimal
Caravan sites	Varied. Mainly regional and national/ international	Varied. In certain cases attached to pubs and facilities	Varied from minimal, i.e. maintenance only, to significant numbers
Hotels and restaurants	In many cases a significant part of trade was local	Sourcing was varied. Significant levels of cash and carry, national catering supply companies and supermarkets	For the most part significant employers
Other tourism attractions	Varied depending on nature of attraction	Varied, although predominance of national suppliers	In many cases a significant employer

recoupling the supply chain are attempting to source locally, thus adding value through tourism. Yet some of the major employers are indeed the 'service' sector, such as hotels and restaurants. There are a number of interesting phenomena here. Those offering the core products, e.g. accommodation, but particularly catering in this context, have limited resource to local supply, while they are potentially critical in the local environment in terms of offering employment. Their lack of a local sourcing strategy unfortunately reduces their impact on the local multiplier. Drawing on resources from primary and preferably also secondary suppliers would add more value within the region, yet the service providers' primary concern, given the real margins on the provision of food, is cost.

There is a further issue to note, given the nature of the locations of particularly north Yorkshire and south-west Wales, hospitality outlets do not appear to identify tourists as their core business. Some of the reasons might be related to how the tourist uses the tourism product.

Scenario

Remembering that there is a wealth of different scenarios on an individual level, hypothetically a married couple arriving at a country cottage for a weekend break could in actual fact bring virtually no benefit to a region.

They have rented a cottage in the Cotswolds through a national agency on the Internet; the cottage belongs to professionals in London who have hopes one day of retiring there. The couple are well organized and, on Thursday night on the way back from work, have bought the food for their stay. They leave their home in Knightsbridge at 4 p.m. on Friday and arrive in time for dinner at the cottage.

They make a late start on Saturday but, taking a packed lunch, they go for a long walk during the afternoon. On their way home they call in at the local hostelry and between them have a pint of beer and a glass of wine, for which they pay the princely sum of £5.50. The hostelry is managed and owned by a national pub company. The alcohol is supplied through a national logistics firm, from a national brewing company owned by a major US brewer. The couple then return to the cottage to have a leisurely evening meal with the food they brought with them.

On Sunday morning, as they are members of the National Trust, they decide to visit the local National Trust establishment. They call back to the local pub on their way home and decide to eat there. Their bill comes to £11.40 for two ploughman's lunches and two pints of lager. The food is supplied to the pub via a major catering supply company. The couple then pack up later in the afternoon of the same day and drive back to their home in Knightsbridge.

It is apparent that in terms of the real value contributed to this village, we have a total expenditure of £16.90. The majority of food is brought from London, the cottage belongs to a London professional couple, and the beer, wine or food served within the pub is not local. Some value may be derived by the village, in wages, for the cottage cleaner, National Trust employees, the bar staff and the pub owner.

This is a fictitious but not unrealistic case. Many pubs are managed, and purchase centrally through national suppliers. Likewise there has been considerable consolidation within the brewing sector. Two of the major UK companies have withdrawn, over the last two years, from the brewing sector.

If we consider variations of the same scenario.

1 The couple was not so organized and has not bought food before they left London, but had to buy it in the nearest supermarket to the village. Or:
2 They stay at a local pub.

What might be the added value generated by their visit? Or:

3 They stay at a local bed and breakfast. In many rural districts there has been a recorded increase in purchases by small independent caterers from supermarkets as the most convenient, efficient source of supplies (Eastham, Ball and Sharples, 2001). Bed and breakfast operations would appear to be particularly supermarket dependent. Interestingly, in the survey identified above, of the limited number of bed and breakfasts that replied, more than half did not realize that they bought food for their customers.

The linkages between cultivation, production and consumption and the traditional structure of supply have to a large extent been broken. The implication in Dwyer *et al.* (2000), Clarke (1999), Elwyn-Owen (1991) and Inskeep (1991) is that significant value from tourism may only be gained if those linkages remain.

While diversification into tourism and tourism products may stem the loss of direct employment for the farming communities, job losses from other parts of the supply chain cannot in reality be reversed under the current supply structure. Furthermore, the real added value from rural tourism is minimized due to lack of an endogenous supply structure and the externalization of funding sources and ownership. In order to maximize value from tourism, supply chain restructuring needs to take place, which requires the active participation of both tourist and core tourism providers. In both cases the barrier to participation is cost.

The role of the private and public sectors in the re-coupling of the food chain

Rural development and the issues around the diverse mechanisms by which the countryside may be made economically viable has become a significant field of academic study. Questions have been raised as to the viability of uncoordinated diversification strategies. Marsden (1995: 291) suggests in the context of north-west Europe that the decline of gross domestic product and employment has been stemmed by the 're-integration of agrarian with non agrarian structures'. Van de Ploeg et al. (2000) explored the relative impact of the diverse forms of rural development strategy found in diverse regions in Europe, namely; pluri-activity/diversification (Kinsella et al., 2000), synergistic networks (Brunori and Rossi, 2000) (in industry terms – new industrial networks), and the shortening of supply chains, (Marsden, Banks and Bristow, 2000). The plethora of research in this area may, in part, have informed government policy.

Agenda 2000 marked a development of agricultural policy when it highlighted the need for the diversification of farming and the integration of 'agricultural structural policy into the wider context of rural areas' (http://europa.eu.int/comm/enlargement/agenda 2000/strong/13,htm). The 1992 CAP Reform stressed the importance of the environmental dimension of agriculture, whereas Agenda 2000, published in 1997, considered wider social issues and recognized the importance of farming communities, encouraging diversification to ensure the stability of farm incomes. Subsequently, Council regulation (EC) No. 1257/1999 of 17 May 1999 introduced the community support framework for sustainable rural development, and Commission regulation (EC). No 1750/1999 of 23 July 1999 set down the guidelines for rural development. These regulations were primarily designed to introduce a sustainable 'integrated' rural development policy, and to promote all aspects of rural development by encouraging the participation of local actors; fundamentally a bottom-up approach. Key foci were issues relating to food safety, fair and stable incomes, the environment and, most importantly in the context of this chapter, the encouragement of complementary and alternative activities that generate employment and strengthen the social and economic fabric of rural communities.

Modernization, diversification, processing and marketing, innovation, provision of services, improvement of infrastructure connected with the development of agriculture, tourism and craft activities and the setting up of young farmers in agriculture were all key debates. Both endogenous development and partnerships/collaboration were emphasized.

As a response the UK government implemented a number of measures. Regional development agencies were established in 1999, where rural areas were for the first time considered in conjunction with urban development areas. The Rural White Paper, (Department of Environment, Food and Rural Affairs, 2000), reflected the objectives set down by the European regulation (EC) No.1257/1999.

Key areas of the White Paper include:

- the support of village services including village shops, pub garages, a renewal of the post office network, and the preservation of rural schools
- modernization of rural services, using technology
- the provision of affordable homes
- local transport solutions
- rejuvenation of market towns
- a new direction for farming – including redevelopment of small abattoirs, and diversification of farming methods
- preservation of rural England
- access to the countryside
- local power to country towns and villages
- promotion of community-based schemes
- broadening of the economy in rural areas.

The implementation of the EU regulation 1257/99 in England came in the form of the England Rural Development Programme (ERDP) implemented through The Department of Environment, Food and Rural Affairs (DEFRA). The ERDP offers a range of funding opportunities, as does its Welsh, Scottish and Northern Irish counterparts. These range from countryside stewardship grants and organic farming initiatives through to processing and marketing grants, i.e. grants designed to facilitate the diversification of farming into processing and aiding farmers' access to markets. Strict guidelines are provided and the grants are offered to sole traders, private and public limited companies, and groups of producers. In the context of this programme, as laid down by the EU commission regulation, there is a strong ethos of sharing best practice, in which collaboration and farmers' co-operatives feature strongly.

Other agencies involved in the Rural White Paper include the Countryside Agency, English National Parks and the National Trust, who are working in apparent collaboration to support rural activities and farming.

A final measure implemented by the UK government, was somewhat forced upon them, following the Foot and Mouth epidemic in the UK in 2001. The government appointed a commission to investigate and advise it on:

> How we can create a sustainable, competitive and diverse farming and food sector which contributes to a thriving and sustainable rural economy, advances environmental, economic, health and animal welfare goals and is consistent with the Government's aims of Common Agricultural policy reform, enlargement of the EU and increased trade liberalization. (Commission Report, 2001: 5)

Sir Don Curry, who headed up the Commission has advised against 'cherry picking' from over 100 recommendations the report puts forward. Critical to the report is the view that the delivery of food to the plate should be a collective activity of players from all links in the food chain. The report also recommends that farming populations should find solutions to market access through co-operatives, that caterers and retailers should source locally and that food production should be based on supply contracts, i.e. longer-term relationships between all purveyors within the supply chain. In essence, the report suggests the importance of the recoupling of the supply chain, and the value of collaboration for small and large farmers, enabling them to get more out of the market. It is suggested that a newly formed 'Food Chain Centre' (to be headed by the Institute of Grocery Distribution) should be formed in order to improve collaboration along the food chain, and help reconnect 'the whole supply chain'. However, the implementation of the whole of the recommendations will cost around £500 million, which may not be made available by the current Labour government.

While the recoupling of the supply chain may not fully solve the 'leakage' problems, it may go some way to retaining greater levels of income generated through tourism within the community. Interestingly, prior to the publication of the Commission Report, partly in response to public opinion, and partly in response to Foot and Mouth, many of the major multiples, e.g. Tesco, Sainsbury's, Asda and Somerfield, had begun to source more produce locally although many question the extent to which local sourcing can take place. A local sourcing manager at Asda claims that, regardless of strategy, local produce cannot exceed 2 per cent of stock. It is doubtful whether this level of local sourcing can sustain local rural economies.

Best practice and the diversity of collaborative models

Government policy is therefore designed, in large part, to create economically and socially sustainable rural communities. One of the key messages to farming communities is that they should meet market needs more effectively. The emphasis on processing and marketing would suggest that the government is interested in recoupling the supply chain, bringing the primary source of food closer to the consumer – an issue, particularly important given the reputed impact of the food logistics systems on the spread of the recent epidemic of Foot and Mouth.

Re-coupling the supply chain also enables the retention of greater levels of added value generated from rural/food tourism, *if core tourism services draw from local food resources.*

It would appear that key to the success of rural development is the participation of local people, and through the valorization of local resources – by no means a new pathway for tourism development (see Bramwell and Sharman, 1998; Jamal and Getz, 1995; Marien and Pizam, 1997; Perdue, Long and Allen, 1990).

Government policy is reflective of their earlier initiatives in industrial contexts of promoting the development of new industrial districts/innovative milieus, which stemmed from the EU (1989) Outsourcing Directive (EC) No. 402/1989. Key to this directive was that close proximity, and interdependence of businesses, within a given geographical environment, produced synergies, even though the scale of employment or the value generated is not alone significant.

Research into the development of new industrial districts focused on their successes and attempted to identify how, and why, networks had emerged as an organizational structure and what, more importantly, made them successful (Pyke et al., 1990). A significant body of research focused upon network classification. Sengenberger, Loveman and Piore (1990) identify two forms of network: *kingdoms*, where small and medium-sized enterprises work closely with large enterprises, which provides market access, and *republics* in which firms collaborate on an equal footing and bring their particular strengths to products and production processes. In Hinterhuber and Levin (1994) a similar differentiation is made but they refer to *vertical* (farm to plate) and *horizontal* relationships, i.e. across same-tier organizations. It is the latter model which is more frequently applied. For example, Murdoch (2000) refers to a vertical network as the way 'in which agriculture is incorporated into a much broader set of processes which exist beyond rural areas', and horizontal as 'forms of rural development' which integrate 'non-agricultural rural economies into a set of processes that straddle both urban and rural spaces'. While these models are helpful there is little reason why vertical cannot be used to describe any upstream or downstream partnership.

Other models of industrial districts focus on different characteristics. Rosenfeld's (1996) model distinguishes the object of exchange, in which *hard* refers to the case where firms join forces to achieve a task, i.e. co-produce, co-market, co-purchase, and *soft* networks which primarily relate to networks for information and knowledge. In contrast, Grandori and Soda (1995) have identified three types of network based on the mechanisms of co-ordination and management:

- *Social* – based on social/personal relationships.
- *Bureaucratic* – more formal centrally controlled collaborative initiative, e.g. some forms of co-operatives or certain holiday cottage associations (see Exhibit 13.2).
- *Proprietary* – includes inter-firm cross-holding of equities and property rights, e.g. joint ventures.

What is apparent from the various models is that there are any number of functions, and manners in which networks might be managed/configured. While the search for 'best practice' is intrinsic in much of government policy, the value of the wealth of literature in this research area is as a means of inspiring entrepreneurs towards further innovative development in rural areas. There is, however, a recurrent viewpoint across the literature that industrial clusters/networks are based on personal relationships, trust, information sharing and shared vision (Mohr and Spekman, 1994; Pyke et al., 1990; Rosenfeld, 1996; Williamson, 1975;). Rosenfeld (1997) writes about 'working clusters' and suggests that 'successful clusters are aware of their interdepend-ence, 'value each other' and 'collectively operate as a system to produce more than the sum of their parts'. It appears that successful collaborative activities are embedded in social relationships (Williamson, 1975) and successful networks are embedded within the community (Bellandi, 1989; Granovetter, 1992; Pyke et al., 1990; Rosenfeld, 1997).

Cases of reintegration of the supply chain

In the following section, two distinctly diverse examples of recoupling the supply chain are identified. Exhibit 13.1 looks at a diversification strategy in a non-peripheral rural area where diversification into food production has contributed to the local economy through job creation. Drawing on local resources, cheeses are produced and sold nation-wide with a Yorkshire brand. In this case there is no direct link and no intention to link food to tourism. Exhibit 13.2 focuses on the activities of a small network of micro-businesses who now supply a range of tourism facilities, e.g. holiday cottages, local shops. In this case the holiday cottages draw upon local sources to add value to the experience of their clients and add value to the local economy.

Exhibit 13.1 Shepherd's Purse

Shepherd's Purse is a North Yorkshire cheese producer, based in 400 acres of beautiful farmland, near Thirsk. Until the late 1980s the land was exclusively farmed, producing wheat, barley, sugar, beef and oil seed rape. However, as the younger members of the Bell family reached school age, Judy Bell sought to replace the task of managing three small children with another equally challenging occupation. Being acutely aware of the number of people with an intolerance to bovine products, she determined there was a niche for non-bovine products. As there was no ewe's milk readily available she acquired a number of sheep and set up a milking parlour with a view to producing cheese.

Her initial challenges included deficits in skills, problems of finding buyers and a lack of knowledge of marketing – issues often experienced by small and medium-sized enterprises that are extending their business into value-adding activities. With a view to addressing these issues, in 1989 Shepherd's Purse became a member of the local food and drink network, Yorkshire Pantry. Judy Bell saw immediate benefits. She was able to gain a whole raft of business advice relating to packaging and marketing, training, and marketing opportunities. She now employs eight people, including her son and daughter, and produces seven diverse cheeses made from sheep's milk, buffalo milk and cow's milk. Her pride and joy is Mrs Bell's Blue which is similar to Roquefort.

Shepherd's Purse now supplies a whole range of operations, both locally and nationally. Some of her national accounts include, Euro-Star, P&O, Virgin and the Houses of Parliament. In conjunction with fifteen other cheese producers under the umbrella brand name of Regional Hand-made Cheeses she supplies five of the major multiple retailers with a unique selling point of 'Quality Fine Cheeses' which are sold on the stores' delicatessen counters. Multiple retailers have

---

been keen to encourage specialist cheese-makers like Judy Bell because of their ability to offer a 'point of difference', therefore attracting customers to delicatessen counters which are currently losing market share at around 10 per cent per annum. Judy Bell is actively involved in the development of delicatessen business for retailers, offering retailers the opportunity to send sales staff to the plant in order to familiarize themselves with the process of producing cheese and the particular characteristics of the Shepherd's Purse cheeses. The current turnover from this enterprise alone is £500 000 plus.

Shepherd's Purse for the most part uses local or regional suppliers. Sheep's and buffalo's milk comes from local North Yorkshire farmers, while Zenith, one of the largest UK dairy farmers co-operatives, supplies all their requirements for cow's milk under a tailored contract, where only a selected number of local farms who can supply milk of the highest quality are involved.

Local delivery of the cheeses is managed in-house. However, to deliver to the larger retailers they draw upon the logistic skill of organizations such as Long Clawson, the co-operative based in Lincolnshire which specializes in Stilton production. This enables direct supply into the regional distribution centres of the multiple retailers.

The Bell family has redefined their core business to food manufacturing. Discussions with the family clearly indicate their reluctance to provide a 'farm holiday' or be more vertically integrated with the tourism industry. They see their key opportunity to be adding value to locally grown produce to sell both to local markets and through networks of other farmers' shops. They are also enthusiastic about a planned plant expansion, which would enable them to supply into the increasing number of multiple retailers who were demanding their products. Fears are that expansion would be difficult due to the restrictions placed on farm buildings. However, in 2002 they were awarded a processing and marketing grant to build new production facilities, which would include refrigerated stores and packing room. The English Rural Development programme would provide 30 per cent the total cost of the project over £514 000. The expanding business will further benefit the surrounding area: the new facilities will enable Shepherd's Purse to operate more efficiently, generate eleven to sixteen more jobs and increase by 400 per cent, the volume of milk bought from local suppliers.

Jane Eastham

Exhibit 13.2 Peak Eats Ready Meals

Peak Eats Ready Meals has resulted from a collaborative initiative, 'Peak District Foods for Tourism', which has involved the joint activities of the Heart of England Tourist Board, the Peak District Rural Development Partnership, the Regional Enterprise Development Office at the University of Derby (RED), the Peak District National Park Authority and the North-East Staffordshire single regeneration budget.

The Peak District Foods for Tourism initiative was part of one of four pilot schemes which have taken place under the 'Food and Drink in Tourism' banner, a national pilot project, aimed at developing the distinctiveness of the Heart of England through its food and drink culture. The national project has been promoted and co-ordinated through the Heart of England Tourist Board, with funding from the English Tourism Council. Other pilot areas which have also been involved are Herefordshire, Staffordshire and Leicestershire.

This particular project was funded from November 2001 to April 2002. Funds were put forward by the Heart of England Tourist Board (50 per cent), the Peak District Rural Development Partnership (25 per cent) and the North-East Staffordshire single regeneration budget (25 per cent). The project was managed through RED office which subcontracted the work to Sue Prince. It is supported by the Peak District National Park Authority's new Environmental Economy scheme.

Sue Prince, a local farmer at Beechen Hill farm at Ilam, has a variety of interests including two holiday cottages, a bed and breakfast business offering home-grown food, an organic farm and a lively interest in local produce. She has been an active member of Peak District Farm Holidays for seventeen years, an organization designed to co-market farm-based cottages and bed and breakfast in the Peak District. At the start of this initiative she had been involved in trying to establish a number of collaborative ventures between food producers and tourism businesses. These included the first 'Savour the Flavour of the Peak District' pamphlet which was launched 1998–99, and a system where people arriving to stay in holiday cottages could order food and lamb from farmers before they arrived. This was seen to be of value to all parties; the farmer knew in advance when to get the lambs ready, tourists could enjoy a flavour of local produce and the holiday cottage owners could offer additional value. However, farmers found this initiative too complicated and at this time did not need the income. Her contacts and the experience that she had gained within these projects, however, proved to be invaluable in the management of the Peak District Foods for Tourism (PDFT) initiative.

The purpose of the PDFT project was to investigate potential links between local foods and the local tourism market in order to determine the scope for new business activity. It was intended that thirty food producers and thirty tourism businesses should be targeted with a view to develop a simple food catalogue and a new 'Savour the Flavour of the Peak District' leaflet. As a result of the five-month project, several other outcomes emerged in addition to the targeted outputs:

- **Peak Eats Ready Meals** – a new collaborative business was formed with the assistance of three other businesses to provide ready meals for holiday cottages and caravan parks in the area.
- **Wake Cakes** – 'local' biscuits were developed that could be sold and presented in packs of two for bed and breakfast operations.
- A collaborative group of small local primary producers was developed.

The emergence of Peak Eats Ready Meals came from the very early stages of the project. After an initial presentation to the Peak District Tourism Conference about the nature of the pilot initiative, a local woman, who owned five holiday cottages, suggested that she would like to offer ready meals to holidaymakers. The idea was that guests would be provided with a pamphlet on booking from which they could order meals before their arrival.

Karen Beresford was also present at the initial presentation. She and her husband own a sheep farm, and specialize in producing ready meals including lamb dishes and home-made English desserts.

In discussion with the holiday cottage owner Karen identified that there might be a market for a greater variety of dishes than just lamb and home-made puddings, so Karen contacted two other micro-businesses in the area who had an interest in ready meals: Arthur Gee and Carol Burns of Dovedale Traditional Beef who, in addition to their rare breeds of beef, which they sell direct to consumers, produce a variety of beef dishes, e.g. braised beef in stout, and Julie Shotton who specializes in innovative vegetarian meals and unusual organic cakes, e.g. courgette and hazelnut, roast pepper and chocolate. After discussion they put together a range of dishes that they could promote.

Together they offer a unique service to tourists in the Peak District. As their pamphlet states, 'When you have been out holidaying or walking in the Peak District all day, come home and put your feet up and enjoy food grown and prepared in the Peak District'. Ingredients are sourced as locally as possible and from environmentally sensitive farming methods if possible, prepared and cooked locally, and stocked in the freezer of the cottage owner or in nearby shops. The cottage owner promotes the meals with posters or pamphlets in the accommodation and makes a small profit on each sale.

Interest has grown in this venture. At the time of writing, two months since their launch in February, Peak Eats Ready Meals are being sold in three village shops, a coffee shop in Eyam, two holiday cottage businesses in Ilam and one in Hope, and one caravan site. Twelve further contracts are expected from cottage businesses in Wootton, Millers Dale, Waterhouses, Alstonefield and Stanshope when micro-waveable packaging has been developed.

Funding for Peak District Foods for Tourism has now come to an end, but there are a range of initiatives emerging, e.g. collaboration of a local food distribution system to co-ordinate supply to tourism businesses and much potential for future development.

Jane Eastham

Localized threads

There are recognizable distinctions in the two cases above. Shepherd's Purse, once a farm, has now completely diversified into food production. Peak Eats Ready Meals is a joint venture in which two of the businesses involved had previously diversified into food production. However, unlike Shepherd's Purse, they have determined the local tourism sector to be their key target. The local sourcing of food is seen to be important in both cases.

Shepherd's Purse relationship with major retailers is supported through 'Regional Cheeses', a horizontal network strategy which has facilitated market access and also helped supermarkets to stem the decline of delicatessen sales. In return Shepherd's Purse provides retailers staff with the opportunity to learn about the cheeses they are to sell.

Judy Bell does sell on to local suppliers but the development of twenty to twenty-five jobs is contingent on the larger contracts provided by five key major multiples. The issue is how much cheese can one sell in a region as a niche product, with small-scale production facilities and minimal demand. The development of the larger contracts may place Shepherd's Purse in the position, as unit of production costs are reduced, to tempt core tourism businesses such as restaurants and/or hotels to profit from local food.

In comparison Peak Eats Ready Meals offers products of greater perceived added value geared primarily to add value to tourism accommodation/ facilities. Production units are significantly smaller. The issue is not an alternative source of income but pluri-activity/economies of scope through collaborative practice. Further involvement of networks of relationships is also evident in Shepherd's Purse membership of Yorkshire Pantry. This has been primarily a knowledge transfer network, but has provided some invaluable marketing opportunities for Shepherd's Purse.

In the case of Peak Eat Ready Meals, once again there are a range of networks in which the numerous players are involved. For example, Peak Holiday Cottages offers the opportunity for co-marketing both within the Peak Holiday cottage network, but also nationally. There may be a strong potential for vertical networks to emerge in the context of Peak Eats and Peak District Foods for Tourism which will enable core tourism services to source increasing quantities of produce locally.

Thus, while apparently different scenarios, both cases have used collective gain to extend market access and branded their products to be recognizable from a specific region. The most notable aspect of the both case studies is the plethora of linkages between local/regional organizations and the key players within the case studies. Endogenous economic growth through tourism does not appear to be standing at a farm gate selling melons.

Conclusion

The importance of rural tourism to rural communities cannot be under-estimated; it is an invaluable additional source of revenue to a region. Yet, as has been recognized by policymakers both in the EU and in the UK, the level to which consumables are imported to rural areas, due to the de-coupling of food production and supply during the twentieth century, limits the regional multiplier. In order to generate a significant multiplier from tourism action needs to be taken to reduce leakage. In certain agricultural regions (Marsden, 1995) the decline of gross domestic product and employment has been stemmed by the reintegration of agrarian with non-agricultural structures, and greater upstream, downstream linkages in order to enable tourism to 'valorize' the region as a whole. European Union and UK funds, available under the Objective 1 and 2 regional strategy initiatives, have helped this cause. In essence, reintegration, i.e. the development of an alternative supply chain, requires a co-ordinated approach from the local stakeholders: the local community, businesses and government bodies.

It is interesting to note that while five years ago, reintegration/recoupling of the supply chain was in a sense unknown as an idea, the need for change among rural areas and farming communities is now being driven home. However, unfortunately, despite the publicity of the multiple retailers and the advent of farmers' markets, if there is real value to be gained from tourists, the loop needs to be closed. Both caterers and tourists need to buy locally.

14

Restaurants and local food in New Zealand

Angela Smith and C. Michael Hall

One of the key components of the relationship between food and tourism and regional development is that of the promotion of local foods (Hall, 2002). As well as direct purchase by consumers, the use of local food by restaurants is also significant in enhancing local food production, while branding menus in terms of their local food content may also be significant in marketing the menu and the restaurant as well as potentially leading to ongoing purchase of regional food-stuffs by consumers (Henchion and McIntyre, 2000) (see also Chapter 2 in this volume). Additionally, the use of local foods may add to the perceived authenticity of the restaurant experience as well as the wider experience of the destination (Symons, 1999).

New Zealand has increasingly begun to promote food as a component of its destination attractive-ness at both the international and domestic level. New Zealand wines have achieved a very high profile in the international quality wine market, while its foodstuffs such as kiwifruit, lamb, apples and pears, venison and seafood have also established a strong presence in some international markets. The meat sector is the second largest generator of export income, with 91 per cent of lamb, 79 per cent of mutton and 83 per cent of beef produced between 1997 and 1999 being exported. According to Statistics New Zealand, meat production currently accounts for NZ$3.2 billion in export earnings. Trade New Zealand states that New Zealand is responsible for 40 per cent of the world's traded sheep meat and about 8 per cent of the world's beef production. Dairy and honey products are also important, with 90–95 per cent of milk and 27 per cent of honey production exported. New Zealand is also recognized for its 'aqua culture' industry. In 1998 Greenshell mussel exports totalled NZ$118.2 million, and salmon NZ$35.6 million; while other seafood exported (including fish, lobster and shellfish) totalled NZ$1236 million in 1998. New Zealand is also diversifying its agricultural and food production base from domestic and international consumption to include high-value produce as diverse as avocado oil, olives, chestnuts, truffles and wasabi. Undoubtedly, food production is going to continue to remain a very important component of the New Zealand economy for many years. Although identifying what exactly New Zealand cuisine is, there is no doubt that the provision of food and wine is a significant part of the New Zealand tourism experience (Mitchell and Hall, 2001a,b,c). However, while wine has become recognized as a significant component of the tourism experience in New Zealand and a means of reinforcing local economic relationships and local identity (Thorsen and Hall, 2001), it is only recently that the broader food dimension has become explicitly promoted, for example through the development of regional brands as well as a producer developed national wine and food tourism strategy (Hall, Mitchell and Smith, 2001).

In order to increase returns to farmers and add value to produce, a number of rural regions are looking at the development of direct supplier and marketing relationships between local food producers and restaurants. In Australia, for example this has become most pronounced in wine regions such as the Barossa, the Yarra Valley and the Margaret River, while the Niagara wine region in Canada has also been developing such relationships under the Taste of Niagara umbrella (see Chapter 9). In the case of Iowa in the USA, Scanlan & Associates et al. (2000) reported that upscale and high-end restaurants appeared to offer the best potential for local-grown food products, particularly organic or sustainably grown meat and produce. Significantly, in terms of adding value to farm produce, their research suggested that upscale and high-end restaurants were willing to pay 10–20 per cent more for these types of products from local sources. Gibson (1995: 35) noting that,

Chefs are increasingly willing to buy directly from growers in order to find field-ripened vegetables and tree-ripened fruits that are difficult to purchase from distributors and purveyors. Although many restaurants buy directly from growers hoping to get a lower price, white-linen restaurant chefs often pay top-dollars for hard-to-find, quality produce.

Several reasons can be provided as to the reason for this premium:

- Most restaurants are locally owned, allowing them to purchase wherever they choose.
- Restaurants change menus frequently, therefore making the use of special or seasonal products easier.
- Restaurant volume demands are lower than those of other institutions or supermarkets, which means the ability of local producers to meet these demands is easier.
- Restaurants are in a position to 'attach status to eating Iowa product', which they are willing and able to promote through their service staffs and menu notations.
- Restaurant customers are willing to pay more for menu items featuring high-quality locally grown products (Scanlan & Associates et al., 2000).

Furthermore, direct selling to restaurants by growers can also have some significant advantages for growers:

- *Market certainty* throughout the production season. If a relationship is established with a restaurant then a price can be agreed to for the purchase period for a certain amount of supply. This degree of certainty of return may allow for innovation with other products and/or provide a basis to break into other markets.
- *Greater product returns*. According to Gibson (1995: 35), 'A minimum of 10% over wholesale terminal prices for standard items at mainstream restaurants; much more from upper scale restaurants for speciality items that they can't get wholesale'.
- *Personal contact* with the restaurant owner, manager or chef allows greater flexibility in products grown as well as providing information from customers as to the quality of the product.
- *Brand recognition*. If restaurants emphasize their locally grown produce on their menus, by mentioning the names of their farm suppliers, then increased brand recognition and market opportunities may follow (Gibson 1995).

This chapter presents the findings of a restaurant survey conducted on restaurants in leading food and wine regions in New Zealand. The survey was conducted to analyse the relationship restaurants have with suppliers in their region, as well as the willingness and ability of those in the industry to use local products. Restaurants were also asked about the relevance of tourism to their business, and how interested they are in creating regional products, dishes and brands to promote regional food and wine tourism. Additionally, restaurants were asked what relationship they have with other businesses and how willing they are to provide regional tourism information to tourists. Support levels for local and New Zealand wines were also assessed to evaluate the potential for a cohesive food and wine brand both regionally and nationally.

Methodology

In the first half of 2002 a survey was sent to restaurants in four New Zealand wine and food regions: Canterbury (including the city of Christchurch), Central Otago, Hawke's Bay and Marlborough. A total of 197 restaurants returned usable surveys, providing a response rate of 29.2 per cent out of 675 surveys distributed. While this is not a very high response rate, it can still be considered satisfactory for a postal survey (Veal, 1992). The survey was sent to all businesses listed under the restaurant category in the regional telephone books while additional restaurants were identified through local business directories, brochures and visitor information centres. The origin of completed surveys were relatively consistent with the distribution of surveys to each region. Where some respondents failed to answer a question, this is noted in the responses, in order to provide accurate results.

Typology of responding restaurants

Over all four survey regions, three key restaurant 'typologies' were prevalent (see Table 14.1), fifty-six (28.4 per cent) were classified as 'family style', forty-six (23.4 per cent) 'casual style/bistro' and forty-four (22.3 per cent) were 'fine dining' restaurants. These results were relatively consistent across the regions, although there was some variation in the most prominent 'type' of restaurant in each region. As Table 14.2 indicates, there was some variation across the four regions; in Central Otago, twelve (34.3 per cent) restaurants were classified as 'fine dining', eleven (31.4 per cent) 'family style', and an additional six (17.1 per cent) were 'casual style/bistro' restaurants. In Canterbury, thirty (27.8 per cent) restaurants were 'family style', twenty-seven (25.0 per cent) 'casual style/bistro', and twenty-one (19.4 per cent) were

Table 14.1 Restaurant type

Restaurant type	No.	%
Family style	56	28.4
Casual style/bistro	46	23.4
Fine dining restaurant	44	22.3
Other	29	14.7
Pub/bar	12	6.1
Banquet service	3	1.5
Chain/franchise restaurant	3	1.5
Catering and off premises sales	2	1.0
Not stated	2	1.0
Total	197	100.0

fine dining. In Marlborough, 'casual style/bistro' restaurants were the most common type of establishment with eight (36.4 per cent) restaurants responding, while in the Hawke's Bay, 'family style' restaurants were the most prominent with eleven (37.9 per cent) of respondents identifying with this typology.

Type of cuisine describing food emphasis

Respondents were asked to identify the main type of cuisine matching their restaurant's food emphasis; the results are shown in Table 14.3. The most common style of cuisine served at restaurants was 'contemporary New Zealand cuisine', with eighty-one (41.1 per cent) restaurants across the survey sample identifying this as their main cuisine typology. Significantly, twenty-six (13.2 per cent) restaurants served mainly Asian cuisine (this result being consistent with Thorsen and Hall, 2001) while 17 (8.6 per cent) restaurants served Pacific Rim cuisine. Twenty-one (10.7 per cent) respondents indicated that an 'other' cuisine style was favoured by their restaurant. Included in this group of respondents were four Indian restaurants, three Mexican restaurants, other South American 'style' restaurants as well as a number of restaurants which indicated that they provided a variety or mixture of cuisine styles depending on demand.

Across the regions 'contemporary New Zealand' cuisine remained the most common cuisine style in restaurants. Marlborough had the highest proportion (54.5 per cent) of restaurants with this style of dish, whereas Hawke's Bay had the smallest portion (29.6 per cent). In Canterbury, Asian restaurants (15.6 per

Table 14.2 Restaurant type by region

Restaurant type	Central Otago (18%)		Canterbury (55.7%)		Marlborough (11.3%)		Hawke's Bay (14.9%)	
	No.	%	No.	%	No.	%	No.	%
Family style	11	31.4	30	27.8	4	18.2	11	37.9
Catering and off premises sales	–	–	1	0.9	1	4.5	–	–
Casual style/bistro	6	17.1	27	25.0	8	36.4	5	17.2
Fine dining restaurant	12	34.3	21	19.4	4	18.2	6	20.7
Banquet service	–	–	3	2.8	–	–	–	–
Pub/bar	2	5.7	6	5.6	1	4.5	3	10.3
Chain/franchise restaurant	–	–	3	2.8	–	–	–	–
Other	4	11.4	17	15.7	4	18.2	4	13.8
Total restaurants	35	100.0	108	100.0	22	100.0	29	100.0

Table 14.3 Cuisine style of restaurants

Cuisine style	No.	%
Contemporary New Zealand cuisine	81	41.1
Asian	26	13.2
Other	21	10.7
Pacific Rim	17	8.6
Mediterranean	10	5.1
Continental	9	4.6
Italian	8	4.1
Seafood speciality	7	3.6
Steakhouse	5	2.5
American	4	2.0
French cuisine	3	1.5
Vegetarian	3	1.5
Not stated	3	1.5
Total	197	100.0

cent) were the second most frequent in the region, whereas in Central Otago, Pacific Rim (14.3 per cent) and Italian (11.4 per cent) were more popular.

Overall, average restaurant seating was 109.7 patrons. A majority (75.2 per cent) of restaurants in the sample had a seating capacity of 100 or less, with sixty (30.5 per cent) of the sample being forty-one to sixty-seat restaurants. Restaurants employed an average of almost six (5.8) full-time employees, with eighty-three (54.8 per cent) restaurants stating they had less than five employees. Restaurants had an average of 9.2 part-time employees, with fifty-eight (31.4 per cent) restaurants employing over nine part-time/casual employees. In some cases, restaurants indicated they had no 'full-time employees', just part-time employees; this was most likely to be in situations where owners did not include themselves.

Description of food origin

Less than half of all restaurants describe the origin of food on their menu in terms of being local (39.1 per cent) or New Zealand produce (40.1 per cent). This perhaps highlights the potential for further promotion by all within the food industry towards branding and promoting local, regional and New Zealand cuisine. However, restaurants were even less willing to describe the origin of international produce on their menus, with just twelve (6.1 per cent) of restaurants describing the origin of certain foodstuffs used in dishes. Of the twelve restaurants who chose to describe the origin of international produce, one was Mediterranean, four were Asian, two contemporary New Zealand cuisine, one Italian and four 'other' cuisine providers. Indicating, perhaps not surprisingly, that most of those who were willing to describe international origin were most likely to be those producing 'international' cuisine.

Restaurants in the Marlborough region were the most successful in describing local produce items on the menu, with 60.0 per cent of restaurants willing to do so. In Hawke's Bay, just seven (26.9 per cent) responding restaurants chose to describe local produce items on the menu. Restaurants from Canterbury were also more likely not to (58.5 per cent) describe local produce items on the menu; however an encouraging four out of ten restaurants in the Canterbury region were willing to describe local produce items on their menu. Central Otago (56.3 per cent) and Canterbury restaurants were the most likely to describe New Zealand produce items on the menu. While, restaurants in all four regions generally had little interest in describing international produce used on the menu, with Hawke's Bay (11.5 per cent) being the most likely.

Restaurants tended not to bring attention to the local or New Zealand cuisine characteristics of items on the restaurant menu. Just fifty-three (29.9 per cent) restaurants identified items by their particular local characteristics (i.e. 'Classic Marlborough lamb roast'), and forty-nine (28.7 per cent) by New Zealand cuisine characteristics (i.e. 'Classic New Zealand lamb roast'). In comparison, almost half (48.3 per cent) of responding restaurants stated they identified international cuisine characteristics (i.e. Moroccan-style lamb) on menu items. This seems to indicate that either there are fewer stigmas attached to identifying overseas cuisine styles, or there is simply not the range of local and New Zealand styles to provide descriptions of. If this is the case, it indicates there is scope for further development and creation of cuisine styles.

When these results are evaluated regionally (see Table 14.4), Marlborough (40.9 per cent) and Central Otago (33.3 per cent) restaurants were the most proactive towards describing dishes on the menu with local cuisine characteristics. Twenty-eight (29.2 per cent) Canterbury restaurants described local cuisine characteristics, while Hawke's Bay restaurants were less enthusiastic, with just five (19.2 per cent) of restaurants choosing to give a description of local cuisine.

Central Otago (45.2 per cent) restaurants were most likely to describe New Zealand cuisine characteristics on the menu, whereas less than 30 per cent of Canterbury, Marlborough and Hawke's Bay restaurants chose to. Canterbury

Table 14.4 Region of origin and description of cuisine characteristics in menu items

| | Local | | | | New Zealand | | | | International | | | |
| | Yes | | No | | Yes | | No | | Yes | | No | |
	No.	%	No.	%	No.	%	No.	%	No.	%	No.	%
Central Otago	11	33.3	22	66.7	14	45.2	17	54.8	15	46.9	17	53.1
Canterbury	28	29.2	68	70.8	24	25.5	70	74.5	53	52.0	49	48.0
Marlborough	9	40.9	13	59.1	5	27.8	13	72.2	7	38.9	11	61.1
Hawke's Bay	5	19.2	21	80.8	6	21.4	22	78.6	11	42.3	15	57.7
Total	53	29.9	124	70.1	49	28.7	122	71.3	86	48.3	92	51.7

restaurants (52.0 per cent) were the most likely to describe international characteristics of food items on the menu, while Marlborough restaurants had the lowest number of descriptions. Arguably this is because of the larger and more culturally and ethnically diverse population base of the Canterbury region which includes the city of Christchurch.

Nevertheless, almost half (47.3 per cent) of responding restaurants indicated that over 70 per cent of items on their menu are representative of produce available in the local region, the average (mean) representation of local products on restaurants menus was 63.2 per cent. Twenty-six (13.2 per cent) restaurants indicated that 100 per cent of items on their menu were representative of produce available in the local region. These results are positive, as it indicates both an awareness of produce available in the area, as well as a ready market for local produce. While the results are not necessarily reflective of actual product usage in cooking, they do indicate the potential for usage of local products. It also indicates the potential for creating and identifying items as unique regional cuisine. Canterbury and Marlborough restaurants have the highest levels of representation of local products on their menus, with 57 per cent of Marlborough, and 53.3 per cent of Canterbury restaurants having over 70 per cent representation of local products on their menus. In comparison, just 30.4 per cent of Central Otago restaurants managed this level of representation.

Restaurants would like to increase usage of local products?

Positively, just over two-thirds (134) of restaurants indicated they would like to increase usage of local products. But when asked whether it was currently possible to increase usage of local products under the current supply arrangements for their restaurant, just 29.9 per cent stated that it would actually be possible to increase usage. This appears to support the idea that restaurants are willing to use local produce within their dishes, but are in some situations being prevented by either lack of access, bad supply networks, unwilling central distributors, unreliable local growers or issues of seasonality.

Percentage of ingredients used sourced locally

Respondents were asked to indicate through an open-ended response, what percentage of the ingredients used in their dishes were sourced locally, elsewhere in New Zealand and from overseas. On average, 65.2 per cent of ingredients were sourced locally, a positive sign for the support of local producers. Restaurants had previously indicated that on average 63.1 per cent of items on their menu were representative of ingredients available locally, thus the finding that an average of 65.2 per cent of ingredients are sourced locally is extremely positive.

A cross-tabulation was performed to evaluate whether any particular cuisine 'type' tended to use local products more than others. It was found that steakhouse restaurants most commonly used local produce, with 60 per cent using 100 per cent local products in their dishes. However, the small sample size makes this result a little unreliable but perhaps reflects well on the availability of local New Zealand beef. It was also deemed important to establish whether restaurants claiming to be purveyors of New Zealand cuisine (i.e. 'Contemporary NZ cuisine') were actually using local and New Zealand produce in their dishes (Table 14.5). The analysis showed that a large number (53.9 per cent) restaurants providing contemporary New Zealand cuisine used over 70 per cent of local products in their dishes. The most interesting result, however, was the 26.7 per cent of the same cuisine type for whom local produce makes up only 20 per cent of their ingredients.

If restaurants are able to identify local cuisine on the menu this can assist in the development of a regional food brand. Furthermore, if customers/tourists can be assured they are actually consuming local food products rather than produce sourced elsewhere, but cooked in a regional style, the benefits are twofold: producers are supported and customers are ensured a genuine 'product'.

Frequency of change of menu content

In order to establish whether local food supply potentially impacts on the changes in the menus, respondents were asked to indicate how often in a year they changed their restaurant menus. Uncovering the frequency of menu changes is important for a number of reasons: it indicates a level of innovation in the production of meals, as well as potentially illustrating the variety of produce (albeit local or otherwise) used in dishes. Most responding restaurants changed their menus one (18.3 per cent), two (18.3 per cent), three (14.2 per cent) or four (27.4 per cent) times a year; these findings seem to support the suggestion that at least some proportion of restaurants change their menus due to the seasonality and availability of local produce. Fifteen restaurants (7.6 per cent) indicated that they never changed their menu, while three suggested they only changed their menus once every couple of years. At the other end of the

Table 14.5 Cuisine style by percentage of local products used in dishes

	% of local products used											
	0	1–10	11–20	21–30	31–40	41–50	51–60	61–70	71–80	81–90	91–99	100
Continental (n = 9)	–	–	11.1	11.1	–	11.1	11.1	11.1	11.1	33.3	–	–
Mediterranean (n = 10)	–	–	–	30	30	10	10	10	–	–	–	10
Asian (n = 24)	4.2	–	–	8.3	4.2	16.7	12.5	12.5	16.7	12.5	12.5	–
Pacific Rim (n = 17)	–	–	5.9	–	5.9	17.6	11.8	17.6	23.5	11.8	–	5.9
Contemporary NZ (n = 78)	2.6	3.8	10.3	–	6.4	10.3	7.7	5.1	15.4	16.7	10.3	11.5
Seafood specialty (n = 7)	–	14.3	–	–	14.3	14.3	14.3	–	14.3	28.6	–	–
French (n = 3)	–	–	33.3	–	–	–	–	–	33.3	33.3	–	–
Italian (n = 7)	–	14.3	–	14.3	–	–	–	42.9	28.6	–	–	–
American (n = 4)	–	–	25.0	25.0	–	–	–	–	25.0	25.0	–	–
Steakhouse (n = 5)	–	–	–	–	–	–	20.0	–	20.0	–	–	60.0
Vegetarian (n = 1)	–	–	–	–	–	–	–	–	–	100.0	–	–
Other (n = 24)	4.2	4.2	12.5	–	8.3	4.2	8.3	12.5	16.7	12.5	8.3	8.3
Total (n = 189)	2.1	3.2	7.9	4.2	6.9	10.1	9.0	9.5	16.4	15.3	6.9	8.5

spectrum, two restaurants indicated that they changed their menu daily, and four changed their menus weekly.

Restaurants were asked to indicate whether changes in menu were reflective of locally available produce. Two-thirds (129) of respondents indicated that menu changes were often a result of variances in foods available locally, while the remainder (68) indicated that the availability of foods locally had little impact. The region with the most significant variation was Central Otago with twenty-seven (77.1 per cent) of the responding restaurants indicating menu changes were reflective of produce available locally. The most surprising result, given its increased branding emphasis on its food and wine, was that of the Hawke's Bay, with just 58.6 per cent of responding restaurants (seventeen) indicating the changes were a result of the availability of local produce.

Reliability of local produce supply

Respondents were asked to indicate on a scale of one to five how reliable local producers were in supplying fresh produce. Respondents indicated a high level of reliability among local producers. Almost a quarter of respondents considered their local producers to be totally reliable in supplying fresh produce, while 42.1 per cent (eighty-three) were very reliable. Slightly over a quarter (26.4 per cent), of respondents stated that their local producers were only sometimes reliable, while just 7.1 per cent considered local producers to be unreliable. Regionally, Central Otago, Canterbury and Hawke's Bay all indicated a high level of reliability, while Marlborough respondents were least impressed with the reliability, with 54.5 per cent stating the suppliers were only somewhat reliable.

Ability to source local products

Generally, respondents indicated it was relatively easy to source local products, with 102 (51.8 per cent) stating it was very or extremely easy to source local products (Table 14.6). This is an important finding, as it indicates that there is a reasonable level of reliability in sourcing local products. This finding was similar across the food and wine regions with the exception of Marlborough, where 31.8 per cent of restaurants indicated it 'can be difficult' or 'very difficult' to source local products. This seems to indicate there may be problems in supply within the local food distribution networks within the Marlborough region. However, this situation may have changed with the establishment of a farmers' market in the region in late 2001. The farmers' market is significant not so much because restaurants will purchase directly

Table 14.6   Difficulty/ease of sourcing local products

	No.	%
Extremely easy	27	13.7
Very easy	75	38.1
Sometimes easy	65	33.0
Can be difficult	22	11.2
Very difficult	7	3.6
Not stated	1	0.5
Total	197	100.0

from it, but because it gives visibility to producers whom restaurants may otherwise have been unaware of, thereby establishing the opportunity for direct supplier–purchaser relationships to be established.

Importance of unique regional cuisine brands to promote food and wine tourism

Overall over half of the respondents rate the importance of regional cuisine brand as being extremely or very important (Table 14.7). However, there was significant regional variation in response. Restaurants in the Marlborough region were the most enthusiastic about the creation of a regional brand for food and wine, with 71.4 per cent of restaurants feeling it was somewhat, very or extremely important to create a brand for their region. Restaurants in the Canterbury region were less interested in establishing a regional food and wine brand, with a quarter (24.8 per cent) indicating it was not very, or not at

Table 14.7   Importance of regional cuisine brand

	No.	%
Extremely important	63	32.0
Very important	47	23.9
Somewhat important	46	23.4
Not very important	20	10.2
Not at all important	18	9.1
Not stated	3	1.5
Total	197	100.0

all important to create a food brand, although half (53.2 per cent) did indicate a high level of importance. Arguably, this again may relate to the metropolitan context of many restaurants in the Canterbury region and the relative size of their market. For rural regions, particular ones such as Marlborough which already has a strong brand presence as a wine region (Hall et al., 2000c), food branding may be a more significant factor in encouraging consumption.

Importance of buy local campaigns and farmers'/growers' markets in the promotion of the use of local produce

Restaurants showed a high level of support for 'buy local' campaigns to promote the use of local produce, with 82.7 per cent indicating they believed it was important to promote buy local campaigns in promoting local produce. Similarly, over two-thirds (68 per cent) of respondents agreed it was very or extremely important to support farmers markets (see Table 14.8). In addition,

Table 14.8 Importance of supporting farmers'/growers' markets and buying local

How important is it to support	Farmers'/ growers' markets		Buy local campaigns		Local products	
	No.	%	No.	%	No.	%
Extremely important	77	39.1	68	34.5	89	45.2
Very important	57	28.9	53	26.9	32	31.5
Somewhat important	33	16.8	42	21.3	34	17.3
Not very important	14	7.1	17	8.6	4	2.0
Not at all important	9	4.6	10	5.1	4	2.0
Not stated	7	3.6	7	3.6	4	2.0
Total	197	100.0%	197	100.0%	197	100.0%

most (76.7 per cent) restaurants indicated an implied importance in the support for restaurants to support local products; agreeing it is very (31.5 per cent) or extremely (45.2 per cent) important for their business to support local products.

Relevance of food and wine tourism

In order to gauge restaurants' level of involvement or a belief that they have a role in food and wine tourism, restaurants were asked to indicate how important food and wine tourism is to their business. This is particularly relevant considering that the restaurants are located in four key food and wine tourism regions.

Almost half (48.7 per cent) of all respondent restaurants stated that food and wine was of maximum relevance to their business, with an additional seventy-one (36.1 per cent) also indicating that tourism is somewhat (17.8 per cent) or quite relevant (18.3 per cent) to their business (Table 14.9). Restaurants in

Table 14.9   Relevance of food and wine tourism to respondents' business

	No.	%
Extremely relevant	96	48.7
Quite relevant	36	18.3
Somewhat relevant	35	17.8
Not very relevant	18	9.1
Not at all relevant	10	5.1
Not stated	2	1.0
Total	197	100.0

Central Otago indicated the highest level of relevance to their business, with 77.1 per cent in the region stating tourism was extremely important to their business.

Willingness to co-operate

Most respondents indicated a level of willingness to work with others to promote food and wine tourism within their region. Just over a quarter of respondents (27.9 per cent) were extremely interested in working with others to promote food and wine tourism, while 25.4 per cent (fifty) were quite interested, and 24.4 per cent (forty-eight) were somewhat interested. One out of five responding restaurants were not particularly interested in working with others (Table 14.10). Respondents were also asked to indicate how interested they would be in being part of a branded and marketed food and wine trail within their region. Just over two-thirds (68.5 per cent, n = 135), stated they would be willing to be part of such a trail.

Table 14.10   Interest in working with others in region to promote food and wine tourism

	No.	%
Extremely interested	55	27.9
Quite interested	50	25.4
Somewhat interested	48	24.4
Not very interested	30	15.2
Not at all interested	11	5.6
Not stated	3	1.5
Total	197	100.0

Support of a local food and wine brand within a region also involves some level of support of local wines. Almost all (90.4 per cent, n = 178) responding restaurants held an off-licence allowing them to sell alcohol. Of those restaurants providing alcohol to their diners, 84.8 per cent (151) actively promoted local wines to their diners, while 92.7 per cent (165) actively promoted New Zealand wines to their diners. A majority (73.0 per cent, 130) of restaurants indicated that the origin of the wine affected their decision to stock it. This result was similar to previous research by Thorsen and Hall (2001) on New Zealand restaurant policies with respect to local wine purchase. Overseas wines accounted for 10 per cent or less of wines served for 66.9 per cent of restaurants. In comparison usage of local and New Zealand wines was considerably higher.

Distribution of regional tourism information to diners

As part of their service, almost all (89.3 per cent, n = 176) restaurants provided information on aspects of the local region. As Table 14.11 demonstrates, the most common aspect of the local region for which information was given were the local tourist attractions and activities. A number of restaurants also gave information on local wines, accommodation, and local vineyards and wineries. This level of support is important if food and wine businesses within a region are to work satisfactorily together in the promotion of food and wine tourism within their region. Restaurants appear to be least willing to provide information on local cafés and restaurants, which is perhaps not overly surprising (although still disappointing) due to the perceived competitive nature of the restaurant business. Three-quarters (148) of businesses preferred to use 'word of mouth' to communicate information

Table 14.11   Information provided at restaurant

Information on	No.	%
Local tourist attractions/activities	132	67.0
Local wines	124	62.9
Local vineyards/wineries	107	54.3
Accommodation	106	53.8
Local restaurants	81	41.1
Local cafés	67	34.0

about the local region to customers. However, a large proportion (59.4 per cent) of businesses also had brochures available to provide information about different aspects of the local region to their patrons.

Conclusions

The results of this chapter indicate that there is substantial support by New Zealand restaurants in the survey areas for the purchase of local food. However, significantly for the future development of direct relationships between producers and restaurants, two-thirds of restaurants would like to increase their local food content, slightly less than 30 per cent believed that this was actually possible under current arrangements.

The results of this New Zealand survey are also similar to that undertaken by Scanlan & Associates et al. (2000) in Iowa. In that

- price needs to be competitive
- supply needs to increase
- quality/freshness are extremely important
- product availability and consistency are very important.

In the Iowa study it was also suggested that there must be consistency in the size of what is supplied, and the product must be packed in standard industry containers. This issue has not surfaced in any of the interviews undertaken in conjunction with the New Zealand research. Furthermore, the New Zealand respondents appear to be more supportive of regional cuisine brands and wine and food tourism, although this may be an artefact of the means by which the research was conducted. Nevertheless, the study does suggest a number of key areas which need to be addressed. However, perhaps most importantly, the issues of creating supply relations between restaurants and producers and a value chain from producer to restaurant to consumer need to be addressed. In undertaking this research it is apparent that local producers and restaurants often do not get together enough to discuss how their relationship could be improved or how to improve the customer experience. As Gibson (1995: 35) noted in the USA, 'Chefs stress that they welcome sales calls from farmers, but are rarely approached. As one chef said: "We are in the yellow pages; the farmers are not, so it is up to them to contact us"'. For example, several restaurants responded that they had never thought to note on their menu where some of the ingredients in the meal were from. With one respondent replying, 'What a fantastic idea, I'm going to do it right away'. He had been using local lamb and other meats all along, but had never told his customers. But perhaps this instance also indicates that, despite attention being paid at a policy level to the creation of improved relationships between producers and restaurants, there is a real need for such information to be tackled at a local level through the provision of information and participants actually talking to each other.

15

Linking food, wine and tourism: the case of the Australian capital region

Brock Cambourne and Niki Macionis

Introduction

Wine and culinary tourism, particularly with a regional flavour, is becoming big business in Australia. Indeed, a number of Australian States and regions have placed substantial emphasis on the development of the food and wine product as 'the bait to bring visitors back for seconds' (Langton, 1996: 3). What, however, are the culinary tourism options of a region or destination that does not have a long gastronomic history? How can such destinations cash in on the tourists' hunger for regional tastes – of both food and wine?

In the absence of a well-developed regional food produce sector, a thriving wine industry can provide an important catalyst in the development of a regional cuisine and culinary identity

(Howard, 1997). However, wine and food tourism are often viewed as separate entities, confined to the cellar door, farm gate or festival, with little consideration placed on linking and weaving culinary tourism throughout all aspects of a destination (Cambourne et al., 2000). In fact, many tourists' first experience with local or regional food and wine is often far removed from its place of production, occurring at their hotel or at a restaurant (Macionis and Cambourne, 1999). Integrating the culinary [food and wine] tourism experience through all aspects of the destination experience by, for example, ensuring that local wines are readily available on restaurant wine lists, would do much to enhance the regional wine and culinary image (see Chapter 2).

Such practices assume particular significance, if one considers that dining out at restaurants and trying different foods and wines consistently ranks among one of the top domestic holiday activities in Australia, with 89 per cent of international visitors dining in restaurants when in Australia (Market Attitude Research Services 1999; South Australian Tourist Commission, 1997). In the Australian Capital Territory (ACT) the Canberra 2000 Visitor Satisfaction Study (Espinoza et al., 2002) shows that 72 per cent of domestic visitors to the ACT dine out in restaurants or cafés during their visit, further highlighting the importance of the food and beverage industry to the regional tourism product. In addition, research conducted by the ACT Cultural Facilities Corporation, notes that wining and dining is becoming a strong motivational factor in choosing Canberra as a short-break destination (Market Attitude Research Services, 1999).

With an increasing consumer focus on regionalism and culinary 'appellations' the wine industry can provide an opportunity for the restaurant and catering sector to develop or strengthen a regional culinary heritage and identity (Downey 1998; Ohlsson 1998). This is particularly important where, due to natural resources or historical development, the development of gastronomic tourism has not been a practical proposition, or indeed, possible. With a reportedly strong correlation between regular wine drinkers and the frequency of their dining experiences (Cambourne and Espinoza, 2000; Faulks and Cambourne, 2001; Weigand, 1995; 1997), a strong regional wine industry presence and focus on culinary tourism development also makes good economic sense for restaurants.

From the wine industry's perspective, the restaurant sector represents substantial opportunities for the marketing and distribution of the regional wine and wine tourism product. This is particularly important in a developing area, dominated by small to medium-sized 'boutique' producers with limited external distribution channels (Centre for Tourism and Leisure Policy

Research, 1998). If properly marketed and integrated, the restaurant sector also provides a secondary opportunity to introduce a winery's and a region's product to a wider audience – becoming, in effect, a de facto cellar door (Hilton, 1998). Importantly, it also provides opportunities for expanding backward economic linkages, by increasing the amount of regional wines used by the hospitality and restaurant sectors. In addition, strengthening linkages between the wine and food industries can facilitate the development and marketing of a regional culinary image, further diversifying the destination product portfolio (Bessière, 1998; Ohlsson, 1998). However, despite the increasing recognition of the role of food and wine in attracting visitors and the often quoted synergy and complementary nature of the food, wine and tourism sectors, there has been relatively little specific focus on wine, food and tourism linkages and opportunities.

This chapter reports on an exploratory study of the nature and extent of linkages and relationships between the wine, restaurant and tourism sectors in Canberra, Australia's national capital. Based on extensive interviews with regional restaurants, the study examines the potential of food and wine tourism in a developing wine region, with no significant culinary heritage, and highlights the perceptions and practices that restrict the development of productive linkages between the wine and food sectors. It also explores opportunities for strategic marketing and product development activities that will benefit both industries at a micro (individual enterprise) and macro (destination product development and marketing) level.

Culinary tourism development in Canberra, Australia's national capital

As a relatively young capital city, with a predominant administrative focus and lacking any traditional agricultural base, it would appear that Canberra has limited culinary tourism potential. In recent years, however, the Canberra District has developed a reputation as a premium and super premium cool climate wine producer, attracting major investment in the area by global wine companies such as BRL Hardy (Cambourne and Macionis, 2000). The growth in and success of the regional wine industry and the subsequent growth in wine tourism has stimulated interest in developing the culinary tourism potential of the region, with for example, substantial investment currently being made in olives in and around the ACT, and the development of a major annual food and wine festival, 'A Taste of Canberra and the Region'.

As Australia's national capital, and home to seventy-seven embassies and High Commissions the culinary tourism potential of the Canberra District is further enhanced by strong multicultural foundations, including staging a national multicultural festival, with a major emphasis on multicultural food and wine (Cambourne et al., 2001) and more restaurants per head of population than anywhere else in Australia (Canberra Tourism and Events Corporation, 2001). Despite these opportunities, the Canberra region lacks a traditional producer base and supply chain networks. There has, however, been a recognition that a successful regional wine industry can be used to develop and leverage culinary tourism opportunities, with the Canberra Tourism and Events Corporation (CTEC) and ACT government currently developing an integrated wine and food tourism strategy as a component of the territory's 'Tourism Master Plan'.

Background

To examine opportunities for culinary tourism opportunities in the ACT, structured personal interviews were conducted with sixty-five Canberra restaurateurs. These interviews focused on:

- perceptions of the regional culinary tourism potential
- restaurant wine management and marketing practices
- the use of regional produce.

Interviewees were selected from the total population of 232 licensed restaurants in the ACT (Jackson, 1998).

Trends and issues in the development of a culinary tourism image in the ACT

A prevailing perception in the tourism industry is that few people choose a destination based on food and wine alone. According to food writer and journalist, John Newton, this may be so, 'but ask anybody for their impressions of a destination, and somewhere along the line they'll tell you . . . 'and the food was sensational' (Tourism New South Wales, 1996: 2). However, as previously noted, due to natural resources and historical development, wine and food tourism might not be a practical proposition, or even possible, for all regions. This would indeed seem to be the case in the Canberra region, with a general perception among Canberra restaurateurs that while they would like to keep their 'money within the regional community',

- 'there was very little available in the way of food'
- 'that regional produce is difficult to source'

- 'there are not enough suppliers'
- 'consumers are willing – but it's too hard to find'
- 'why bother – Sydney is so close and much cheaper'.

Despite such perceptions, 44 per cent of regional restaurateurs stated that they actively try to source and use regional produce. However, with a limited produce base to develop a regional culinary image, the ACT restaurant and catering sector has looked to the wine industry to develop their competitive culinary edge. Indeed, when questioned about culinary tourism opportunities in the region, and trends driving the development of their own industry, the synergies between wine and food and the opportunities presented by the wine industry were the most frequently mentioned issues. For example, 91 per cent of restaurants interviewed stated that they believed there were significant opportunities for both the ACT restaurant sector and wine industry in developing the regional food and wine product and image. In addition, restaurateurs frequently articulated sentiments such as:

- 'cooperative marketing would be fantastic for the food, wine and tourism industries'
- 'raising the profile of local wines will surely increase restaurant sales'
- 'it [developing and marketing the food and wine tourism product] would enhance Canberra's reputation'.

In this context, ACT restaurateurs also identified a number of consistent themes influencing the development of their own industry and the evolution of a culinary tourism image (Table 15.1).

Table 15.1   Trends in the development of food and wine tourism

	% responses
Wine is ahead of food as a lifestyle product	41.5
Increasing consumer sophistication	24.6
Consumers drinking less overall, but drinking more wine	13.8
Increasing consumer experimentation	12.3
Influence of BYO	12.3
Casual dining/outdoor dining/café culture	10.8
Trend towards lighter/healthier food	7.7
Increasing interest in communal dining	4.6
Growing potential of food tourism	3.1
Customer focus on the complete dining experience	3.1

The importance of (Canberra) wines in the regional produce chain

It is clear that the bulk of regional produced used by the ACT restaurant and catering industry comprises local wines. Indeed, 54 per cent of the restaurants interviewed, explicitly identify regional wines as the primary local produce component that they used. Locally produced wines also comprise the bulk of local products requested by and consumed by patrons at ACT restaurants, with comments such as the ones listed below commonly recorded:

- 'We get a lot of consumer enquiries about local produce – especially regional wines – people are interested.'
- 'There is a definite interest in local wines by consumers at restaurants – they want to be educated about them.'
- 'Tourists look for local wines, before they look for local food.'

This is also reflected by the fact that 64 per cent of restaurants interviewed stated that they at least occasionally receive requests for Canberra wines in their establishments, while 41 per cent report that customers at least occasionally bring Canberra wines as bring your own (BYO) alcohol to their restaurants (Table 15.2).

As such, in the case of the ACT, locally produced wines obviously form the backbone of the regional produce chain and provide the foundations for the development of a regional culinary image.

Table 15.2 Consumer demand for Canberra wines in Canberra restaurants

Requests for Canberra wines		*Canberra wines as BYO*	
Response	*% respondents*	*Response*	*% respondents*
Often	9	Often	2
Occasionally	55	Occasionally	39
Never	30	Never	34
Don't know	6	Don't know	3
		Not Applicable	22

Note: because of the opportunity for multiple responses the total does not add up to 100 per cent.

Impediments to development of a food and wine tourism image

Despite being an integral, if not vital, component of the regional produce image and chain, the widespread use of Canberra District wines in the development of a culinary tourism image is faced by a number of significant problems. Foremost among these is a 'general perception that they [regional wines] are too expensive, or not good value for money' (Centre for Tourism and Leisure Policy Research, 1998: 106). The remainder of this chapter examines issues surrounding the use of regional wines by the Canberra restaurant and catering sector. It also identifies a range of considerations that should be considered to increase the use of regional wines in the restaurant setting, thereby facilitating the development of a regional culinary image.

Perhaps the primary impediment to the greater use of locally produced wines in the regional restaurant and catering sector revolves around issues of cost. Indeed, in this study, 23 per cent of restaurants interviewed noted that they did not believe that regional wines provided 'good value for money', with 34 per cent of restaurants stating that they believed the quality of Canberra wines was quite variable noting that there were 'some good and some bad' regional wines. It is obvious that the emergent nature of the Canberra District wine industry and a subsequent varying reputation leads to a perception they can be 'too high risk' for some restaurants. Specific reasons reported by Canberra restaurants for not using Canberra wines are provided in Figure 15.1.

Such perceptions would appear to result from a general lack of knowledge and understanding of the regional wine industry product and business environment among restaurateurs. Indeed, a significant proportion of establishments interviewed reported little formal contact with Canberra wines. Sixty-three per cent of restaurants stated that Canberra District wines were simply not marketed to their establishment. In the context of marketing, many of the reasons noted in Figure 15.1 for restaurants failing to use regional wines could be mitigated via a simple and cohesively articulated communications strategy which addresses misconceptions and issues such as cost of production, availability and supply and general awareness.

Restaurant wine list management and marketing

The restaurant and catering sector, like the wine industry, is largely composed of small, diverse and dispersed businesses where the proprietor is often the main contributor to the operation – that is, making all management decisions

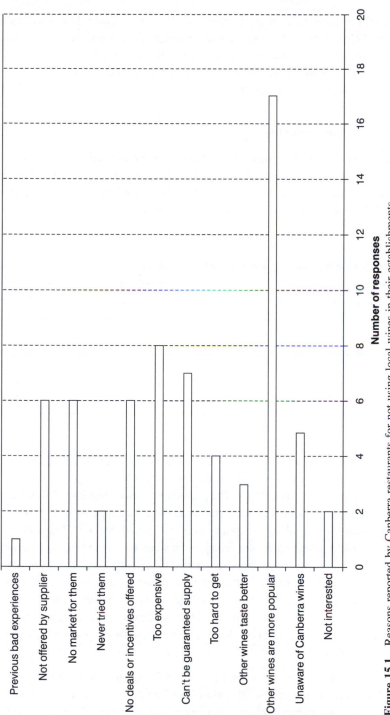

Figure 15.1 Reasons reported by Canberra restaurants for not using local wines in their establishments

without the assistance of paid expertise (Edwards, 1986; Macionis, 1997; 1998; Welsh, 1994). As such, an understanding of who the key decision makers are, and how they develop, manage and market their wine lists can assist wine producers in formulating effective marketing and distribution strategies targeted at this sector.

Wine list management

In the majority of restaurants interviewed, the product mix of the wine list appears to be based primarily on management preference, with owner or restaurant manager constructing the wine list in 82 per cent of surveyed establishments. These data are presented in Table 15.3.

Table 15.3   Responsibility for wine list construction

Who constructs the wine list?	% of sample
Owner	60
Restaurant manager	22
Food and beverage manager	8
Combined input of staff	6
Professional wine consultant	5

Canberra restaurateurs were also asked to nominate which factors influence their choice of wines on a four-point scale (with 0 being 'of no influence' to 3, being 'extremely influential'). The primary factors influencing the choice of wines for wine lists by Canberra restaurateurs are presented in Figure 15.2. Predominant among these are price, availability and previous knowledge of wines. While reinforcing the need to articulate a message of quality, availability and value for money, these data concur with the findings of previous studies (Barrows, 1996; Fattorini, 1996; Ochsner et al., 1988) and practices recommended in industry trade journals and beverage management texts which note that the primary considerations in developing and or adjusting a wine list should be clientele, restaurant menu, price compatibility and availability.

There are a number of simple activities that wine producers and marketers can employ to encourage the use of regional wines by the restaurant and catering sector. Ensuring efficient reliable delivery of wines and providing information

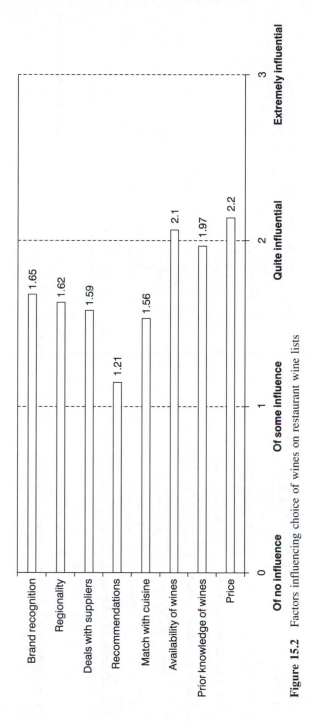

Figure 15.2 Factors influencing choice of wines on restaurant wine lists

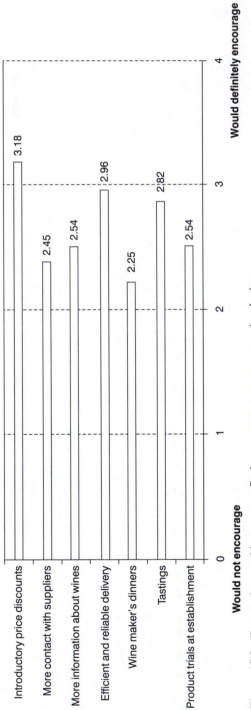

Introductory price discounts — 3.18

More contact with suppliers — 2.45

More information about wines — 2.54

Efficient and reliable delivery — 2.96

Wine maker's dinners — 2.25

Tastings — 2.82

Product trials at establishment — 2.54

0   1   2   3   4

Would not encourage   **Would definitely encourage**

Figure 15.3   Factors that would encourage Canberra restaurateurs to use regional wines

about wines, opportunities to taste and trial the product, and introductory price discounts would provide the greatest encouragement for Canberra restaurateurs to include Canberra wines on their wine list (Figure 15.3).

Small, boutique wine producers and/or their distributors should also maintain regular and frequent contact with restaurateurs. On average, wine lists are altered every 3.7 months. Several restaurants noted that they adjust their wine list on a daily basis, while one restaurant stated that they never changed their wine list. The availability (or unavailability) of particular wines was also cited as the most common reason for changing wine lists in Canberra restaurants (Table 15.4).

Table 15.4   Reasons nominated for changing wine lists in Canberra restaurants

Reason for changing wine list	Frequency of response
Availability of certain wines	56
To introduce new wines	49
To try different wines	47
It is always changed regularly	28
Change in restaurant menu	24
Deals and incentives to stock particular wines	17
Seasonality	10
Poor performance of wines on the list	3
Price increases of wines on the wine list	2
Customer requests	2
Wine list is not changed	2
To specifically stock boutique wines	1
Personal taste	1

It is interesting to note that 75 per cent of interviewees stated that they altered their wine list in order to introduce new wines, while poor performance of wines on the list and price increases were noted as catalysts for altering the wine list by only 5 and 3 per cent of respondents respectively. It would thus appear easier to have a wine placed on a wine list than have it removed.

Wine list marketing

Dodd (1997) notes that wine consumption in a restaurant setting is not based solely on a diner's predetermined decision to purchase a quantity or quality of wine, and that consumers can be influenced by a range of implicit or supplementary marketing cues employed by the restaurant. Furthermore, he notes that supplementary wine marketing activities, such as personal selling by staff and merchandising such as the use of 'tent cards' or 'table talkers', serving wine by the glass and matching particular wines with specific menu items, can substantially influence restaurant wine sales.

Offering wine by the glass is becoming an important restaurant wine marketing technique, which can account for up to 50 per cent of a restaurant's wine sales (Ripe, 1998). All restaurants interviewed reported that they served wine by the glass with 87 per cent of them noting that wine by the glass was popular with customers. Only 6 per cent stated that wine by the glass was not popular with customers, while the remainder noted that it was at least moderately or somewhat popular. Interestingly, few other supplementary wine-marketing activities were reported by interviewees. The nature of supplementary wine marketing techniques employed by Canberra restaurateurs is detailed in Table 15.5.

Table 15.5 Supplementary wine marketing techniques used by Canberra restaurateurs

Wine marketing activity	Number of restaurants frequency of response
Wine of the month promotions	11
Table talkers/tent cards	10
Food and wine specials	9
Winemaker's dinners	8
Staff recommendations	8
Wine displays in restaurant	5
Wine tastings	3
Give-away promotions	2

Personal selling and staff recommendations can have a significant effect on restaurant wine sales, by influencing the decision-making behaviour of customers (Dodd, 1997). As such staff training also represents an important restaurant wine marketing technique. Indeed, 80 per cent of restaurants interviewed provide some form of wine training for their staff. Given these reported levels of training it is surprising that only eight restaurants explicitly identified staff recommendations as a supplementary wine marketing activity. The majority of restaurant staff wine training consisted of informal discussions and tastings of wines on the wine list, however, some

Table 15.6 Nature and focus of restaurant wine training provided by Canberra restaurants

Nature of training	*% of restaurants*	*Focus of wine training*
Informal	63	Informal tastings and/or discussions Staff encouraged to taste widely and frequently Impromptu tastings Education re 'best sellers'
Formal	14	Wine tastings with wine reps or wine makers Wine appreciation courses with wine maker/viticulturalist Formal tasting nights for staff and management Provision of wine maker's notes Food and wine pairing instruction

establishments provided formal wine training opportunities. The nature and range of restaurant wine-training opportunities are detailed in Table 15.6.

In addition, 21 per cent noted that they at least attempted to involve either wine makers or distributors in some form of either formal or informal wine training for their staff.

Discussion

It is obvious that Canberra District wines are an important component of the regional tourism product and that they represent a significant part of the local produce chain in Canberra restaurants. It is also clear, that in order to increase distribution opportunities within the restaurant and catering sector, and facilitate the development of a regional culinary image, the Canberra District wine industry needs to overcome a number of seemingly ingrained misconceptions among Canberra restaurateurs, including:

- a general perception that regional wines do not provide value for money
- a reputation of varying quality
- a general lack of awareness.

The lack of a cohesive marketing strategy, directed at the restaurant and catering sector also restricts wine sales and the development of an industry profile in this sector.

At a micro, or individual enterprise level, these data do, however, highlight a range of simple marketing and communication approaches which could greatly assist the penetration of regional wines into the restaurant and catering sector. Recalling that 63 per cent of Canberra restaurants stated that Canberra wines were not marketed to them at all, simply increasing both the level of overall wine marketing and sales activity to the restaurant sector will undoubtedly increase the profile of Canberra District wines. Marketing activity and the articulation of the sales message needs to emphasize quality for money, guaranteed availability and regionality.

With 80 per cent of restaurants interviewed offering some form of training to their staff, the provision of training opportunities and/or material for restaurant management and staff would further increase the profile and sales opportunities of Canberra wines as well as providing a mechanism for the articulation of a cohesive marketing strategy to 'front-line' sales people and ambassadors. This is particularly important with prior knowledge of particular wines being a 'quite influential' factor determining the choice of wines on a restaurant wine list. Empowering restaurant staff to make specific wine suggestions with meals can also substantially increase wine sales. In order for staff to feel comfortable suggesting wines, they first have to feel confident about their wine knowledge (Ochsner et al., 1988). With the product mix on Canberra wine lists being largely determined by management preference, identifying and targeting appropriate restaurant personnel will greatly enhance this range of activities. Reducing the perceived risk to the restaurant (and its customers) by offering introductory price discounts, requesting that wines be offered for sale by the glass, and providing direction in suggesting food and wine combinations should be considered by wine producers when developing restaurant wine marketing strategies.

From a restaurant's perspective, wine sales are an important source of revenue. As an appurtenance to the enjoyment of a meal, wine can significantly enhance the overall dining experience, increasing satisfaction, repeat business and per customer yield (Barrows, 1996; Dodd, 1997). As such, wine lists represent a significant marketing and merchandising opportunity for restaurants. However, an ever-increasing consumer interest in wine means that restaurants have to scrutinize the structure and management of their wine lists in order to maximize its profit potential.

As restaurant consumers increasingly view wine as an everyday commodity, the composition and structure of restaurant wine lists will come under increasing pressure (Barrows, 1996; Fattorini, 1996). This is a legitimate concern of Canberra restaurateurs, with a considerable number noting that the average consumer was becoming more sophisticated and knowledgeable (particularly with regard to wine), while at the same time demanding better value for money. With a reportedly strong correlation between regular wine drinkers and the frequency of their dining-out experiences, an increased focus on wine list structure can have significant impacts on developing a loyal customer base and increasing the amount each customer spends (Wiegand, 1995; 1997). An added benefit to both the wine and restaurant sector, of actively pursuing the development of a regional culinary and wine image via cross-marketing alliances and practices is the so called 'demonstration effect' whereby the domestic market demands a greater quantity, or similar products as those consumed by tourists (Telfer and Wall, 1996).

At a macro, or destination marketing, level it is clear that the regional wine industry currently occupies an important place in the regional produce chain and that the existence of a thriving boutique wine industry provides a good culinary tourism product base. As the 'Embassy City', with a plethora of ethnic eateries, and simply taking a more expansive view of where regional produce can be sourced, the opportunities for the use of regional food products in developing culinary tourism are substantially increased. The capital region, for example, includes smoked trout and goats cheese from Jindabyne, South Coast seafood and cheeses, Gundagai venison, Murrumbateman lamb, stone fruits and pome fruits from Batlow and Pialligo, berries from Crookwell, a developing regional olive industry and the superb smoked meats from Poachers Pantry in Canberra (Brander, 1997). As noted previously however, many tourists' first experience with local or regional food and wine is often far removed from its place of production, occurring at their hotel or at a restaurant. In this context the restaurant and catering sector represents a significant opportunity to facilitate the development of a regional culinary image and, thereby, an increased use of regional produce.

Conclusion

A broader range of stakeholders such as those noted above, need to be actively and explicitly brought into the wine/culinary tourism chain. By doing so, these stakeholders become both actors in and ambassadors for the regional wine tourism product. This is exemplified in the Languedoc-Roussillon region of France, where more than 1000 restaurants display the 'Hostevin' seal of approval, signifying that they have at least five regional wines on their wine list, which are served under appropriate conditions by staff with a minimum level of knowledge about the local wines (Comite Regional du Tourisme, n.d.). By actively developing broader linkages, and weaving the wine (and food) product through every aspect of the tourism and destination experience, the wine, food and tourism sectors can develop a strong regional culinary image while at the same time greatly increasing their share of the tourist dollar.

16

Managing food and tourism developments: issues for planning and opportunities to add value

Steven Boyne and Derek Hall

Introduction

As the number of destination areas employing locally produced food and beverage products to strengthen their tourism products increases, so too there has been a growing interest in this topic on the part of academic researchers and development agencies. Academic studies of tourism and food relationships have examined a range of issues including: caterers' use of local foodstuffs (Telfer and Wall, 1996); competition for land and labour between the tourism and food production sectors (Belisle, 1983); the role of food in destination image (Hughes, 1995); agriculture's role in creating touristic landscapes (Buchgraber, 1996); and tourists' food choices (Reynolds, 1993).

Studies such as these have been undertaken from a variety of disciplinary perspectives including economics, marketing, regional development and anthropology, and have variously examined the interrelationships between tourism and food and the economic, social, cultural and physical impacts which are manifested in tourism food contexts. These impacts can be found in both supply and demand side domains and can be felt simultaneously in both. Some food and tourism initiatives, for example, seek to generate positive outcomes for both the tourism and food production sectors – through increased economic activity – and tourists – by enhancing their visitor experiences.

In the UK, the potential for the tourism and food sectors to work together to achieve mutual benefit at local and regional levels has also been endorsed in recent strategy documents for agricultural, tourism and regional development. Examples include: the Department of Media, Culture and Sport (DCMS, 1999: 67, 100); Department of the Environment, Transport and the Regions (DETR, 2000: 84); English Tourism Council (2001: 3); and Scottish Executive (2001: 23). The general theme of these policy recommendations can be usefully summarized in the recent Visit Scotland strategy document, *Tourism Framework for Action 2002–2005*, which notes the requirement to create 'stronger links between tourism and sectors such as retail, food and drink and transport that have a major influence on the tourism "experience", and which also benefit from tourism' (Scottish Executive, 2002: 19).

This case study-based contribution takes a management perspective and highlights issues for strategic planning and opportunities to enhance the value of local and regional food-related tourism initiatives. The authors do not attempt to make concrete recommendations, as, owing to these areas' heterogeneity, any such recommendations would be rendered, at best, impractical.

Thinking of a food analogy, we are reminded of Escoffier's (1907) enduring classic *Le Guide Culinaire*: first published in 1903. This cooking guide places a greater emphasis on listing dishes' ingredients while devoting little energy to describing methods for preparation. In a similar way, we provide details of potential 'ingredients' for development and suggest some methods which may be employed to create a finished product. The exact nature of both the development process and the final product will, however, be dependent on what's available locally and what the 'cooks' are aiming to create. It is our intention that his contribution should be viewed as a thinkpiece for those with an interest in or who are engaged in such a task, rather than providing a transferable 'recipe for development'.

286

The context for this contribution is food-related destination area development initiatives and the authors draw upon their own experiences of project development and related research to describe a range of planning-related issues and opportunities which may arise. The type of initiative being described is one which aims to strengthen the linkages between local tourism and food-related sectors. Initiatives of this type typically employ some form of literature (a guidebook, pamphlet or Internet web site) to promote the area based on the quality and distinctiveness of its local food and beverage products. Areas enjoying greater gastronomic notoriety can use this to attract first-time visitors to the area while initiatives in areas not so endowed may seek to influence visitors upon their arrival.

Underpinning such developments is the rationale that, in order to maintain and enhance local economic and social vitality (often in rural areas – hence the food production dimension), creating back-linkages between the tourism and food-production sectors can add value within an area's local economy. Value is also added to the tourism product as this is strengthened and visitors' experiences are enhanced – hopefully sufficiently to engender repeat visits. While the contribution is contextually grounded in tourism- and food-related development initiatives, many of the points made are germane to other types of tourism development, particularly where industry participants are typically small or micro-businesses and a variety of agencies are involved in the development process.

Setting aims and engaging stakeholders

As with any strategic plan, the broad aims and specific objectives of the initiative should be unambiguous and such that relevant stakeholders should be afforded the opportunity to have an input into their formulation at the earliest possible opportunity.

Objectives which are specific and clear will help strengthen funding applications for development assistance and provide indicators for objective measurement in subsequent monitoring and evaluation exercises. In addition, aims and objectives which are clearly stated from an early stage can help avoid disappointment from participating stakeholders (i.e. member businesses) who may hold unrealistic expectations.

With regard to stakeholders, engaging these at an early stage of project planning is likely to have a significant degree of importance, both during the initial stages and in terms of the project's longer-term continuity and success. Major issues relating to stakeholder participation include the role of community members in fostering sustainable development processes and the institutional (i.e. agencies') support for the initiative.

'Community members', at this stage of the food-related tourism development, is likely to mean members of the 'local business community', although in the longer term, members of the wider community may also 'participate' in the tourism development through sharing in the resultant economic and social benefits (see, for example, Timothy, 1999: 372). With regard to the importance of the local business community: first, they provide a locally participatory dimension which is important for contributing to sustainable development objectives such as minimizing economic leakages; militating against overdependence on outside influences; keeping the initiative small scale and therefore less environmentally damaging; and maintaining consonance with local needs (see, for example, Murphy, 1985; Richards and Hall, 2000). In addition, participants in the development process (and ultimately the wider community and the tourism product) benefit from the educational dimension of their participative experience.

Second, responsibility for the longer-term management of the initiative may fall to this group of stakeholders as public sector financial support is withdrawn – as often happens following an initial kick-start period. Engaging the local business community at an early stage of development, in the formulation of aims and objectives and in providing them with a sense of ownership over these, can, therefore, be a key factor influencing the success of the initiative (see, for example, Caffyn, 2000: 90).

In relation to the role of the local and regional agencies (local authority, business support networks, development agencies and tourist boards), which, together, constitute the institutional support network, it is important that they too feel some sort of ownership over the project in order that they will continue to support it over time. Support from the local or regional tourism authority is more likely to be forthcoming – and sustained – if, for example, it has been involved in the development of the project.

The authors have noted from previous research (Boyne, Hall and Williams, forthcoming) that while in any locale there may be many tourism-related development initiatives which wish to be represented in the area tourist board's promotional material, owing to limited promotional space and the requirement to promote quality goods and services to visitors, the tourist board is likely to entertain only those initiatives/projects which:

- are considered major and enjoy national or international recognition
- can demonstrate acceptable or exceptional levels of quality assurance, or
- have achieved the tourist board's endorsement in some other way.

Engaging the tourist board in the development process can act positively in forcing the issue of achieving acceptable levels of quality assurance and/or in contributing significantly to the initiative securing the tourist board's endorsement.

Support for training and development

Satisfying quality assurance requirements will, then, be a key objective for the initiative. As discussed above, securing promotional support from the local tourist board may require the initiative to meet certain criteria stipulated by the tourist board. Participant businesses may be required to be tourist board members and/or comply with statutory or discretionary legislation (e.g. health and safety, disabled access, customer service, environmental accreditation). At the initiative-wide level, the tourist board may reasonably expect assurances that information provided for dissemination (via brochures, web sites, etc.) is valid at the time of publication. Such a requirement generates another management task – that is, maintaining up-to-date information on, for example, participant businesses, special events, special offers and themed activities. In addition to satisfying external agencies' requirements, invitation to individual businesses to participate in the scheme may be on an exclusionary basis in order to maintain quality and satisfy the objectives of the initiative (in this example to encourage the use of locally produced goods, strengthen the local tourism product and enhance the visitors' experience). Criteria for membership may relate to quality of produce and service, and focus to a greater or lesser extent on applicants' commitment to locally produced goods.

Two drivers for quality assurance have therefore been identified: on the one hand, the local or regional tourist board may insist on participant businesses meeting certain standards and, on the other hand, if the initiative is aiming to create a first-class product, then it must maintain its own quality-related criteria for selecting member businesses. Whatever quality assurance criteria are set to achieve this second task, it is likely that some businesses which wish to participate in the initiative will fail to meet some or all of them.

Following on from this, the opportunity therefore exists for the initiative to perform an important locally based quality/training-related role. Having engaged local industry members and development agencies in the initiative – and therefore having access to these participants' pooled knowledge of training/skills needs and opportunities – it may be possible for the initiative to act as a signposting organization for training materials and services. An operational framework for this activity might require applicants for project membership to be assessed based on a set of criteria including quality of goods and service. Having undertaken this assessment, the applicant is either granted membership or offered training-related advice as regards achieving the requisite awards or levels of competence required. If appropriate, several categories of membership may even be available so that members joining at 'lower rungs' are motivated to undertake training in order to progress through improving their skills and product quality. Although this method may be less appropriate for non-catering businesses. (The efficacy of such an approach will depend, however, upon the participants' perceiving benefit from 'moving up the scale'. For example, while this approach may work with catering establishments where the notion and meaning of a 'star-based' rating system is well understood by both businesses and consumers, in a non-catering context, such a rating system may not, in fact, be appropriate.)

Therefore, using the opportunity to draw upon the pooled knowledge of the network of local agencies and participating stakeholders, the potential exists for the initiative to put together a portfolio of training opportunities complete with information on how and where to access these. In this way, value is added to the initiative in so far as it can act as a skills/quality auditing and training signposting agency, heightening businesses' and individuals' aware-ness of the need for, and positive consequences of, improved service provision and helping individual businesses to recognize and address their training needs and upgrade their skills levels accordingly.

Realizing this opportunity will represent a tangible output for the initiative and will help add value to it in terms of the resultant local-area benefits. Examples of benefits related to the training dimension include improved skills levels in the locale, heightened awareness of training-related issues among practitioners and fostering a training culture within the business community. This latter point can be especially useful where local businesses are typically small and micro in scale – particularly as it is these types of business which often have less appreciation of the positive role which training and staff development can play in strategic business management.

Other less tangible outputs

From the consumers' perspective, any training-related dimension of the tourism food initiative will not be a visible part of the tourism product, although they should enjoy its benefits. In that respect we may consider the training-related dimension a less tangible output of the initiative. Other less tangible outputs might include:

- Enhanced levels of professionalism and awareness of local heritage. That is, through their involvement in the initiative, local business people and staff members become more engaged with the needs and expectations of visitors and the wider local tourism-related product.
- To facilitate the use of locally produced food and beverages, a local or regional trading network may be established which connects users of local products with producers, processors and existing distributors. Such a network can help overcome supply-related difficulties which can be experienced by caterers, such as inconsistency of product availability or specification from small local producers.
- Local tourism food initiatives can act as catalysts for the formation of strategic alliances between local producers, processors, retailers and distributors. Joint working has been shown to enhance the ability of small and often peripherally located food-related businesses to access external markets. Meanwhile, creating an awareness of and demand for the locally-produced food and beverage products – both during visitors' tourism trips and following their return home – is accomplished by more tangible outputs such as the guidebook and other promotional material.

From the perspective of participating businesses, outputs may also appear, respectively, more and less tangible. More tangible outputs for this constituency might include increased turnover for businesses and associated decreasing economic leakages – in addition to the tourist products which are created, such as the guidebook describing the food route, food way or taste trail and other promotional material, special events and themed activities. Less tangible outputs might include the creation of strategic alliances, improved local supply chain and business networking, and increased entrepreneurial confidence.

Project planners should make *both* the more and less tangible outputs clear to participant businesses at an early planning stage, as participants' awareness of these is likely to be critical for the longer-term continuation of the initiative. Specifically, this concern relates to the need to plan for an exit strategy – adding this dimension to the wider development strategy will provide funding agencies with a time-bound period within which to commit financial support. Because a realistic exit strategy is likely to involve stakeholder support and input, their appreciation of the potential benefits and subsequent expression of commitment to sustaining the initiative in the longer term may be a key dimension in securing start-up funding.

Funding and the exit strategy

So, in the context of longer-term financial planning for the project, it is necessary to demonstrate the potential benefits of the initiative to participant members of the local business community. As described above, this constituency should be brought on board from an early stage of development – in order to increase their sense of ownership over the development process and its outputs. This sense of ownership will hopefully engender a more positive attitude as regards participants' willingness to take control of the initiative in the longer term. Securing participants' commitment to such longer-term management of the initiative may prove key to attracting initial funding assistance as, increasingly, funding agencies wish to commit their support over a predetermined period following which they are relieved of funding responsibility.

Challenges which may face initiatives at this stage of their evolution include: (a) losing members as fees for participation are introduced to cover the shortfall in public sector support; and/or (b) compromising quality standards as inclusion by membership fee may displace (by financial necessity) inclusion on merit of quality. Negative impacts from situation (a) may be ameliorated by new members joining as others leave, while avoiding scenario (b) is a matter for the respective steering group or management committee to deal with at an initiative-specific level. In general, potential negative impacts arising from both these situations will be most effectively combated by the initiative producing benefits that outweigh whatever membership fees are levied and by making participation attractive to new members. In addition, successful initiatives will, most likely, inherently encourage the maintenance of a selective membership policy based on quality of goods and service.

The analysis above illustrates something of a chicken and egg situation. Participant businesses are unlikely to commit time and/or finances unless the initiative is providing positive benefits, yet in order to gain start-up funding it may be necessary to secure businesses' future commitment before any benefits are realized. In this situation it would be useful to have a body of research – describing similar initiatives' successes – to draw upon. Unfortunately, such a research literature is not currently available – perhaps owing to the relative newness of this type of development initiative.

Following this then – and adopting for a moment a researchers' and planners' perspective rather than that of a project manager – it should be incumbent upon planners and developers engaged in such initiatives to undertake monitoring and evaluation towards providing indicators of success and failure.

The data generated from such efforts can then be used in future and to the benefit of other areas facing economic and social development challenges.

Monitoring and evaluation

Tourism expenditure, in general terms, is difficult to identify, as many products only become 'tourism products' at the point of sale. At an individual business level, disaggregating tourists' expenditure from that of residents is often not possible. If, therefore, the following question was asked of a retailer or caterer, 'what proportion of your turnover is attributable to expenditure by visitors who have been influenced to visit your premises by the tourism food initiative promotional material?' they would, we suggest, have some difficulty in providing a quantifiable answer.

In the light of these difficulties, how, then, should the monitoring and evaluation of the economic and wider impact(s) of food-related tourism development initiative be undertaken? One possible approach is to canvass the visitors themselves using a questionnaire survey. Interviewer-completed questionnaires are the most effective type, however, achieving a representative sample (roughly 200–400 depending on the level of accuracy required) would involve a significant – but not unrealistic – effort in collecting the data. Alternatively, short questionnaires for respondents' completion could be included with the guidebooks, other promotional literature or be distributed by participant businesses on their premises. Data collected from visitors in this way may not only relate to economic dimensions of the initiative, but also to experiential data on, for example, visitors' preferences and satisfaction.

Another source of data with which to assess initiatives' economic and wider impacts is the participating businesses. More quantifiable indicators include businesses' turnover and profit levels, proportion of locally produced goods being sold, length of season for extended opening and number of visitors/patrons. However, if participating businesses are to contribute to the monitoring and evaluation process effectively, then the requirement to monitor their respective business's performance using these or other suitable indicators must be made clear, both in the development strategy and to the individual participant businesses.

Participant members' 'more subjective' assessments of the initiative's performance can also be used to maximize the relevance of their feedback. If this type of response is to be sought, then it will be useful if the broader aims of the development initiative are clearly laid out and understood by members. To help clarify and maintain awareness of the aims of the initiative among members, it may be desirable to hold regular members' meetings or to set up some form of communication forum/fora to stimulate debate and discussion. Regular meetings of this sort would assist the monitoring and evaluation process in addition to helping provide an ongoing performance profile.

Summing up

Much of this chapter may appear to be restate the same or similar points as the reader moves through it. This reflects, however, the interlinkages between stages in the development process and the way in which the dynamic relationship between aims and objectives and outputs is linked by the monitoring and evaluation process. Underpinning the contribution is the emphasis on start-up funding and the relationship between this, stakeholder support and the expected benefits of the initiative.

Planning issues have been described and opportunities for locally or regionally based food and tourism development initiatives to generate added value for both the tourism- and food-related products highlighted. In addition, the authors have attempted to emphasize the interwoven nature of different elements of the development process. Drawing on our research- and development-based experience, we have described:

- the importance of setting clear and unambiguous aims and objectives and engendering stakeholder, development agency and tourism board support
- the opportunity for the initiative to act at a local or regional level in a training-related capacity to improve skills, heighten training awareness and foster a training culture
- the way in which initiatives can contribute to increasing local actors' product- and consumer-related knowledge, act as a focus for creating linkages between local producers and processors and caterers using their products, and act as catalysts for the formation of intra- and inter-sectoral strategic alliances
- the interlinkages between negotiating start-up funding, planning for the longer-term financial sustainability of the initiative and securing stakeholder involvement in and commitment to the initiative
- the critical role of monitoring and evaluation in informing and assisting all stages in the development process.

It is intended that this chapter should provide a practical and useful thinkpiece for those interested or engaged in destination area development processes which aim to draw together local tourism and food production/processing sectors. The content is intended to be transferable in nature and it is for this reason that firm recommendations and conclusions are not made. We hope readers can take what is useful to them in the context of their respective regions and interests, and that this short piece acts both as a practical planning guide and as a 'springboard' for new and locally appropriate ideas to be generated.

17

New global cuisine: tourism, authenticity and sense of place in postmodern gastronomy

Rosario Scarpato and Roberto Daniele

What is the future of global gastronomy tourism? Reports from the industry around the world indicate that, no longer accessory or marginal as in the past, the food and wine experience is now increasingly the principal – if not the only – motivation in the selection of a tourist destination (BITEG, 2001). At the same time, however, we are warned that 'we are facing the grim perspective of having the heart taken out of gourmet travel' due to 'the emerging dining-out sector within the global food industry' (Symons, 1999: 336). In particular, it has been argued that 'when menus become the same the world over, gastronomic tourism becomes redundant'. Gastronomy scholar Michael Symons has blamed the *new global cuisine* for this situation arguing that this new approach to cooking 'leads to increased sameness' (Symons, 1999: 336).

Other authors have gone even further with their criticism. According to Barbara Santich, the co-ordinator of the first Graduate Program in Gastronomy at the University of Adelaide in Australia, the buzzword today is globalization, 'an intermingling of various cuisines and multiple reciprocal influences' (Santich, 2000). She attacks such culinary hybridizations by noting that 'when several culinary cultures are put together on the one plate (as, for example, in spaghetti with black bean sauce) the result is "fusion" – or perhaps confusion: in company with others, each culture loses something of itself and its impact is reduced' (Santich, 2000). Thus, for this author 'global cuisine might be interpreted as the foods and dishes which can be found anywhere in the world. By extrapolation, it means the same food and dishes throughout the whole world. And this is precisely the reproach, that globalization results in homogenization' (Santich, 2000).

Globalization last hurrahs?

These positions are not too dissimilar from those of critics who – according to the Peruvian-born writer Mario Vargas Llosa – condemn globalization as 'a nightmare or negative utopia' in which the world 'is losing its linguistic and cultural diversity' (Vargas Llosa, 2001). Food and cuisine globalization are not spared by the condemnation since they are analogous to languages, as Lévi Strauss (1978: 471) pointed out 'Cooking ... is with language a truly universal form of human activity'.

In general terms anti-globalization's views gained momentum in the aftermath of the 11 September 2001 ('9–11') events, with some scholars going as far as proclaiming that the era of globalization is at its last hurrah (Anonymous, 2002). An intrepid statement, in truth, considering that the decade ending in 2000 has seen the most remarkable growth in global activities, including tourism.

> Worldwide, travellers made an additional 50 million trips across national borders in 2000 to reach 698.8 million international arrivals, up from 457.2 million a decade before ... Cross-border telephone traffic ... saw a steady growth of roughly 10 billion minutes ... Internet hosts (computers that allow users to communicate with one another along the Internet) continued to climb, growing by 44 per cent. (Anonymous, 2002: 38)

In the aftermath of 9–11 events tourist numbers in fact went down for the first time since 1982 but the prevailing consensus among experts is that global tourism is poised to achieve 'tremendous growth' in the foreseeable future (Foroohar, 2002: 36). The World Tourism Organization predicts an increase in the number of tourist arrivals to more than 1 billion by 2010 (Foroohar, 2002: 36). In other words, as far as tourism is concerned, globalization is far from being dead. Other aspects of globalization, however, 'are likely to sustain their forward momentum' (Anonymous, 2002: 38) according to the *Kearney Globalization Index*, which ranks the twenty most global nations. Call rates will keep falling 20 per cent per year and the international telephone traffic will grow at the same pace it has since 1997. Internet traffic also will continue its expansion, particularly in developing countries like China and India (Anonymous, 2002).

On the other hand, at a cultural level, too, more balanced analyses which reject radical anti-globalization positions are gaining ground. For Vargas Llosa the inflexible defence 'of cultural identity reveal a static conception of culture that has no historical basis'. As he puts it, no cultures have ever remained identical and unchanged over time. For this reason, he argues, 'globalization must be welcomed because it notably expands the horizons of individual liberty'. Accordingly, he suggests that 'the fear of Americanization of the planet is more ideological paranoia than reality'. The reality is, instead, that 'the vanishing of borders and an increasingly interdependent world has created incentives for new generations to learn and assimilate to other cultures'. 'Globalization will not make local cultures disappear', on the contrary, in a framework of worldwide openness; 'all that is valuable and worthy of survival in local cultures will find fertile ground in which to bloom' (Vargas Llosa, 2001).

In some ways, Vargas Llosa is on the same side of those thinkers who first saw a *euphoric* dimension to globalization, a concept evoking 'a cybernetic dance of cultures, 'one planet under a groove', the transcendence of rigid ideological and political divisions, and the worldwide availability of cultural products and information' (Shohat and Stam, 1996: 146).

It is against this backdrop that food globalization and gastronomy tourism are analysed in this chapter, which is articulated in three parts. The first part is an introduction to the issues of authenticity and sense of place in postmodern gastronomy tourism. The focus of the second part is new global cuisine (NGC) as a paradigm for gastronomy tourist products (GTP), which are not only the traditional 'bricks and mortar' gastronomic poles, as restaurants, wineries or food outlets, but also a new breed of gastro-attractions within established tourist destinations, including food and wine events and festivals based on virtual clustering. Finally, remarks on the possible evolution of gastronomy globalization and its implications for tourism are contained in the conclusion.

The topics of this chapter are approached with the tools of tourism research but also seen through the transdisciplinary perspective of gastronomy studies (Scarpato, 2000). Within this emerging theoretical framework gastronomy is the pursuit of the best possible eating and drinking, but in a *reflective* mood. A pledge implying, for example, an awareness of underlining *eatimologies,* a neologism borrowed by Rushdie (1999: 61, in Parasecoli, 2002) referring 'to the analysis of the origin and the development of specific products, their spreading through commerce, cultural expansion, colonization, tourism, and their hybridization'. However, it also implies a paramount work towards how communities can evolve socially and economically, keeping an eco-nutritional commitment to environmental sustainability and community's members optimal health (Scarpato, 2000: 186).

Gastronomy authenticity and modern tourists

Within this approach, concepts such as *authenticity* and *sense of place* have to be reworked and the huge changes occurred in cuisines taken into account, as does the evolution of gourmet travel around the world. Our analysis pertains mainly to the cuisine provided by quality independent restaurants whose culinary globalism is an example of the complexity of food globalization (Hall and Mitchell, 2002) and cosmopolitanism (Thompson and Tambyah, 1999) as opposed to the uniform industrial global cuisine of either fast-food chains or that staged by large hotels, in 'restaurants resembling Chianti cellars, ancient Chinese pagodas, and so on' (Symons, 1999: 336), which do represent a widespread homogenization or society's *McDonaldization* as Ritzer (1996) has argued.

It has been suggested that, in gastronomic terms, sense of place is the 'respect for local climate' and that, to be authentic, meals 'have to be true to place' (Symons, 1999: 336). Only climatically sensitive cooking favours the sense of place and the quest for authenticity of gastronomic tourists, 'who have long sought local cooking and so avoid international hotel fare and the increasingly inevitable McDonald's'. According to Symons even air conditioning is untrue to the places because it 'adds distance of another kind, by taking restaurant customers out of local environment' as it does sound-conditioning with Vivaldi, which restores 'the calm of a far-off age' (Symons, 1999: 336).

The gastronomic tourists described here are clearly those identified as 'modern tourists', for whom reality and authenticity 'are thought to be elsewhere; in other historical periods and cultures, in purer, simpler lifestyles' (MacCannell, 1989: 3). Symons's gastronomic tourists, too, are motivated by 'the paradoxical and seemingly inexhaustible hope that they can discover authentic cultures', and therefore cuisines, 'uncontaminated by the very market forces' that by using air and sound conditioning in restaurants enabled them to experience the authentic (Thompson and Tambyah, 1999). Several authors have also pointed out that the tourist industry frequently deploys this stereotypical image through promotional narratives that promise a world of adventure, personal enrichment and unique cultural experiences not available to conventional tourists or at conventional tourist sites (Craik, 1997; Urry, 1995).

The media, particularly in New World countries, has deployed similar modern stereotypes of culinary authenticity through a fascination with the *good old food* and the traditional local cuisines, and their supposed simplicity and authenticity, in opposition to *modern bad food and eclectic cuisines*. In doing so media have joined and driven the modern tourists in their 'nostalgia rush' (Urry, 1990: 109), generating powerful romantic culinary myths that, like most myths, have little historical basis. Most *old food*, for example, is not very old at all. In a plea for culinary modernism, Rachel Laudan (2001: 36) has noted that 'for every prized dish that goes back two thousand years, a dozen have been invented in the last two hundred'. Scarpato (1999) had previously argued, that authentic old food often implied:

> lack of choice, affordability of other foods, awareness of health issues and many other pitfalls. Ox carcasses slaughtered in a village two kilometres away from Paris, reached the French capital after 3 or 4 days and before selling them, the butcher had to cut away 3 or 4 inches of rotten meat infested by worms.

Sense of place and post-tourists

Enter the scene the post-tourist (Urry, 1990: 109) and the gastronomic correspondent, with his or her intellectually detached approach to leisure travel, and authenticity no longer carries the 'quasi sacred meaning that had for modern tourists'. 'The post-tourist embodies the reflexive, ironising, playful spirit of post modernity' and is aware that the authentic 'could not survive without the income from tourism' (Urry 1990: 100). 'Whereas the modernist is a pilgrim who wants to return home to a mythologized, sacralized site, the masculinized postmodernist is portrayed as an enthusiastic nomad whose only real home is the open expanse of the road and whose raison d'etre is mobility and the pursuit of excitement and novelty' (Thompson and Tambyah, 1999: 214).

Of course, the post-tourist is far from being ubiquitous and his or her condition is permanently shifting. 'Some tourists may be post-tourists most of the time, and most tourists may be post-tourists some of the time' (Thompson and Tambyah, 1999: 214). In any case, for the post-tourist, in full, part or casual time, the hybridization of cuisines generated by globalization is not perceived as a frightening homogenization. It is seen instead as a challenge, another game to play, an enhancement of individual freedom, the 'construction' of personal authenticity.

It is undeniable that the 'sense of place' has a fundamental relevance for the gastronomic tourist experience. However, as suggested by Parasecoli (2002) in the postmodern turn, the eatimology of place as 'a foundation for identities – individual and cultural, local and national' has lost the energy of the past. As argued by Jameson (1984: 83), for instance, a 'postmodern hyperspace has finally succeeded in transcending the capacity of the individual human body to locate itself, to organize immediate surroundings, perceptually and cognitively to map its position in a mappable external world'. Thus it is highly questionable to evaluate gastronomic authenticity in the postmodern world only against the geographical, climatic or historical sense of place. With the borders between local, national and global cuisine increasingly blurred, neat distinctions are possible only on paper, because each single regional cuisine is undergoing endless changes and transformation. In regional contexts, today or in the future, any possible cuisines will never again be limited to local ingredients, as in the past.

The relationship among food, places and cultural identity, in the current era, has a totally new significance as in the case of the global sushization:

> Just because sushi is available, in some form or another, in exclusive Fifth Avenue restaurants, in baseball stadiums in Los Angeles, at airport snack carts in Amsterdam, at an apartment in Madrid (delivered by motorcycle), or in Buenos Aires, Tel Aviv, or Moscow, doesn't mean that sushi has lost its status as Japanese cultural property. Globalization doesn't necessarily homogenize cultural differences nor erase the salience of cultural labels. Quite the contrary, it grows the franchise. In the global economy of consumption, the brand equity of sushi as Japanese cultural property adds to the cachet of both the country and the cuisine. (Bestor, 2000)

The sense of place has completely been reshaped in a global village that is no longer only a geographic dimension but, instead, the result of a new cartography drawn according to the characteristics of different lifestyles. 'Cultural' factors have paralleled and often ousted the traditional territorial aggregations of people. 'The village is an immense consumer zone, transversally criss-crossing idioms, local traditions, religious affiliations, political ideologies, folk and traditional sexual roles' (Scarpato, 2000: 88). What has been labelled as 'new global cuisine' is catering for this village precisely as the *international cuisine* of the French chef Auguste Escoffier (1957) catered for the army of well-off tourists, at the beginning of the twentieth century. Escoffier appealed to those tourists dazzled by the travelling wonders of the first automobiles and trains that crowded the European grand hotels, welcoming a cuisine that re-created the grandeur of their aristocratic houses (Smith, 1990: 31):

> His [Escoffier's] medium was the grand hotel. Their customers were his ... The Savoy and the Carlton gave him space, investments, huge brigades and rich customers. Here was a scale similar to that of the grand aristocratic houses. The well off were moving. They needed places to travel by boat, train, car; and places to stay when they arrived ... The tyre company Michelin launched its guide to hotels and restaurants in 1900. The railways invested heavily in resorts to persuade people to travel ... The whole of the cookery bent to the iron will of the codification ... The (Escoffier) Guide's 5000 recipes became as functional as a medical textbook. If it was not in the book, it was not cuisine. The rigidity of the codification meant the cooking could travel. It was international. And it not depends overly on the individual skills of a single man. It was team cooking. The real boundary was only one of climate. Too far south, and the batteries of stockpots and sauce became dangerous in the heat. To the north, it was a tradable commodity.

The importance that NGC has for global tourism today is similar to that which international cuisine had for the tourism of 100 years ago, though the two styles are totally different. More than from trains and cars, NGC has benefited from the 'lionization of travel' as a key to self-enhancement and the attainment of a sophisticated, worldly outlook (Belk, 1997). These are common features of contemporary cosmopolitanism, which is fuelled by a 'travelling trope' with a state of intellectual freedom and independence, based on nomadic travels (both literal and metaphoric) that do not follow conventional paths (Deleuze and Guattari, 1987). Cosmopolitanism is a 'proteanism', a permanent desire 'to explore and experience the panoply of transcultural diversity' (Hannerz, 1990: 240).

New global cuisine

It is widely acknowledged that *modern* cooking began after the French revolution, with the famous chef Carême, at the beginning of the nineteen-century (Smith, 1990:9). Its latest update, instead, stemmed from France's *cuisine nouvelle* spreading all over the world in the 1970s (Courtine, 1996) and then, with the early American movement of *East-meets-West* in the 1980s. These were times when existing definitions still made some sense and the history of cuisine was following the pattern of Western history, a unified stream stemming from the West, which the rest of the world had inevitably to flow into.

Today, Western models of modernity and progress are no longer universal (Vattimo, 1988). Pre-existing classifications are worthless. In cuisine, as in other arts, cultural syncretism and democratization have led us towards the unified undirectional history or a plurality of histories of the twenty-first century. In NGC *anything is possible* and at the same time, contingent, often incoherent and ambivalent, like the postmodern era in which it has developed. In this sense, NGC is cooking at the end of history, as Vattimo (1988) deemed the end of the universality of the Western modernity model.

The definition of NGC was first adopted at the end of the 1990s (Scarpato, 1998) to portray an already well-established worldwide culinary trend, thriving in our days. In 1996 the US magazine *Bon Appetit* had already described it in the following terms: 'Call it multicultural, cross-cultural, intercontinental, fusion or world cuisine – it's what's happening in food today. Creative cooks are combining styles, techniques, ingredients and flavours from every corner of the globe, often in a single dish' (Anon. 1996: 86).

At about the same time, restaurants began to state their global philosophy on the frontispiece of menus, as *Pangaea*, in the Hotel Nikko (La Cienega, Los Angeles) did in 1997: 'Before there was Europe, the Americas, Africa and Asia, then there was Pangaea. Over times continents were created as cultures evolved and melded, our dining experience has growth into a diverse medley of staples and cuisines'. At about the same time a menu of *China Grill*, in New York City, explained to the customers that the restaurant 'gathers ingredients from around the globe to compose its signature world cuisine. To best enjoy a dinner here, consider it a journey to be taken together'.

New global cuisine's chefs' philosophy is a pledge in favour of a basic rule, which is really an anti-rule, since it advocates that cuisine has 'no rules' or, as Ephraim Kadish, former chef at China Grill, says: 'rules are meant to be broken' (Scarpato, 2000: 126). While in traditional cuisines chefs were highly regarded as guardians of traditions, in the new cuisine the appreciation goes to both the creative chef and diner. It is a huge shift from the comfort of cooking and eating traditional tandoori chicken, *spaghetti alla bolognese*, a *pot au feu* or a *Big Mac*. In these dishes there is an intense pleasure in anticipating, morsel after morsel, the expected taste perhaps emerging with individuals' pleasant memories. It is a completely different story to cook or eat dishes such as a 'steamed bouillabaisse custard in saffron fish consommé with fennel puree' or 'lobster nachos with Boursin cheese, Asian tomato relish and guacamole', or 'chicken ravioli with wild mushrooms and Australian macadamia nuts pesto' or 'cake-kasu seared scallops on a butternut squash risotto with a pomegranate reduction'. Every morsel in these dishes is an exploration; the diner cannot anticipate the flavour and must question himself or herself because all is new and stimulating. As Scarpato pointed out: 'New Global Cuisine is in gastronomic terms what jazz has been for classic music. Like jazz, New Global Cuisine stands and falls on being alive, and whatever lives, changes. As soon as a style starts to gain popularity, new chefs turn in a brave or sometimes opposite direction' (Scarpato 2000: 137).

And like jazz, NGC represents liberation from the chains of traditional culinary codes and in particular the supremacy of international-French cuisine. The 'culinary mish-mash', the frightening hybridization, match up with the anti-grammatical, anti-syntactical tendencies of writers in modern literature, including James Joyce.

Cheong Liew, a Malaysian-born Australian chef, is credited with giving birth to a global cuisine, in Adelaide, in 1975, five years before Ken Hom and Jeremiah Tower launched their *East-meets-West* cuisine in California (Ripe, 1996). What happens with Liew represents one of the many similarities between NGC and jazz. The music played in New Orleans at the beginning of the twentieth century was jazz but it was not dissimilar from that played by the blues composer W. C. Handy since 1905. However, it was only in 1917 that Handy became aware of it. Similarly, when Liew began the culinary experiments at his restaurant, *Neddy's*, other chefs around the world were adopting or close to adopting a style of cooking similar to his. However, Cheong's style remains exemplary because it was generated by a genuine although unconscious globalist approach.

By the end of the 1990s, NGC, was 'an obvious and demonstrable style of cuisine', to use the words that in 1972 the French writers Gault and Millau wrote in regard to *Cuisine nouvelle* (Courtine, 1996: 868). The *global culinary equation* begins to be evident when American media write that Australian chefs are like Californian ones and at the same time Australian (and New Zealander) cooks are requested to shape the *modern British* or *modern European* style in London restaurants.

New global cuisine is a consequence of the spreading global culture which reflects 'the sense of heaps, congeries, and aggregate of cultural particularities juxtaposed together on the same field' (Featherstone, 1996: 70). Therefore, its definition is inherently complex and the phenomenon may be better understood by describing what it is not. New global cuisine has nothing to do with *international cuisine*, which internationalized a strictly codified number of haute cuisine dishes. No cooking books have today the importance that Auguste Escoffier's *Guide to Modern Cookery* had for the cooks of his time. No chefs today would rely on a single book – without photos – as their work reference. In fact, chefs practising NGC, and particularly young chefs, are accused of reading too many cookery books and food magazines and copying too much, according to the Australian chef Stephanie Alexander (Scarpato, 2000).

New global cuisine has also little to do with *East meets West,* although the latter was its immediate antecedent. In the new style of cooking, serving and eating, not only does East meet West but both meet North and South, and South meets South-East and so on, often simultaneously. Any traditional, geographic divisions have been overcome. Ingredients, techniques, equipment and cooking philosophies come from every corner of the world and are melted by global cooks – everywhere – with those from around the corner, in one dish. New global cuisine is much more than a phase of *fusion cuisine*, which was chiefly a spontaneous movement of the late 1980s. Today, cooks join NGC willingly, knowing that the adjective global is used in its larger meaning of comprehensive, all embracing.

The argument that transnational cuisine is just an ultimate point of progressive culinary exoticisms (Montanari, 1994) is contradicted by the global consciousness of chefs from around the world participating in a research on NGC (Scarpato, 2000), including experienced practitioners such as Gray Kunz, former chef at Lespinasse (New York City), Cheong Liew, Nobuyuki Matsuhisa, chef and owner of fourteen Nobu's restaurants around the world and Hugh Carpenter, chef and cookery book author. Exoticism always had a geographic dimension, meaning in the culinary instance the adoption of 'foreign', not native ingredients coming from abroad, neither acclimatized nor naturalized. With chefs and diners seeing the world as one and without borders, concepts such as 'abroad' have lost a large part of their traditional significance. Increasingly, geographic factors are only residually influencing cultural behaviours and/or consumer choices.

In reality, the translational chefs working in London, the USA, Australia, London, Hong Kong, Singapore, São Paulo and Tokyo have established a culinary global 'third culture', one of the many generated by globalization. Featherstone (1996) argues that third cultures are sets of practices, bodies of knowledge, conventions and lifestyle, which have developed in ways increasingly independent of nation-states. Television productions, modern music, advertising and fashion have all set their third cultures. Hundreds of television mini-series can be viewed in opposite corners of the globe without fear of cultural rejection. Advertising agencies plan global television campaigns; film producers, advertisers, actors, fashion designers and musicians no longer share the culture of a specific nation, alongside corporate tax accountants, financial planners and management consultants who deal with the problems of cultural communications in the global village.

A 'transnational imaginary' (Wilson and Dissanayake, 1996) created by the spread of electronic media and mass-tourist experiences have integrated the individual capacity of personal memories with collective memories. An illiterate of the twenty-first century, exposed to media, would have been an erudite of the nineteenth century. Sushi does not belong to the background of a Spanish youth, but the first time he or she eats it, his or her mind is likely to recall either natural or artificial memories: a transcontinental trip, a movie or a television documentary. Furthermore, we continuously 'reconstruct' our 'perceptions' (Ewen, 1988: 41) and, as a consequence, the new meanings of old feelings influence new ways of thinking about food, both from the point of view of those cooking and those eating it. The new dimension of desire, for example, has greatly contributed to the formation of non-geographic NGC. In contemporary life, we are able to remember not only images of events that we did not witness (Leavy, 1999), but thanks to the effects of 'global motions of people (and therefore culture)' (Dirlik, 1996: 32) we become aware of flavours not belonging to the geographic space we inhabit. New global cuisine has been built upon desires no longer generated exclusively 'within given historical time and geographic location', indeed, not even the strictly private memories coming to the mind of the French writer Marcel Proust (1981), when he dipped the famous *madeleine* in his tea.

New global cuisine is another *ethnic* way of cooking, being the local cuisine of the global village, as French cuisine was for France or Chinese for China. However, today's global village is no longer made up of only geographic places like France or China. A new cartography of the world has been drawn according to the characteristics of lifestyles and *cultural* factors, both often ousting the traditional territorial aggregations of people. Thus consumption patterns, television ratings, musical tastes, fashion, motion picture and concert attendances, home video rentals, magazines' readership, home computer software selection and shopping mail participation, Internet navigation all have an increasingly greater impact on the kitchen of the future.

The *consumer zones* have dominated the non-geographical mapping of the world for the purposes of marketing and communications strategies since the end of the 1980s. New global cuisine is catering for consumer zones composed by diners that have been exposed for more than forty years to television, are computer and telephone addicted, post-tourists who fly regularly to every destination in the world and live side by side with the offspring of 150 different ethnic groups, such as in Australia or in the USA.

The new 'localism'

In the new culinary global landscape, cuisines and food preparation procedures can no longer be read as within the theoretical schemes of the past, to which tourism referred too. Divisions of cuisines in *paysanne, bourgeoisie* and *haute*, as devised by Revel (1982a,b) and to which Symons's reading of NGC is inspired, are obsolete. Food, cuisines and food-ways have to be assessed in the real context of our days in which globalization thrives and signifies technological advance, progress in communications, modern versus past. Globalization, for instance, has increased the speed of kitchen modernization. All over the world, kitchen spaces have quickly adapted to the new environmental influences and provoked changes; and in doing so, they have followed the patterns of their history.

The romantic defence of localism, too, which in the world of cooking is vested as a resistance to the new cuisine, is obsolete. This is not to say that that local produce and ingredients do not have importance in NGC: quite the opposite. This cuisine has a strong local vocation: creative global chefs, in their pursuit of quality and 'competitive advantage', encourage and commonly use fresh, local, non-industrialized and organic ingredients. But they do not feel bound to the area where they work because 'local has been redefined in the jet age', as alleged by Thomas Keller, chef and owner of *The French Laundry*, in the Napa Valley (California):

> I mean, local to me is anything I can get here by jet . . . in a few hours . . . I mean, our scallops come from Maine . . . We get lobsters from Maine every day . . . they are local to me because they're coming in my back door every day, fresh, live, vibrant. (As) The hearts of palm from Hawaii that we just started getting, for example. (Bryant, 2001)

Accordingly, the regional appeal for gastronomy tourists, particularly in metro-politan contexts, is no longer just the climatic or productive vocation of the area, but also, and often mostly, the presence of one or more particular chefs on that specific territory. It is the original combination of ingredients in the chef's dishes that shape the new culinary *local* dimension. Thus, although a result of globalization, the hybridization inherent to NGC does not represent homogeni-zation but in its place supports biological and cultural diversity. In fact, it also represents 'the expansion of consumer and life-style choices' (Kellner, 1999) and promotes a cosmopolitan aesthetic (Joy and Wallendorf, 1996; Wilk, 1995) which 'prominently stands in a mutually supportive relation to the dynamics of cultural globalization, which, contrary to the still popular homogenizing thesis, have precipitated an increasing heterogeneity of cultural forms in music, food, fashion, and art' (Thompson and Tambyah, 1999: 215).

In terms of gastronomy tourism as well, NGC belongs to the realm of 'euphoric globalization'; in other words, the fulfilment of the old global dream of cooks and diners of any time, that is, to be able tocook and eat dishes with ingredients coming from different seasons and all over the world freely combined (Scarpato, 2000). On the other hand, it cannot be denied that within the neo-global culinary 'third culture' stemmed from the latest transformation of capitalism and its further development toward de-territorialization and abstraction, some negative aspects of globalization also flourish. In food terms, for instance, homogenized and often unhealthy fast and industrial cuisine (Schlosser, 2001) belongs to a 'melancholic' globalization, insensitive to the warnings of 'ecological catastrophe', which translates into unsustain-able gastronomy.

Global gastronomy and tourism

Several years ago Beardsworth and Keil (1997: 257) asked the following questions:

> Are we about to witness (or indeed, are we now witnessing) the emergence of what might loosely be termed a 'postmodern' food system and 'postmodern' eating patterns? Can we say that the monolith of the modern food system, with its emphasis on large scale, intensive production and standardized manufacturing, on mass marketing and retailing, is in the process of giving ground to a more diversified and fragmented situation in which idiosyncratic, even 'playful', combina-tions of aesthetic, ethical, culinary and gustatory preferences can be assembled by individual consumers or group of consumers?

Today we can give a positive answer to these questions. New global cuisine is a postmodern cuisine with characteristics of mixed codes, fragmentation, incoherence, disjunction and syncretism. At the same time, it signals the emergence of a generalized postmodern culinary taste because the phenomenon is not limited to upmarket restaurants, in which neo-global chefs work, and their customers. These figures have been only the avant-garde of the attack against 'the monolith of modern food', as well as instrumental to the diffusion of the process at grassroots level.

The neo-global style of cooking has entered the mainstream of cafés, bistros, brasseries and, even, pizzerias. The American chef and food writer, Hugh Carpenter, noted that even manufacturers of frozen pre-cooked food, sold widely in supermarkets, resort usually to 'fusion' cuisine recipes. In Buenos Aires's *Tenedor libre*, multi-ethnic all-you-can-eat restaurants, people freely assemble their dishes picking bits and pieces from the vast and affordable multi-culinary buffet (Scarpato, 2000).

New global cuisine is also a medium to be 'a tourist everyday and everywhere' (Bauman, 1996: 55), one of the many ways that postmodern consumers have to live as 'tourist citizens' who delight in traversing the world, via travel, media consumption, and immersion in hyperrealist simulations, gladly paying for the 'right to spin webs of meaning all their own' (Bauman, 1996: 53). Not by chance, but by deconstructing the cuisine of a neo-global chef like Cheong Liew, we find the dream of a long trip.

When we were designing a new menu the courtyard at Neddy's often gave us inspiration. We could have been anywhere. We dreamed in the 'Land of the Dreaming' as my good friend John Ho said, and the courtyard led us to the Middle East along the spice routes, to the Greek Islands, to Tuscany, Provence, Singapore, Sichuan and, last but not least, to the Australian back garden (Liew, 1996: 45).

Of course, as Bauman (1996: 54) noted, this form of tourist citizenship 'is reserved for those having the requisite degree of class privilege in the global economy' and Liew again seem particularly aware of it:

> People are travelling more to expand their business, that means they will be experiencing more . . . their palates will demand more and more. We actually have a group of people that have been travelling around the world, whether they're musicians, entertainers, lawyers, corporate businessman or educators (and their travelling) develop an influence of their palate instinct. (In Scarpato, 2000: 127)

Chefs as gastronomy tourism designers

Food and recipes of chefs practising NGC contribute to a culture and lifestyle that does not belong to one nation but to the world, exactly like a suit tailored by Giorgio Armani, a film directed by Steven Spielberg, a poster drawn by Neville Broadie or software packaged by Bill Gates. In comparison to the traditional cuisines, the cooking style of global chefs is what traditional Lappish dress is to an Armani model or what a silent movie of the 1920s is to *Titanic* (the movie), or what an old handwritten account-book is to the most up-to-date office organization software.

Similar to those working in the film, television, music, advertising, fashion and consumer industries, global chefs are 'design professionals' (Featherstone, 1996: 61). They play a key role in the future of human nourishment but also in the orientation of gastronomy tourism flows. The significance of their work is amplified by the often aggressive marketing of their innovative restaurants that feeds the collective imaginary. Historically, restaurants' marketing has been a major instrument 'for smashing old eating habits' (Zeldin, 1980: 147). Its influence, as noted by Kivela (1998), has been postulated by a number of scholars, including Finkelstein (1989) and Wood (1995).

The role of chefs in NGC, however, is decisive and cannot be seen as limited to their indispensable, but just technical, abilities in successfully combining ingredients like garam masala and Italian parmigiano, or Thai fish-sauces and New Zealand truffles. New global cooks are cultural specialists and, as such, reflect values, philosophies and aesthetics of their common culture, as do architects when designing a building or a painter when painting a picture. With them the restaurant is increasingly belonging to the realm of cultural industries (Scarpato and Daniele, 2000).

As argued by Scarpato (2000: 176) the aesthetic of new global cuisine prompts chefs to have a clear conscience of their 'designing' role towards the various dimensions of their activity, from the public taste to the environment in which they work. These chefs are 'change agents' (Rogers, 1995) and are influencing work practices and sociocultural changes including tourism motivations. The neo-global chefs are set to replace the role of peasants and fishermen once had in the past in the formation of new cuisines. An example is given by the phenomenon of New Asia cuisine (NAC), which also is a case of how new cuisines develop in the contemporary extra geographic situation. New Asia cuisine, in particular, has stemmed from the marketing needs of both the hospitality industry and the agencies promoting tourist destinations, in this case the Singapore Tourism Board (STB).

A quick look at the history of NAC may be useful. The first public discussions on the 'concept' of NAC occurred at the end of 1995. However, the birth of this cuisine

> took place many years ago when chefs (professionals and home cooks alike) ventured into the realm of combining flavours and techniques, coupled with the right ingredients, into a different entity that had one important objective in mind: variety, the so-called spice of life. Human beings cannot happily function without a variety of any number of things, especially when it comes to their dietary intake. (Knipp, 1998)

Fresh ingredients available in Singapore, coming from *localities* all around Asia (agriculture in Singapore is a very limited industry) imparted some degree of distinctive flavour to NAC, which enjoyed wide publicity and the support of a magazine carrying the same name, published by Peter Knipp, himself a former chef.

The name NAC became official in 1996, in a meeting in St Moritz attended by the Singapore Tourist Promotion Board chief executive officer (Mosley, 1997). A neo-global gastronomy tourist product (GTP) was born. Soon after the St Moritz meeting, the STB began to promote Singapore as New *Asia*, a brand name still used today to market the city-state. New Asia cuisine reinforces the image of Singapore as a food and wine destination, but at the same time reflects its postmodern spirit: 'A truly inspiring city where East meets West, Asian heritage blends with modernity and sophistication happily co-exists with nature'. (Mosley, 1997)

In 1997, by organizing the Singapore Food Festival and the World Gourmet Summit specifically to launch NAC (Mosley, 1997), the STB set a historical precedent. It was perhaps the first national tourism body in the world promoting a form of transnational NGC as part of its destination offer. Likely, in the near future, any real or fictitious cuisine *distinctiveness* will also depend on the amount of money injected into its promotion by tourism promotion bodies.

Since then, NAC has been practised in many restaurants, mainly in five-star hotels, and promoted as an 'authentic' tourist attraction of the city. The STB's official guide to the city lists 'New Asia–Singapore Cuisine' among the array of traditional ethnic cuisines, from the Chinese to the Indian, from the peculiar *Peranakan* to the Arab. 'The latest entrant to our food paradise is New Asia–Singapore cuisine. An attempt to marry the best of both Asian and Western, New Asia–Singapore cuisine is for more adventurous palates. Let your adventures begin in Doc Cheng's at the Raffles Hotel and Club Chinois at Orchard Parade Hotel' (Singapore, 2001: 82).

What is the future?

What then is the future of global gastronomy cuisine? The rise of NGC shows that in contemporary GTPs, the overlapping local and global dimensions tend to prevail. Thus, for example, in the GTP's *glocal* model there is little room for the national identity in the classical terms of nation-state. A meal no longer reflects only the history of nation-based aggregation of people. While its prosody in the past 'permitted a person to partake each day of the national past' (Barthes, 1979: 170), in the current phase of global capitalism it may permit individuals to chip instead into transnational consumer zones.

This situation is leading to new forms of 'localizations' within NGC that should be further investigated by future research in global gastronomic tourism. It appears that to provide with competitive advantage a neo-global GTP, such as a restaurant, a gourmet resort or a festival, will increasingly need to specialize in the catering to one or more 'global nations' – aggregations of people sharing cultural and consumption similarities but not belonging to the same country (Scarpato, 2000).

Worldwide spa users represent one of these global nations and spa cuisine caterers to them. The boom of this style has been impressive: spa restaurants have sprung up all over the world inside and outsides spas, with specialized chefs. A corpus of thousands of spa recipes has become readily available in dozens of books, web sites and videos. These recipes can be prepared regardless of the location of the spa, because they have been built only with the aim of gratifying the 'desire for full-scale pampering': 'Unlike traditional spas, which have long been in the business of "cures" . . . today's vacation spas focus simply on pampering both body and spirit' (Thomas, 2002: 58).

The desire for pampering is not to be underestimated, since it is a unifying cultural and social motivator: 'Spa cuisine can work on the inside while the other healers at spas work on the external body for total healing and pampering . . . we are going to make the world a better place, step by step, making each individual we touch healthier in body and mind' (Hartsough, 1999).

The trend in the past few years has been that spas no longer are true to their natural places such spring waters and volcanic areas. Yoga, hydrotherapy, aquacranial massages, grape seeds frictions, new spas are built 'on the hippest new treatment' (Thomas, 2002: 58). Spa cuisine is following the evolution and gastronomic tourists will move accordingly, even if their favourite spa restaurant is in a day spa, in the heart of a cosmopolitan city centre, like the *banya* in Moscow.

Cyber social aggregations are also playing an important function in the building of global nations as imagined communities. Web sites are being invested with collective memories and have such emotional power to generate a sense of community, exactly like the role that, according to Featherstone (1996), was played by national monuments in the nation-states. Indeed, web sites like gay.com, which features over 1 million individual profiles around the world, with its editorial on food preferences and wines, may prompt the establishment of a *pink neo-global cuisine*: a corpus of recipes and an authentically gay culinary philosophy both created and realized by gays but not only for gay customers.

It is with these possible scenarios that gastronomic tourism planners, researchers and operators have to deal in the near future. For this reason a good knowledge of the case NGC, with its inherent issues of authenticity and sense of place in the current postmodern turn, may prove very helpful for future research.

18

The experience of consumption or the consumption of experiences? Challenges and issues in food tourism

C. Michael Hall, Liz Sharples and Angela Smith

This final chapter examines forthcoming issues and challenges with respect to food tourism at the level of both the firm and the region. It reviews a number of SWOT (strengths, weaknesses, opportunities, threats) analyses that have been conducted on food and wine tourism, and identifies a number of common elements in these studies and their relationship to issues identified in the present book. The chapter concludes with identifying potential research issues for the future.

The advantages of wine and food tourism for producers and wineries

At the beginning of our companion book on wine tourism (Hall et al., 2000b), the authors identified a number of advantages and disadvantages of tourism for wineries. In this book we seek to conclude with such an observation. As many of the chapters in this book have identified, from the perspective of food business development, tourism can be part of the core business activities for many producers. Many small-scale businesses can use direct marketing and sales through cellar door, farm gate or farmers' and produce markets to gain an essential source of cash flow in the early stages of business development, particularly as there are usually greater returns from direct sales than from selling through retail outlets. Door sales also provide an opportunity to develop a mailing list of customers, which can then be used for direct-marketing purposes. Some businesses also produce a newsletter and/or web site as a means of maintaining customer relationships.

For established businesses, visitors provide a test-bed for new products. Wine and food tourism also facilitates producer–consumer interaction and involves education about and experience of products and regions. For example, as Chapter 3 indicated, there is a substantial market of food interested visitors. The Enteleca Research and Consultancy (2000) report on tourist attitudes towards regional and local food in the UK also recognized the significance of the market. Enteleca Research and Consultancy (2000) conducted national face-to-face in-home survey of 1600 English residents, to examine current awareness and interest in regional foods while on holiday and values associated with local food and drink. This produced information on current use of local food and drink and awareness of local food and drink products in their region (Exhibit 18.1).

Exhibit 18.1 Tourist attitudes towards regional and local food in the UK

- Between 61 and 69 per cent of holidaymakers and visitors to the four sample regions (the South West, Cumbria, Yorkshire and the Heart of England) recognize that food makes a positive contribution to their holiday – 39 per cent said it contributed 'a lot'.
- Overall 72 per cent of people visiting the four regions took an interest in local foods during their visit. The vast majority were not

---

actively seeking it out but were happy to try it when they came across it.

Respondents were divided into five groups:

- *Food tourists*: 6–8 per cent of UK holidaymakers and visitors (day visitors as high as 11 per cent) and 3 per cent of international visitors – seeking local food and drink is a particular reason for choosing their holiday destination.
- *Interested purchasers*: 30–33 per cent of UK holidaymakers and visitors – those in this group believe that food in general can contribute to their enjoyment of their holiday and they purchase/eat local foods when the opportunity arises.
- *Un-reached*: 15–17 per cent of UK holidaymakers and visitors – people in this group believe that food and drink can contribute to their enjoyment of their holiday, are happy to try local food if they come across it, but at present are not purchasing local foods.
- *Un-engaged*: 22–24 per cent of UK holidaymakers and visitors – these people do not perceive food and drink as adding to the enjoyment of their holiday but they are not negative about trying local foods.
- *Laggards*: 28–17 per cent of UK holidaymakers and visitors – these people say they have no interest in local food and are unlikely to have purchased any on holiday.

Values associated with local food and drink

There is a widely held perception that the purchase of local foods helps the local economy (82 per cent) and that purchase of local produce helps the local environment (65 per cent). Sixty-seven per cent of holidaymakers say that they are prepared to pay more for quality food and drink.

Twenty-six per cent of people express a strong interest in seeing restaurant menus that identify food that has been locally produced.

Image of local foods

The majority of visitors make little distinction between 'local produce' and 'local specialities' – definition, largely driven by place and geography rather than a full understanding of the uniqueness of the product.

Tourists purchase of local foods

Between 32 per cent and 66 per cent of tourists either purchase or eat local foods during their visit. The proportion is strongly linked to their length of stay.

Shopping: 39 per cent of tourists make at least one purchase of local foods during their visit. Seventeen per cent of purchases included items bought as gifts.

Eating out: the most popular venues for eating out are

- pubs – 64 per cent
- tearooms – 43 per cent
- cafés and snack bars – 32 per cent
- fish and chip shops – 31 per cent.

The 'Food tourists' and 'Interested purchasers' were more interested in upmarket restaurants, foreign food and gourmet restaurants.

Source: after Enteleca Research and Consultancy (2000)

Liz Sharples and C. Michael Hall

For both large- and small-scale food and wine businesses, tourism can be very important in terms of brand development. However, tourism needs to be seen as part of the overall development of a food or wine business rather than necessarily an end in itself. The manner in which food and wine tourism is used as a component of the business mix will therefore depend on the stage of business development, overall business goals, location and target markets. In other words, food and wine tourism needs to be seen within the context of the business plan, desired lifestyles and values of participants, and good business decision-making.

In summary, the advantages of food tourism at the level of the food operator are:

- *increased consumer exposure* to product and increased opportunities to sample product
- *building brand awareness and loyalty* through establishing links between producer and consumer, and purchase of company branded merchandise
- *creating relationships with customers*: the opportunity to meet staff and to see 'behind the scenes' can lead to positive relationships with consumers which may lead to both direct sales and indirect sales through positive 'word of mouth' advertising

- *increased margins* through direct sale to consumer, where the absence of distributor costs is not carried over entirely to the consumer
- an *additional sales outlet*, or for smaller producers who cannot guarantee volume or constancy of supply, perhaps the only feasible sales outlet
- *marketing intelligence on products*: producers can gain instant and valuable feedback on the consumer reaction to their existing products, and are able to trial new additions to their product range
- *marketing intelligence on customers*: visitors can be added to a mailing list which can be developed as a customer database to both target and inform customers
- *educational opportunities*: visits help create awareness and appreciation of specific types of foods and food as a whole, the knowledge and interest generated by this can be expected to result in increased consumption.

Some of the disadvantages of tourism for small operators are:

- *increased costs and management time*: the operation of a tasting room or direct sales may be costly, particularly when it requires paid staff. While the profitability gap is higher on direct sales to the consumer, profit may be reduced if wineries do not charge for tastings
- the *capital required*: suitable facilities for hosting visitors may be prohibitively expensive for some small operators, especially as some types of added value production are capital intensive
- *inability to substantially increase sales*: the number of visitors a business can attract is limited and if a business cannot sell all of its stock, it will eventually need to use other distribution outlets
- *opportunity costs*: investments in tasting rooms and tourist facilities means that capital is not available for other investments
- *seasonality*: tourism as with the production of food is seasonal. It is important to ensure that demand periods are complimentary.

Tourism and hospitality operators, and the wider region, can also benefit from wine and food tourism (Hall, Mitchell and Smith, 2001):

- There is an association with a *quality product* (Henchion and McIntyre, 2000).
- *Food tourism is not a standardized product.* Reinforcement of 'authentic' tourist experiences allows visitors to see beyond the shop front and establish strong relationships with a destination.
- *Food tourism is an attraction*: The existence of the product, such as markets and wineries, provides a motivation for visiting an area, staying in accommodation and eating at restaurants.

■ The existence of the product also helps extend visitors' length of stay because it gives them places to visit and activities to engage in.

Regional tourism organizations and economic development and promotion organizations can also benefit from food and wine tourism because of branding opportunities, the creation of backward economic and employment linkages, and the role that wine and food tourism plays in attracting higher-spending visitors into a region. Indeed, as several of the chapters in this book have illustrated, these factors underlie government policies towards tourism while the growth of food tourism is also perceived as having environmental and social benefits as well (Exhibit 18.2). Nevertheless, despite much enthusiasm from a number of interests for the development of food tourism, substantial issues still remain and we shall turn to these in the next section.

Exhibit 18.2 Farmers' markets in the UK

The number of farmers' markets that regularly take place in the UK has risen dramatically over recent years. At the time of the establishment of the National Association of Farmers Markets (NAFM) in 1999, delegates from fourteen of the sixteen markets that were then in operation attended a meeting jointly organized by the Soil Association and the Bath Environment Centre. They estimated that by the year 2000, the total number of UK farmers' markets would exceed fifty. However, their estimate proved to be conservative as, by March 2000, over 140 markets had been registered on the Soil Association web site (http://www.soilassociation.org) and in 2002 the NAFM reported that farmers' markets had taken place in over 380 towns and cities throughout the UK by the end of 2001.

The NAFM is a non-profit-making limited company owned by the Soil Association, the Farm Retail Association, the National Farmers Union and 'Envolve', an organization that deals with partnerships for sustainability. The Countryside Agency and Barclays Bank are also keen supporters of the NAFM venture.

Not all the farmers' markets that take place within the UK are members of the NAFM (it is estimated that around half belong to the association) but there is a definite drive to encourage membership in an attempt to reassure consumers about the quality of foods that are being sold. Indeed, in 2002 the Minister for Food and Farming, Lord Whitty, launched a scheme to crack down on market traders who attempt to sell poor-quality foods as home-grown produce at farmers' markets. The Certification of Farmers' Markets scheme will accredit genuine farmers who fulfil certain criteria with a distinctive logo. Part funded by the Department of Environment, Food and Rural Affairs (DEFRA), it should assure consumers about the standards of goods that they are buying and protect traders from unfair competition (see http://www.farmersmarkets.net).

The NAFM define a farmers' market as one in which 'farmers, growers or producers from a defined local area are present in person to sell their own produce, direct to the public. All products sold should have been grown, reared, brewed, pickled, baked, smoked or processed by the stallholder' (http://www.farmersmarkets.net). The 'defined local area' is usually within a 30-mile radius, although there is some 'leeway' in certain geographical areas.

Farmers' markets have a number of benefits for the producers, the consumers, the environment and the local community/economy in which the market takes place. As the Countryside Alliance states 'By selling directly, consumers can obtain specific, seasonal produce, the farmers can stay in touch with their markets, and both can enjoy the social, energetic, atmosphere that is unique to a farmers' market' (http://www.farmers-markets.org). These benefits are also available for the tourist who can gain much from attending a farmers' market either as a day visitor, indeed it can be the main reason for the journey, or as part of a longer visit to a specific area in order to stock up with supplies. By buying from a farmers' market a tourist may not only have an interesting and enjoyable shopping experience, but also the opportunity of learning more about the local food culture while supporting suppliers/producers in the region.

Liz Sharples and C. Michael Hall

The strengths, weaknesses, opportunities and threats for food and wine tourism: an international comparison

The following discussion presents a review of SWOT analyses conducted on four wine and regions: British Columbia, Canada (Wilkins and Hall, 2001); Victoria, Australia (Victorian Wineries Tourism Council, 1997); Western Australia (Edith Cowan University, 1999) and New Zealand (Hall, Mitchell and Smith, 2001; Smith, 2001; Smith and Hall, 2002). The findings of each

SWOT analysis were formulated using different methods: the Canadian, New Zealand and Western Australian analyses were formulated through communication with stakeholders in the industry, while the Victoria, Australia analysis was formulated by the writers of the state's wine and food tourism strategy. The different methods used in the SWOT formulation of each region may have resulted in slightly different approaches towards interpreting stakeholder responses; however, when the various SWOTs are compared, some key similarities and differences can be identified.

Strengths

All four regions identified the growing recognition by wineries and small food producers of their role in tourism as a key strength for their region; indicating the importance of the enthusiasm of producers in maintaining as well as nurturing and growing wine and food tourism (Figure 18.1). The quality of the product(s) on offer was also recognized as an important strength and asset to all four regions. The uniqueness and/or beauty of the environment in which the industries are based was seen as a key strength in the SWOT analysis for British Columbia, New Zealand and Western Australia. The 'personal approach' often provided by smaller/boutique wineries was mentioned in the Australian and Canadian studies, but did not rank as an important strength for stakeholders in the New Zealand wine tourism industry. This may be due to the perception by some in the industry that smaller boutique wineries are less able to cater for larger groups, and thus will be less supportive of growth.

The role of events in the promotion of wine tourism was also considered to be an important strength of the Victorian and Western Australian wine tourism industries; this is probably due to the profile these events can give to a wine and food region. Additionally, specific wine and/or food events and festivals also give producers the ability to 'showcase' their produce to a large group of people at one event.

Government support is seen by many as an important strength for the wine tourism industry, obviously due to the support that government bodies (such as local councils to central government) are able to give to infrastructure, policy, funding and promotion. New Zealand was the only wine 'region' where this was not listed as a key strength, potentially related to the concern from some stakeholders that there is a lack of government interest in the industry (Hall, Mitchell and Smith, 2001; Smith and Hall, 2002).

In addition to the common strengths of the four regions, there were also a number of strengths unique to each destination. In British Columbia, the

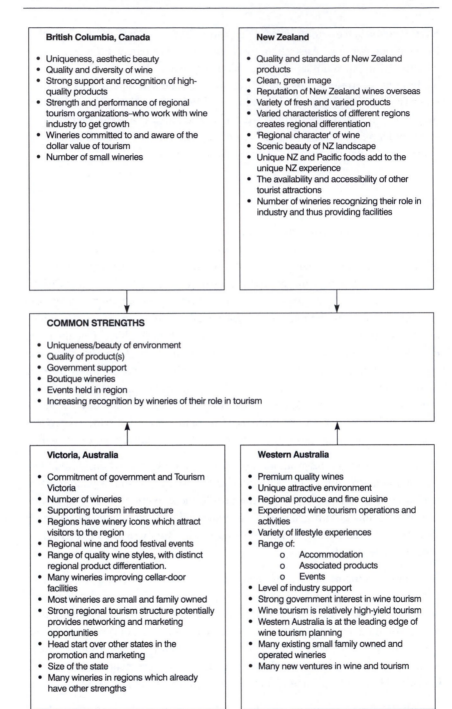

British Columbia, Canada

- Uniqueness, aesthetic beauty
- Quality and diversity of wine
- Strong support and recognition of high-quality products
- Strength and performance of regional tourism organizations–who work with wine industry to get growth
- Wineries committed to and aware of the dollar value of tourism
- Number of small wineries

New Zealand

- Quality and standards of New Zealand products
- Clean, green image
- Reputation of New Zealand wines overseas
- Variety of fresh and varied products
- Varied characteristics of different regions creates regional differentiation
- 'Regional character' of wine
- Scenic beauty of NZ landscape
- Unique NZ and Pacific foods add to the unique NZ experience
- The availability and accessibility of other tourist attractions
- Number of wineries recognizing their role in industry and thus providing facilities

COMMON STRENGTHS

- Uniqueness/beauty of environment
- Quality of product(s)
- Government support
- Boutique wineries
- Events held in region
- Increasing recognition by wineries of their role in tourism

Victoria, Australia

- Commitment of government and Tourism Victoria
- Number of wineries
- Supporting tourism infrastructure
- Regions have winery icons which attract visitors to the region
- Regional wine and food festival events
- Range of quality wine styles, with distinct regional product differentiation.
- Many wineries improving cellar-door facilities
- Most wineries are small and family owned
- Strong regional tourism structure potentially provides networking and marketing opportunities
- Head start over other states in the promotion and marketing
- Size of the state
- Many wineries in regions which already have other strengths

Western Australia

- Premium quality wines
- Unique attractive environment
- Regional produce and fine cuisine
- Experienced wine tourism operations and activities
- Variety of lifestyle experiences
- Range of:
    - o Accommodation
    - o Associated products
    - o Events
- Level of industry support
- Strong government interest in wine tourism
- Wine tourism is relatively high-yield tourism
- Western Australia is at the leading edge of wine tourism planning
- Many existing small family owned and operated wineries
- Many new ventures in wine and tourism

Figure 18.1   Strengths

'strength and performance of the local Regional Tourism Organization' was seen as a significant strength to the region. In New Zealand the clean green image, and the range of fresh foods was a common perceived strength, in addition to the strength to New Zealand of the 'unique New Zealand and Pacific' style foods. New Zealand stakeholders also considered that the 'varied characteristics' of the different wine regions in New Zealand helped to establish a differentiated regional food and wine product.

In Australia, there were some variations between the analyses of the Victorian and Western Australian wine industries. In Victoria, for example, there is particular emphasis on the strength of the state's supporting infrastructure and marketing and promotional ability. While in Western Australia there was an emphasis on the experience of those in the industry, the range of accommodation, associated products and events as well as the perceived strength that 'Western Australia is at the leading edge of wine tourism planning' (Edith Cowan University, 1999).

Weaknesses

There were a number of similarities between 'weakness' analyses of the four wine regions (Figure 18.2); however, not all regions faced the same issues. The most common perceived weakness was the lack of industry research, the lack of support infrastructure and the lack of co-operation/co-ordination and/ or networking between those in the industry. Interestingly, these three issues are arguably interrelated to each other, as the lack of industry research may be a contributing factor to the lack of support infrastructure (be that in the form of tourist facilities such as accommodation or assistance offered by government bodies), as research can help identify the shortfalls of support within the industry. Similarly, the lack of co-operation and co-ordination is likely to be a contributing factor to both the lack of research as well as the lack of support structures in place (Hall et al., 1998).

The lack of and/or poor quality of signage was seen as a problem, particularly within the Australian wine tourism industry; while service quality was seen as a key weakness in the Western Australian and New Zealand analyses. Both these issues are important, as the lack of (or the lack of clarity of) signage can have a particular impact on the visitor experience as well as visitor numbers, while service quality could have a significant impact on the success of the food tourism industry in a region as a result of poor visitor experiences.

In British Columbia, the politics between organizations, the impact of government policy and the actual government support were seen as the

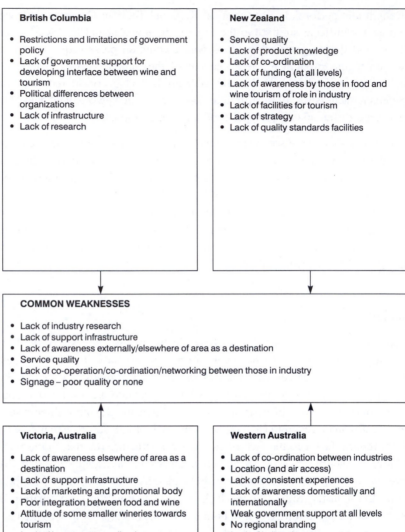

British Columbia

- Restrictions and limitations of government policy
- Lack of government support for developing interface between wine and tourism
- Political differences between organizations
- Lack of infrastructure
- Lack of research

New Zealand

- Service quality
- Lack of product knowledge
- Lack of co-ordination
- Lack of funding (at all levels)
- Lack of awareness by those in food and wine tourism of role in industry
- Lack of facilities for tourism
- Lack of strategy
- Lack of quality standards facilities

COMMON WEAKNESSES

- Lack of industry research
- Lack of support infrastructure
- Lack of awareness externally/elsewhere of area as a destination
- Service quality
- Lack of co-operation/co-ordination/networking between those in industry
- Signage – poor quality or none

Victoria, Australia

- Lack of awareness elsewhere of area as a destination
- Lack of support infrastructure
- Lack of marketing and promotional body
- Poor integration between food and wine
- Attitude of some smaller wineries towards tourism
- Lack of investment to cellar door
- Little co-operation and networking between all involved in wine, food and tourism
- Lack of winery tourism signage
- Inadequate market research to assist in the formulation of marketing plans

Western Australia

- Lack of co-ordination between industries
- Location (and air access)
- Lack of consistent experiences
- Lack of awareness domestically and internationally
- Weak government support at all levels
- No regional branding
- Lack of hallmark events
- Lack of tour routes and organized tours
- Lack of signage
- Lack of linkages
- High prices and poor service quality at cellar door
- Infrastructure
- Funding
- Limited awareness of tourist needs ventures in the wine and tourism

Figure 18.2 Weaknesses

defining weaknesses. In New Zealand, industry stakeholders suggested that the biggest weaknesses related to the lack of facilities, funding and (at that stage) no wine and food tourism strategy to guide the industry. The two Australian regions had relatively different weaknesses. In Victoria the biggest issues were perceived to be the lack of investment, the lack of a central marketing body and the 'attitude of some smaller wineries towards tourism'. In Western Australia the key identifiable weaknesses were related to the remote location, branding issues and the problem of ensuring consistent reasonably priced experiences which cater to visitors' needs.

Opportunities

All four regions identified that increasing linkages between the food and wine tourism industry was an important opportunity (Figure 18.3). Additionally, the importance of adequate promotion and marketing of the destination and its products both domestically and internationally was seen as a key opportunity for the wine and food tourism industries in Western Australia and British Columbia. The importance of events and festivals as promotional tools were also suggested as an important opportunity for those in Victoria and Western Australia, as, too, was closer collaboration between different stakeholders within the wine and food tourism industry. All destinations identified a need for increased external recognition of their destinations and products – the various stakeholders by working collaboratively together (e.g. food and wine providers at a regional food and wine festival) to promote the region could potentially improve this.

In British Columbia, there is the perceived opportunity to increase the number of wineries to provide more variety in the visitor experience, as well as the specific opportunity to exploit the US market to a higher degree. In New Zealand, there was a key emphasis on the need for a change in the visitor experience, particularly in ensuring a reasonable level of product knowledge, to enable better education of visitors. Additionally, the development of a 'unique' New Zealand food and wine experience was recognized as an area to be developed, perhaps through the opportunity to create regionally 'distinct' food and wine experiences. An opportunity to increase visitor length of stay was also suggested, something which could be encouraged through increased international exposure. The opportunities identified in Victoria focused mainly on the development and investment into infrastructure and promotion to the domestic market. Also suggested was the use of exports to lift the region's profile, and an emphasis being placed on attracting new markets.

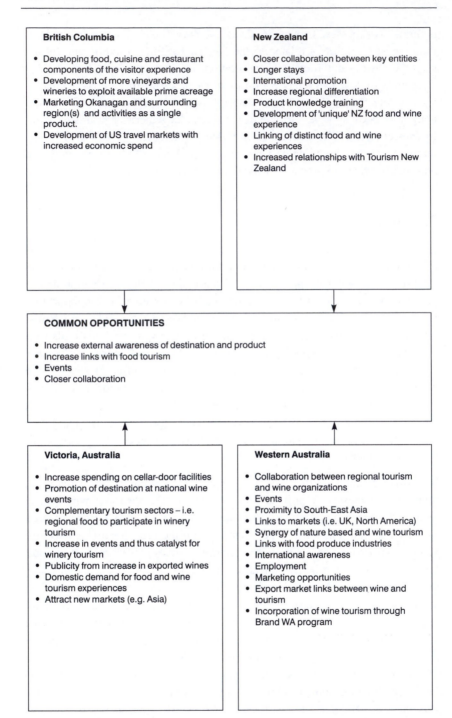

British Columbia

- Developing food, cuisine and restaurant components of the visitor experience
- Development of more vineyards and wineries to exploit available prime acreage
- Marketing Okanagan and surrounding region(s) and activities as a single product.
- Development of US travel markets with increased economic spend

New Zealand

- Closer collaboration between key entities
- Longer stays
- International promotion
- Increase regional differentiation
- Product knowledge training
- Development of 'unique' NZ food and wine experience
- Linking of distinct food and wine experiences
- Increased relationships with Tourism New Zealand

COMMON OPPORTUNITIES

- Increase external awareness of destination and product
- Increase links with food tourism
- Events
- Closer collaboration

Victoria, Australia

- Increase spending on cellar-door facilities
- Promotion of destination at national wine events
- Complementary tourism sectors – i.e. regional food to participate in winery tourism
- Increase in events and thus catalyst for winery tourism
- Publicity from increase in exported wines
- Domestic demand for food and wine tourism experiences
- Attract new markets (e.g. Asia)

Western Australia

- Collaboration between regional tourism and wine organizations
- Events
- Proximity to South-East Asia
- Links to markets (i.e. UK, North America)
- Synergy of nature based and wine tourism
- Links with food produce industries
- International awareness
- Employment
- Marketing opportunities
- Export market links between wine and tourism
- Incorporation of wine tourism through Brand WA program

Figure 18.3   Opportunities

Threats

The SWOT analyses of all four regions identified that other wine and food tourism destinations were identified as the biggest threat to their region's wine and food industry (Figure 18.4). The issue of competition coming from other regions domestically is mentioned in the SWOT analyses of both Victoria and Western Australia. In comparison, New Zealand stakeholders seemed less concerned about competition domestically, but were concerned about competing with Australia for international visitors.

The growth of the wine and food industry was itself seen as a major threat. There was concern among many that the growth will bring with it 'cowboys' and others who have more interest in profit and quantity than maintaining quality products. If such a drop was to occur, this could potentially taint the 'quality' image of a destination. There is also the issue of oversupply making the product less 'unique' and, thus, potentially less desirable. Service quality and the visitor experience were also perceived as a threat to the industry if they are not maintained. This is no doubt linked again to the image and the motivation of visitors wanting to visit being affected. Some stakeholders in the New Zealand wine industry suggested that there is already an issue with service quality and the visitor experience that needed to be addressed.

Finally, future environmental factors and the resulting impacts on the industry were considered a threat to the wine and food tourism industries of New Zealand, British Columbia and Western Australia. These environmental factors included: climate change; damage from vineyards; breaches of biosecurity and their potentially devastating consequences; and, in New Zealand, the loss of the 'clean, green' image. In British Columbia there was concern about monopolies and the purchasing of smaller vineyards by larger companies, which have the potential to disturb the 'diversity of the visitor experience'. Also considered a key threat was potential negative economic conditions. In New Zealand there were a number of concerns, however, the 'perceived complacency and laziness within the food and wine industry' and the resulting missed opportunities as a result of inaction was considered the key threat. In Western Australia, there were issues relating to land use, inadequate planning and even the cost of land itself. Additionally, the 'cheap wines' available locally from other regions are considered a threat, as is the Asian recession (especially with Asia being one of the closest markets to this region). Also of concern was/is the issue of alcohol abuse and drink driving. In Victoria, health issues and the social implications of alcohol were also a concern, and there was unease that a 'shift in lifestyle activities away from wine and food' and the 'growing pressure for the regional tourism dollar'

British Columbia, Canada

- Inconsistent wine quality
- Inconsistent quality of visitor experience
- Difficult economic environment
- Larger producers buying out boutique and/or small producers and resulting decreased diversity of visitor experience
- Environmental conditions/fluctuations
    - Climatic
    - Economic
- Development of competing regions

Western Australia

- Conflicting land use
- Inadequate local planning for wine and tourism
- Rising costs of land
- Oversupply and resulting threat to integrity and quality
- Global competition
- Cheap wines from elsewhere
- Asian recession
- Other regions
- Alcohol abuse
- Environmentally damaging vineyard developments

COMMON THREATS

- Competing destinations
- Integrity and quality of wine due to oversupply and/or 'cowboys' (rogue operators).
- Service Quality/Visitor Experience
- Environmental factors

Victoria, Australia

- Health issues
- Lack of customer/service quality
- Bad/poor signage
- Increase in competition from other states
- Decline in domestic travel
- Market domination from conglomerates
- A shift in lifestyle activities away from wine and food as well as growing pressure for the regional tourism dollar
- Social implications of alcohol
- Health issues

New Zealand

- Biosecurity
- Drop in quality standards
- Service quality
- Loss of personal approach through size
- Low profile of region internationally
- Competing destinations overseas
- Perceived complacency and laziness within the food and wine tourism industry causing missed opportunities
- Loss of clean, green image
- Change in New Zealand dollar

Figure 18.4 Threats

could have a major impact on the industry. The threat of domination by conglomerates, and bad/poor signage were also considered important threats to the success of the industry.

The future

Hall et al. (1998) noted several barriers to creating effective links between wine producers and the tourism industry in Australia and New Zealand which can be extended to the wider food and tourism relationship, including:

- the often secondary or tertiary nature of tourism as an activity in the wine and food industries
- a dominant product focus of food and wine producers, and food and wine marketers
- a general lack of experience and understanding within the food and wine industry of tourism, and a subsequent lack of entrepreneurial skills and abilities with respect to marketing and product development
- the absence of effective intersectoral linkages, which leads to a lack of inter- and intra-organizational cohesion within the food and wine industry, and between the wine and food industries and the tourism industry.

The review of the SWOT analyses conducted above as well the insights in many of the chapters in this volume identify a strong set of commonalities that need to be addressed (Figure 18.5) for the ongoing development of wine and food tourism. In many ways the problems which face wine and food tourism are little different from those addressing many parts of the wider tourism industry. In particular, the attempt to balance sustainable business and economic growth with concerns over damaging the resource, which attracts consumers in the first place, is clearly important. However, also of significance is recognition of the role that research may be able to play not only in tackling immediate practical business problems, but also deeper and more difficult issues with respect to identity, culture and heritage, and what the food we eat tells us about ourselves. Such issues lie at the heart of sustainable local food and economic systems.

Food and travel have long been related. National and regional cuisines are never constant and always experience change as new foodstuffs arrive. This process has been going on for hundreds of years. However, now people also move in numbers almost undreamed off and their taste buds go with them. When they return home new patterns of consumption and production are created, while food shows and ethnic restaurants only serve to reinforce the taste of the exotic. What was once foreign is now local. Indeed, the various chapters of this book, particularly that of Scarpato (Chapter 17), highlight the contested nature of the

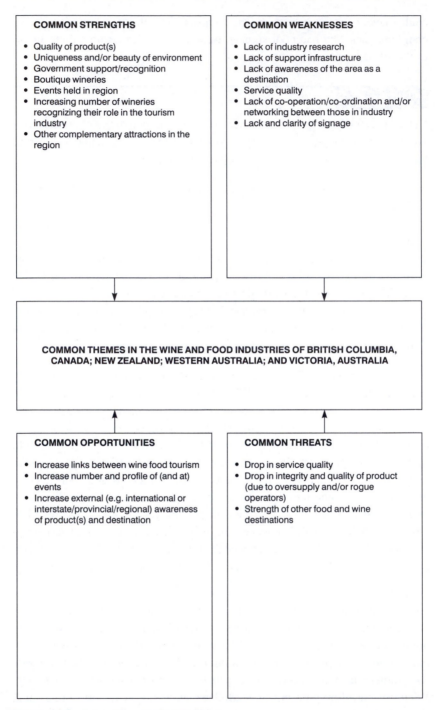

COMMON STRENGTHS

- Quality of product(s)
- Uniqueness and/or beauty of environment
- Government support/recognition
- Boutique wineries
- Events held in region
- Increasing number of wineries recognizing their role in the tourism industry
- Other complementary attractions in the region

COMMON WEAKNESSES

- Lack of industry research
- Lack of support infrastructure
- Lack of awareness of the area as a destination
- Service quality
- Lack of co-operation/co-ordination and/or networking between those in industry
- Lack and clarity of signage

COMMON THEMES IN THE WINE AND FOOD INDUSTRIES OF BRITISH COLUMBIA, CANADA; NEW ZEALAND; WESTERN AUSTRALIA; AND VICTORIA, AUSTRALIA

COMMON OPPORTUNITIES

- Increase links between wine food tourism
- Increase number and profile of (and at) events
- Increase external (e.g. international or interstate/provincial/regional) awareness of product(s) and destination

COMMON THREATS

- Drop in service quality
- Drop in integrity and quality of product (due to oversupply and/or rogue operators)
- Strength of other food and wine destinations

Figure 18.5 International commonalities

local and the extent to which the notion of local can expand for some in the provision and consumption of food.

Tourism is intimately bound up in these patterns of change. Indeed, we need to realize that such changes are normal. As Janiskee outlines in Exhibit 18.3, Oktoberfests have spread beyond Germany all over North America, and while some of their 'traditional' cultural functions may have disappeared they are still important and meaningful to the people who go, whether for culture or just to be with friends and to have a good time. Yet this does not mean that all change is good and should remain uncommented on. Indeed, in the case of the food industry perhaps far too many things have been left uncontested. Neither can all matters of consumption be easily bundled under the heading of lifestyle – as important as it is. There is also perhaps something of an irony that we produce a book about food tourism at a time when many people around the world are starving. Yet, arguably, it is a concern with the nature of the food system which drives interest in food tourism as much as it does those seeking to develop improved programmes of food security.

Instead, it is appropriate that many people are now becoming acutely interested in what they are eating, where it comes from and how sustainable it was to produce. Many people are also discovering more traditional and seasonal dishes made with produce which, if not organic, may at least have had a minimum of human interference. These things are worthwhile and people will travel to experience and learn about them. Ultimately, food is about attachment to place and to the local; it is also tied in with memories, tastes, friends, family and, perhaps, comfort and security. These experiences provide commercial opportunities for hospitality, tourism and production, yet they also provide a chance to reflect on what food actually means in contemporary society. For many people food tourism is an opportunity to find something real, traditional and meaningful, something which is produced by artisans and which says something about heritage and identity, whether our own or somebody else's. Therefore, in looking at food and tourism we are not only thinking about travel to somewhere, we also have to consider what it means to come home, and the implications of the journeys that both we and food have taken.

Exhibit 18.3 Oktoberfest in America

Oktoberfest was born in October 1810 when the townspeople of Munich threw a big party to celebrate the wedding of Bavaria's Crown Prince Ludwig and Princess Theresa. An annual party emerged from this event, and beer stands were added by 1818. Today, Munich's annual two-week Oktoberfest is one of the world's biggest and best known community celebrations. Each year about 6 million people gather in the Bavarian capital's beer tents and Festhallen to celebrate the festival the locals call 'Wies'n.' Celebrants at the Haufbrauhaus and associated venues, sit at long wooden tables, drink 5 million litres of beer, consume 200 000 pairs of pork sausages, sway to oompah music, do the Chicken Dance, and share the joyous state of being what the Germans call 'Gemuetlickheit'.

The largest Oktoberfest outside Germany apparently is an annual gathering of about 700 000 in the Kitchener-Waterloo area of Ontario, Canada. German immigrants also brought the Gemuetlickheit recipe with them to the USA. At least 430 Oktoberfest celebrations are produced in America each year.

American Oktoberfests are given an American twist (Janiskee, 1996). The Bavarian Oktoberfest of modern times is a September event, but nearly all the Oktoberfests held in America are produced during October. More importantly, Oktoberfests produced in the USA seldom create an environment conducive to the free-spirited, drink-and-dance revelry that typifies an authentic Bavarian celebration. Many of these tamed-down American Oktoberfests look suspiciously like generic 'family fun' festivals supplemented by adults-only beer tents. Mixed in with the Oktoberfests on the festival calendar are 'Octoberfests' that trade on the name but have nothing to do with the Oktoberfest tradition.

Oktoberfest is celebrated in one form or another in nearly every part of America, including Alaska and Hawaii. Festivals with this theme are most common, however, in areas that have German-settled towns and many people of German ancestry. Thus, for example, there are plenty of Oktoberfests in the cities of the eastern seaboard megalopolis, a region that welcomed millions of pre-First World War European immigrants. Other conspicuous clusters exist in German-settled areas like south-eastern Wisconsin, south-western Ohio, the hill country of eastern Texas and the upper Mississippi river valley. Oktoberfest celebrations can be produced nearly anywhere that people want to get together and have a good time. They are staged in urban regions as different as Los Angeles, Dallas, Tulsa, St Louis and Miami.

America's oldest and most authentic Oktoberfest is the Bavarian Oktoberfest in Glendale, Wisconsin, a suburb of Milwaukee. Five Bavarian clubs began producing this event over six decades ago, and it has had a permanent venue since 1943. Although there has been significant public participation since the 1960s, the Bavarian Oktoberfest is overshadowed by the much larger (c. 100 000 attendance) German Fest that is produced each July by the nearly three dozen German clubs of Milwaukee.

The larger German-themed festivals tend to be produced in metropolitan areas that attracted numerous German settlers and have historic German neighbourhoods. Given that Germans figured prominently in the settlement of the Ohio river valley, it is not surprising that Cincinnati stages the largest Oktoberfest in the USA. Oktoberfest-Zinzinnati, which is produced by the Downtown Council, was established in 1976. Now, on a single weekend each autumn, the event attracts over 500 000 people to a lively downtown venue with more than half a dozen entertainment stages. The comprehensive programme of activities and attractions – largely funded by major corporate sponsors such as Coca-Cola, Miller Lite and Lowenbrau – is provided with the help of about 1700 volunteers and includes delights such as the 'Biggest Bavarian Buffet This Side of Munich' (serving over 80 000 bratwurst) and the 'World's Largest Chicken Dance and Kazoo Band' (over 30 000 participants).

There are big Oktoberfest productions in many other places. An Oktoberfest staged in the Mainstrasse Village district of Covington, Kentucky, draws over 300 000 people each year. The Berghoff, a famous German restaurant established in Chicago in the late 1880s, attracts 100 000 or so to its annual Oktoberfest bash. In Columbus, Ohio, about 75 000 gather for the Oktoberfest produced in the city's historic German Village district. Among the larger West Coast events of this type is the Oktoberfest that is staged each year at the Bavarian-themed Old World Village in Huntington Beach near Los Angeles.

Some of America's most heavily publicized Oktoberfest celebrations are produced in smaller communities with tourism-orientated economies. Prominent among them are self-consciously ethnic tourist destinations like Frankenmuth (Michigan), Helen (Georgia), New Ulm (Minnesota), New Glarus (Wisconsin), Hermann (Missouri), Fredericksburg (Texas) and the Amana colonies (Iowa). Oktoberfest celebrations in these and many other towns are tied skilfully into broader tourism destination marketing strategies (Janiskee and Drews, 1998). Producing an Oktoberfest helps to create or strengthen a community's image as a bona fide ethnic attraction. Nowhere is this more evident than in Helen, Georgia, a southern Appalachian mountain town that employed an Alpine village makeover to attract tourists and rescue its moribund economy. Today, people from near and far flock to Helen to browse the little shops, buy fudge and immerse themselves in the faux-alpine ambience of the place. No one seems to mind that Helen's Oktoberfest, now one of the most prominent events on the regional festival calendar, is staged in a community that lacks German roots. German-heritage tourist destinations elsewhere fit Oktoberfest productions into comprehensive, widely advertised programmes of events and activities that attract people to the community throughout the year. In this sense, Oktoberfest functions as a tool for bolstering the trade of restaurants, wineries, speciality shops, and related means of entertaining visitors and separating them from some of their money.

Food and drink play a central role in any Oktoberfest worthy of the name. It is a given that most legal-age participants will want to enjoy beer or wine, and not necessarily in moderation. Alcoholic beverages are dispensed and consumed only in authorized places, with stringent measures being used to prevent underage drinking. Many structures will suffice, but the archetypal venue has one or more large tents equipped with long tables and benches, food and drink serving areas, a bandstand or stage, and a wooden dance floor. Corporate sponsorships, which typically include brewers or distributors, usually determine which domestic and/or imported brands are served.

The typical American Oktoberfest offers celebrants a choice among several German heritage foods. Bratwurst sausage ('brat') links are standard Oktoberfest fare. It is easy to understand why, since the hotdog-like brats are tasty, affordable and convenient to serve and eat. Most of the larger or more authentic Oktoberfests offer a large selection of German foods. In addition to bratwurst, a celebrant might have his or her choice of spanferkel, rollbraten, sauerbraten, schnitzel, sauerkraut and pretzels. For a sweet tooth, he or she could choose strudel, kuchen or other German heritage pastries and cakes.

The distinctive sounds of polka and oompah music permeate the typical Oktoberfest setting. Delivered enthusiastically by lederhosen-clad musicians, this live music underlines the ethnic quality and festive mood of the occasion. The USA has hundreds of competent German bands, but the producers of the bigger and better Oktoberfest celebrations boost the appeal of their events by importing big-name bands from Germany.

Projecting current trends suggests that America will have twice as many Oktoberfests within fifteen years. There are good reasons to expect vigorous growth. Oktoberfest not only embraces the concept of high-spirited fun, but also takes place when the weather is cool and autumn foliage is at its scenic best. Producers like the fact that Oktoberfest celebrants gladly pay for admission, food, beverages and other Gemuetlichkeit necessities, and can be accommodated with big-top tents, pavilions, community centres, restaurants, or other sheltered venues that eliminate rainouts and ease the task of collecting admissions and keeping alcohol away from underage drinkers.

On a less sanguine note, some event producers, promoters and event tourism researchers have pointed to trends that might stifle the further growth of community celebrations like Oktoberfest. The festival boom that began in America during the 1970s has loaded the national calendar with over 26 000 community festivals, leaving little room for new Oktoberfests or similar events in many locales (Janiskee and Drews, 1998). At the very least, more competition for sponsorships and attendees will weed out the less viable Oktoberfest celebrations and make the rest work harder.

Another limiting factor for Oktoberfest production is the central role of beer and wine consumption. While no one complains about celebrants eating brats and mustard-slathered pretzels, the consumption of alcoholic beverages in public places is quite another thing. Just about anywhere in America – and especially in the Deep South, Kansas and Utah – any festival with a 'beer party' image is likely to draw criticism. Such events are seen as encouraging alcoholism and drug addiction, disorderly conduct, spousal beatings, child abuse and impaired driving. Oktoberfest producers must vigorously discourage the irresponsible or underage consumption of alcoholic beverages at their events or risk public relations disasters and costly lawsuits. Prudent producers employ special measures such as designated driver programmes and a free taxi service.

Robert Janiskee

References

Abel, J., Thomson, J. and Maretzki, A. (1999).
Extension's role with farmers' markets: working with farmers, consumers, and communities. *Journal of Extension*, **37**(5), available
online: joe.org/joe/1999october/a4.html

ACP Publishing (2002). *Australian Gourmet
Traveller* readership profile: www.acp.com.au/
Entertaining/AGT/read.htm (accessed 17 May
2002).

Al Mujaddid (2001). FIANZ requests government regulate halal food. *Al Mujaddid*, **1**(13),
July, 9.

Al Qaradawi, Y. (1995). *The Lawful and the
Prohibited in Islam*, trans K. El-Hebawy, M.
Moinuddin Siddiqui and S. Shukry. Islamic
Book Trust.

Allen, S. (2001). Changes in the supply chain
structure: the impact of expanding consumer
choice, in *Food Supply Chain Management,
Issues for the Hospitality and Retail Sectors*
(Eastham, J. F., Sharples, L. and Ball, S. D.,
eds), Butterworth-Heinemann.

American Chamber of Commerce (2002).
Tradenz North America regional monthly
report – June 2002. *AmCham News*, **1**(6), 7.

Anon. (1996). Cuisine of the world. *Bon Appetit*,
41(1), 86.

Anonymous (1991). Teasers Burlesque Palace.
Cheri, November, 27–30.

Anonymous (1999). Great Canadian centrefold
search '99. *Cheri*, December, 148–153.

Anonymous (2002). Globalization's last hurrah?
Foreign Policy (128), January–February,
38–51.

Arce, A. and Marsden, T. (1993).The social construction of international food: a new research agenda. *Economic Geography*, **69**(3), 293–311.

Arkwright Society, The (1974). Cauldwell's Mill, Rowsley. The Arkwright Society.

Attenborough, D. (1960). *Quest for Paradise*. The Quality Book Club.

Audretsch, D. B. and Feldman, M. P. (1997). *Innovative Clusters and the Industry Life Cycle*. CEPR. Discussion Papers 1161, Centre for Economic Policy Research.

Australian Bureau of Statistics (2000). *ABS Tourism: International Inbound Tourism – Expenditure*: www.abs.gov.au/Ausstats/ABS@.nsf/94713ad445ff1425ca25682000192af2/fbebbf4a54c25a59ca256b360004a306!OpenDocument

Bar-On R (2001). East Asia and the Pacific, and WTO's international tourism summary for 2000. *Tourism Economics*, **7**(2), 191–208.

Barrows, C. W. (1996). Evaluating the Profit Potential of Restaurant Wine Lists. *Journal of Restaurant and Foodservice Marketing*, **1**(3/4), 161–177.

Basu, P. K. (2000). Conflicts and paradoxes in economic development – tourism in Papua New Guinea. *International Journal of Social Economics*, **27**(7/8/9/10), 907–916.

Bauman, Z. (1996). Morality in the age of contingency. In *Detraditionalization* (Heelas, P. et al., eds), pp. 49–58, Blackwell.

Beardsworth, A. and Keil, T. (1997). *Sociology on the Menu: An Invitation to the Study of Food and Society*. Routledge.

Beer, S. (2001). The future of the food supply chain: a perspective looking the chain. In *Food Supply Chain Management, Issues for the Hospitality and Retail Sectors* (Eastham, J. F., Sharples, L. and Ball S. D., eds), Butterworth-Heinemann.

Belisle, F. J. (1983). Tourism and food production in the Caribbean. *Annals of Tourism Research*, **10**(4), 497–513.

Belk, R. W. (1997). Been there, done that, bought the souvenirs: of journeys and boundary crossing. In *Consumer Research: Postcards from the Edge* (Brown, S. and Turley, D., eds), pp. 22–45, Routledge.

Bell, D. and Valentine, G. (1997). *Consuming Geographies: We Are Where We Eat*. Routledge.

Bellandi, M. (1989). The industrial district in Marshall. In *Small Firms and Industrial Districts in Italy* (Goodman, E. and Bamford, J. eds), pp. 136, 152, Routledge.

Bellew, V. (2002). The world's their oyster. *Foodtown Magazine* (4), April.

Bello, D. C. and Etzel, M. J. (1985). The role of novelty in the pleasure travel experience. *Journal of Travel Research*. Summer, 20–26.

Bergmann, U. (ed.) (1982). *Save Na Mekim*. Liklik Buk Information Centre.

Bessière, J. (1998). Local development and heritage: traditional food and - cuisine as tourist attractions in rural areas. *Sociologia Ruralis*, **38**(1), 21–34.

Bestor, T. C. (2000). How sushi went global. *Foreign Policy* (121), November–December, 54–63, available online: proquest.umi.com/pqdlink-?Ver=1&Exp=09–20 (accessed August 2002).

Blackler, F. B. (2002). Halal. Slow the international herald of tastes. *Magazine of the Slow Food Movement*, **2**, 32–37.

Blandy, R. (2000). *Industry Clusters Program: A Review*. South Australian Business Vision 2010, Government of South Australia.

Bode, W. K. H. (1994). *European Gastronomy, The Story of Man's Food and Eating Habits*. Hodder and Stoughton.

Boyne, S., Hall, D. R. and Williams, F. (2002). Policy, support and promotion for food-related tourism initiatives: a marketing approach to regional development. *Journal of Travel and Tourism Marketing*, forthcoming.

Bramwell, B. (1994). Rural tourism and sustainable rural tourism. *Journal of Sustainable Tourism*, **2**(1/2), 1–6.

Bramwell, B. and Sharman, A. (1998). Collaboration in local tourism policy making. *Annals of Tourism Research*.

Brander, M. (1997). *Capital Taste: The A–Z of Good Food In and Around Canberra*. Wakefield Press, South Australia.

British Tourist Authority (2001). Outbound Statistics for 2000. www.britishtouristauthority.org

Brotherton, B. and Himmetoglu, B. (1997). Beyond destinations – special interest tourism. *Anatolia*, **8**(3), Fall, 11–30.

Bruhn, C. M., Vossen, P. M., Chapman, E. and Vaupel, S. (1992). Consumer attitudes toward locally grown produce. *California Agriculture*, July–August, 13–16.

Brunori G. and Rossi A. (2000). Synergy and coherence through collective action: some insights from wine routes in Tuscany. *Sociologia Ruralis*, **40**(4), 409–423.

Bryant, H. (2001). *Interview with Chef Thomas Keller, The French Laundry*, in Small Business School online: smallbusinessschool.org/webapp/sbs/sbs/index-ie.jsp?Size=800&Speed=250&page=http%3A//sbschool.net/keller.html (accessed August 2002).

Buang, A. H. (2001). Islam and Muslims in New Zealand. Unpublished research paper, Malay Studies, Victoria University, Wellington, New Zealand.

Buchgraber, K. (1996). Grünland – Bewirtschaftung – Grundlage für Milch- und Fleischproduktion und Basis der Produktion für Landschaft und Fremdenverkehr. *Stocarstvo*, **50**(6), 439–448.

Bureau of Industry Economics (1991a). *Networks: A Third Form of Organisation*. Discussion Paper 14, Bureau of Industry Economics, Canberra.

Bureau of Industry Economics (1991b). Networks: a third form of organisation. *Bulletin of Industry Economics*, **10**, 5–9.

Burns, J. (2002). Superstores in spotlight, *Farmers Weekly*, 3 May, 10.

Butler, R. (1998). Rural Recreation and Tourism. In *The Geography of Rural Change* (Illberg, B. ed.), Longman, London.

Butler, R. and Clark, G. (1992). Tourism in rural areas: Canada and the United Kingdom. In *Contemporary Rural Systems in Transition, Vol. 2 Economy and Society*, (Bowler, I. R., Bryant, C. R and Nellis, M. D., eds), CAB International.

Butler, R., Hall, C. M. and Jenkins, J. (eds) (1998). *Tourism and Recreation in Rural Areas*, Wiley.

Caffyn, A. (2000). Developing sustainable tourism in the Trossachs, Scotland. In *Tourism and Sustainable Community Development* (Richards, G. and Hall, D., eds), pp. 83–100, Routledge.

Cambourne, B. and Espinoza, M. (2000). 2000 Kamberra Wine Show Evaluation. Unpublished Research Report, Centre for Tourism Research, University of Canberra, Canberra ACT Australia.

Cambourne, B. and Macionis, N. (2000). Meeting the wine-maker: wine tourism product development in an emerging wine region. In *Wine Tourism Around the World: Development, Management and Markets* (Hall, C. M., Sharples, L., Cambourne, B. and Macionis, N., eds), Butterworth-Heinemann.

Cambourne, B., Macionis, N., Hall, C. M. and Sharples, L. (2000). The future of wine tourism. In *Wine and Tourism from Around the World* (Hall, C. M., Sharples, L., Cambourne, B. and Macionis, N., eds), pp. 297–320, Butterworth-Heinemann.

Cambourne, B., Cegielski, M., Espinoza, M. and May, C. (2001). National Multicultural Festival Evaluation. Unpublished Research Report, Centre for Tourism Research, University of Canberra, Canberra ACT Australia.

Canadian Tourism Commission (CTC) (2000). Cuisine as a Canadian tourism product, developing beyond the wine country. Minutes of the Tourism and Cuisine Round Table Niagara Region, Niagara Falls, Ontario, 8–9 March.

Canadian Tourism Commission (CTC) (2001). *National Tourism and Cuisine Forum*. Canadian Tourism Commission.

Canberra Tourism and Events Corporation (2001). ACT Tourism Master Plan, 2001–2005. Canberra Tourism and Events Corporation, Canberra Australia.

Caraher, M., Dixon, P., Lang, T. and Carr-Hill, R. (1999). The state of cooking in England: the relationship of cooking skills to food choice. *British Food Journal*, **101**(8). 590–609.

Carpenter, F. R. (ed.) (1974). *The Classic of Tea by Lu Yu*. Little, Brown and Company.

Cawley, M. E., Gaffey, S. M., Gillmor, D., McDonaugh, P., Commins, P., McIntyre, B. and Henchion, M. (1999). *Regional Images and the Promotion of Quality Products and Services in the Lagging Regions of the European Union*. FAIR3-CT96–1827, Final Regional Report, University College Galway, Ireland.

Center for Economic Development Research and Assistance (1997). *Las Cruces International Airport, New Mexico, USA, Airport Master Plan – 1997, Final Report Economic Impact Study For The Las Cruces International Airport*. Submitted by the Center for Economic Development Research and Assistance at New Mexico State University, prepared for Coffman Associates, Airport Consultants, 24 July 1996.

Centre for Environment and Society (1999). *Local Food Systems: Lessons for Local Economies Conference Proceedings*. University of Essex.

Centre for Tourism and Leisure Policy Research (1998). *The Canberra District Wine Industry*. Unpublished Research Report, ACT AusIndustry, Canberra, Australia.

Chapman, P. (1994). Agriculture in Niagara: an overview. In *Niagara's Changing Landscape* (Gayler, H., ed.), pp. 279–299, Carlteon University Press.

Chaudry, M. M. (2001). *Eating by the Book: Halal Food – Worth the Extra Investment?* FoodFen: www.foodfen.org.uk/fflibrary/consumer/021reHalal.htm (accessed 20 August 2001).

Chidley, J. (1998). Haute Canuck. *Maclean's*, 26 August, 36–40.

Chun, F. Y. (1987). The dynamics of the halal meat trade in New Zealand and Australia. In *New Zealand and the Middle East* (Macintyre, R., ed.), pp. 149–176, Australasian Middle East Studies Association.

CIA (2001). *The World Factbook*: http://www.odci.gov/cia/publications/factbook/

Clarke, J. (1999). Marketing structures for farm tourism: beyond the individual provider of rural tourism. *Journal of Sustainable Tourism*, **7**(1).

Cloke, P. J. (1993). The countryside as commodity: new spaces for rural leisure. In *Leisure and the Environment* (Glyptis, S., ed.), pp. 53–70, Belhaven.

Coates, B. J. (1977). *Birds in Papua New Guinea*. Robert Brown and Associates.

Coffee and Beverage (2002). Tea 101. *Coffee and Beverage*, **6**(3), Winter, 16–17.

Collier, A. (1995). *Principles of Tourism: A New Zealand Perspective*. 3rd edn. Longman Paul.

Comite Regional du Tourisme (nd). *Region Languedoc Roussillon: Wines and Wine Growing Areas*. Regional Tourist Guide.

Commission Report (2002). *Farming and Food: A Sustainable Future*. Report of the Policy Commission on the Future of Farming, January.

Cong, Yan (2001). Tea and tourism. Unpublished paper, University of New Brunswick–Saint John.

Connell, C. M., Beierlein, J. G. and Vroomen, H. L. (1986). *Consumer Preferences and Attitudes Regarding Fruit and Vegetable Purchases from Direct Market Outlets*. Report 185. Pennsylvania State University, Department of Agricultural Economics and Rural Sociology, Agricultural Experiment Station.

Cook, I. and Crang, P. (1996). The world on a plate: culinary cultures, displacement and geographical knowledges. *Journal of Material Culture*, **1**(2), 131–153.

Coopers and Lybrand Consulting (1996). *Domestic Tourism Market Research Study: Main Report*. Canadian Tourism Commission.

Cotter, A. (1992). Green image and marketing Irish beef. In *Environment and Development in Ireland* (Feehan, J., ed.), pp. 179–181, Environment Institute, University College Dublin.

Countryside Agency (2001). *Eat the View: Promoting Sustainable, Local Products*. Countryside Agency. (www.eat-the-view.org.uk).

Coupe, C. (1991). *Shellfish – Australian Cookery Series*. Hodder and Stoughton, p. 107.

Courtine, J. B. (ed.) (1996). *Larousse Gastronomique*. Lewis Esson.

Craik, J. (1997). The culture of tourism. In *Touring Cultures: Transformation of Travel and History* (Rojek, C. and Urry, J., eds), pp. 113–136, Routledge.

Crang, P. (1995). The world on a plate: or, making a meal out of culture, economy, place and space. Paper presented during Academic Study Group visit to Israel.

Crompton, J. L. (1979). Motivations for pleasure vacations. *Annals of Tourism Research*, **6**(4), 408–424.

Culligan, K. (1992). *Developing a Model of Holidaytaking Behaviour: Leisure and Tourism Futures Conference Proceedings*. Henley Centre for Forecasting.

Cusack, I. (2000). African cuisines: recipes for nation building? *Journal of African Cultural Studies*, **13**(2), 207–225.

Cutforth, F. (2000). Pacific Rim cuisine. *Pacific Tourism Review*, **4**, 45–52.

Daley, G. (2001). The intangible economy and Australia. *Australian Journal of Management*, **26**, 3–20.

De Selincourt, K. (1997). *Local Harvest: Delicious Ways to Save the Planet*. Lawrence and Wishart.

DEFRA (2002). http://www.defra.gov.uk/esg/work_htm/publications

Deleuze, G. and Guattari, F. (1987). *A Thousand Plateaus: Capitalism and Schizophrenia*. University of Minnesota Press.

Department of Environment, Food and Rural Affairs (DEFRA) (2000). *Introduction, the Countryside– the Challenge, ch1, Our Countryside: The Future, a Fair Deal for Rural England* (Rural White Paper, November 2000). DEFRA and MAFF.

Department of Media, Culture and Sport (DCMS) (1999). *Tomorrow's Tourism*. DCMS.

Department of the Environment, Transport and the Regions (DETR) (2000). *Our Countryside: The Future. A Fair Deal for Rural England*. HMSO.

Dirlik, A. (1996). The global in the local. In *Global/Local: Cultural Production and the Transnational Imaginary* (Wilson, R. and Dissanayake, W., eds), Duke University Press.

Dodd, T. (1997). Techniques to Increase Impulse Wine Purchases in a Restaurant Setting. *Journal of Restaurant and Foodservice Marketing*, **2**(1), 63–73.

Dodd, T. H. (1997). Factors that influence the adoption and diffusion of new wine products. *Hospitality Research Journal*, **20**(3), 123–136.

Douglas, N. (1998), Tourism in Papua New Guinea: past, present and future. *Pacific Tourism Review*, **2**(1), 97–104.

Downey, E. (1998). Triple Treat. *The Land Magazine*, September 10, 1998, 6–7.

Du Rand, G. E., Heath, E. and Alberts, N. (2002). The role of local and regional food in destination marketing: a South African situation analysis. *Journal of Travel and Tourism Marketing*, in press.

Dwyer, L., Forsyth, P., Madden, J. and Spurr, R. (2000). Inbound economic impacts of tourism on the macroeconomy. *Current Issues in Tourism*, **3**(4), 325–363.

Eastham, J. F., Ball, S. D. and Sharples, L. (2001). The catering and food retail industries: a contextual insight. In *Food Supply Chain Management, Issues for the Hospitality and Retail Sectors* (Eastham, J. F., Sharples, L. and Ball, S. D., eds), Butterworth-Heinemann.

Eastwood, D. B., Brooker, J. R. and Gray, M. D. (1995). *An Intrastate Comparison of Consumers' Patronage of Farmers' Markets in Knox, Madison and Shelby Counties*. Research Report 95–03. University of

Tennessee, Department of Agricultural Economics and Rural Sociology, Institute of Agriculture, Agricultural Experiment Station.

Economic Planning Group of Canada (EPG) (2001). A strategy for wine and culinary tourism in Ontario: background report. Unpublished report, available online: www.wineroute.com/Iplan.htm) (accessed 23 May 2002).

Economic Planning Group of Canada (EPG) (2002). *Wine and Culinary Tourism in Ontario – Executive Summary.* EPG.

Economics Research Associates (1996). *1995 Survey of San Francisco Visitors.* Conducted for the San Francisco Convention and Visitors Bureau by Economics Research Associates: www.sfvisitor.org/memberinfo/html/VisitorStats.html

Edith Cowan University (1999). *Draft Western Australian Wine Tourism Strategy.* Edith Cowan University.

Edwards, F. (1986). *The Marketing of Wine from Small Wineries.* Unpublished Masters Thesis, Faculty of Commerce and Economics, University of Queensland, St Lucia.

El Mouelhy, M. (1997). *Food in the Quran.* Halal helpline: www.geocities.com/Athens/Acropolis/1950/quran.htm (accessed 23 July 2001).

Elmont, S. (1995). Tourism and food service: two sides of the same coin. *Cornell Hotel and Restaurant Administration Quarterly,* February, 57–63.

Elwyn-Owen, R. (1991). Strategies for sustainable tourism: the theory and the practice. International conference on tourism development, trends and prospects in the 1990s, Universiti Teknologi Malaysia, Kuala Lumpur, Malaysia, September.

English Tourism Council (ETC) (2001). *Working for the Countryside: A Strategy for Rural Tourism in England, 2001–2005.* ETC.

Enright, M. and Roberts, B. (2001). Regional clustering in Australia. *Australian Journal of Management,* **26**, 65–86.

Enteleca Research and Consultancy (2001). *Tourist's Attitudes Towards Regional and Local Food.* Prepared for the Ministry of Agriculture, Fisheries and Food and the Countryside Agency by Enteleca Research and Consultancy.

Erbil, C. (2001). *Why is Slaughtering Animals Prescribed as It Is?*: www.afi.org.uk/miscon/G2SLAU1.htm (accessed 17 August 2001).

Escoffier, A. (1907). *Le Guide Culinaire: Aide-mémoire de Cuisine Pratique.* Avec la collaboration de Gilbret et Fétu, Deuxi'eme édition. Emile Colin et Cie.

Escoffier, A. (1957). *A Guide to Modern Cookery.* London: Heinemann.

Euromonitor (2001a). *Restaurants and Cafes in France.* Global Market Information Database (GMID), online edition.

Euromonitor (2001b). *Restaurants and Cafes in the United Kingdom*. Global Market Information Database (GMID), online edition.

European Union (2002). *Food Quality: Commission Proposes Better Protection for Geographical Names*. IP/02/422, Brussels, 15 March.

Eurostat (2000). *A Community of Fifteen Key Figures*. European Commission.

Ewen, S. (1988). *All Consuming Images: The Politics of Style in Contemporary Culture*. Basic Books.

Express Travel and Tourism (2000). Editorial, 16–30 April, available online: www.expresstravelandtourism.com/2001d0403/travelindia5.htm (accessed 3 August 2002).

Farmers Markets Ontario (2001). *History*: www.fmo.reach.net/history.html

Fattorini, J. E. (1996). *Managing Wine and Wine Sales*. International Thomson Business Press.

Faulks, P. and Cambourne, B. (2001). 2001 Kamberra Wine Show Evaluation. Unpublished Research Report, Centre for Tourism Research, University of Canberra, Canberra ACT Australia.

Featherstone, M. (1996). Localism globalism, cultural identity. In *Global/Local: Cultural Production and the Transnational Imaginary* (Wilson, R. and Dissanayake, W., eds), Duke University Press.

Federation of Islamic Associations of New Zealand (FIANZ) (2001). Press release, 31 May.

Ferguson, C. (1995). Our northern bounty. In *Northern Bounty* (Powers, J. and Stewart, A., eds), pp. 3–6, Random House of Canada.

Ferguson, C. (2000). Foreword. In *The Flavours of Canada* (A. Stewart), p. 9, Raincoast Books.

Fernandez-Armesto, F. (2001), *Food: A History*. Macmillan.

Ferretti, F. (1999). Canadian arcadia: Southern Ontario's table and vine. *Gourme*, **61**(8), 68–75.

Finkelstein, J. (1989). *Dining Out: A Sociology of Modern Manners*. Polity.

Fishwick, M. (1995). Ray and Ronald girdle the globe. *Journal of American Culture*, **18**(1), 13–29.

Flognfeldt, T. (2002). Second homes in Norway. In *Tourism and Migration: New Relationships between Production and Consumption* (Hall, C. M. and Williams, A. M., eds), Kluwer Academic.

Fockler, R. (2002). Viewpoint: tea talk. *Coffee and Beverage*, **6**(3), Winter.

Folk Arts Council of Winnipeg (1998). *Annual Report*. Folk Arts Council of Winnipeg.

Folklorama (2000). *Folklorama*: www.folklorama.ca/know.html (accessed 19 May 2000).

Font, X. and Ahjem, T. E. (1999). Searching for a balance in tourism development strategies. *International Journal of Contemporary Hospitality Management*, **11**(2/3), 73–77.

Food and Travel (2002). www.foodand travel.com (accessed 11 July 2002).

Foroohar, R. (2002). Travel and tourism: getting off the beaten track. *Newsweek*, **160**(4), 22 July–29 July, 34–38.

Francis, A. (2001). Now one in three women forced to find extra work. *Farmers Weekly*, 9 November, 17.

Frechtling, D. C. and Horvath, E. (1999). Estimating the multiplier effects of tourism expenditures on a local economy through a regional input–output model. *Journal of Travel Research*, **37**, May, 324–332.

Fridgen, J. D. (1984). Environmental psychology and tourism. *Annals of Tourism Research*, **11**, 19–39.

Frochot, I. (2002). An analysis of regional positioning and its associated food images in French tourism regional brochures. *Journal of Travel and Tourism Marketing*, in press.

Fuller, D. (1978). *Maori Food and Cookery*. A. H. and A. W. Reed.

Galston, W. A. and Baehler, K. J. (1995). *Rural Development in the United States: Connecting Theory, Practice and Possibilities*. Island Press.

Gardner, B. (1996). *European Agriculture, Policies, Production and Trade*. Routledge.

Germov, J. and Williams, L. (1999). *A Sociology of Food and Nutrition: The Social Appetite*. Oxford University Press.

Gerrard, M. (1999). Eat your heart out in Paris. *Independent on Sunday*.

Getz, D. (1997). *Event Management and Event Tourism*. Cognizant Communication Corporation.

Gibson, E. (1995). Selling to restaurants. In *Direct Farm Marketing and Tourism Handbook*, pp. 35–40, University of Arizona College of Agriculture, Cooperative Extension.

Good Earth Cooking School (n.d.). Brochure.

Goodman, D. and Watts, M. J. (1997). *Agrarian Questions, Globalising Food, Agrarian Questions and Global Restructuring*. Routledge.

Goody, J. (1982). *Cooking, Cuisine and Class*. Cambridge University Press.

Gourmet on Tour (2002). www.gourmet on tour (accessed 25 June 2002).

Government of South Africa (1996). *The Development and Promotion of Tourism in South Africa* (White Paper). Department of Environmental Affairs and Tourism.

Govindasamy, R. (1996). Characteristics of farmer-to-consumer direct market customers: an overview. *Journal of Extension*, **34**(4), available online: http://www.joe.org/joe/1996august/rb1.html

Govindasamy, R., Italia, J. and Adelaja, A. (2002). Farmers' markets: consumer trends, preferences and characteristics. *Journal of Extension*, **40**(1), available online: http://joe.org/joe/2002february/rb6.html

Grandori, A. and Soda, G. (1995). Inter-firm networks: antecedents, mechanisms and forms. *Organisation Studies*, **16**(2), 183–214.

Granovetter, M. (1992). Problems of Explanation in Economic Sociology. In *Networks and Organizations: structure, form and action*. (Nohria, N. and Eccles, R., eds.), pp. 25–56, Harvard Business School Press.

Hall, C. M. (1992). *Hallmark Tourist Events. Impacts, Management and Planning*. Bellhaven Press.

Hall, C. M. (1996). Wine tourism in New Zealand. In *Tourism Down Under II: Towards a More Sustainable Tourism, Conference Proceedings* (Kearsley, G., ed.), pp. 109–119, Centre for Tourism, University of Otago.

Hall, C. M. (2001). The development of rural wine and food tourism networks: factors and issues. In *New Directions in Managing Rural Tourism and Leisure: Local Impacts, Global Trends*, Scottish Agricultural College.

Hall, C. M. (2002). Local initiatives for local regional development: the role of food, wine and tourism. In *Tourism and Well Being* (Arola, E., Kärkkäinen, J. and Siitari, M., eds), pp. 47–63, Jyväskylä Polytechnic. Second Tourism Industry and Education Symposium, held at Jyväskylä Polytechnic, Jyväskylä, Finland 16–18 May.

Hall, C. M. (2003). *Introduction to Tourism in Australia*. 4th edn. Pearson (in press).

Hall, C. M. and Jenkins, J. (1998). Rural tourism and recreation policy dimensions. In *Tourism and Recreation in Rural Areas* (Butler, R., Hall, C.M. and Jenkins, J., eds), pp. 19–42, Wiley.

Hall, C. M. and Johnson, G. (1998). Wine and food tourism in New Zealand: difficulties in the creation of sustainable tourism business networks. In *Rural Tourism Management: Sustainable Options, Conference Proceedings, 9–12 Sept 1998* (Hall, D. and O'Hanlon, L., eds), pp. 21–38. Scottish Agricultural College.

Hall, C. M. and Kearsley, G. W. (2001). *Tourism in New Zealand: An Introduction*. Oxford University Press.

Hall, C. M. and Macionis, N. (1998). Wine tourism in Australia and New Zealand. In *Tourism and Recreation in Rural Areas* (Butler, R. W., Hall, C. M. and Jenkins, J., eds), pp. 197–224, Wiley.

Hall, C. M. and Mitchell, R. (2000). We are what we eat: food, tourism and globalisation. *Tourism, Culture and Communication*, **2**, 29–37.

Hall, C. M. and Mitchell, R. (2001). Wine and food tourism. In *Special Interest Tourism: Context and Cases* (Douglas, N., Douglas, N. and Derrett, R., eds), pp. 307–329, Wiley.

Hall, C. M. and Mitchell, R. (2002a). Tourism as a force for gastronomic globalization and localization. In *Tourism and Gastronomy* (Hjalager, A.-M. and Richards, G., eds), Routledge.

Hall, C. M. and Mitchell, R. (2002b). The tourist terroir of New Zealand wine: the importance of region in the wine tourism experience. In *Food and Environment: Geographies of Taste* (Montanari, A., ed.), pp. 69–91, Societá Geografica Italiana.

Hall, C. M. and Page, S. (2002). *Geography of Tourism and Recreation: Environment, Place and Space*. 2nd edn. Routledge.

Hall, C. M. and Williams, A. M. (eds) (2002). *Tourism and Migration: New Relationships between Production and Consumption*. Kluwer Academic.

Hall, C. M., Cambourne, B., Macionis, N. and Johnson, G. (1998). Wine tourism and network development in Australia and New Zealand: review, establishment and prospects. *International Journal of Wine Marketing*, **9**(2/3), 5–31.

Hall, C. M., Johnson, G. and Mitchell, R. (2000). Wine tourism and regional development. In *Wine Tourism Around the World: Development, Management and Markets* (Hall, C. M., Sharples, E., Cambourne, B. and Macionis, N., eds), pp. 196–225, Butterworth-Heinemann.

Hall, C. M., Mitchell, R. and Smith, A (2001). *New Zealand Draft Food and Wine Tourism Strategy*. Working paper no. 1, Department of Tourism, University of Otago.

Hall, C. M., Johnson, G., Cambourne, B. Macionis, N., et al. (2000a). Wine tourism: an introduction. In *Wine and Tourism Around the World: Development, Management and Markets* (Hall, C. M., Sharples, E., Cambourne, B. and Macionis, N., eds), pp. 1–23, Butterworth-Heinemann.

Hall, C. M., Longo, A. M., Mitchell, R. and Johnson, G. (2000c). Wine tourism in New Zealand. In *Wine Tourism Around the World: Development, Management and Markets* (Hall, C. M., Sharples, E., Cambourne, B. and Macionis, N., eds), pp. 150–174, Butterworth-Heinemann.

Hall, C. M., Sharples, E., Cambourne, B. and Macionis, N. (eds) (2000b). *Wine Tourism Around the World: Development, Management and Markets*. Butterworth-Heinemann.

Halliday, J. (1998). *Wine Atlas of Australia and New Zealand*. HarperCollins.

Halliday, S. (2000). Food and regional wine tourism: Yarra Valley experience. Unpublished presentation at All for One and One For All, a meeting of minds on the development of food and wine in Hawke's Bay, Ormlie Lodge, July.

Halstead, B. (1996). *The Dive Sites of Papua New Guinea*. New Holland.

Hamal, K. and Yomapisi, J. (2001). Abstract from 2001 CAUTHE National Research Conference, Australia.

Hamel, D. (2001). Tea: a silk road odyssey. *Student Traveler*, **24**(2), Fall, 10–11.

Hamilton, L. M. (2002). The American farmers market. *Gastronomica*, **2**(3), 73–77.

Hammond, P. W. (1993). *Food and Feast in Medieval England*. Alan Sutton.

Hannerz, U. (1990). Cosmopolitans and locals in a world culture. *Theory, Culture and Society*, **7**, June, 237–251.

Harler, C. R. (1956). *The Culture and Marketing of Tea*. Oxford University Press.

Harmer, J. (2000). The fame game. *Caterer and Hotelkeeper*, 6–12 April.

Harris, M. (1974). *Cows, Pigs, Wars and Witches: The Riddles of Culture*. Vintage Press.

Harris, M. (1985). *Good to Eat: Riddles of Culture*. Waveland Press.

Hartsough, C. (1999). The future of spa cuisine – millennium eating, the newest nutrition. *Pulse*, July–August, (the official magazine of the International Spa Association).

Hashimoto, A. and Telfer, D. J. (1999). Marketing icewine to Japanese tourists in Niagara: the case of Inniskillin Winery. *International Journal of Wine Marketing*, **11**(2), 29–41.

Havitz, M. E and Dimanche, F. (1999). Leisure involvement revisited: drive properties and paradoxes. *Journal of Leisure Research*, **31**(2), available online.

Heart of England Tourist Board (2001). *Food and Drink in Tourism Motivations and Attitudes Survey*. Heart of England Tourist Board.

Heath, E. and Wall, G. (1992). *Marketing Tourism Destinations: A Strategic Planning Approach*. Wiley.

Henchion, M. and McIntyre, B. (2000). Regional imagery and quality products: the Irish experience. *British Food Journal*, **102**(8), 630–644.

Henderson, T. (2002). Trust to open farm shop, *Newcastle-upon-Tyne Journal*, 9 March.

Henton, D. and Walesh, K. (1997). *Grassroots Leaders for a New Economy: How Civic Entrepreneurs Are Building Prosperous Communities*. Jossey-Bass.

Hilton, M. L. (1998). The Partnership of Food and Wine: A Relationship Still in Therapy. *Wine Business Monthly*, November 1998, http://smart wine.com.wbm/1998/November/bmk9823.htm (accessed November 2, 1998).

Hinterhuber, H. H., and Levin, B. M., (1994). Strategic networks – the organisation of the future. *Long Range Planning*, **27**(3), 43–53.

Hjalager, A.-M. (1996). Agricultural diversification into tourism. *Tourism Management*, **17**(2),103–111.

Hjalager, A. and Richards, G. (2002). *Tourism and Gastronomy*. Routledge.

Hjalager, A. and Corigliano, M. A. (2000). Food for tourists: determinants of an image. *International Journal of Tourism Research*, **2**, 281–293.

Holbrook, M. B. and Hirschman, E. C. (1982). The experiential aspects of consumption: consumer fantasies, feelings, and fun. *Journal of Consumer Research*, **9**, 132–140.

Howard, P. (1997). Capital Invasion. In *Enjoy Australian Food and Wine*. Gore and Osmet Publications, pp. 62–65.

Hudson, W. J. (ed.) (1971). *Australia and Papua New Guinea*. Sydney University Press.

Hughes, G. (1995). Authenticity in tourism. *Annals of Tourism Research*, **22**(4), 781–803.

Hughes, M. E. and Mattson, R. H. (1995). *Farmers Markets in Kansas: A Profile of Vendors and Market Organization*. Report of progress 658. Kansas State University, Agricultural Experiment Station.

Hummelbrunner, R. and Miglbauer, E. (1994). Tourism promotion and potential in peripheral areas: the Austrian case. *Journal of Sustainable Tourism*, **4**(3), 41–50.

Ikeda, J. (1999). Culture, food and nutrition in increasingly culturally diverse societies. In *A Sociology of Food and Nutrition: The Social Appetite* (Germov, J. and Williams, L., eds), pp. 149–168, Oxford University Press.

Ilbery, B. (1998). *The Geography of Rural Change*. Longman.

Ilbery, B. and Kneafsey, M. (2000a). Registering regional specialty food and drink products in the United Kingdom: the case of PDOs and PGIs. *Area*, **32**(3), 317–325.

Ilbery, B. and Kneafsey, M. (2000b). Producer constructions of quality in regional speciality food production: a case study from south west England. *Journal of Rural Studies*, **16**, 217–230.

Independent on Sunday (2001). Twelve best foodie holidays, *Independent on Sunday*, 4 March, p. 4.

Inflight Catering Association (2002). http://www.ifcanet.com/ (accessed 23 June 2002).

Inskeep, E., (1991). *Tourism Planning: An Integrated and Sustainable Development Approach*. Van Nostrand Reinhold.

Jackson, S. (1998). Just Bring Yourself, BYO's Off the Menu. *Weekend Australian*, 19–20 September, 1998, p. 5.

Jackson, P. (2000). Old MacDonald had a farm … *Independent*, 7 October, available online: www.the independent.co.uk

Jamal, T. B. and Getz, D. (1995). Collaboration theory and community tourism planning. *Annals of Tourism Research*, **22**, 186–204.

Jameson, F. (1984). Postmodernism, or the cultural logic of late capitalism. *New Left Review*, **146**, July–August, 53–92.

Janiskee, R. (1996). Oktoberfest – American style. *Festival Management and Event Tourism: An International Journal*, **3**, 197–199.

Janiskee, R. and Drews, P. L. (1998). Rural festivals and community reimaging. In *Tourism and Recreation in Rural Areas* (Butler, R. W., Hall, C. M. and Jenkins, J., eds), pp. 157–175, Wiley.

Jenkins, J., Hall, C. M. and Troughton, M. (1998). The restructuring of rural economies: rural tourism and recreation as a government response. In *Tourism and Recreation in Rural Areas* (Butler, R. W., Hall, C. M. and Jenkins, J., eds), pp. 43–68, Wiley.

Johnson, G. (1998). Wine tourism in New Zealand – a national survey of wineries. Unpublished Diploma in Tourism dissertation, University of Otago.

Jolly, D. A. (1999). 'Home Made' – the paradigms and paradoxes of changing consumer preferences: implications for direct marketing. Paper presented at the Agricultural Outlook Forum 1999, 22 February, available online: http://www.usda.gov/agency/oce/waob/outlook99/speeches/025/JOLLY.TXT

Joy, A. and Wallendorf, M. (1996). The development of consumer culture in the third world. In *Consumption and Marketing: Macro Dimensions* (Belk, R. et al., eds), pp. 104–142, Southwestern College Publishing.

Ju-Ping, C. (2001). Pinglin honors the ancient tradition of tea. *Taipei Times*, 24 July, available online: http://taipeitimes.com/news/2001/07/24 (accessed 23 march 2002).

Just-food.com (2002). *Republic of Ireland/USA: Irish Food Board Launches Major Programme in Western US*. Just-food.com (accessed 21 January 2002).

Kastenholz, E., Davis, D. and Paul, G. (1999). Segmenting tourism in rural areas: the case of north and central Portugal. *Journal of Travel Research*, **37**, May, 353–363.

Kellner, D. (1999). *The Frankfurt School and British Cultural Studies: The Missed Articulation*, available online: www.popcultures.com/theorists/kellner.html

Kezis, A., Gwebu, T., Peavey, S. and Cheng, H. (1998). a study of consumers at a small farmers' market in Maine: results from a 1995 survey. *Journal of Food Distribution Research*, February, 91–98.

Kezis, A. S., King, F. R., Toensmeyer, U. C., Jack, R. et al. (1984). Consumer acceptance and preference for direct marketing in the Northeast. *Journal of Food Distribution Research*, September, 38–46.

King, D. (1993). *Tea Time: New Ways to Serve Tea*. Kenan Books.

Kinsella, J., Wilson, S., de Jong, F. and Renting, H. (2000). Pluriactivity as a livelihood strategy in Irish farm households and its role in rural development. *Sociologia Ruralis*, **40**(4), October, 481–496.

Kivela, J. (1998). Dining satisfaction and its impact on return patronage. PhD thesis, RMIT University.

Knipp, P. (1998). New Asia cuisine: revolution or evolution. *New Asia Cuisine*, March, available online: www.asiacuisine.com/

Koo, L. C., Tao, F. K. C. and Yeung, H. C. (1999). Preferential segmentation of restaurant attributes through conjoint analysis. *International Journal of Contemporary Hospitality Management*, **11**(5), 242–250.

Korchok, K. (2002). Niagara's cooking. *Toronto Star*. 8 June, L2.

Kotler, P., Ang, S. H., Leong, S. M. and Tan, C. T. (1999). *Marketing Management: An Asian Perspective*. 2nd edn. Prentice-Hall.

Kotler, P., Bowen, J. and Makens, J. (1999). *Marketing for Hospitality and Tourism*. 2nd edn. Prentice-Hall.

Krogt, C. van der (1996). Islam. In *Religions of New Zealanders* (Donovan, P., ed.), pp. 189–208, Dunmore Press.

Krotz, L. (1993). Food for the soul. *Harrowsmith Country Life*, **105**, October, 54–59.

Kuzenof, S., Tregear, A. and Moxey, A. (1997). Regional foods : a consumer perspective. *British Food Journal*, **99**(6) 199–206.

Lane, B. (1994). What is rural tourism? *Journal of Sustainable Tourism*, **2**(1/2), 7–21.

Lang Research (2001). *Travel Activities and Motivation Survey: Interest in Wine and Cuisine*. Canadian Tourism Commission.

Langton, B. (1996). News. *Tourism New South Wales Newsletter*, Spring, 3.

Laudan, R. (2001). A plea for culinary modernism: why we should love new, fast, processed food. *Gastronomica Quarterly*, 2–01, 36–45.

Le Grys, G. A., Dholakia, N. and Venkatesh, A. (1988). Developments in the processing and marketing of food crops in Papua New Guinea. *Proceeding of the ASEAN Conference*, pp. 523–527.

Le Grys, G. A. (1991). The food industry in Papua New Guinea. *Food Australia*, **43**(8), 361–364.

Le Manoir de Ecole de Cuisine, available online: http://www.goodfood.co.uk/le-manoir-ecole-de-cuisine.htm (accessed 13 February 2002).

Leavy, P. (1999). Grande, decaf, low fat, extra dry cappuccino: postmodern desire. *M/C: A Journal of Media and Culture*, **2**(5), available online: http://www.uq.edu.au/mc/9907/grande.html

Lee, D. (2002). Appeal of real meals. *The Times*, 8 August, pp.18–19.

Lee, T. H. and Crompton, J. (1992). Measuring novelty seeking in tourism. *Annals of Tourism Research*, **19**, 732–751.

Leiper, N. (1989). *Tourism and Tourism Systems*. Occasional paper no.1, Department of Management Systems, Massey University.

Leicestershire Farm Tourism Association (1993). *Leicestershire Farms*. Brochure. LFTA.

Leith's (2002): http://www.leiths.co.uk (accessed 13 July 2002).

Leones, J. (1995). Farm outlet customer profiles. In *Direct Farm Marketing and Tourism Handbook*, pp. 1–3, University of Arizona College of Agriculture, Cooperative Extension.

Leones, J., Dunn, D., Worden, M. and Call, R. (1995). A profile of visitors to fresh farm produce outlets in Cochise County, AZ. In *Direct Farm Marketing and Tourism Handbook*, pp. 5–12, University of Arizona College of Agriculture, Cooperative Extension.

Lévi Strauss, C. (1978). *The Origin of Table Manners*. HarperCollins, p. 471.

Liew, C. (1996). *My Food*. Allen and Unwin.

Line, S. (1995). *A Passion for Oysters: The Art of Eating and Enjoying*. Reed International, p. 7.

Linstrom, H. R. (1978). *Farmer to Consumer Marketing*. Report no. ESCS–01, U.S. Department of Agriculture, Economics, Statistics, and Cooperative Service.

Lipscomb, A., McKinnon, R., Wheeler, T. and Murray, J. (1998*). Papua New Guinea: A Travel Survival Kit*. 6th edn. Lonely Planet.

Lipton, T. J. (1930). *Leaves from the Lipton Logs*. Hutchinson.

Lockeretz, W. (1986). Urban consumers attitudes toward locally grown produce. *American Journal of Alternative Agriculture*, **1**(2), 83–88.

Lofman, B. (1991). Elements of experiential consumption: an exploratory study. *Advances in Consumer Research*, **18**, 729–734.

MacCannell, D. (1989). *The Tourist: A New Theory of the Leisure Class*. Schocken Books.

Macdonald, R. and Swales, J. (1991). The local employment impact of a hypermarket: a modified multiplier analysis incorporating the effect of lower retail prices. *Regional Studies*, **25**(2), 155–162.

Macdonald, C. (1987). *More Seasonal Cooking*. Bantam Press.

MacDonald, H. (2001). *National Tourism and Cuisine Forum: 'Recipes for Success' Proceedings and Final Report*. Canadian Tourism Commission.

Macionis, N. (1997). *Wine Tourism in Australia: Emergence, Development and Critical Issues*. Unpublished Masters Thesis, Faculty of Communication, University of Canberra.

Macionis, N. (1998). Wineries and Tourism: Perfect Partners or Dangerous Liaisons. In *Proceedings of the First Australian Wine Tourism Conference, Margaret River, Western Australia 5–9 May, 1998*. Bureau of Tourism Research, Canberra.

Macionis, N. and Cambourne, B. (1999). Wine and Food Tourism in the ACT: Exploring the Links. *International Journal of Wine Marketing*, **16**(3), 5–21.

Macionis, N. and Cambourne, B. (2000). The development of a national wine tourism plan? Wine tourism organisations and development in Australia. In *Wine Tourism Around the World: Development, Management and Markets* (Hall, C. M., Sharples, E. Cambourne, B. and Macionis, N., eds), Butterworth-Heinemann.

MacKay, R. D. (1976). *New Guinea*. Time-Life International.

MacLaurin, T. L. (2001). Food safety in travel and tourism. *Journal of Travel Research*, **39**(3), 332–333.

MacLaurin, T. L., MacLaurin, D. J., Loi, S. L. and Steene, A. (2000). Impact of food-borne illness on food safety concerns of international air travellers. *Tourism Economics Special Issue: Tourism Safety and Security*, **6**(2), 169–185.

Malecki, E. (1997). *Technology and Economic Development*. 2nd edn. Longman.

Manitoba Restaurant Association (2000): http://www.dinemanitoba.com (accessed 30 December).

Marien C. and Pizam A. (1997). Implementing sustainable tourism development through citizen participation in the planning process. In *Tourism, Development and Growth: The Challenge of Sustainability* (Wahab, S. and Pigram, J. J., eds), pp. 164–178, Routledge.

Market Attitude Research Services (1999). *Canberra Arts Marketing Final Report*. Unpublished Research Report, ACT Cultural Facilities Corporation.

Marsden, T. (1995). Beyond agriculture? Regulating the new rural spaces. *Journal of Rural Studies*, **11**(3), 285–296.

Marsden, T., Banks, J. and Bristow, G. (2000). Food supply chains approaches: exploring their role in rural development. *Sociologia Ruralis*, **40**(4), October, 424–439.

Marsh, I. and Shaw, I. (2000). *Australia's Wine Industry: Collaboration and Learning as Causes of Competitive Success*. Australian Business Foundation.

May, R. J. (1984). *KaiKai Aniani: A Guide to Bush Foods, Markets and Culinary Arts of PNG*. Robert Brown and Associates.

McDonnell, I., Allen, J. and O'Toole, W. (1999). *Festival and Special Event Management*. Wiley, p.10.

Meat New Zealand (2002). *NZ Lamb Focus of Campaign in Middle East*, Meat NZ, http://www.meatnz.co.nz/wdbctx/corporate/docs/ARCHIVES_PR_1997/970942.htm (accessed 18 April 2002).

Meikle, S. (2001). Middle Eastern growth. *Tourism News*, September.

Mennell, S., Murcott, A. and Van Otterloo, A. H. (1992). *The Sociology of Food: Eating, Diet and Culture.* Sage.

Mickler, D. L. (2000). *Halal Foodways.* Unichef: http://www.unichef.com/Halalfood.htm (accessed 22 July 2001).

Miller, A. (1988). *The Artifacts and Crafts of Papua New Guinea.* SPATF.

Mills, F. (1991). *Pasin Bilong Papua Niugini.* Video. Frank Mills and Associates.

Mintel (2001). *Tourism Catering Habits.* December.

Mintel (2002). *British on Holiday at Home.* February.

Mitchell, R. D. (1998). Learning through play and pleasure travel: using play literature to enhance research into touristic learning. *Current Issues in Tourism*, **1**(2), 176–188.

Mitchell, R. D. (in progress). 'Scenery and Chardonnay': a visitor perspective of the New Zealand winery experience. Unpublished doctoral thesis, University of Otago.

Mitchell, R. and Hall. C. M. (2000). Touristic terroir: the importance of region in the wine tourism experience. Paper presented at the IGU Conference, Cheju.

Mitchell, R. and Hall, C. M. (2001a). The influence of gender and region on the New Zealand winery visit. *Tourism Recreation Research*, **26**(2), 63–75.

Mitchell, R. and Hall, C. M. (2001b). Lifestyle behaviours of New Zealand winery visitors: wine club activities, wine cellars and places of purchase. *International Journal of Wine Marketing*, **13**(3), 82–93.

Mitchell, R. and Hall, C. M. (2001c). Wine at home: self-ascribed wine knowledge and the wine behaviour of New Zealand winery visitors. *Australia and New Zealand Wine Industry Journal*, **16**(6), 115–122.

Mitchell, R. and Hall. C. M. (2001d). Taking advantage of the relationship between wine, food and tourism: joint marketing activities. In *Tourism in New Zealand: An Introduction* (Hall, C. M. and Kearsley, G. W., eds), Oxford University Press.

Mitchell, R. D. and Mitchell, C. J. (2000). Sydney Wine Region: regional marketing strategy 2000–2005. Unpublished report.

Mitchell, R., Hall, C. M. and Johnson, G. (2001). Food and drink in the New Zealand tourism experience. In *Innovations in Cultural Tourism* (Butcher, J., ed.), pp. 75–91, ATLAS.

Mitchell, R. D, Hall, C. M. and McIntosh, A. J. (2000). Wine tourism and consumer behaviour. In *Wine Tourism Around the World: Development, Management and Markets* (Hall, C. M., Sharples, E., Cambourne, B. and Macionis, N., eds), pp. 115–135, Butterworth-Heinemann.

Mohr and Spekman (1994). Characteristics of partnership success, partnership attributes, communication behaviour and conflict resolution. *Strategic Management Journal*, **15**, 135–152.

Montanari, M. (1994). *The Culture of Food*. Blackwell.

Moran, W. (1993). Rural space as intellectual property. *Political Geography*, **12**(3), 263–277.

Moran, W. (2000). Culture et nature dans la geographie de l'industrie vinicole néo-zélandaise. *Annales de geographie*, **614–615**: 525–551.

Moran, W. (2001). Terroir – the human factor. *Australian and New Zealand Wine Industry Journal of Oenology, Viticulture, Finance and Marketing*, **16**(2), 32–51.

Morrow-Brown, C. (2000). Have some trifle – it's 200 years old. *Independent Weekend Review*, 22 July.

Mosley, J. (1997). New Asia cuisine Singapore. *New Asia Cuisine*, September, available online www.asiacuisine.com/

Murdock, J. (2000). Networks, a new paradigm of rural development. *Journal of Rural Studies*, 407–419.

Murphy, P. (1985). *Tourism: A Community Approach*. Methuen.

Mycologue: www.mycolgue.co.uk (accessed 14 August 2002).

National Animal Welfare Advisory Committee (NAWAC) (2001). *Discussion Paper on the Animal Welfare Standards to Apply When Animals Are Slaughtered in Accordance with Religious Requirements*. Ministry of Agriculture and Forestry.

National Restaurant Association (1997). The impact of international tourism. *Restaurants USA*, available online www.restaurant.org/rusa/magArticle.cfm?ArticleID=461 (accessed 6 April 2002).

National Restaurant Association (1998). Summer travel heats up restaurants. *Restaurants USA*, available online www.restaurant.org/rusa/magArticle.cfm?ArticleID=306 (accessed 6 April 2002).

National Restaurant Association (2002). *Travel and Tourism Facts*. www.restaurant.org/ tourism/facts.cfm (accessed 6 April 2002).

National Trust (2002). From plot to plate. *East Midlands News*, Spring/ Summer.

National Trust (2001). *Farming Forward*. Leaflet. National Trust.

Nayga Jr, R. M., Fabian, M. S., Thatch, D. W. and Wanzala, W. N. (1994). *Farmer-to-Consumer Direct Marketing: Characteristics of New Jersey Operations*. Publication no. P–02453–1–94), Rutgers University, New Jersey Agricultural Experiment Station.

Nelson, H. (1990). *Taim Bilong Masta*. Australian Broadcasting Organisation.

Nettleton, J. S. (1999). *The New Farmers/New Markets 1998/9 Project Highlights*. Cornell University, Cooperative Extension.

New Zealand Tourism Board (NZTB) (2001). Interview with NZTB conducted by Siti Hajjar Sulaiman, Wellington, July.

New Zealand Tourism News (NZTN) (1994). New Zealand's wines attract Canadian visitors. *New Zealand Tourism News*, February, 8.

New Zealand Tourism News (NZTN) (1997). Increasing focus on destination marketing. *New Zealand Tourism News*, December, 6–7.

New Zealand Way (1998): www.nzway.co.nz/Media/discover_nzway.html

Nield, K., Kozak, M. and Le Grys, G. A. (2000). The role of food service in tourist satisfaction. *International Journal of Hospitality Management*, **19**, 375–384.

Nightingale, N. (1992). New Guinea: An Island Apart. BBC Books.

Novak, T. (1998). A fresh place. *Oregon's Agricultural Progress*, Fall/Winter, available online: http://eesc.orst.edu/agcomwebfile/Magazine/98Fall/OAP-98%20text/OAPFall9802.html anchor1926968

Nunavut Tourism: www.nunatour.nt.ca/BUS/BUS5a_1.htm

Observer Food Monthly (2002). Available online: www.observer.co.uk/foodmonthly (accessed 11 July 2002).

Ochsner, K. T., Folwell, R. J. and Lutz, S. (1988). *Marketing Wine in Washington Restaurants and Hotels*. Extension Bulletin, Cooperative Extension, College of Agriculture, Washington State University, Research Report EB 1492.

Oddy, D. J. (1990). Food, drink and nutrition. In *The Cambridge History of Britain 1750–1950, Vol. 2* (Thompson, F. M. L., ed.), Cambridge University Press.

Office of Travel and Tourism Industries (2000). *Profile of U.S. Resident Traveler Visiting Overseas Destinations Reported From: Survey of International Air Travelers*: www.tinet.ita.doc.gov/view/f–2000–101–001/index.html?ti_cart_cookie=20020904.064052.22943

Ohlsson, T. (1998). Regional Culinary Heritage – A European Network. *Nordic Workshop on Regional Small Scale Food Production, Bodo, Norway 25–26 May, 1998*. http://www.culinary-heritage.com (accessed March 17, 1999).

Ontario Government (2002). Ontario's wine industry is poised for greatness. Press release.

Oriental Times (2001). Teesta Tea Tourism Festival. *Oriental Times*, **3**(33–34), available online: www.nenanews.com/OT%20Jan.7-%2001/0h11.htm

Otago Daily Times (2001). *Muslims Seek Trip after Bacon Pizza*, Otago Daily Times Online Edition: www1.odt.co.nz/cgi-bin/getitem?date=17Ju-l2001&object=0716531365&type=html (accessed 30 July 2001).

Page, S. and Hall, C. M. (2003). *Managing Urban Tourism*. Prentice-Hall.

Page, S. J. and Getz, D. (1997). *The Business of Rural Tourism: International Perspectives*. Thomson International Press.

Page, S. J., Brunt, P., Busby, G. and Connell, J. (2001). *Tourism: A Modern Synthesis*. Thomson.

Parasecoli, F. (2002). Tourism and taste: towards a semiotics of food. Unpublished manuscript, special lecture at the Florence Summer School, Food and Nutrition Department of New York University, 24 June.

Paxton, A. (1994). *The Food Miles Report: The Dangers of Long Distance Food Transport*. SAFE Alliance.

Peak District Foods for Tourism Project (2002). Savour the Flavour of the Peak District. The RED Office, University of Derby.

Perdue, R. R., Long P. T. and Allen, L. (1990). Resident support for tourism development. *Annals of Tourism Research*, **17**, 586–599.

Peters, G. L. (1997). *American Winescapes*. Westview Press.

Pilcher, J. M. (1996). Tamales or timbales: cuisine and the formation of Mexican national identity. *The Americas*, **53**(2), 193–216.

Pitkänen, R. (2002). *The World of Objects in a Sociologist's Eyes*, available online: www.hackmangroup.fi /hackman/website_new.nsf/pagesbyid/ 2B3783BF3DCFB62AC2256B820057992D?OpenDocument (accessed 6 June 2002).

PNG Tourism Promotion Authority (1995). The National Tourism Strategy for Papua New Guinea. Tourism Promotion Authority, Port Moresby.

Policy Commission on the Future of Farming and Food (2002a). *Farming and Food: A Sustainable Future*. Policy Commission on the Future of Farming and Food.

Policy Commission on the Future of Farming and Food (2002b). *Farming and Food: A Sustainable Future*, Crown Copyright, available online: www.cabi-net-office.gov.uk/farming

Porter, M. (1990). *The Competitive Advantage of Nations*. Macmillan.

Power, T. M. (1996). *Lost Landscapes and Failed Economies: The Search for a Value of Place*. Island Press.

Pratt, J. N. (n.d.). *Essay: Pilgrimage to the Holy Land of Tea*. Imperial Tea.

Pratt, J. N. (1982). *The Tea Lover's Treasury*. 101 Productions.

Pratt, S. J. (1994). Special event tourism: an analysis of food and wine festivals in New Zealand. Unpublished Diploma of Tourism dissertation, University of Otago.

Prentice, R. (1993). *Tourism and Heritage Attractions*. Routledge.

Prince, S. (2002). Peak District foods for tourism. The RED office, University of Derby.

Probyn, E. (1998). McIdentities: food and the familial citizen. *Theory, Culture and Society*, **15**(2), 155–173.

Proust, M. (1981). *Remembrance of Things Past*. Trans Scott Moncrief, C. K. and Kilmartin, T. Chatto and Windus.

Purvis, A. (2002). So what's your beef? *Observer*, 14 April available online: http://www.observer.co.uk/foodmonthly/story/0,9950,681828,00.html

Pyke, F. and Sengenberger, W. (1990). Introduction. In *Industrial Districts and Inter-Firm Co-operation in Italy* (Pyke, F., Becattini, G. and Sengenberger, W., eds), pp. 1–9, International Institute for Labour Studies, Geneva.

Rasheed, Z. A. (1992). The halal market: food for thought. Speech delivered at the International Halal Conference (INHALCON '92), Singapore World Trade Centre, 20 August.

Rasmussen, W. and Rhinehart, R. (1999). *Tea Basics*. Wiley.

Relph, E. (1996). Place. In *Companion Encyclopedia of Geography: The Environment and Humankind* (Douglas, I., Huggett, R. and Robinson, M., eds), Routledge.

Restaurant Association of New Zealand (2001a). Reflection that industry sales affected by September 11. http://www.restaurantnz.co.nz/news.asp?view=yes&pageID=216 (accessed: 7/4/02).

Restaurant Association of New Zealand (2001b). *USA Terror Attacks Have Bigger Impact on Restaurant Industry than Earlier Forecast*, available online: www.restaurantnz.co.nz/news.asp?view=yes&page ID=198 (accessed 7 April 2002).

Revel, J. F. (1982a). *Culture and Cuisine: A Journey through the History of Food*. Da Capo.

Revel, J. F. (1982b). *Culture and Cuisine*. Doubleday.

Reynolds, P. (1993). Food and tourism: towards an understanding of sustainable culture. *Journal of Sustainable Tourism*, **1**(1), 48–54.

Rhodus, T., Schwartz, J. and Haskins, J. (1994). *Ohio Consumers' Opinions of Roadside and Farmers' Markets*. Ohio State University, Department of Horticulture, May, pp. 1–7.

Riaz, M. N. (2001). *Halal Food: An Insight into a Growing Food Industry Segment*. International Food Marketing and Technology: http://www.icbc-s.org/Halal.htm (accessed 25 July 2001).

Richards, G. (1996). Production and consumption of European cultural tourism. *Annals of Tourism Research*, **23**(2), 261–283.

Richards, G. and Hall, D. (2000). *Tourism and Sustainable Community Development*. Routledge.

Rimmington, M. and Yüksel, A. (1998). Tourist satisfaction and food service experience: results and implications of an empirical investigation. *Anatolia*, **9**(1), 37–57.

Ripe, C. (1996). *Goodbye Culinary Cringe*. Allen and Unwin.

Ripe, C. (1998). Wine by the Dish. *The Weekend Australian*, 21–22 March, 1998, p. 41.

Ritchie, J. B. R. and Zins, M. (1978). Culture as a determinant of the attractiveness of a tourist region, *Annals of Tourism Research*, **5**, 252–267.

Ritzer, G. (1993). *The McDonaldization of Society*. Pine Forge Press.

Ritzer, G. (1996). *The McDonaldization of Society*. Pine Forge Press.

Rivers, M. (1995). *Time For Tea; Tea and Conversation with Thirteen English Women*. Crown.

Robinson, M. (1999). Cultural conflicts in tourism: inevitability and inequality. In *Tourism and Cultural Conflicts*. (Robinson, M. and Boniface, P., eds), pp. 1–32, CABI.

Rogers, M. E. (1995). *Diffusion of Innovations*. Free Press.

Rosenfeld, S. (1966). Does co-operation enhance competitiveness: assessing the inputs of interfirm collaboration. *Research Policy*, **25**(2), 247–263.

Rosenfeld, S. S. (1997). Bringing business clusters into the mainstream of economic development. *European Planning Studies*, **5**(1), February, 9–22.

Ross, G. F. (1994). *The Psychology of Tourism*. Hospitality Press.

Rowe, M. (2000). Townies flock to join farmers' union. *Independent*, 24 December, available online: www.independent.co.uk

Roy Morgan Research (1997). Roy Morgan Value Segments, roymorgan.com.au/products/values (accessed 10 October 2000).

Rushdie, S. (1999). *The Ground Beneath her Feet*. Picador USA.

Saeter, J. A. (1998). The significance of tourism and economic development in rural areas a Norwegian case study, In *Tourism and Recreation in Rural Areas* (Butler R., Hall, C. M. and Jenkins, J., eds), Wiley.

Saleh, A. R. (1996). Marketing strategy for halal food. In *First International Halal Food Conference (INHAFCON 96): Conference Proceedings* (Ayan, A., ed.), pp. 35–45, Arabic Society of Victoria.

Sami'ullah. M. (2001). *The Meat: Lawful and Unlawful in Islam,* eat-halal.com and IHFM, Canada: http://www.eat-halal.com/articles/0300.htm (accessed 29 July 2001).

Santich, B. (2000). Global cuisine(s)? In *Mietta's Australian Food Website*, available online: www.miettas.com/food_wine_recipes/food/food_opinions/globalcuisine.html (accessed August 2002).

Scanlan and Associates, Huber, G. and Karp, R. (2000). *Practical Farmers of Iowa: Grocery and Hotel, Restaurant and Institutional Study*, Practical Farmers of Iowa, available online: www.pfi.iastate.edu/HRI%20report.htm

Scarpato, R. (1998). The cuisine of the future. *Divine: Food and Wine*, **17**, December–February.

Scarpato, R. (1999). Food globalisation, new global cuisine and the quest for definition. Paper presented at Cuisines: Regional, national or global? Research Centre for the History of Food and Drink, University of Adelaide.

Scarpato, R. (2000). New Global Cuisine: The perspective of postmodern Gastronomy Studies. Unpublished masters thesis, Royal Melbourne Institute of Technology.

Scarpato, R. and Daniele, R. (2000). Effects of media reviews on restaurants: the perception of the industry. Unpublished working paper for Peak performance in tourism and hospitality research CAUTHE Conference, La Trobe University Mount Buller Campus, 2–5 February.

Schiffman, L. G., and Kanuk, L. L. (1987). *Consumer Behavior*. 3rd edn. Prentice-Hall.

Schlosser, E. (2001). *Fast Food Nation. What the All-American Meal Is Doing to the World*. Allen Lane, The Penguin Press.

Scholliers, P. (ed.) (2001). *Food, Drink and Identity. Cooking, Eating and Drinking in Europe Since the Middle Ages*. Berg.

Scottish Executive (2001). *A Forward Strategy for Scottish Agriculture*. Scottish Executive.

Scottish Executive (2002). *Tourism Framework for Action: 2002–2005*. Scottish Executive.

Scottish Food Strategy Group (SFSG) (1993). *Scotland Means Quality*, SFSG.

Seligman, I. (1994). The history of Japanese cuisine. *Japan Quarterly*, **41**(2), 165–180.

Sengenberger, W., Loveman, G. W. and Piore, J. J. (eds) (1990). *The Re-emergence of Small Enterprises Geneva*. International Institute of Labour Studies.

Seydoux, J. (1986). L'avenir de la gastronomie suisse: La gastronomie regionale, element de promotion touristique, *AIEST Conference Proceedings*. AIEST.

Shalleck, J. (1972). *Tea*. Viking Press.

Shapira, J. (1975). *The Book of Coffee and Tea*. St Martin's Press.

Shohat, E. and Stam, R. (1996). From the imperial family to the transnational imaginary: media spectatorship in the age of globalization. In *Global/Local: Cultural Production and the Transnational Imaginary* (Wilson, R. and Dissanayake, W., eds), Duke University Press.

Shumway, J. M. and Otterstrom, S. M. (2001). Spatial patterns of migration and income change in the Mountain West: the dominance of service-based, amenity rich counties. *Professional Geographer*, **53**(4), 492–502.

Sillitoe, P. (2000). *Social Change in Melanesia: Development and History.* Cambridge University Press.

Silverman, E. K. (2000). Tourism on the Sepik River of Papua New Guinea: favoring the local over the global. *Pacific Tourism Review*, **4**, 105–119.

Simon, I. (1999). Fall suppers. *Winnipeg Free Press*, 22 September, D1.

Simpson, T. (1999). *A Distant Feast: The Origins of New Zealand's Cuisine.* Random House New Zealand.

Singapore (2001). *Singapore New Asia: An Insider Guide.* Singapore Tourism Board.

Smith, A. (2001). A stakeholder generated SWOT analysis of the New Zealand food and wine tourism industry. Working paper presented at 2nd New Zealand Food and Wine Tourism Conference, Hawkes Bay.

Smith, A. and Hall, C. M. (2002). A SWOT analysis of the New Zealand food and wine tourism industry. Working paper presented at the CAUTHE conference, Fremantle, 9 February.

Smith, D. (1990). *Modern Cooking: From the First Back-Street Bistros of Lyons to the Finest Restaurants of Today.* Sidgwick and Jackson.

Smith, G. P. (2002). *Growing up with Tok Pisin.* Battlebridge.

Smith, L. J. S. (1983). Restaurants and dining out: geography of a tourism business. *Annals of Tourism Research*, **10**, 514–538.

Smith, M. (1986). *Michael Smith's Afternoon Tea.* Macmillan.

Smith, S. S. (1988). *Tourism Analysis.* Longman Scientific and Technical.

Soil Association (2002). http://www.soilassociation.org

Sokolov, R. (1991). *Why We Eat What We Eat: How the Encounter Between the New World and the Old Changed the Way Everyone on the Planet Eats.* Summit Books.

Sommer, R., Stumpf, M. and Bennett, H. (1984). Quality of farmers' market produce: flavor and pesticide residues. *Journal of Consumer Affairs*, **16**, 130–136.

Sommers, R. (1980). *Farmers Markets of America: A Renaissance.* Capra Press.

Sopade, P. A. (1997). Mumu, a traditional method of slow cooking in Papua New Guinea. *Boiling Point*, **38**, 34–45.

Sopade, P. A. (2000). The fate of cyanogens during the cooking of cassava in mumu, a traditional oven in Papua New Guinea. *International Journal of Food Science and Technology*, **35**(2), 173–182.

Sopade, P. A., Isaro, J., Kantecka, M., Birual, S. et al. (1998). Temperature distribution in mumu, a traditional slow cooking method in Papua New Guinea. Proceedings of 6th. ASEAN Food Conference, Singapore, pp. 170–180.

South Australian Tourist Commission (1997). *Wine and Tourism: A Background Research Report*. Research and Planning Group, South Australian Tourist Commission, Adelaide.

South Pacific Commission (1983a). *Banana: A Tropical Treat*. Leaflet no. 7.

South Pacific Commission (1983b). *Green Leaves: Nutritious Pacific Plants*. Leaflet no. 6.

South Pacific Commission (1985a). *Mango: A Fruit for the Family*. Leaflet no. 3.

South Pacific Commission (1985b). *Taro: A South Pacific Speciality*. Leaflet no. 1.

South Pacific Commission (1986). *Pumpkin: A Valuable Food*. Leaflet no. 12.

Southland Spirit of a Nation (2002): http://www.spiritofanation.co.nz/facts/default.asp (accessed 14 July 2002).

Spina, J. (1998). Winnipeg's Little Italy: a developmental model. Unpublished MA thesis, Department of Geography, University of Manitoba.

Statistics Canada (1998). Canadian travel survey. Unpublished survey.

Statistics Canada (1998). *Snapshots*, Statistics Canada.

Statistics New Zealand (2001). *2001 Census Snapshot 1 (Cultural Diversity): Media Release*, Statistics New Zealand, available online: www.stats-.govt.nz/domino/external/pasful . . ./Media+Release+2001+Census+Snapshot+1+Cultural+Diversity?ope (accessed 17 April 2002).

Stewart, A. (2000). *Flavours of Canada: a celebration of the finest regional foods*. Raincoast Books.

Stimmell, G. (2002). Grape escapes. *Toronto Star*. 12 June, D6.

Sulaiman, S. H. (2001). Following in the Footsteps of Allah. *The Dominion*, 6 August, p. 9.

Swarbrooke, J. (1995). *The Development and Management of Visitor Attractions*. Butterworth-Heinemann.

Swarbrooke, J. and Horner, S. (1999). *Consumer Behaviour in Tourism*. Butterworth-Heinemann.

Symons, M. (1999). Gastronomic authenticity and sense of place. In *Proceedings of the 9th Australian Tourism and Hospitality Research Conference, Council for Australian University Tourism and Hospitality Education – Part Two* (Molloy, J. and Davies, J., eds), pp. 333–340, Bureau of Tourism Research.

Tannahill, R. (1973). *Food in History*. Stein and Day.

Tannahill, R (1988). *Food in History*. Revd edn. Penguin.

Tastes of Niagara (2000). *6th Annual Showcase*. Brochure. Tastes of Niagara.

Tastes of Niagara (2002). *Summer Showcase 2002*. Brochure. Tastes of Niagara.

Tastes of Niagara (n.d.). *Tastes of Niagara: Niagara Fruit Stands and Markets*. Brochure. Tastes of Niagara.

Taylor, C. N. and Little, H. M. (1999). Alternative enterprises on New Zealand farms: obstacles, challenges and potential. Paper prepared for the 1999 NZARES/AARES Conference Christchurch, New Zealand, *Agribusiness Perspectives*, Paper 23, available online: www.agrifood.info/

Taylor, D. (1996). *The Café Cookbook: Great Eating from New Zealand's Best Cafés*. Penguin Books.

Tea Council of Canada. Available online: www.tea.ca

Teatime Travel to England (2000). Available online: www.teatime.cc/travel.shtml

Teeman, T. (2001). The restaurant at the top of the world, *Times Weekend*.

Telfer, D. J. (2000a). Tastes of Niagara: building strategic alliances between tourism and agriculture. *International Journal of Hospitality and Tourism Administration*, **1**, 71–88.

Telfer, D. J. (2000b). The Northeast Wine Route: wine tourism in Ontario, Canada and New York State. In *Wine Tourism Around the World: Development, Management and Markets* (Hall, C. M., Sharples, E., Cambourne, B. and Macionis, N., eds), pp. 253–271. Butterworth-Heinemann.

Telfer, D. J. (2001a). Strategic alliances along the Niagara Wine Route. *Tourism Management*, **22**, 21–30.

Telfer, D. J. (2001b). From a wine tourism village to a regional wine route: an investigation of the competitive advantage of embedded clusters in Niagara, Canada. *Tourism Recreation Research*, **26**, 23–33.

Telfer, D. J. (2002). Tourism and regional development issues. In *Tourism and Development; Concepts and Issues*. (Sharpley, R. and Telfer, D. J., eds), pp. 112–148, Channel View Publications.

Telfer, D. J. and Wall, G. (1996). Linkages between tourism and food production. *Annals of Tourism Research*, **23**(3), 635–653.

Thomas, D. (2002). The quest for the herbal Holiday. *Newsweek*, **160**(4), 22 –29 July, 58–59.

Thompson, C. J. and Tambyah, S. K. (1999). Trying to be cosmopolitan. *Journal of Consumer Research*, **26**(3), 214–241.

Thompson, L. (1989). Kaikai bilong Sepik. *Paradise*, **76**, 39–42.

Thompson, W. (2000). West Auckland restaurants to support local wineries. *New Zealand Herald*, 13 December.

Thomson, J. S. and Kelvin, R. E. (1994). A community systems approach to sustain agriculture in urbanizing environments: developing a regional market infrastructure. Pennsylvania State University, Department of Agricultural and Extension Education.

Thorsen, E. and Hall, C. M. (2001). What's on the wine list? Wine policies in the New Zealand restaurant industry. *International Journal of Wine Marketing*, **13**(3), 94–102.

Timmer, J. (2000). Huli Wigmen engage tourists: self adornment and ethnicity in the Papua New Guinea Highlands. *Pacific Tourism Review*, **4**, 121–135.

Timothy, D. (1999). Participatory planning: a view of tourism in Indonesia. *Annals of Tourism Research*, **26**(2), 371–391.

Tourism Concern, Fair Trade in Tourism Bulletin 1 (2001). *Developing 'tea tourism' in Sri Lanka*, available online: www.tourismconcern.org.uk/fair%20trade/Bulletin%20issue%201/srilanka.htm (accessed 23 November 2001).

Tourism KwaZulu-Natal (2002*). Statistics of our Tourism Industry, Wozani: Our Kingdom Calls*. 3rd edn. Tourism KwaZulu-Natal.

Tourism New South Wales (1996). *Food and Wine in Tourism – A Plan.* Tourism New South Wales, Sydney, Australia.

Tourism New Zealand (2000). *Growing New Zealand's Share of the UK Travel Market.* Available online: www.tourisminfo.co.nz/documents/UKLong-haulMarket.pdf (accessed: 7 April 2002).

Tourism New Zealand (2001a). Tourisminfo: www.tourisminfo.govt.nz/cir_home/index.cfm (accessed 6 April 2002).

Tourism New Zealand (2001b). *Tourism New Zealand Market Tracking Research UK Market, January 2001*. Available online: www.tourisminfo-.co.nz/documents/TRUK.pdf accessed:7 April 2002).

Tourism New Zealand (2002). *Activities Undertaken and Attractions Visited (Top 15)*. Available online: www.tourisminfo.govt.nz/cir_randd/index.cfm-?fuseaction=Survey&subaction=NationalOnly&item=DisplayReport (accessed 6 April 2002).

Tourism New Zealand (n.d.). *Understanding the Japanese Long Haul Travel Market*. Available online: www.tourisminfo.co.nz/documents/JapanLong-haulMarket.pdf (accessed 6 April 2002).

Tourism Strategy Group (2001). *The New Zealand Tourism Strategy 2010*. Tourism Strategy Group.

Tourism Victoria (2000). Domestic market segmentation: understanding your consumer. Unpublished leaflet, available online: www.tourismvictor-ia.com.au/research/docs/market_research/ understanding_your_consumer.pdf (accessed 17 May 2002).

Tourism Winnipeg (1999a). *1999 Visitor's Guide*. Tourism Winnipeg.

Tourism Winnipeg (1999b). *Taste: Winnipeg Restaurant Guide 1999*. Fanfare Publications.

Town of Altona (1999). *Millennium Diary*. Town of Altona.

Town of Winkler (2000). *Harvest Festival and Exhibition*. Brochure.

Travel Manitoba (1995). *Travel Report*. No. 2. Travel Manitoba.

Travel Manitoba (1999a). *Manitoba Explorer's Guide*. Travel Manitoba.

Travel Manitoba (1999b). *Manitoba Spring/Summer/Fall Events Guide*. Travel Manitoba.

Travel Manitoba (2000). *Manitoba Events Guide: 2000 Things to Do in Fall, Winter and Spring*. Travel Manitoba.

Tregear, A., Kuzenof, S. and Moxey, A. (1998). Policy initiatives for regional foods: some insights from consumer research. *Food Policy*, **23**(5), 383–394.

Trossolöv, A. (1995). *Psychophysiological Messages in Marketing: Symbolic Aspects of Food*. Lunds Universitet, Institute of Economic Research.

Tuorila, H., Meiselman, H. L., Bell, R., Cardello, A. V. and Johnson, W. (1994). Role of sensory and cognitive information in the enhancement of certainty and liking for novel and familiar foods. *Appetite*, **23**(3), 231–246.

Twaigery, S. and Spillman, D. (1989). An Introduction to Muslim Dietary Laws. *Food Tech*, **43**(2), 88–90.

Twining, S. (1956). *The House of Twining, 1706–1956*. R. Twining and Company.

Twohig, A. (ed.) (1986). *Liklik Buk: A Source Book*. Liklik Buk Information Centre.

United States Congress (1976). *Farmer-To-Consumer Direct Marketing Act*. Government Printing Office.

Urry, J. (1990). *The Tourist Gaze: Leisure and Travel in Contemporary Societies*. Sage.

Urry, J. (1995). *Consuming Places*. Routledge.

Van der Ploeg, J. D. and Renting, H. (2000). Impact and potential: a comparative review of European rural development practices. *Sociologia Ruralis*, **40**(4), October, 529–543.

Van der Ploeg, J., Renting H., Brunori, G., Knickel, K., Mannion, J., Marsden, T., de Roest, K., Sevilla-Guzman, E. and Ventura, F. (2000). Rural development from practices towards theory. *Sociologia Ruralis*, **40**(4), October, 391–408.

Van Fleet, P. (1988). Crocodile farm. *Paradise*, **70**, 15–19.

Vargas Llosa, M. (2001). The culture of liberty. *Foreign Policy* (122), January–February, available online: www.foreignpolicy.com/issue_janfeb_2001/vargasllosa.html (accessed August 2002).

Vas, A. C. (1999). Jobs follow people in the rural rocky Mountain West. *Rural Development Perspectives*, **14**(2), 14–23.

Vattimo, G. (1988). *The End of History*. Polity Press.

Veal, A. (1992). *Research Methods for Leisure and Tourism: A Practical Guide*. Longman.

Vermeulin, J. (1998). Report to birdtours.co.uk, 4–16 October.

Victorian Wineries Tourism Council (1997). *Victoria's Wine and Food: Victorian Wineries Tourism Council Strategic Business Plan 1997–2000*. Victorian Wineries Tourism Council.

Visser, M. (1991). *The Rituals of Dinner: The Origins, Evolution, Eccentricities and Meaning of Table Manners*. Penguin Group.

Von Reichart, C. and Rudzitis, G. (1992). Multinomial logistic models explaining income changes of migrants to high-amenity counties. *Review of Regional Studies*, **22**, 25–42.

Von Reichart, C. and Rudzitis, G. (1994). Rent and wage effects on choice of amenity destinations of the labor and nonlabor force. *Journal of Regional Science*, **34**, 445–455.

Wagner, H. A. (2001). Marrying food and travel ... culinary tourism. *Canada's Food News, Foodservice Insights*, March.

Waits, M. J. (2000). The added value of the industry cluster approach to economic analysis strategy development, and service delivery. *Economic Development Quarterly*, **14**, 35–50.

Walker C. (2000). To see some real poverty, visit the countryside. *Independent*, 15 October, available online: www.independent.co.uk

Walker, J. R. (2001). *Introduction to Hospitality*. Prentice-Hall.

Waugh, A. (1950). *The Lipton Story*. Doubleday.

Webster, S. (2001). Magical mystery tour. *Sunday Telegraph*, 7 October, p. 3.

Weinreich, M. (1980). *The Tea Lover's Handbook*. Intermedia Press.

Welsh, A. (1994). *An Analysis of Marketing Factors Contributing to Success Amongst Geographically Clustered Small Businesses in the Australian Wine Industry*. Unpublished Masters Thesis, University of South Australia, Adelaide.

Wiegand, R. (1995). Moderate Wine Pricing Helps Market Leading Hotel. *Restaurant Wine*, http://www.restaurantwine.com/promo.html (accessed September 16, 1998).

Wiegand, R. (1997). Meritage's Integrated, Dynamic Wine Program is Key to its Success. *Restaurant Wine*, http://www.restaurantwine.com/oper-prof.html (accessed September 16, 1998).

Wilk, R. (1995). Learning to be local in Belize: global systems of common difference. In *Worlds Apart. Modernity through the Prism of the Local* (Miller, D., ed.), pp. 110–131, Routledge.

Wilkins, M. and Hall, C. M. (2001). An industry stakeholders SWOT analysis of wine tourism in the Okanagan Valley, British Columbia. *International Journal of Wine Marketing*, **13**(3), 77–81.

Williams, A. and Hall, C. M. (2000). Tourism and migration: new relationships between production and consumption. *Tourism Geographies*, **2**(1), 5–27.

Williams, A. M. and Hall, C. M. (2002). Tourism, migration, circulation and mobility: the contingencies of time and place. In *Tourism and Migration: New Relationships Between Production and Consumption* (Hall, C. M. and Williams, A. M., eds), pp. 1–52, Kluwer Academic.

Williams, L. and Warner, K. (1990). *Oysters: A Connoiseur's Guide and Cookbook*. Ten Speed Press, p. 41.

Williams, P. (2001). The evolving images of wine tourism destinations. *Tourism Recreation Research*, **26**(2), 3–10.

Williamson, O. E. (1975). *Markets and Hierarchies: Analysis and Antitrust Implications*. New York Press.

Wilson, R. and Dissanayake, W. (eds) (1996). *Global/Local: Cultural Production and the Transnational Imaginary*. Duke University Press.

Wilton, D. (1997). *Recent Developments in Tourism as Revealed by the National Tourism*. Tourism Indicators, Canadian Tourism Commission, Research Report 1998–1. Canadian Tourism Commission.

Wolf, E. (2002). *Culinary Tourism: A Tasty Economic Proposition*. International Culinary Tourism Task Force.

Woman's Food and Farming Union (2002). A Taste of Derbyshire and the Peak District. Women's Food and Farming Union, Derbyshire.

Wood, N. E. (2001). The interdependence of farming and tourism in Vermont: quantifying the value of the farm landscape. Unpublished Masters thesis, Department of Community Development and Applied Economics, University of Vermont.

Wood, R. (ed.) (2000). *Strategic Questions in Food and Beverage Management*. Butterworth-Heinemann.

Wood, R. C. (1995). *The Sociology of the Meal*. Edinburgh University Press.

World Bank (1997). *Papua New Guinea: Accelerating Agricultural Growth, an Action Plan*. Report No. 16737-PNG.

World Muslim Population (2001). *World Muslim Population*, available online: www.a1realism.com/english/others/worldmuslimpopulation.htm (accessed 9 August 2001).

Younge, C. M. (1960). *Oysters*. Collins.

Zeldin, T. (1980). *France 1848–1945: Taste and Corruption*. Oxford University Press.

Zelinsky, W. (1987). You are where you eat. *American Demographics*, **9**(7) (online version).

Useful web sites

Arblaster and Clarke: www.arblaster_and clarke.com/ (accessed 22 June 2002).

Ballymaloe Cookery School: www.cookingisfun.re/school/ (accessed 25 May 2002).

Ballymaloe House: www.ballymaloe.com/ (accessed 10 July 2002).

Carnelian Rose Tea Company: http://www.teatime.cc/travel.shtml (accessed 10 October 2000).

Court/China Tea Tour Essay: www.imperialtea.com/tea/tours/TheTour.html (accessed 20 March 2002).

Daniel Butler's Fungi Forays: www.raptor-rambles.co.uk (accessed 13 August 2002).

Delia on Line: www.deliaonline.com (accessed 13 February 2002).

El Mouelhy, M. (2001). *Modern Products*, Halal helpline: www.geoci-ties.com/Athens/acropolis/1950/modern.html (accessed 25 October 2001).

European Union: http://europa.eu.int

Focus on Food Campaign: www waitrose.com/focusonfood_(accessed 2 August 2002).

Food Illustrated: www.wfi-online.com (accessed 25 June 2002).

Gastronomy of Portugal: http://www.manorhouses.com/food.htm

Good Earth Cooking School: www.goodearthcooking.com

International Culinary Tourism Task Force: www.culinarytourism.org

International SPA Association: http://www.experienceispa.com/conferences/articles/future.html (accessed August 2002).

Lifestyle at Supanet: http://www.supanet.com/lifestyle/food/topstory.htm (accessed 16 August 2002).

New Zealand Seafood Industry: http://www.seafood.co.nz/educat.cfm?SEC_ID=69&DOC_ID=142

Padstow Seafood School: www.rickstein.com/school_course (accessed 10 April 2002).

Patanegra: http://www.patanegra.net/home.html (accessed 22 June 2002).

Proquest Information and Learning: http://proquest.umi.com/pqdlink?Ver-=1&Exp=09–20 (accessed 23 August 2002).

Tante Marie School of Cookery: www.tantemarie.co.uk (accessed 13 July 2002).

Tastes of Niagara: www.tastesofniagara.com/index.cfm

Tasting Places: http://www.tastingplaces.com/ (accessed 25 July 2002).

Venture Southland: http://www.venturesouthland.co.nz/venture/eco/profile_pages/AgricultureF.html

What's Hot: http://districts.nic.in/Jorhat/whats_hot.htm (accessed 23 November 2001).

Wine Country Cooking School: www.winecountrycooking.com/about.html

Wine Country Tours: www.winecountrytours.ca

Index

Airlines, *see* In-flight catering
Appellations, 33–6, 52
Australia, 3, 39. 67–8, 269–84
    Australian Capital Territory, 269–84
    New South Wales, 2
    South Australia, 38
    Victoria, 7, 320–9
        Yarra Valley, 7, 43
    Western Australia, 320–9
Austria, 149–57
Authenticity, 297–313

Ballymaloe Cookery School, 104–6
Bestor, T.C., 301
Biodiversity, 30
Brand, 52–6

Canada, 65–7, 129, 159–77, 178–91
    British Columbia, 320–9
    Manitoba, 178–91
        Winnipeg, 180–2
    Ontario, 38, 47, 65–7
        Niagara, 38, 159–77
        Toronto, 8
    Prince Edward Island, 130–1
        Charlottetown, 130–1
Cheese rolling, 6–7
Cheese trail, 152
China, 3, 126–7, 132
Cider trail, 152
Clusters, 37–9, 172–7, 223–7, 314–31
Consumer behaviour, 60–80, 164–5,
    273, 315–17

Cookery schools, 102–20, 174–5
Cooperation, 38, 43, 149, 153–6,
    172–7, 223–7, 228–48, 264–5,
    286–95, 314–31
Countryside, *see* Rural regions
Countryside Agency, The, 29–32
Cuisine, 6, 61, 129–31, 159–60, 179,
    253–5, 297–313
Cuisine tourism, 11
Culinary tourism, 11, 162
Culture, 5, 72, 106, 143, 161, 198,
    297–313

Daley, G., 32, 52
Direct marketing, 40, 41, 42
Diving, 142–3

Eat the View project, 29–32
Entrepreneurship, 37–9, 57
Environment, 20–30
European Union, 35–6, 47, 230
Events, 6–7, 28, 49–52, 134, 180–9,
    193–205, 331–5

Falk, P., 73
Farm tourism, *see* Rural tourism
Farm value, 42
Farmers' markets, 32, 40, 43–6, 62,
    319–20
Farmers' Markets Ontario, 47
Ferguson, A., 162

Festivals, *see* Events
Finland, 57
Food, the study of, 1–3
Food education, 102–20, 135
Food gathering, 115
Food safety, 30, 222
Food tourism, defined, 9–12
Food tourists, *see* Consumer behaviour
France, 6, 118
    Paris, 115
    Provence, 7
Fusion cuisine, 303–13

Gastronomic tourism, 11
Gender, 114
Germany, 3, 332
Globalization, 6, 159, 297–313
Gourmet tourism, 11
Government of South Africa, 4–5

Halal food, 81–101
Hall, C.M., 61, 73
Heart of England Tourist Board, 49
Hong Kong, 73–4
Hotel sector, 4, 26–8, 144–5

Identity, 5, 6, 297–313
India:
    Darjeeling, 129
Indonesia, 3
In-flight catering, 20–4
Intellectual capital, 56–7, 156–7,
    289–90
Intellectual property, 33–6
Ireland, 53, 55–6
    Ballymaloe, 104–6
Islam and food, 81–101
Italy, 118
    Tuscany, 7

Japan, 132

Le Manoir Ecole de Cuisine, 111–12
Leones, J., 63

Liew, C., 309
Lifestyle, 2, 30, 57, 70, 113–15
Local, conceptions of, 10, 307–8
Local economic development strategies,
    28–9, 40–3, 57–9, 203–5, 223–7,
    228–48, 286–95, *see also* Regional
    development
Local food, 25–59, 104–6, 110–11,
    145–8, 165–71, 206–27, 228–48,
    249–67, 307–8, 315–17

McDonaldization, 6, 299
McIntosh, A., 61, 73
Media, 2, 76, 108, 113–15, 222–3
Mitchell, R., 61, 73
Moran, W., 33–4
Motivation, 69
Museums, 132–3

National Association of Farmers'
    Markets, 44, 319–20
National parks, 206–27
National Restaurant Association, 74
National Trust, 47–8
Networks, 37–52, 153–6, 172–7,
    223–7, 314–31
New Zealand, 3, 47, 53–4, 56, 63,
    81–101, 249–67, 320–9
    Bluff, 193–205
    Canterbury, 252–67
    Central Otago, 252–67
    Hawkes Bay, 48–9, 252–67
    Marlborough, 47, 252–67
    West Auckland, 47
New Zealand Way, 54–5
Norway, 57

Oktoberfest, 331–5
Oysters, 193–7

Padstow Seafood School, 106–8
Papua New Guinea, 138–48
Partial industrialization, 40
Portugal, 14–19, 118
Postmodernity, 297–313

Pratt, J.N., 133
Pure Ireland, 55

Quality, 31, 55, 57–8

Regional development, 2, 25–59,
    203–5, 228–48, 286–95, 314–31,
    see also Local economic
    development strategies
Relationship marketing, 40–2
Restaurant sector, 4, 5, 8–9, 47, 52, 62,
    73–4, 88, 174–5, 249–67, 269–84
Risk management, 201–3
Rural policy, 27–32, 47–52
Rural regions, 2, 7, 26, 29–32, 45–52,
    104–6, 128, 206–27, 228–48
Rural tourism, 11, 32, 40, 43–6, 62,
    104–6, 128, 228–48

Scarpato, R., 300
Second homes, 57
Shopping, 5
Singapore, 310–2
Smith, D., 302
South Africa, 3, 4–5, 75
    KwaZulu-Natal, 75
Spa cuisine, 312
Spain, 118
Special interest tourism, 10, 11, 26,
    109–10, 119
Sri Lanka, 135–6
Stewart, A., 161–2
Supermarkets, 30, 43, 231–2
Sustainability, 31

Taiwan, 129, 130, 132
Taste, *see* Tourist experiences
Tea, 121–36
Terroir, 34–5
Tourism marketing, 7–8, 27, 31, 40–2,
    52–5, 153–6, 164–5, 178–91,
    209–21, 274–84, 314–31
Tourism planning and policy, 4–5,
    162–3, 167–70, 228–48, 286–95,
    314–31
Tourism Victoria, 71–2
Tourist activities, 5, 102–20

Tourist attractions, 7, 8, 102–20, 131–4,
    135, 152–3, 172–3, 178–91
Tourist experience, 7, 14, 72–7
Tours, 119, 173–4
Tradition, 125–6
Trails, 149–57, 167, *see also* Wine
    roads
Transport, 30

United Kingdom, 14–19, 26, 29–32, 43,
    128–9, 131, 203–5, 228–48,
    315–17, 319–20
    Bath, 43
    Brockworth, 6–7
    Elan Valley, 115
    Great Milton, 111–12
    Knightwick, 26
    Ludlow, 49–52
    Padstow, 106–8
    Peak District, 206–27
    Wallington Hall, 48
United States of America, 3, 5, 36, 43,
    63, 64, 65–7, 331–5
    Arizona, 64
    California, 45
        Napa Valley, 7
        San Diego, 45
        San Francisco, 3, 132
    Illinois, 64
    Maine, 45
        Orono, 45
    Michigan, 64
    New Mexico, 4
        Las Cruces International Airport, 4
    New York, 64
    Oregon, 45
        Albany, 45, 46
        Corvallis, 45, 46
    Perryville, 135
    Vermont, 7
    Wisconsin, 64
Urban tourism, 11

Wine roads, 149–57, 167
Wine routes, *see* Wine roads
Wine tourism, 9–10, 149–57
World Trade Organization, 35–6